THE TAOIST EXPERIENCE

RECEIVED

| DATE DUE | | |
|---|---|---|
| 12/8/97 | | |
| MAY 1 5 1996 | | APR 0 6 2015 |
| APR 1 6 1997 | | |
| Xpr 27, 1997 | | |
| OCT 1 1997 | | |
| NOV 3 1997 | | |
| NOV 1 8 1997 | | |
| DEC 1 2 2000 | | |
| | | |
| | | |
| | | |

Taoist Experience: an anthology
Livia Kohn

vii, 391 p.; ill.; 24 cm.

Includes bibliographical references and index

1. Taoism, China

*SUNY SERIES IN CHINESE PHILOSOPHY AND CULTURE*
*DAVID L. HALL AND ROGER T. AMES, EDITORS*

# THE TAOIST EXPERIENCE

## AN ANTHOLOGY

*Livia Kohn*

STATE UNIVERSITY OF NEW YORK PRESS

*Permissions*

The translation from the *Yufang bijue* in Section 20 is reprinted with minor adaptations from *The Art of the Bedchamber: The Chinese Sexual Yoga Classics Including Women's Meditation Texts*, by Douglas Wile, copyright 1992 by State University of New York Press. Used by permission.

The translation of the *Shishuo xinyu* in Section 40 is reprinted with minor adaptations from *A New Account of Tales of the World: The Shih-shuo hsin-yü*, by Richard B. Mather, copyright 1976 by University of Minnesota Press. Used by permission.

The translation from the *Yongcheng jixian lu* in Section 44 is reprinted with minor adaptations from "Practice Makes Perfect: Paths to Transcendence for Women in Medieval China," by Suzanne Cahill (*Taoist Resources* 2.2 (1990), 23–42). Used by permission of the author.

The translation from the *Shizhou ji* in Section 7 is reprinted with minor adaptations from "The Record of the Ten Continents," by Thomas E. Smith (*Taoist Resources* 2.2 (1990), 87–119). Used by permission of the author.

The translations from the *Zuowanglun* in Section 31 and from the *Cunshen lianqi ming* in Section 43 are taken from *Seven Steps to the Tao: Sima Chengzhen's Zuowanglun*, by Livia Kohn, copyright 1987 by Monumenta Serica. Used by permission.

The translation from the *Neiguan jing* in Section 22 is reprinted from *Taoist Meditation and Longevity Techniques*, ed. Livia Kohn, copyright 1987 by the University of Michigan, Center for Chinese Studies. Reprinted by permission.

The translation of the *Jiude song* in Section 40 is reprinted from *Early Chinese Mysticism: Philosophy and Soteriology in the Taoist Tradition*, by Livia Kohn, copyright 1992 by Princeton University Press. Reprinted by permission.

Published by
State University of New York Press, Albany

©1993 State University of New York

For information, address State University of New York
Press, State University Plaza, Albany, N.Y., 12246

Production by Diane Ganeles
Marketing by Dana E. Yanulavich

Library of Congress Cataloging-in-Publication Data

Kohn, Livia, 1956–
    The Taoist experience : an anthology / Livia Kohn.
        p.  cm.—(SUNY series in Chinese philosophy and culture)
    Includes bibliographical references.
    ISBN 0-7914-1579-1 (alk. paper).—ISBN 0-7914-1580-5 (pbk. :
alk. paper)
    1. Taoism—China.  I. Title.  II. Series.
BL1910.K64   1993
299'.514—dc20                                        92-32933
                                                     CIP

10 9 8 7 6 5 4 3 2 1

# CONTENTS

# ACKNOWLEDGMENTS

The first roots of this work were planted in the context of a graduate seminar in Taoism I taught at the University of Michigan in Winter 1987. Pulling together a collection of hitherto untranslated texts on Taoist mythology and religious practice, I developed the rudiments of a compendium and tried it for the first time in a teaching context.

The idea of a full anthology came in the summer of 1990, when I reread Stephan Beyer's *The Buddhist Experience: Sources and Interpretations* for an introduction to Eastern religions at Boston University. Following Beyer's inspiration, I decided to attempt a vision of the Taoist religion that follows its path and gives an integrated picture of Taoism beyond the boundaries of historical periods and sectarian divisions. His example also encouraged me to try for more creative translations and easy introductions. Unlike him, however, I decided to turn the work into a resource tool by including ample bibliography, especially of works in English, and a detailed index.

Around the core complex of texts prepared originally in Michigan, I assembled translations I had prepared in other contexts, both published and unpublished, and went on to collect materials that would give the best representation of the religion. The aim was to have both newly translated materials of a more esoteric nature and classical passages that were already well-known so as to provide samples of mythological descriptions, philosophical discourse, and practical religious instructions. I found suitable texts, over a period of time, both unknown and never translated as well as well-known and translated one or more times before.

In cases when a previous translation was available, my attention was usually drawn to the material by this translation. I read it and found its contents suitable to my purpose, then went to the original to develop my own rendition. Generally the Taoist terminology I had developed in my research and used in my own translations was not identical with that used by other authors. In all cases I therefore standardized the language in order to avoid confusion. Beyond that in some cases, especially in concrete descriptions and technical instructions, there was little room for disagreement on the meaning of the text or even on the choice of English words. Inevitably some translations that I include in this volume are therefore closer to previously published works than others.

I am deeply indebted to all the excellent translators and meticulous scholars whose work has made this compendium possible. My most heartfelt gratitude goes to the work of Suzanne Cahill, Richard B. Mather, Thomas E. Smith, and Douglas Wile, whose outstanding renditions have been reprinted with little change. Their pioneering work has opened dimensions of excellence in Taoist translation that I can only humbly follow. Their renditions so closely suit the tenor and feeling of the originals that any alteration could only have created an inferior product.

I have also relied heavily on Burton Watson, *The Complete Works of Chuang-tzu*; Lionel Giles, *A Gallery of Chinese Immortals*; James Ware, *Alchemy, Medicine and Religion in the China of A.D. 320: The Nei P'ien of Ko Hung*; and Percifal Yetts, "The Eight Immortals" in presenting texts they translated. Their renditions are eminently accurate and excellent in their choice of English equivalents. In reworking the original texts, I chose my own terminology to bring out the religious Taoist content and occasionally saw a different meaning in the text. Overall, however, I found their work so powerful and inspiring that my own abilities could not compete.

Other inspiring and meticulous translations are found in the following: Stephen Bokenkamp, "Death and Ascent in Ling-pao Taoism;" Suzanne Cahill, "The Image of the Goddess: Hsi Wang Mu in Medieval Chinese Literature;" Thomas Cleary, *Understanding Reality: A Taoist Alchemical Classic by Chang Po-tuan*; Ilza Veith, *The Yellow Emperor's Classic of Internal Medicine*; and Tao-chung Yao, "Chüan-chen: A New Taoist Sect in North China."

I am indebted to them all for giving me a first impression of the texts and providing guidance and support when my own reading faltered. Their often superb choice of vocabulary and phrase at times left me at a loss for improvement or even change. Still, overall my reading differs considerably, not only in terminology but also in grammatical analysis and ultimate understanding.

Other previous English translations of texts I used mainly as reference points, as mirrors that helped clarify my own vision and choice of terminology. To be more precise, I found Poul Andersen's *The Method of Holding the Three Ones* incompatible with my understanding of the meditation practice and in many points disagreed with his reading. In the case of the *Yuanyou*, I substituted a reading of Taoist religious practice for the superb literary vision David Hawkes provides in his *Ch'u Tz'u: The Songs of the South*. In Edward H. Schafer's translation of the visualization practice of "The Jade Woman of Greatest Mystery" (*History of Religions* 17), I added the introductory part of the text, placed a higher emphasis on the verses, and applied a less esoteric language.

The *Daode jing* I translated without consulting prior works. However, since I commonly use Wing Tsit-chan's excellent and most insightful translation, contained in his *A Source Book in Chinese Philosophy*, for teaching and quick reference, some of his terms and phrases have made their way into this work.

I also consulted Henri Maspero's rendition of the *Daoyin jing* in *Taoism and Chinese Religion*, translated by Frank Kierman, and Kenneth DeWoskin's translation of Hugong's biography in his *Doctors, Diviners, and Magician's in Ancient China*. Both are based on different original versions than the ones I used as my basis, but I found them helpful in understanding the texts better through their variants.

In two cases, more than one English version exists. I therefore also examined the translations in Russell J. Kirkland's "Huang Ling-Wei: A Taoist Priestess in T'ang China" and in Florian C. Reiter's "Ch'ung-yang Sets Forth His Teachings in Fifteen Discourses," relying on them to gain a wider context and deeper understanding of the texts.

I only found Eva Wong's version of the *Qingjing jing* in her *Cultivating Stillness: A Taoist Manual for Transforming Body and Mind* and Lu Kuan-yü's translation of the *Yinshizi jingzuo fa* in his *The Secrets of Chinese Meditation* after I had prepared my own rendering. Still, the two aided my project by providing an opportunity for comparison and correction.

Other works that were very helpful in reading the classical immortals' biographies were Gertrud Güntsch, *Das Shen-hsien-chuan und das Erscheinungsbild eines Hsien*, and Maxime Kaltenmark, *Le Lie-sien tchouan*. Last but not least, I am indebted to Hou Ching-lang for inspiring me to translate, with the help of his French rendition, the *Luku shousheng jing* on the workings of the celestial treasury.

My translation of the *Tianyin zi* in section 11 was first published in the *Journal of Chinese Religions* (Kohn 1987a) and later reprinted in *Seven Steps to the Tao* (Kohn 1987). The translations presented in chapter 7 on "The One" are expanded from materials first used in my article "Guarding the One: Concentrative Meditation in Taoism" (Kohn 1989a). The translation of Chen Tuan's sleep practice in Section 36 is adapted from the German version in my dissertation (Knaul 1981).

# INTRODUCTION

What is Taoism? Is it a degenerate form of a highly sophisticated ancient philosophy? Is it an organized form of popular religion? Or has it nothing much to do with either?

Is Taoism found mostly in a messianic movement of mass salvation that began in the second century C.E.? Is it most essentially present in the elaborate performance of majestic rituals of renewal and ancestral salvation? Or, again, is it found first of all in the leisurely play of immortals, sitting under pine trees, sipping elixirs of immortality?

Is Taoism a political force, developed and supported by the imperial court for its own ends? Or is it the physical retention of youth, the attainment of longevity and health in the body? Is it, in the end, maybe just an unstructured mass of beliefs, doctrines, and practices that have changed from century to century, from school to school, even from believer to believer?

Taoism, of course, is all these things and none of them. It is an unknown and enigmatic, yet pervasive and ubiquitous aspect of Chinese, even East Asian, religion and culture. It is a force that has influenced Eastern thinking like few others; it is an organized religion, a philosophy, and also the attitude that individuals have toward their lives and the world.

Taoism plays a central part in the development of East Asian culture, and yet it is not a religion in our sense that can be easily defined in terms of founder, doctrines, pantheon, practices, and scriptures. Only the latter are relatively well delineated through the corpus of the Taoist canon, published in 1445, and its various supplements. Still, even there confusion prevails.

Most of the materials are undated and do not contain clear references to an author or sectarian affiliation. Many documents contained in the canon come from non-Taoist traditions, such as

1

ancient philosophers or works on divination. And even within the texts that can be identified in terms of lineage and roughly dated, beliefs, doctrines, and deities appear in an apparently incoherent jumble, mixing Buddhism and Confucianism, Chinese medicine and divination, alchemy and shamanism into a wondrous and multifaceted combination.

The study of Taoism in recent years has done much to unravel its doctrinal intricacies and historical developments, making inroads into the complexity of the religion from a variety of different angles. Methodologically centered on the philological study of texts and the identification of historical context, Taoist studies has made enormous progress, and the full complexity of the religion has come to be appreciated.

This progress is reflected in recent publications: several new histories of Taoism have appeared (Seidel 1990, Robinet 1991); a number of specialized bibliographies are available now (Loon 1984, Thompson 1985, Boltz 1987, Pas 1988, Dragan 1989; for earlier lists, see Soymié 1968 and 1969); a survey of the development of Taoist studies in the West has come out (Seidel 1990a), and there is even a journal devoted entirely to its study (*Taoist Resources,* Indiana University).

However, there is as yet no scholarly presentation of Taoist texts in Western languages. There is no textbook that makes the materials of the religion easily accessible to students of religion and the interested lay reader. This volume, an anthology containing altogether about sixty translations from a large variety of Taoist texts, is a step toward filling this lacuna. It is meant as an easy and yet thorough introduction to the major concepts, doctrines, and practices of Taoism, presenting the philosophy of the ancients as much as the practices and ideas of Taoists today.

The organization of the work follows the Taoist path. It begins with the Tao, the most fundamental power of the Taoist universe, and its role in the creation of the heavens and the world. Moving on to an outline of the overall teaching, the work then divides according to the three distinct stages of long life, eternal vision, and immortality. "Long life and eternal vision" is the way in which the *Daode jing* already describes the central concern for the Tao. The two terms distinguish physical and meditational practices, longevity and spiritual attainment.

Still, however ancient the distinctions, however clear and integrated the organization, any systematic description of the Taoist path can never do justice to the actual experience of the religion.

The way of the Tao is always a totality. Unravelled into sentences, transposed into the linear nature and logical structure of language, divided into chapters and sections, it can only be a mere shadow, a trace of itself, a pointer to its essence. Although presented as a logical succession, it must be understood that the concepts and practices described in actual reality are interwoven and mingled in a highly complex way. They are not to be followed in as simple and linear a manner as their presentation may suggest.

The texts translated below are selected from many different periods and cover all the major schools of the religion (see below). They are texts chosen because they are most suitable to demonstrate certain concepts and doctrines and illuminate most clearly certain practices. They are not necessarily the most classic of Taoist texts, nor do they represent the historical development of the religion. Rather, the documents are assembled here in order to provide a phenomenological approach to Taoism, to convey a sense of identity and being in the world that is particular to this religion as opposed to all others.

About eighty percent of the selections are taken from the Taoist canon of 1445, with the remainder chosen from later supplements to the canon, from Taoist manuscripts discovered at Dunhuang, and from literary sources. They are mostly given in the rendering of the author, with about half translated here for the first time. Introductions to individual sections describe the concept or practice at hand, provide some data on the text, and contain references for further reading. The references are strictly limited to works in Western languages, with preference given to materials in English whenever available. Translations are geared toward readability more than toward technical detail. The numbering system for texts from the Taoist canon follows K. M. Schipper, *Concordance du Tao Tsang: Titres des Ouvrages* (Paris, 1975). For a conversion to the Harvard-Yenching Index, see Boltz 1987.

A summary of the major dates and events that punctuate the history of Taoism helps to put the materials presented below into a general historical perspective.

Taoism as a religion began in the year 142 c.e. with the revelation of the Tao to Zhang Daoling by the personified god of the Tao, Taishang laojun, the Highest Venerable Lord. This deity is the Tao, but also a mythological development of the ancient philosopher Laozi. He appears also as Huanglao jun, the Yellow Venerable Lord, a title that indicates the close association of Laozi with the Yellow Emperor in the centuries preceding the revelation.

Zhang Daoling, by virtue of this divine endowment, became the first Celestial Master and founder of the first organized Taoist school, called Orthodox Unity or Celestial Masters after his title. Still continuing the tradition, the sixty-fourth Celestial Master resides today in Taiwan. The school is a form of communal religion, with a heavy emphasis on morality, ritual, purifications, and exorcism.

There were various precursors of this first organized school of Taoism. First, in terms of doctrine, there were the ancient philosophers of the Tao, Laozi and Zhuangzi with their major works *Daode jing* (Scripture of the Tao and the Virtue) and *Zhuangzi* (fourth and third centuries B.C.E.). Describing the world as created and supported by the Tao, encouraging people to pursue simplicity and spiritual cultivation in order to recover and realize this all-encompassing force, and developing the ideal of the sage and the perfect human being, these works furnished the conceptual framework for the later religion. Also, the *Daode jing* became its first sacred scripture, to be recited at regular intervals and to almost magical purposes (see Seidel 1969).

Second, in terms of practice, there were the magico-technicians (*fangshi*) of the Former Han dynasty (206–6 B.C.E.), a group of ascetics and wandering healers who strove for personal refinement and immortality. They were mainly known for their expertise in a variety of arts: forms of divination, such as astrology, physiognomy, numerology, milfoil analysis after the *Yijing* (Book of Changes), dream interpretation, etc.; medical techniques, such as acupuncture, moxibustion, pharmacology, dietetics, and the like; shamanistic practices, such as purifications, exorcisms, travels to the other world, and spirit mediumship. Using these methods, the goal of the magico-technicians was to attain immortality, a longevity in the body and a free spiritual access to the world of the gods and spirits. They were in many ways the earliest active Taoists in Chinese history (see DeWoskin 1983).

Third, in terms of organization, there were a number of similar messianic movements and religious groups that emerged around the beginning of the Common Era. Driven by the increasingly disastrous political and economic situation at the time and inspired by the belief in the utopian realm of Great Peace, thousands of people took to the roads, numerous revelations of texts and sacred talismans were received by gifted visionaries, and again and again rebellions against the existing order had to be quelled—as for example the big insurrection of the Yellow Turbans or Tao of Great Peace in 184. The Celestial Masters, far from being a special and unique movement at the time, were one among many, different mainly in that they did not get quite as deeply involved in political disputes and somehow managed to survive (see Levy 1956, Seidel 1969a).

The first Taoist movement thus combined in its foundation the ancient worldview of the Taoist philosophers, the practices of the magico-technicians of the Former Han, and the messianic, millenaristic dimensions of the popular cults of the Later Han. Successive Taoist schools, usually inspired by further and new revelations from the heavens, continued with the same combination, emphasizing different aspects in accordance with the times and circumstances of their emergence.

The second major Taoist school was the school of Highest Clarity (Shangqing). It began with a revelation from the Heaven of Highest Clarity received by the medium Yang Xi in 364–70. Yang Xi was a member of a southern aristocratic clan, and the new scriptures and insights into the realms of the otherworld transmitted to him remained at first limited to this select group. Highest Clarity in its teaching combined the new visions with the practices of the magico-technicians as they were continued in the south and specifically associated with a family named Ge. Shangqing practice was highly individual and aimed at transferring the practitioner into the realms of the immortals, first by visualizations, then by ecstatic journeys, and finally through the ingestion of a highly poisonous alchemical elixir (see Strickmann 1978 and 1981, Robinet 1984).

A few decades after the Shangqing revelations, Ge Chaofu, a member of the Ge family, proceeded to develop his own vision of the otherworld. Calling his new understanding Numinous Treasure (Lingbao), he integrated the Highest Clarity scriptures with Han-dynasty thinking, Buddhist cosmology and doctrine, as well as the magico-technical practices transmitted within his family. The new group of scriptures, compiled from the last decade of the fourth century onward, soon became widespread and very popular. Much simpler than the practice of Highest Clarity, Numinous Treasure required merely the recitation of its scriptures and participation in its rites to guarantee a place among the perfected. Since only initiates were allowed to own the necessary documents and join the ceremonies, the group placed a high emphasis on secrecy and the proper transmission of the scriptures (see Bokenkamp 1983, Seidel 1983).

With the Lingbao movement spreading, Taoism emerged for the first time as an organized religion of all China, expanding vastly over the limited sphere of influence of the Celestial Masters. Copying readily from the fast-growing Buddhist community, Taoists in the fifth century built the first monasteries of their own, compiled their first catalogues and canons of scriptures, and established proper rank and file among their membership. Throughout the sixth century, scriptures continued to be received in revelation and compiled by human beings; commentaries and discourses grew. Soon also the first encyclopedias were collected, and there appeared the first statues and pictural representations of Taoist gods.

The Tang dynasty (618–906) saw the heyday of Taoist splendor and influence. The leading church of China, especially in the eighth century, Taoism with Highest Clarity at the top continued to produce scriptures, texts and art works and gained an ever increasing influence on the political scene of the day. The great splendor of courtly Taoists was matched by the high spiritual attainments of masters on isolated mountains. The widespread impact throughout the country was enhanced by the political support of the Tang rulers, who claimed descent from Laozi himself (see Kohn 1987, Benn 1991).

The rebellion of An Lushan in 755 was the beginning of a great break in the fortunes and development of the religion as well as in all of Chinese culture, a hiatus which ended only with the founding of the Song dynasty in 960. Turning their eyes on the origins of Chinese greatness, thinkers and practitioners in the following centuries placed a strong emphasis on the teachings of Confucius and on integrating all the various strands of their heritage lost in two centuries of disorder. The "harmonization of the three teachings" of Confucianism, Buddhism, and Taoism was the order of the day and main guideline for the development of new Taoist doctrine. At the same time, the evolving practice of inner alchemy integrated all the various earlier techniques into a highly sophisticated complex under an umbrella of alchemical and divinatory symbolism (see Baldrian-Hussein 1984, Needham et al. 1983).

Many new Taoist schools sprang up, especially in the twelfth century under the Southern Song, a period of great political distress due to the conquest of the north by the Central Asians but also a time of rapid modernization and new economic developments. Most important among them was Complete Perfection (Quanzhen), a monastic and ascetic school that emphasized the integration of the three teachings and the practice of inner alchemy. Supported by the Yuan (Mongol) rulers, Complete Perfection attained a position of high influence which it has maintained until the present. In fact, the monastic group of Complete Perfection and the communal school of the Celestial Masters are the two surviving forms of Taoism today (see Tsui 1991).

In the first decades of the twentieth century, Taoism was a colorful mixture of the monastic, communal, and individual, a fascinating combination of spiritual, ritual, and shamanistic practices. Much of this has been destroyed in the People's Republic and is only making a slow and rather hesitant comeback, though many ancient techniques are popular again under the shield of medical practice (see Goullart 1961, Blofeld 1973, Pas 1990).

# Part One

## THE TAO

# Chapter One

## THE TAO

The Tao is what gave Taoism its name, both the ancient philosophy and the later religion; the Tao is their most fundamental concept, what occupies the place of the sacred in their very center.

The Tao is ineffable and beyond human comprehension; thus it is spoken about as nameless, formless, and obscure, with the help of contradictory metaphors and paradoxes. To speak about the Tao is, in fact, to "tao" it—something that cannot possibly succeed, yet has to be continuously attempted if there is to be a teaching in its name.

The Tao, if we then try to grasp it, can be described as the organic order underlying and structuring and pervading all existence. It is organic in that it is not willful, but it is also order because it changes in predictable rhythms and orderly patterns. If one is to approach it, reason and the intellect have to be left behind. One can only intuit it when one has become as nameless and as free of conscious choices and evaluations as the Tao itself.

The Tao cannot be described in ordinary language, since language by its very nature is part of the realm of discrimination and knowledge that the Tao transcends. Language is a product of the world; the Tao is beyond it—however pervasive and omnipresent it may be. The Tao is transcendent and yet immanent. It creates, structures, orders the whole universe, yet it is not a mere part of it.

Crucial to the religious experience of Taoism, the Tao is always there yet has always to be attained, realized, perfected. It creates the world and remains in it as the seed of primordial harmony, original purity, selfless tranquility. When outwardly active, it manifests as Virtue, an orderly, measurable power of

11

vitality that supports and rectifies the world, pervading life with a hue of the Tao's radiance deep within. Virtue can be practiced and followed, but only so far. Perfect Virtue is too close to the Tao itself to be fully practiced or understood. To realize it one must go truly beyond.

All Taoism centers around the Tao and its Virtue, around the ever transforming power of vitality and its deep and dark yet brilliant source. Different schools and traditions, down to individual practitioners, have understood and experienced this Tao and its Virtue differently, organizing their religious activities accordingly and building different theoretical frameworks for its comprehension. There is no one Taoism and no one single Taoist experience. Yet there are patterns, manifestations, to be observed. Like the Tao, the experience is and and yet is not, remains hidden and only occasionally emerges from the shadows.

The selections on the Tao are representative of varied approaches to this difficult and most fundamental of all Taoist concepts. The four texts come from three different periods and schools and give an impression of four different approaches to the enigma of the Tao and its formulation in human language.

First, the *Daode jing* (Scripture of the Tao and the Virtue) is the classic of all Taoism, the oldest and most important of its works. Dated to the third century B.C.E., it belongs to philosophical Taoism and represents the ancient philosophical and speculative view of the Tao.

Second, the *Daoti lun* (On the Embodiment of the Tao) is a medieval (eighth century) exegesis of the ancient text, highly theoretical and sophisticated, yet strongly informed by the beliefs of the religion and geared toward the needs of the religious practitioner. It stands for the scholastic approach to the Tao.

Third, the *Qingjing jing* (Scripture of Purity and Tranquility) represents the liturgical formulation of the Tao. The text, originally from the Song dynasty (960–1260), has been and still is used in the ritual devotions of monastic Taoism. It is chanted regularly and represents a devotional attitude to the Tao.

Fourth, then, the selection from the *Zhuangzi*, another text of philosophical Taoism that at the same time is recognized as China's first major literary work, shows the Tao in a story, clarified by literary tales, by metaphors and narrative events. It represents another ancient angle, yet at the same time shows the literary and metaphorical approach to the Tao.

## 1. The Tao That Can't Be Told

The *Daode jing*, known also as the *Laozi* after its alleged author, a philosopher of the sixth century B.C.E., is a short text of about five thousand characters. It is divided into eighty-one chapters and two major sections, dealing with the Tao and the Virtue respectively.

Although the concepts expressed in the text are recognized as quite ancient, the actual document dates from approximately 250 B.C.E. A manuscript copy from before 168 B.C.E. was found recently. Due to the rather legendary nature of its alleged author Laozi, the text is now assumed to consist of varied sayings of ancient masters, transmitted orally. Interpreted in many ways—politically, symbolically, as cultural criticism, allegory, popular sayings, etc.—the text in its religious reading has maintained a strong influence over Taoism for the past 2,500 years.

English translations of the text abound—more than one hundred to date. Frequently used versions are, for example, Waley 1934, Bynner 1944, Lin 1948, Legge 1962, Chan 1964, LaFargue 1992. Translations of the recently excavated manuscript are found in Lau 1982 and Henricks 1989. On the problems surrounding Laozi, see Fung and Bodde 1952, Seidel 1969, Kaltenmark 1969, Graham 1990. For commentaries of the text, see Ch'en 1981, Robinet 1977, Bergeron 1986, Chan 1991, Wagner 1980, 1986, and 1989.

---

### *Daode jing* (Scripture of the Tao and the Virtue)

The Tao that can be told
Is not the eternal Tao.
The name that can be named
Is not the eternal name.

The nameless is the origin of heaven and earth;
The named is the mother of the myriad beings.

Always remain free from desires—
And you can see its wonder.
Always cherish desires—
And you can only observe its outcome.

Both these develop together
But have different names;
They are part of the mystery.

Mysterious and more mysterious—
The gate of all that's wondrous. (chap. 1)


The Tao is empty.
Use it,
It will never overflow;
Abysmal it is—
The ancestor of all beings.

Blunting blades,
Opening knots,
Joining light,
Merging with dust.
Profound it is—
Like something eternal.

I do not know.
Whose child is it?
Its appearance precedes the gods. (chap. 4)


Heaven and earth are not benevolent,
They take the myriad beings as mere straw dogs.
The sage is not benevolent,
He takes the hundred families as mere straw dogs.

The space between heaven and earth,
Isn't it like a bellows?
Empty, yet never bent;
Active, yet reaching ever farther.

Speak much, repeat again—
No, much better to guard it in your midst! (chap. 5)


The valley spirit does not die,
It is called the mysterious female.
The gate of the mysterious female
Is called the root of heaven and earth.

Forever and ever, it exists continuously,
Use it, yet you'll never wear it out. (chap. 6)

Highest goodness is like water.
It benefits the myriad beings
And never contends.
By never contending
It is without fault.

It rests in what the multitude disdain,
Thus it is close to the Tao.

Rest in goodness like you stand on the earth,
Make your mind as good as the abyss is deep.
Join goodness to become fully benevolent,
Speak pure goodness for mutual trust.

Be straight in goodness when you govern,
Serve goodness as much as you can,
Then you will move with goodness at all times. (chap. 8)

Look at it and do not see it:
We call it invisible.
Listen to it and do not hear it:
We call it inaudible.
Touch it and do not feel it:
We call it subtle.

These three cannot be better understood,
They merge and become one.

Infinite and boundless, it cannot be named.
It belongs to where there are no beings.
It may be called the shape of no-shape,
It may be called the form of no-form.

Call it vague and obscure.
Meet it, yet you cannot see its head,
Follow it, yet you cannot see its back.
Grasp the Tao of old and control existence now.
Know the beginnings of old—
And have a thread to the Tao. (chap. 14)

Attain utmost emptiness,
Maintain steadfast tranquility.

The myriad beings are alive,
And I see thereby their return.
All these beings flourish,
But each one returns to its root.

Return to the root means tranquility,
It is called recovering life.

To recover life is called the eternal.
To know the eternal is called enlightenment.

If you don't know the eternal,
You will fall into error and end in disaster.

Know the eternal and forgive;
Forgive and be altruistic.
Be altruistic and embrace all;
Embrace all and be like heaven.

Be like heaven and merge with the Tao,
One with the Tao, you will last long.
You may die but will never perish. (chap. 16).


Forgiveness of great virtue
Flows from the Tao alone.
The Tao may appear as a being,
Yet is just vague, only obscure.

Obscure it is! It is vague!
In its midst, some appearance.
Vague it is! It is obscure!
In its midst, some being.

Serene it is! It is profound!
In its midst, some essence.
True this essence, nothing but so true!
In its midst, some trust.

From the old to today
Its name never vanished,
To open the beginnings of all.

How do I know what those beginnings are?
From this alone. (chap. 21)


There is a being, in chaos yet complete;
It preceded even heaven and earth.

Silent it is, and solitary;
Standing alone, it never changes;
It moves around, yet never ends.
Consider it the mother of all-under-heaven.

I do not know its name.
To call it something, I speak of Tao.
Naming its strength, I call it great.

Great—that means it departs.
Depart—that means it is far away.
Far away—that means it will return.

Therefore the Tao is great,
Heaven is great,
Earth is great,
The king, too, is great.

In this enclosure, there are these four greats,
And the king rests as one of them.
The king follows earth,
Earth follows heaven,
Heaven follows the Tao.
The Tao follows only itself. (chap. 25)


The Tao—eternal, nameless, simple.
Although small,
It is subject to neither heaven nor earth.

Kings and lords maintain it,
And the myriad beings come to them.
Heaven and earth are in harmony,
And sweet dew falls.

People do not order it,
It is everywhere equally.

First you control it, then names appear.
Yet once there are names,
Knowledge must arise of when to stop.
Know when to stop
And you will never perish.

Compare how the Tao is in all-under-heaven
To the converging of rivers and valleys
Toward the great streams and endless oceans. (chap. 32)


Great Tao—overflowing!
Can be left and right!

The myriad beings rely on it to be born.
It never turns them away.
Its merit, so perfect—
Yet claims no fame for its existence.

It clothes and nurtures the myriad beings—
Yet claims no position as their chief.
Always free from desires—
Call it small!

The myriad beings return to it—
And yet never make it their chief.
Call it great!

To its very end
It does not think itself great.
Thus
It can perfect its greatness. (chap. 34)

## 2. The Tao in the World

The *Daoti lun* (DZ 1035, fasc. 704) is a short scholastic treatise not studied or translated to date. It is commonly associated with Sima Chengzhen (647–735), the twelfth patriarch of Highest Clarity (Shangqing) Taoism at its height under Emperor Xuanzong of the Tang. Invited to court several times, Sima was the leading Taoist figure of his time. Several important works of his remain today, including the *Zuowang lun* (On Sitting in Oblivion) and the *Fuqi jingyi lun* (On the Essential Meaning of the Absorption of Energy). Both texts deal with Taoist practice, meditation and longevity techniques.

For more on Sima Chengzhen, see Kohn 1987, Engelhardt 1987 and 1989. For a study of Taoist soteriology, see Kohn 1992. For other scholastic interpretations of the *Daode jing*, see Robinet 1977.

---

### *Daoti lun* (On the Embodiment of the Tao)

DISCUSSING LAOZI'S *DAODE JING*

[1a] The Tao is all-pervasive; it transforms all from the beginning. Virtue arises in its following; it completes all beings to their end. They thus appear in birth and the completion of life. In the world, they have two different names, yet fulfilling their activities, they return to the same ancestral ground. They are two and yet always one.

They are two and yet always one. Therefore there is no Tao outside of the omnipresence of Virtue. There is no Virtue different from the completion of life through the Tao. They are one and still appear as two.

The Tao is found in endless transformation and pervasive omnipresence. Virtue shines forth in the completion of life and in following along. They are always one; they are always two.

Two in one, they are all-pervasive. All-pervasive, they can yet be distinguished. Thus their names are the Tao and the Virtue.

Question: You said, "The Tao is all-pervasive; it transforms all from the beginning." Whose beginning does this refer to?

Answer: The beginning of the inner natures of all beings. How do we know this? Because the text says, "Virtue arises in its following; it completes all beings to their end." Thus we know. [1b] Inner nature arises from the Tao. The outer body is brought forth by Virtue.

Question: This being so, why then does the scripture say, "The Tao brings them forth, Virtue nurtures them"?

Answer: They follow the root and rely on the prime, thus the text says, "the Tao brings them forth." The body is established only gradually, thus the text speaks of "nurture."

Question: There is a root that lies at the beginning of inner nature. Does it have a name or is it nameless?

Answer: Both.

Question: If it is both, why then does the scripture say that the nameless is at the root of the myriad beings? Why does it not say that it has a name?

Answer: The Tao is an expression for that which pervades all life. When something pervades all life, there are bound to be outer manifestations. Once there are such manifestations, one can name them. Therefore one can attach names to the Tao, but none of these names will ever be truly permanent.

Indeed, the Tao embodies all, wide and encompassing; its meaning is not limited to one name. Today we use language to dispel its engulfing obscurity. But language only makes the rough outer manifestations of the Tao appear more clearly. It is only by going beyond these that one can awaken to the wondrous depths. [2a]

Question: The Tao is wide and encompassing. Is it the same or different from beings?

Answer: The Tao is always there, yet eternally other. Beings need the Tao to embody themselves. At the same time, the Tao needs beings to embody itself. Beyond the inherent oneness of all, there are good and evil, right and wrong, life and death, opposition and conformity.

Compare it to a fish. The fish depends on water to live; it also depends on water to die. Similarly people depend on the earth to walk on; they depend on the earth to fall down on; and they depend on the earth to get up on.

Question: The scripture says, "The Tao brings them forth, Virtue nurtures them." It also says, "That which brings forth and nurtures beings is called the Mysterious Virtue." First it says, the Tao brings them forth. Then it says, Virtue does so. How does this go together?

Fig. 1. The Empty Tao and the Tao in the World. Source: *Laojun bashiyi huan tushuo.*

Answer: When the text first says that the Tao brings them forth, it refers to the fact that beings first receive cosmic empowerment from the very root of all existence. When it then says that

Virtue brings them forth, it indicates that afterwards beings receive their concrete life and are duly shaped into separate entities. How do we know this is so?

Yin and yang embody each other in harmony and engender manifold transformations. With the establishment of these transformations yang comes to predominate, just as ruler and minister jointly govern the world. When their task is fulfilled, they return to the primordial beginning.

The embodiment of the myriad beings as concrete living entities comes through Virtue. [2b] But in its ancestral roots, this goes all the way to the deepest ground [of the Tao].

The text says, "The Tao brings them forth." What the Tao does in fact bring forth is the embodiment of chaos complete, the beginning that has no name. It structures and encompasses the myriad beings in their original state. Wondrous it is in the extreme, the tranquil center of all developments.

Obscure it is, indistinct! One cannot say it is really there. Yet all beings are there, right in its midst! One cannot say it is not there either. Above it shines, yet there is no light. Below it hides, yet there is no darkness. Meet it and you cannot see its head; pursue it and you cannot see its back.

None knows where it comes from; it cannot be investigated and searched out. It is shape without shape, image without being. It is a word that is no word, yet this wordless word fills the universe. Through the Tao, bodies and names become apparent, and it separates the ordinary from the sagely.

Indeed, the ordinary cannot awaken of themselves. They must accumulate outer impulses and painstakingly seek the omnipresent pervasion underlying all. The sagely thus do not abandon beings to themselves, but instead make use of favorable opportunities to establish the teaching.

The opportunities of teaching are irregular; therefore a myriad differences arise. But they all have in common that they are manifestations of the unifying harmony of all—the Tao and the Virtue.

The Tao's deepest roots lie in its omnipresent pervasion. Virtue most of all means spontaneous realization. In omnipresent pervasion, there is no principle that is not pervaded. In spontaneous realization, there is no trait of inner nature that is not fully realized.

Omnipresent pervasion has no name. Nameless, it can be affirmatively named. [3a] Spontaneous realization is nonrealization. Therefore its activity manifests and duly becomes known in appellations. Appellations thus contain the manifestations of active Virtue.

In Virtue, diligent practice is foremost, affirmatively naming the originally nameless. In the Tao, diminishing daily is essential, diligently pursuing and practicing it. Without this practice, nothing can be achieved.

Diminish and again diminish, and there will be no fetter that does not dissolve. As Tao and Virtue are both forgotten, one mysteriously joins beings and oneself in pervasive oneness. Thus one can be great and overflowing [like the Tao]. Remain moderate in its use and it will never be exhausted.

So great, it has no beyond; so small, it has no within. Flowing and encompassing all, it changes and transforms, leaving nothing that is not done.

Therefore the myriad beings, numerous and varied, in all their shapes and names, their actions and developments, always depend on the Tao and the Virtue. Thus they can complete themselves.

The scripture says, "The Tao is the obscure background of the myriad beings." Thus Laozi the Perfected lived in accordance with its manifestations and, under the Zhou dynasty [6th century B.C.E.], revealed its mysterious aura in order to save the age. Thus he wrote about the Tao and the Virtue. He used these two names to establish the teaching. Thus we know that the teaching does not appear all by itself. To appear in the world, it must have a foundation.

Its first and foremost foundation lies with Laozi, the Old Child. As he was even before symbols and gods, he is called Old. As he goes along with the changes and transforms in ever new births, he is called Child. [3b] As he embodies the teaching in omnipresent pervasion, he is called the Tao. As he represents the perfect principle that never changes, he is called the Scripture. As he has arisen even before these four, he is called the Highest. Thus his name is Old Child; he is embodied in the Highest Scripture of the Tao.

Question: What does chaos complete embody itself in?

Answer: It embodies itself in empty nonbeing as well as in the myriad forms of being.

Question: Chaos is empty nonbeing as well as the myriad forms of being. Now, is this embodiment of chaos the same or different from the Tao?

Answer: It is both different and the same.

Question: Please explain how this is so.

Answer: It is different because, when chaos assembles to obtain embodiment, it becomes apparent and is named the Tao. In its embodiment, chaos pervades all and can thus be named. This is because, in its pervasion, it accumulates and its different aspects are singled out. Then they can be identified. Thus we say, chaos is different from the Tao.

But it is also the same, because the Tao is never separate from its omnipresent pervasion. When one tries to distinguish this pervasion from chaos, there is no real division. Chaos assembles and pervades all. Thus we say, chaos is the same as the Tao.

Question: So, you're saying that chaos can pervade the myriad beings. Pervasion therefore is chaos. Chaos in turn is all beings. [4a] Chaos is the Tao. Therefore all beings are the Tao. Now, if there is no difference between all beings and the Tao, why then should one cultivate it?

Answer: Pure cultivation makes up for the discrepancy, however minor, between the root and its embodiment. It leads back to the original nonbeing beyond and above chaos. The meaning of cultivation must be carefully taught. It is certainly not at all like an investigation and analysis of embodiment.

Question: Is chaos complete the same or different from the Great Emblem?

Answer: It is both different and the same. How do we know this? The Great Emblem is called chaos complete. This is the name of its embodiment. But the actual meaning of this embodiment is something else again. Thus we know that it is different.

Still, if the name is not distinguished from the appellation of this embodiment, then the name is also this very embodiment itself. When thus the embodiment has no other name than chaos, the name is in fact the embodiment. Thus we say they are the same.

### 3. Pure and Tranquil

The *Qingjing jing* (DZ 620, fasc. 341), translated here in full, is a short, verse-like text that rose to prominence in the Song dynasty (960–1260). It was especially popular with the monastic school of Complete Perfection (Quanzhen) Taoism, in whose centers it is still recited as part of the regular devotions today.

The text serves to inspire the active practitioner and believer. It provides an easy handle on the realization of the Tao within the religious life. It is an exhortation to purity and meditation, a warning against bad thoughts and deviant desires. Pious Taoists know this short and rhythmic text by heart.

There is as yet no study of this text or of Taoist monastic liturgy. A recent translation with inner-alchemical commentary is found in Wong 1992. On the history and present circumstances of the Complete Perfection sect, see Yao 1980, Tsui 1991.

---

### *Qingjing jing* (Scripture of Purity and Tranquility)

> The Great Tao has no form;
> It brings forth and raises heaven and earth.
> The Great Tao has no feelings;
> It regulates the course of the sun and the moon.
>
> The Great Tao has no name;
> It raises and nourishes the myriad beings.
> I do not know its name—
> So I call it Tao.
>
> The Tao can be pure or turbid, moving or tranquil.
> Heaven is pure, earth is turbid;
> Heaven is moving, earth is tranquil.
> The male is moving, the female is tranquil.
>
> Descending from the origin,
> Flowing toward the end,
> The myriad beings are being born.
>
> Purity—the source of turbidity,
> Movement—the root of tranquility.
>
> Always be pure and tranquil;
> Heaven and earth
> Return to the primordial.
>
> The human spirit is fond of purity,
> But the mind disturbs it.
> The human mind is fond of tranquility,
> But desires meddle with it.

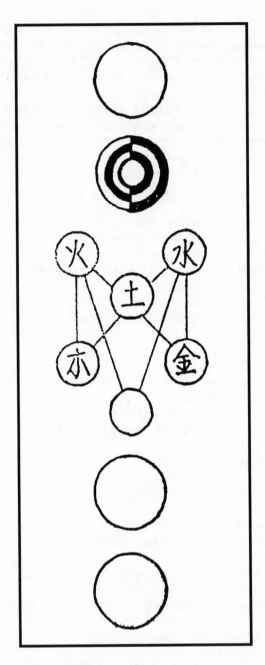

Fig. 2. The Empty Tao Develops into the
World: The Diagram of the Great Ultimate.
Source: *Taiji tushuo.*

Get rid of desires for good,
And the mind will be calm.
Cleanse your mind,
And the spirit will be pure.

Naturally the six desires won't arise,
The three poisons are destroyed.
Whoever cannot do this
Has not yet cleansed his mind,
His desires are not yet driven out.

Those who have abandoned their desires:
Observe your mind by introspection—
And see there is no mind.

Then observe the body,
Look at yourself from without—
And see there is no body.

Then observe others by glancing out afar—
And see there are no beings.

Once you have realized these three,
You observe emptiness!

Use emptiness to observe emptiness,
And see there is no emptiness.
When even emptiness is no more,
There is no more nonbeing either.

Without even the existence of nonbeing
There is only serenity,
Profound and everlasting.

When serenity dissolves in nothingness—
How could there be desires?
When no desires arise
You have found true tranquility.

In true tranquility, go along with beings;
In true permanence, realize inner nature.
Forever going along, forever tranquil—
This is permanent purity, lasting tranquility.

In purity and tranquility,
Gradually enter the true Tao.
When the true Tao is entered,
It is realized.

Though we speak of "realized,"
Actually there is nothing to attain.
Rather, we speak of realization
When someone begins to transform the myriad beings.

Only who has properly understood this
Is worthy to transmit the sages' Tao.

The highest gentleman does not fight;
The lesser gentleman loves to fight.
Highest Virtue is free from Virtue;
Lesser Virtue clings to Virtue.

All clinging and attachments
Have nothing to do with the Tao or the Virtue.

People fail to realize the Tao
Because they have deviant minds.
Deviance in the mind
Means the spirit is alarmed.

Spirit alarmed,
There is clinging to things.
Clinging to things,
There is searching and coveting.

Searching and coveting,
There are passions and afflictions.
Passions, afflictions, deviance, and imaginings
Trouble and pester body and mind.

Then one falls into turbidity and shame,
Ups and downs, life and death.
Forever immersed in the sea of misery,
One is in eternity lost to the true Tao.

The Tao of true permanence
Will naturally come to those who understand.
Those who understand the realization of the Tao
Will rest forever in the pure and tranquil.

## 4. Ineffable Knowledge

The *Zhuangzi* is the second most worthy ancient classic of Taoism after the *Daode jing*. In its present edition it consists of thirty-three chapters. Only the first seven are accepted as being close to the philosopher Zhuangzi himself, a man who lived in the fourth century B.C.E. in the south of China. The remaining chapters are associated with different schools of ancient philosophical Taoism, including the Primitivists, the Hedonists, the Syncretists, and later followers of Zhuangzi's thought. Chapter 22, from which the stories are taken, belongs to the latter.

The *Zhuangzi* is famous for its high literary quality, its humor, and the depths of its insights. Throughout the history of Taoism, the text has never failed to inspire practitioners and poets alike.

The rendition relies on Watson 1968. For other translations, see Graham 1981 and 1982. Discussions are found in Mair 1983, Allinson 1990. On the history and origin of the text, see Graham 1980, Roth 1991a.

The are also two other texts of philosophical Taoism, the *Huainanzi* and the *Liezi*. Like the *Zhuangzi*, they present philosophical concepts in literary and metaphorical format. On the *Huainanzi*, see LeBlanc 1978, 1985, Roth 1992; for a translation of the *Liezi*, see Graham 1960.

---

### "Zhi beiyou" (Knowledge Wandered North), *Zhuangzi*, chap. 22.

Knowledge wandered north to the far side of the primordial waters and climbed the hills of the absconded rise. There he happened to meet Non-Action-No-Words.

Knowledge said to Non-Action-No-Words: "I would like to put some questions to you. By what thinking, by what reflection can I know the Tao? By what setting, by what activities can I be at peace with the Tao? By what procedures, by what way can I attain the Tao?"

He put these three questions, but Non-Action-No-Words did not answer. It was not that he did not answer. He did not know how to answer.

Knowledge thus did not get any answer. He returned to the south of the white waters and climbed the heights of suspicions-at-rest. There he caught sight of Crazy Crouchy. Knowledge, in the same words, put the three questions to Crazy Crouchy.

"Ah! I know!" said Crazy Crouchy. "I'll tell you."

But just as he wished to say something, he forgot what he wished to say.

Knowledge thus did not get any answer. He returned to the imperial palace, where he had an audience with the Yellow Emperor. He posed his questions.

"Only with no thinking nor reflection," said the Yellow Emperor, "can you begin to know the Tao. Only with no setting nor activities can you begin to be at peace with the Tao. Only with no procedures nor way can you begin to attain the Tao."

Knowledge had a further question. "You and I know," he said, "but those other two did not. Which of us is right?"

"Non-Action-No-Words is truly right," the Yellow Emperor explained. "Crazy Crouchy appears to be so. But you and I, after all, don't even come close. Really! Who knows does not speak—who speaks does not know. Therefore the sage practices the teaching without words. The Tao cannot be brought about; Virtue cannot be approached.

"But benevolence," he went on, "can be actively practiced. Righteousness can be lost or gained, and the rites can be considered true or false. Thus we say: Lose the Tao and then there is Virtue; lose Virtue and then there is benevolence; lose benevolence and then there is righteousness; lose righteousness and then there are the rites. Rites are the marginal ornaments of the Tao. They are the beginning of disorder.

"Thus we say," the Yellow Emperor continued, "practice the Tao and decrease day by day. Decrease and again decrease, until you come to non-action. In non-action there is nothing that is not done. Now we already are active beings. To want to go back and recover our root, is this not indeed difficult? Only the great man might find it easy.

"Life is the follower of death; death is the beginning of life. Who knows their patterns? Human life is an assembly of energy. It assembles and there is life; it disperses and there is death. Death and life follow each other naturally. So why should I feel distressed?

"From that perspective the myriad beings are in fact one. We find some beautiful because they are spiritual and strange; others we think of as hateful because they are smelly and rotten. But the smelly and rotten will again change and be spiritual and strange;

and the spiritual and strange will again turn to be smelly and rotten. So we say: Just penetrate the one energy of all-under-heaven. The sage, accordingly, places highest value on absolute oneness."

Knowledge pondered this. "I asked Non-Action-No-Words and he did not give me a reply," he said to the Yellow Emperor. "It was not that he did not give me a reply. He did not know how to reply. I asked Crazy Crouchy and he wished to tell me, but he did not tell me. It was not that he did not tell me. But just as he wished to say something, he forgot what he wished to say. Now I have asked you. You know. Why then do you say you don't even come close?"

"Non-Action-No-Words is truly right. Because he does not know. Crazy Crouchy appears to be so. Because he forgets. But you and I, after all, don't even come close. Because we know."

Crazy Crouchy heard about this. He thought the Yellow Emperor knew what he was talking about.

*

Master Eastwall asked Zhuangzi, "What we call the Tao—where does it exist?"

"There's no place it does not exist," Zhuangzi replied.

"Come on," said Master Eastwall, "you must be more specific!"

"It is in the ant."

"How can it be so low?"

"It is in the grass."

"How can it be even lower?"

"It is in bricks and shards."

"How can it be lower still?"

"It is even in excrement!"

Master Eastwall did not reply.

"Sir," Zhuangzi said in explanation, "your questions do not reach the essence. When Inspector Huo inquired in the market how to examine the fatness of a pig by pressing it with the foot, he was told that the lower one pressed, the better."

"But," he went on, "you must not apply this rule to the Tao. Nothing ever avoids its presence. Such is the perfect Tao. So too are truly great words. Encompassing, universal, including all. These three are different words but mean the same. They all indicate just one reality."

He took a breath, then went on.

"Why don't you wander with me," he asked companionably, "to the Palace of Nothing-At-All? We'll be together and in harmony for our discussions, never ending, never exhausted. Why don't you join me in non-action? Be serene and tranquil, carefree and utterly pure, finely tuned and at leisure? Already my will is open vastness. I go nowhere and do not know where I'm getting to. I go and come and do not know where to stop. I've already come and gone many times, but I do not know when it'll be over. I ramble and relax in endless openness. Great knowledge enters in and I do not know where it will ever end."

He paused to collect his thoughts.

"That which treats beings as beings does not have the limits of beings," he continued with conviction. "Beings have their limits—the so-called limit of beings. The limit of the unlimited ultimately is the limitless end of the limit. We speak of beings filling and emptying, decaying and dying. The Tao makes them full and empty, but is not itself full or empty. It makes them decay and die, but does not itself decay or die. It establishes their roots and branches, but is itself free from roots or branches. It determines when they assemble and disperse, but in itself neither assembles nor disperses."

# Chapter Two

## CREATION

The Tao is responsible for all-that-is; it is at the ground beyond all existence and yet immanent in all its forms. The Tao creates; in its most immediate appearance it is the creation of the universe. First all emptiness and nonbeing, it is formless and vague. Revolving around for long periods of time and through various stages of primordiality and chaos, it eventually divides into two, originally equally formless energies, one light, one heavy, one bright, one dark. These are yin and yang, the original pair of complementary opposites. Through them, there are heaven and earth, the sun and the moon, light and darkness, hot and cold, and all the various distinctions that make up the world of existence.

Combining again, yin and yang then give rise to the myriad beings, plants and living creatures, of which humans are one. Giving different distributions to different beings, the multiplicity of life evolves, patterned according to the scheme of the five agents or phases, which represent yin and yang in the varying stages of lesser and greater.

The first things created, the forces at the very brink of existence, are pure emanations of yin and yang. They are the gods and the heavens, the scriptures and the talismans. These are the Tao in its most original and yet no longer empty and formless shape; they are the world on the threshold of being born. Only due to their existence can everything else come into being; only through the creative and salvational will of the gods in their heavens, through the powerful sacred formulas embedded in the scriptures and the talismans, can the world ever take shape. Not only creating, these forces continue to be part of the wider universe. Forever the same and yet ever new, they descend into the world of humanity to rectify and save, to support and cherish, to reveal the purity of the Tao. They are a canopy of Tao that is always there, that can be called upon in ritual and reached in meditation. They are the source of creation as much as the cause of the world's continued existence and the ultimate hope of the salvation of all.

The selections below give accounts of the original state of the world from different perspectives and traditions.

First, the *Kaitian jing* (Scripture of Opening the Cosmos), is a short account of the origins of the world, beginning with formless nothingness and ending with the Zhou dynasty. Inspired by Highest Clarity Taoism, it dates approximately from the Tang dynasty (618–906). It centers around the figure of the Venerable Lord, the deified Laozi and embodiment of the Tao. It integrates the early myth of the transformations of Laozi (see below)—the notion that he appeared in every age to be the teacher of the dynasty—with the historical vision of classical Chinese mythology.

Next, the *Lingbao lueji* (A Short Record of Numinous Treasure), concentrates on the role of the talismans of Numinous Treasure in the creation and continued salvation of the world. It is inspired by the Numinous Treasure (Lingbao) school and dates back to the third century. The central deity here is the Heavenly Venerable of Primordial Beginning (Yunshi tianzun), an adaptation of the Buddha, as much in the Lingbao school is influenced by Buddhism. The purpose of the document is to establish an integrated connection between the kalpic revolutions at the dawn of time with the emergence of the historical Lingbao tradition in the fourth century. It reinterprets history to this end.

Third, the *Shizhou ji* (Record of the Ten Continents), is an account of the isles and paradises of the immortals. These realms of high purity are part of the original state of the Tao; they house wondrous plants and animals which can bestow salvation upon human beings. The text is related to tales of the marvelous that were popular in the early middle ages (220–589) and was also integrated into the Highest Clarity corpus. It is a description of sacred geography as much as of the concrete conditions of the heavens, in which the pure representatives of the Tao reside.

Fourth, finally, there is biography of the Queen Mother of the West (Xiwang mu). Written by Du Guangting (850–933) in the late Tang and contained in his *Yongcheng jixian lu* (Record of the Assembled Immortals of the Heavenly Walled City), this provides some insight into the nature and daily tasks of the Taoist gods. They, as much as their lands and the celestial scriptures and talismans, are part of the original creation—existing and yet uncreated, formless and yet powers of salvation to be called upon.

## 5. Scriptures Create the Universe

The *Taishang laojun kaitian jing* (The Scripture of How the Highest Venerable Lord Opens the Cosmos) is contained twice in the Taoist canon, in DZ 1437, fasc. 1059, and in chapter 2 of the *Yunji qiqian* (Seven Tablets in a Cloudy Satchel), a Taoist encyclopedia from the early eleventh century (DZ 1032, fasc. 677–702).

Probably dating from the Tang dynasty (618–906), it shows a certain Mahāyāna Buddhist influence. Not only in its initial formula, "Thus I have heard," but also in its contents, for example in the description of the size and heavenly nature of the scriptures, in its phrasing, "as numerous as the sands of the Ganges," and in the final verse or *gatha* of Laozi, it follows the pattern of a Buddhist sutra.

Nevertheless, the text is primarily an indigenous version of the creation. It integrates philosophical views of the stages of the universe, first expressed in the tradition of the *Yijing* (Book of Changes), with the myth of the transformations of Laozi, who appears in every age to be the teacher of the dynasty, and the traditional Chinese understanding of ancient history and the beginnings of culture.

There is no study of Taoist creation myths to date. For a comparative analysis of the myth of chaos (Hundun) in philosophical Taoism, see Girardot 1983. On the mythology and cosmology of Highest Clarity, see Robinet 1984. On Laozi as the body of the Tao, see Schipper 1978, 1982.

---

*Taishang laojun kaitian jing* (**Scripture of How the Highest Venerable Lord Opens the Cosmos**)

[1a] Thus I have heard. Before heaven and earth opened, all was endless beyond Great Clarity; all was limitless in Barren Nonbeing. Desolate and vast it was, and without bounds.

No heaven nor earth : no yin nor yang,
no sun nor moon : no brightness nor radiance,
no east nor west : no green nor yellow,
no south nor north : no soft nor hard,

no cover nor support : no embrace nor closeness,
no wisdom nor sageliness : no loyalty nor goodness,
no going nor coming : no arising nor passing,
no front nor back : no round nor square.

It transformed hundreds of millions of times, all grand and vast, vast and grand! No shape nor sign. Pure so-being and emptiness! Oh , how unfathomable!

No measure nor end : no high nor low
no even nor odd : no left nor right.
Above and below, in pure so-being alone,

THE VENERABLE LORD, the Tao, was at rest in open mystery, beyond silent desolation, in mysterious emptiness. Look and do not see, [1b] listen and do not hear. Say it/he is there and do not see a shape; say it/he is not there, yet all beings follow him for life. Beyond the eight bounds—slowly, slowly—first it divides. Sinks to form the subtle and the wondrous, to make the world.

Then there was Vast Prime [Hongyuan]. In the time of Vast Prime, there still was no heaven and no earth, the empty void had not yet separated, clear and turbid were not yet divided. In mysterious barrenness and silent desolation, Vast Prime continued for a myriad kalpas.

Then Vast Prime divided, and there was Coagulated Prime [Hunyuan]. Coagulated Prime continued for a myriad kalpas until it reached its perfection. Its perfection lasted for eighty-one times ten thousand years.

Then there was Grand Antecedence [Taichu]. In the time of Grand Antecedence,

THE VENERABLE LORD descended from barren emptiness to be the teacher of Grand Antecedence. His mouth brought forth the *Scripture of Opening the Cosmos* in one section and forty-eight times ten thousand scrolls. Each scroll had forty-eight times ten thousand characters. Each character was one hundred square miles in size. Thus he taught Grand Antecedence.

In Grand Antecedence, for the first time he separated heaven and earth, the clear and the turbid. [2a] He divided boundless galaxies and vast nebulae. He set up shapes and signs. He secured north and south. He ordered east and west. He opened the darkness and made light. He positioned the four universal mainstays.

Above and below, inside and out, within and without, long and short, gross and subtle, female and male, white and black, big and small, noble and humble—all were constantly moving along in darkness.

But when Coagulated Prime attained the *Scripture of Opening the Cosmos* of

THE VENERABLE LORD, clear and turbid were separated. Clear energy rose up and formed heaven. Turbid energy sank down and formed earth. The three spheres were established. Then, for the first time, there were heaven and earth. Yet, still no sun nor moon.

Heaven desired to transform beings, to afford them changes without bounds. Therefore it set up the sun and the moon in its midst. They would illuminate the darkness below. In the time of Grand Antecendence, there were thus the sun and the moon. Still no human beings. Slowly, they first came forth. Above he took the essence of heaven. Below he took the essence of earth. He joined them in the middle and made a spirit called human.

Heaven and earth were first void; then there were the three initial divisions. [2b] All species of life were without sign or shape. Each received just one bit of energy and life was complete. Those with raw energy for life were stones and mountains. Those with moving energy for life were birds and beasts. Those with essential energy for life were human beings. Among all the myriad beings, humans are the highest.

Grand Antecedence continued for a myriad kalpas. Then only human beings appeared. Thus this period is called Grand Antecedence. At this time, there were only heaven and earth, the sun and the moon, animals and people. Still no consciousness nor language.

When Grand Antecedence came to an end, Grand Initiation [Taishi] emerged. In the time of Grand Initiation,

THE VENERABLE LORD descended to be its teacher. His mouth brought forth the *Scripture of Grand Initiation* in one section. Thus he taught Grand Initiation. He worked to set up all under heaven for ninety-one times ten thousand years. After ninety-one times ten thousand years, it reached its perfection. The perfection lasted eighty-one times ten thousand years.

Grand Initiation is the beginning of the myriad beings. Thus it is called Grand Initiation. It flowed and revolved, perfected and refined all immaculate signs in its midst. [3a] Energy became solid and transformed into perfect yin and yang.

When Grand Initiation came to an end, there was Grand Immaculate [Taisu]. In the time of Grand Immaculate,

Fig. 3. The Venerable Lord. Source: *Laojun bashiyi hua tushuo.*

THE VENERABLE LORD descended to be its teacher. He taught Grand Immaculate how to order all under heaven. After eighty-one kalpas, it reached its perfection. This lasted eighty-one times ten thousand years. Grand Immaculate is the immaculate state of the myriad beings. Thus it is called Grand Immaculate.

From Grand Antecedence to Grand Immaculate, heaven brought forth sweet dew and earth brought forth sweet wine. People lived on these and attained long life. Upon death they would not bury the corpse, but abandon it in a distant wilderness. This period is called High Antiquity.

Then Grand Immaculate came to an end and there was Chaos [Hundun]. In the time of Chaos, for the first time there were mountains and streams.

THE VENERABLE LORD descended to be its teacher. He taught Chaos how to govern all under heaven. For seventy-two kalpas, he flowed along with Chaos. He completed its mountains and rivers, and there first were the five sacred mountains and four majestic streams. High and low, noble and humble arose for the first time.

From the time of Chaos, there were consciousness and language. With the name of Chaos there were two personages. [3b] The elder was Barbarian Vassal [Huchen]; the younger was Barbarian Soul [Huling]. The elder died and became the god of the mountains. The younger died and became the god of the rivers. They gave names to the five sacred mountains, the four majestic streams, and to all the mountains and rivers, high and low.

Then Chaos came to an end and there was Nine Palaces [Jiugong]. In the time of Nine Palaces,

THE VENERABLE LORD descended to be its teacher. His mouth brought forth the *Scripture of the Heaven and Earth Hexagrams* in one section. Teaching Nine Palaces, he first gave people consciousness and language of heaven and earth. Pure energy formed heaven; turbid energy formed earth. Ever since Nine Palaces, heaven was yang and earth was yin. Yang is hard and strong. It is hard to see from afar. In heaven it forms the signs—sun, moon, stars, and constellations. On earth it forms the shapes—the five sacred mountains and the four majestic rivers. In human beings it forms the five orbs including the heart and the liver. Divided, it receives many names. Joined, it is called the One.

Nine Palaces came to an end and there was the Primordial Sovereign [Yuanhuang]. In the time of the Primordial Sovereign, THE VENERABLE LORD descended to be his teacher. His mouth brought forth the *Scripture of the Primordial Sovereign* in one section. Thus he taught the Primordial Sovereign how to order all under heaven. [4a] For the first time, there was an imperial government. It flowed along to later generations and gradually reached perfection.

After the Primordial Sovereign, there was the Great Highest Sovereign [Taishang huang]. In the time of the Great Highest Sovereign,

THE VENERABLE LORD descended to be his teacher. He taught the Great Highest Sovereign how to order all under heaven.

After the Great Highest Sovereign, there was the Earth Sovereign [Dihuang]. After the Earth Sovereign, there was the Human Sovereign [Renhuang]. After the Human Sovereign, there was the Venerable Lü [Zun Lü]. After the Venerable Lü, there was the Crooked Lou [Gou Lou]. After the Crooked Lou, there was the Glorious Xu [He Xu]. After the Glorious Xu, there was the Great Lian [Tai Lian].

From Chaos to the Great Lian, this is called Middle Antiquity. During this period, heaven brought forth the five energies. Earth brought forth the five flavors. The people lived on these and attained extended years.

After the Great Lian ended, there was the ruler Hidden Vapor [Fu Xi]. He was born at the source of a spring in accordance with heaven. He harmonized yin and yang and established the eight trigrams. Before Hidden Vapor, the five classics had not been recorded and there had not been a system of writing. There had only been [4b]

THE VENERABLE LORD who followed the barren emptiness of heaven, immeasurable as the sands of the Ganges. He rested beyond Great Clarity, unfathomable in its vastness. Since the division of the Great Tao and the existence of heaven and earth, he had established the imperial government and assisted the rulers in their task. With the world he flowed along to later generations and recorded their events.

In the time of Hidden Vapor,

THE VENERABLE LORD descended to be his teacher. He was called Master of Non-Efflorescence or Master of Luxuriant Efflorescence. He taught Hidden Vapor how to expand the old laws and extend yin and yang. He made him order the eight directions and set up the eight trigrams. He produced the *Scripture of Primordial Yang* in order to teach Hidden Vapor.

Before him, there had been no clan names nor personal appellations. Now everywhere there were names. People then were simple and straightforward; they did not yet have the five grains. Hidden

Vapor taught them how to make nets and traps to catch birds and beasts to eat. They all wore furs and lived on blood, smelling rancid and putrid. Men and women were not separated; there was no jealousy between them. In winter they lived in caves; in summer they made their homes on trees.

After Hidden Vapor, there was the ruler Snake Woman [Nügua]. She was followed by the ruler Divine Farmer [Shennong]. In the time of Divine Farmer, [5a]

THE VENERABLE LORD descended to be his teacher. He was called Master of Great Completion. He produced the *Scripture of Great Tenuity*. He taught Divine Farmer about the hundred plants and gave him the five grains. Divine Farmer ordered the people to plant and reap them so that they could eat them instead of taking the lives of birds and beasts.

After Divine Farmer, there was the ruler Fire Drill [Suiren]. Again, THE VENERABLE LORD descended to be his teacher. He taught Fire Drill to drill wood and make fire. This would continue the light of day and allowed the cooking of raw meat. It put an end to the rancid and bloody smells.

After Fire Drill, there was the ruler Blessed Melter [Zhurong]. THE VENERABLE LORD descended to be his teacher. He was called Master of Wide Longevity. He taught Blessed Melter to cultivate the three mainstays of heaven and to harmonize the course of the seven planets. Under the earlier rulers, who had cultivated the Tao, there had been no sickness among the people. Now he produced the *Scripture of Applying Pressure and Guiding Essence* [to help against diseases].

Next there were the rulers High Source [Gaoyuan], High Yang [Gaoyang], and High Toil [Gaoxin]. After them came Dark Knot [Cangjie] whom he taught how to write.

After these rulers, there was the Yellow Emperor [Huangdi]. In the time of the Yellow Emperor, [5b]

THE VENERABLE LORD descended to be his teacher. He was called Master of Wide Perfection. He harmonized yin and yang and produced the *Scripture of Tao Precepts*. In the time of the Yellow Emperor, for the first time there were the formal ranks of ruler and minister, father and son. Venerable and common were divided; noble and humble made a difference.

After the Yellow Emperor, there was Lesser Brilliance [Shaohao]. In the time of Lesser Brilliance,

THE VENERABLE LORD descended to be his teacher. He was called Master of Following in Accordance. He produced the *Scripture of*

*Mysterious Repository*. The times were peaceful, crops grew in abundance, sweet springs gushed forth, unicorns arrived, phoenixes were spotted, and the stars shone bright.

After Lesser Brilliance, there was Good Xu [Zhuan Xu]. In the time of Good Xu,

THE VENERABLE LORD descended to be his teacher. He was called Master of Red Essence. He produced the *Scripture of Tenuous Words*.

After the Good Xu, there was Emperor Ku [Di Ku]. After Emperor Ku, there was Emperor Yao [Di Yao]. In the time of Emperor Yao,

THE VENERABLE LORD descended to be his teacher. He was called Master of Perfected Duty. He produced the *Scripture of Government Service*.

After Emperor Yao, there was Emperor Shun [Di Shun]. In the time of Emperor Shun, [6a]

THE VENERABLE LORD descended to be his teacher. He was called Master of Ruling Longevity. He produced the *Scripture of Great Clarity* .

After Emperor Shun, there was Yu of Xia [Xia Yu]. In the time of Yu of Xia,

THE VENERABLE LORD descended to be his teacher. He was called Master of True Practice. He produced the *Scripture of Virtuous Precepts*.

After Yu of Xia, there was Tang of Yin [Yin Tang]. After Tang of Yin, the Zhou dynasty arrived. In the time of the Zhou dynasty,

THE VENERABLE LORD descended to be its teacher. He was called Master of Adjusting the Regions. He produced the *Scripture of Red Essence*.


THE VENERABLE LORD said:

> At the beginning of the mysterious transformations,
> I embodied emptiness and non-being.
> Passing along through the limitless,
> I changed and transformed myriads of times.
> Then I first came down
> And was the teacher of the world.
> Before the Three Sovereigns
> I was the root of all the spirit transformations.
> Under the Three Sovereigns and Five Emperors

I helped them as their teacher.
Thus it went on, down to the Three Dynasties.
I admonished them all
To cultivate goodness.


## 6. Numinous Treasure—Wondrous History


The school of Numinous Treasure (Lingbao) developed in the wake of Highest Clarity (Shangqing) at the end of the fourth and beginning of the fifth centuries. Its first scripture was compiled by Ge Chaofu, who traced the origin of his revelation back through several generations of his family to Ge Hong, noted alchemist and author of the *Baopuzi*, and to Ge Xuan, a magic master and Taoist of the second century. Later followers integrated Buddhist doctrine and terminology, and the Lingbao scriptures thus created a different vision of the origins and workings of the cosmos.

Creation here is the intertwined development of religion, history, and the Ge-family tradition. It proceeds through the cycles of kalpas, long periods of universal rise and decline, and depends largely on the power of talismans or treasures. Talismans are heavenly symbols or charts that contain the original power of the Tao in graphic form. Not only are they responsible for the creation and continued existence of the world, they also bestow on their bearer magical powers and the divine right to rule. Famous charts of old are the *Hetu* (River Chart) and the *Wuyue zhenxing tu* (Chart of the True Shape of the Five Sacred Mountains). Both convey absolute power over all under heaven, i.e., the empire of China.

The Lingbao tradition traces itself back to the revelation of five central talismans, associated with the five directions. These five are described in the *Lingbao wufu xu* (Explanations of the Five Talismans of Numinous Treasure) contained in DZ 388, fasc. 183. This text is a composite mixture of ancient myths, longevity methods, and descriptions of the talismans. It goes back to the third century C.E.

The *Lingbao lueji,* translated here for the first time, is a summary of the sacred history of Numinous Treasure contained in the *Yunji qiqian* ( 3.9a-11b). It summarizes the myth originally found in the first scroll of the *Lingbao wufuxu.* For a translation of this latter version, see Bokenkamp 1986. On the *Wufuxu* and its development, see Kaltenmark 1981, Yamada 1989. On the historical origin of the Lingbao scriptures, see Ofuchi 1974, Bokenkamp 1983. For Lingbao worldview, see Kaltenmark 1960, Bokenkamp 1989, 1990; Zürcher 1980.

---

### *Lingbao lueji* (A Short Record of the Numinous Treasure)

[9a] It is recorded: When the sacred scriptures of the True Law of Numinous Treasure first arose, our world of measure was just empty void. Infathomable it was! Oh, immeasurable!

Kalpa after kalpa they emerged and transformed. Unimaginable it was! Oh, unthinkable!

In the past, there was then a first kalpa, called Dragon Country. A sage was born. Him we know as the Heavenly Venerable of Brahma Energy. He appeared in the world and with the teaching of Numinous Treasure transformed and saved countless people. His true law radiated through many thousands of worlds.

One revolution of Dragon Country lasted ninety thousand times nine thousand nine hundred and ninety-nine eons. Yet eventually even the energy revolutions of this kalpa came to their end. Heaven collapsed and the earth tumbled down. The four seas merged into one and the trigrams of heaven and earth were destroyed. There was no more light. The era of darkness lasted for one hundred million eons.

Then heaven and earth began anew. Another kalpa emerged; it was called Red Radiance. A sage appeared in the world. Him we know as the Heavenly Venerable of Primordial Beginning. He too used the teaching of Numinous Treasure to transform and save people. His True Law flourished greatly and all was as we have described above. Red Radiance lasted for two eons. Then heaven and earth collapsed again. There was no more light. Darkness reigned for five eons.

[9b] Then heaven and earth began anew. In the first year of the era Opening Sovereign, the Highest Lord of the Tao took birth in the west. He entrusted himself to the womb of Mrs. Hong in the country of Green Jade. For 3,700 years he coagulated his spirit in the repository of her womb. Then he was born in the Green Jade country, on the Peak of Floating Network in the Mountains of Flourishing Growth, on the bank of the Cinnabar Mystery River.

He became known as the Helper to Deliverance, the Highest Who Created the Prime. When he had grown up he first awakened to the truth of the Tao. He thereupon readied his heart for its loftiness.

Once he was sitting under a withered mulberry tree, deep, deep in meditation for a hundred days. The Heavenly Venerable of Primordial Beginning descended into his presence. He transmitted to the Lord of the Tao the true law of the Great Vehicle of Numinous Treasure. The Lord thus received the wondrous sacred scriptures in ten sections.

Thus the Heavenly Venerable came to reside in this country at this time. He spread joy to all its dwellings. He gave his teaching freely to the people of the time. Many were those who through him received the True Law that opens the gates of heaven. The people who attained the Tao in those days were more numerous even than the sands of the Ganges.

Later the Heavenly Venerable and the Lord of the Tao wandered together in all the ten directions of the world, spreading the True Law everywhere. After they had completed this task, the Heavenly Venerable entrusted all matters of the Law to the Lord of the Tao. He formally bestowed the title "Highest" on him.

[10a] The Highest Lord of the Tao continued to widely spread scriptures and records so that they would be properly transmitted for ten thousand generations. At that time, the Great Law had spread far and wide throughout the ten directions. Only to the city and country of Ferghana [in Central Asia] the sound of the law had not yet reached. Yet many people there were destined to have close relations with the law.

In antiquity there once reigned an emperor by the name of Ku. To him the Highest Lord sent the True Sovereign of the Three Heavens with the *True Writ of the Five Chapters of the Numinous Treasure*. He bestowed this sacred text on Emperor Ku. The emperor received them with deep respect and kept them well. He spent his remaining years safeguarding these records of the Law and preparing their proper transmission to the world. When he was about to become an immortal, he sealed the scripture in Copper Mountain. Copper Mountain is in the northwest, beyond a weakwater stream. It is 15,000 miles high.

When Emperor Yu of the Xia dynasty ascended the throne, he climbed all the sacred mountains. On one circuit, he crossed the weakwater stream and went up Copper Mountain. He thus obtained the *True Writ of the Numinous Treasure* that Emperor Ku had sealed in there.

He deeply bowed to the scripture and brought it out of hiding. From then on, in his cultivation and practice he relied on the True Law. But Emperor Yu cultivated only himself with its help. He did not make it accessible to the world at large. Thus he himself obtained the powers of a great spirit immortal. He could chisel open the Dragon Gate of the Yellow River and structure the course of the four streams. When his labors were concluded, all rivers flowed in orderly channels and the empire was firmly secure.

[10b] Later, Emperor Yu allowed his body to undergo a transformation that looked like death. In reality, he never actually died. Even today the wise emulate his traces; the perfected recognize his numinous power.

Before Yu underwent the transformation, he again sealed the sacred scripture away. This time he hid two copies: one in the sacred mountain of the north; the other in a grotto on Packet Mountain.

Time passed. Years later King Helü of Wu wandered around and reached Packet Mountain. There he encountered a man.

"Who are you?" the king asked.

"My name is Mountain; I am called the Hermit."

"In this mountain," the king questioned him further, "you must certainly have found strange things. Will you offer them to me?"

Hermit assented. He entered deep into the mountain grotto, wandering into a separate earth world 1,500 miles large. After a long walk he came to a stone castle. He did not at once dare to enter, but fasted and purified himself for three days at its gates. Only then and with great care did he approach the stone castle. The gate opened to a huge chamber. On a jade table lay one plain scroll, covered with the most extraordinary script. Hermit bowed deeply before it and took it with profound respect. Emerging from the grotto, he presented it to the king.

Helü called his followers. Together they inspected the sacred scroll. The writing was in an ancient seal script which none of them could read. [11a] Therefore the king ordered one of his attendants to take it to Confucius and ask him about the meaning of the text.

Meeting with the sage, the emissary was careless and told a lie about the origin of the manuscript. "My lord, the king of Wu," he said, "was in his hall enjoying an hour of leisure. Suddenly a red bird appeared carrying this text in his beak. It dropped the scroll right before the king. But my lord does not understand its meaning. May I respectfully inquire about it?"

Confucius looked sorrowful and did not answer for a while. Finally he said: "I recently heard a popular ditty. It goes:

The king of Wu went wandering, looked at trembling lakes,
Met the majestic dragon man, known as Mountain Hermit.

North he climbed the Packet Mountain, entering numinous
  remains,
In the end went to the grotto and stole the book of Yu.

The Great Lord of Highest Heaven will not let that go,
These documents are old indeed, passed for a hundred kalpas.
Whoever grabs them by sheer force will lose his state and
  hearth.

"If these are in fact the documents referred to in the ditty I can
say something about them. If they were brought in the beak of a
red bird, I have never heard of them."

The emissary deeply bent his head and apologized. "The facts
are indeed as you state them."

"All right, then," Confucius explained. "This scroll contains the
*True Writ of the Five Talismans of the Numinous Treasure*. For-
merly Emperor Yu of the Xia dynasty obtained them on Copper
Mountain. Later he sealed them in a grotto chamber."

The emissary returned and related the explanation to King
Helü. [11b] The king thereupon sincerely venerated the sacred text.
However, since his nature was wasteful and easy-going, he could
not properly fulfill all the rules of the Tao. Before long the text flew
up to heaven and vanished. Nobody knows where it went.

Later the king's son Fucha inherited the throne. He went to
Labor Mountain and again obtained the scripture. He treated it
with the proper respect and succeeded to keep it in the possession
of his family for many generations.

The time of the Three Kingdoms arrived. During the reign
period Red Bird [238–251], when the land of Wu was ruled by Sun
Quan, a man called Ge Xuan, also known as Xiaoxian, was born in
Langya in the east of China as the son of Secretary Ge Xiaoru. His
father was already eighty years old at the time of his birth.

Ge Xuan was full of numinous power. Even at the early age of
thirteen he was very fond of worshiping the Tao and the Virtue. He
was pure and of loyal faith, staunchly upholding filial piety and
modesty. However, he did not proceed to serve in office, but abandoned all glory, gave up all income, and set his will firmly on the
mountains and rivers. He duly went to the Tiantai mountains to
study the Tao. He concentrated his mind in meditation, penetrating ever deeper. In less than one year he attained full realization.

The Highest Lord thereupon sent three sagely perfected down
to transmit the sacred writings of Numinous Treasure to him. The

first of these perfected was called *Yu Laoqiao*, the First Perfected of Highest Mysterious Unity. [12a] The second was called *Guang Miaoyin*, the Second Perfected of Highest Mysterious Unity. The third was called *Zhen Dingguang*, the Third Perfected of Highest Mysterious Unity.

Before the three perfected descended, the Highest Lord had also ordered Xu Laile, the Perfected of the Great Ultimate, to become Ge Xuan's teacher in the methods of the Three Caverns [teachings of Taoism]. From him Xuan received the sacred writings in twenty-three scrolls, together with instructions and questions in ten scrolls. Altogether he was honored with thirty-three scrolls.

Later Ge Xuan transmitted these to Zheng Siyuan, who in turn passed them on to his nephew Shao. From him they went to Hai Anjun, also known as Xiaoyuan. This person handed the texts to his son Hujun, who gave them to the son of his younger brother. He in turn was none other than Ge Hong or Baopuzi, the famous Master Who Embraces Simplicity.

Baopuzi was a disciple of Lord Zheng, who instructed him on Mount Luofou. About to leave the world, Baopuzi handed the texts to his nephew, known by the name Hai'anzi. Over several generations they eventually reached his descendant Ge Chaofu [the compiler of the Lingbao scriptures]. In the last year of the reign period Eminent Peace [401], Ge Chaofu transmitted the sacred scriptures to a number of Taoists, including Ren Yanqing and Xu Lingqi. For generation after generation the records had thus been handed on.

However, later various schools and different traditions developed. The scriptures were scattered and dispersed and the body of the inheritance was no longer one. [12b] This is what happens during a great kalpa revolution.

Still, those who act in accordance with the original root will find themselves destined to encounter the sacred words in secrecy. With an intention for spirit enlightenment in their hearts, such noble people can still receive the sacred scriptures of the True Law of Numinous Treasure.

### 7. The Lands of the Immortals

The realm of the pure Tao, in which the gods and immortals are at home, consists of ten continents and two paradises. The ten continents are rather late (post-Han) and may, at least in their number, well go back to Buddhist cosmology, which counts ten directions in the world. Traditional Chinese cosmology, on the contrary, has nine as the perfect number.

The two paradises have been part of Chinese mythology since before the Han dynasty (third century B.C.E.). They are the group of five islands around Penglai in the Eastern Sea and the mountain range of Kunlun in the Western Highlands. Some evidence suggests that the earliest visions of these paradises were related to the marvelous gardens built by the First Emperor of the Qin dynasty (221–210 B.C.E.) and his Han-dynasty successors. On the other hand, the paradise visions of the Taoists most certainly colored the Chinese perception of the Buddhist Pure Land, introduced a few centuries later.

The *Shizhou ji* is a record describing the lands of the immortals. It is placed in the mouth of Dongfang Shuo, an immortal and jester in the time of the Han emperor Wu (140–87 B.C.E.) and closely connected with the legends surrounding both personages. The text goes back to these stories, which are first documented in the second century C.E. In its present form, it probably dates from the fourth or fifth century, as does the *Han Wudi neizhuan* (The Secret Story of the Han Emperor Wu). Both texts are connected to the Taoism of Highest Clarity.

The *Shizhou ji* is contained in DZ 598, fasc. 330, with a variant version in *Yunji qiqian* 26. This adapts the translation in Smith 1990, revised in Smith 1992, 536–62. For a study of the legends surrounding the Han emperor Wu, see Schipper 1965, Smith 1992. On traditional Chinese cosmology, see Maspero 1924, Major 1984, Allan 1991.

---

### *Shizhou ji* (Record of the Ten Continents)

[2a] Ancestor Continent is right about in the center of the Eastern Sea. It is five hundred square miles in area and lies seventy thousand miles from the western shore of the ocean.

On this continent, there is a plant of no-death that resembles marsh-reed sprouts and grows to a height of three or four feet. Someone may be already dead for three days but if covered with this plant, he will come back to life in an instant. Its ingestion confers exceeding longevity.

In old times, the First Emperor of the Qin dynasty had a great garden, filled with the corpses of executed people. However, when a flock of crow-like birds brought this plant in their beaks and covered the faces of the dead with it, they rose up immediately and came back to life spontaneously.

An official heard about this and reported it. The First Emperor duly dispatched envoys to take the plant to the Master of the Demon Valley in the northern suburb to inquire about it.

"This is the plant of no-death," the Master said. "It comes from Ancestor Continent in the Eastern Sea. Grown in fields of jasper, it is also called the mushroom of spiritual cultivation. Its leaves are like marsh-reed sprouts; it grows in clusters, and one stalk can easily revive a human being."

"Can it be harvested?" The First Emperor asked eagerly and duly sent out the envoy Xu Fu with five hundred young men and young women. [2b] Led aboard high ships and other vessels, they went to sea in search of the Ancestral Continent. They did not return. Fu, in fact, was a master of the Tao. He was also called Junfang, and later became a perfected.

Ocean Continent is also in the Eastern Sea. It is four thousand square miles in area and located approximately on the same level as Guiji (Zhejiang). It is about seven hundred thousand miles from the western shore of the ocean.

This continent grows divine mushrooms and immortal plants. There is also a jade rock about a thousand fathoms high, from which a sweet spring gushes forth. It is named Sweet Jade Spring. Several pints of it make one gradually drunk. It confers longevity.

Many immortals make their homes on this continent. Their customs are like those of the people of Wu. Mountains and rivers are also like those of the Middle Kingdom.

Mystery Continent is in the northwest of the Northern Sea. It is seven thousand two hundred square miles in area and lies three hundred sixty thousand miles from the southern shore of the ocean.

Its capital, Mystery Metropolis, is governed by immortal worthies and perfected dukes. There are many hills and mountains. There is also Wind Mountain, which makes sounds like thunder and lightning. [3a]

Mystery Continent faces the northwestern gate of heaven. On this continent there are many immortal officials of Great Mystery. The palaces and chambers of these immortal officials are each unique in their own special way. They abound in golden mushrooms and jade plants. This area falls under the lower jurisdiction of the Lords of the Three Heavens. It is very majestic indeed.

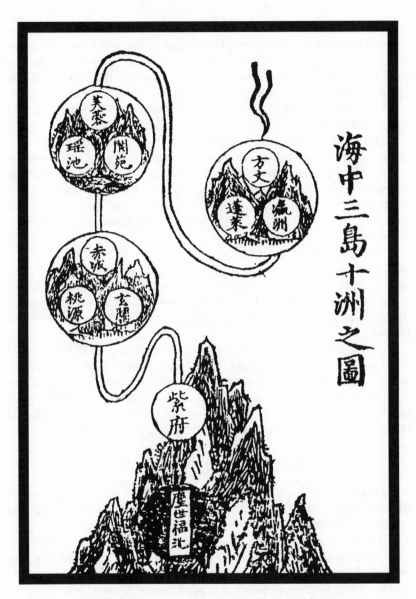

Fig. 4. The Ten Continents. Source: *Xiuzhen taiji hunyuan tu.*

Blaze Continent is in the Southern Sea. It is two thousand square miles in area and lies ninety thousand miles from the northern shore of the ocean.

On this continent are wind-born beasts which look like panthers. They have a fresh complexion and are about as big as a fox. Spread a net, capture one, and pile several cartloads of firewood to cook it. Though the firewood will be consumed, the beast will not catch fire. It just stands amidst the ashes with its fur unsinged. Axes and knives will not penetrate its flesh, and if struck it is just like a leather bag.

But take an iron hammer and hit it over the head several tens of times. Then it will die. Yet, spread its mouth open to the wind, it will revive in a moment. Another method to kill it is by stuffing its nose with calamus wrapped on a stone. One can then remove its brain and eat it mixed with chrysanthemum blossoms. If one eats ten catties of this, one will obtain a life span of five hundred years.

There is also the mountain of Fire Forest. Here lives a beast of fiery radiance. It is the size of a rat. Its fur, sometimes red, sometimes white, is three or four inches long. The mountain is three hundred miles high. [3b] If one can see this mountain forest at night, it is because the animals shine on it with a radiance like that of fire.

Pluck the fur of such a beast and weave it into cloth—this is what people call "fire-washed cloth." The people of that continent wear it. If it becomes soiled and one uses ashes and water to clean it, it never becomes clean. Only when one burns it in fire for the length of time it takes to eat two bowls of rice, one can shake off the dirt. With the dirt naturally falling off, the cloth becomes pure and white as snow.

Many immortals make their homes here.

Long Continent, also named Green Hill, is in the southeast of the Southern Sea. It is five thousand square miles in area and two hundred and fifty thousand miles from the coast.

This continent has an abundance of mountains and rivers as well as numerous big trees. Among them are those that are two thousand arm spans in circumference. There is nothing but forest on the entire continent, hence it is also named Green Hill.

There also grow plants conferring immortality, efficacious medicinal herbs, sweet-juice plants, and flowers with jade blossoms. They are virtually everywhere. In addition, there is a Wind Mountain, which makes a continuous rumbling sound.

In the Palace of the Purple Court on this continent, heavenly perfected and immortal maidens amuse themselves. [4a]

Prime Continent is in the Northern Sea. It is three thousand square miles in area and lies one hundred thousand miles from the southern shore of the ocean.

On this continent grow five kinds of sacred mushrooms; there also flows a dark rivulet. The water of the dark rivulet is thick and tastes like honey. Drinking it bestows a life as long as that of heaven and earth. Eating the five kinds of sacred mushrooms also results in long life and no-death.

Floating Continent is in the Western Sea. It is three thousand square miles in area and lies one hundred and ninety thousand miles from the eastern shore of the ocean.

On this continent are many mountains, streams, and assemblies of a rock called *kunwu*. This may be smelted to make swords. Swords made from *kunwu* radiate as brightly and are as transparent as rock crystal. They cut through jade as if it were mud.

Many immortals make their homes here.

Life Continent is in the northeast of the Eastern Sea. It overlaps Penglai by one hundred and seventy thousand miles. It is two thousand and five hundred square miles in area and lies two hundred and thirty thousand miles from the western shore of the ocean. [4b]

On this continent are several tens of thousands of immortal households. Its natural atmosphere is stable and pleasant, so that mushrooms and plants grow continually all year round. Free from extreme cold and heat, the climate here nurtures the myriad beings in utmost peace. There are numerous mountains and streams, with immortal herbs and clusters of mushrooms. The rivers throughout the entire continent taste like sweet cream.

This is by far the best continent.

Phoenix-Unicorn Continent is in the middle of the Western Sea. It is one thousand and five hundred square miles in area and is encircled by a weakwater stream, which cannot float a swan's feather or be crossed in any way.

On this continent there are many phoenixes and unicorns. They appear in flocks of several tens of thousands. There are also mountains, rivers, ponds, and grasslands that abound in a hundred varieties of divine medicinal herbs.

In addition, there are the households of the immortals. They boil phoenix bills and unicorn horns together and decoct a glue that is called "string-connecting glue" or "metal-fusing paste." This glue can connect snapped bowstrings and fuse the metal of broken knives and swords. Furthermore, if a strong man were made to pull on something mended by the glue, it would only break somewhere else, and never along the mended seam. . . .

[5b] Cave Continent is in the southwest of the Western Sea. It is three thousand square miles in area. In the north it overlaps Kunlun for two hundred and sixty thousand miles. It lies two hundred and forty thousand miles from the eastern shore of the ocean. [6a]

On this continent there are many palaces and mansions of perfected immortals and spirit officials. Their number cannot be counted. There are also wondrous lions, scare-evils, chisel-teeth, heaven-deer, and beasts with long fangs, bronze heads, and iron foreheads.

The continent features a large mountain formed in the shape of people and birds; hence it is called the "People and Bird Mountain." On this mountain grow many large trees that resemble maples, but the fragrance of their flowers and leaves may be smelled hundreds of miles away. They are called Soul-Returning Trees.

Knock on one and it can actually produce a sound by itself that seems like a herd of cattle bellowing. Those who hear it tremble in their hearts and are startled in their spirits.

Yet one can also dig up its root, boil it in a jade cauldron, remove the water, fry the remainder under low heat until it becomes like a black goo, and then shape it into pellets.

The product is called Essence-Alarming Incense, but some also call it Spirit-Shaking Pellets, Life-Restoring Incense, Quaking Sandalwood Incense, People-and-Bird Essence, or Death-Dispelling Incense. This single item with six names is a wondrous thing. Its fragrance may be smelled several hundred miles away. [6b] The dead in the earth who smell this incense return to life and do not perish again. Perfuming the dead with it is even more efficacious. . . .

[10b] Peng Hill is Mount Penglai. It faces the northeast shore of the Eastern Sea and is five thousand miles in circumference.

On its periphery the mountain is surrounded by the Circular Sea. The water of the Circular Sea is perfectly black, so it is also called the Dark Sea. Even when there is no wind, its waves are a hundred fathoms high. It cannot be crossed in either direction.

On the mountain are the palaces of the Nine Elders and the Perfected Kings of the Nine Heavens. Only flying immortals can reach the places where these most exalted perfected reside.

Kunlun is also called Kun Mountain. It lies west-northwest of the Western Sea and north-northwest of the Northern Sea. It is ten thousand square miles in area and is located one hundred and thirty thousand miles from the coast.

Like Phoenix-Unicorn Continent, Kunlun also is completely surrounded by a weakwater stream. The mountain borders on four surrounding mountains: in the southeast there is the Orchard of Assembled Rocks; in the northwest, the Mansion of the Northern House. In the northeast, it borders on the Great Sparkling Well; in the southwest, it extends to the Deep Basin Ravine.

These large mountains on its four corners are actually the branches and supports of Kunlun. The southern tip of the Orchard of Assembled Rocks is where the Queen Mother told King Mu of Zhou that his capital, Xianyang, was four hundred and sixty thousand miles away .

The mountain rises thirty-six thousand miles above the surrounding plain. [11a] Its top has three corners and is ten thousand miles wide. It is shaped like a hanging bowl. Its base is narrow and its top wide, thus it is called Kunlun, "high and precarious."

As for the mountain's three corners, one is due north and shines with the brilliance of a thousand stars. Hence it is called the Peak of Lofty Winds. One corner is due west and is named the Hall of the Hanging Gardens. One corner is due east and is called the Kunlun Palace.

On this latter corner there are heaps of gold which make up the Heavenly Walled City. It is one thousand square miles in area. In the city there are five golden terraces and twelve jade towers.

North of this, there are the Mansion of the Northern House and the Deep Basic Ravine. They also have walled cities with golden terraces and jade towers. All these illuminate each other like the pervading radiance of flowing essence.

There are also halls of luminescent green jade, mansions of carnelian florescence, purple, halcyon, and cinnabar mansions, phosphorescent clouds, a candle sun, and vermilion clouds of ninefold radiance. This is the place governed by the Queen Mother of the West and revered by perfected officials and immortal beings.

## 8. Gods and Goddesses

The gods, as much as the lands of the immortals, are part of the pure realm of the Tao. Next in rank after the highest deities of the religion, who themselves are none other than the Tao—the Heavenly Venerable of Primordial Beginning, the Lord of the Tao, the Highest Venerable Lord—are the pure representatives of yin and yang. Divided according to the system of the five agents into male and female, east and west, wood and metal, light and dark, up and down, they are embodied in two deities: the Lord King of the East and the Queen Mother of the West.

The pair developed first in the Han dynasty (206 B.C.E.–220 C.E.), when the system of the five agents became the general basis for Chinese thought. While the Queen Mother was known as a powerful deity before, associated with fanciful lands and a rather strange, tiger-like appearance, the Lord King developed as her counterpart to fit the overall system.

The Queen Mother is particularly powerful. Residing in the Heavenly Walled City on Mount Kunlun, she is the queen of all the immortals. She is also the chief guardian of the elixir of life and the peaches of immortality that grow in her garden and ripen once in 3,000 years. She is truly highest among the celestials.

The following biography of the Queen Mother of the West (Xiwang mu) is contained in the *Yongcheng jixian lu* (Record of the Assembled Immortals of the Heavenly Walled City). Written by Du Guangting (850–933), eminent court Taoist, liturgist, and chronicler of the late Tang, this text concentrates on the biographies of goddesses, lady immortals, and successful female practitioners. It is unique in this focus.

The text is contained in DZ 783, fasc. 560–61 and in *Yunji qiqian* 114. Only the first few pages are rendered below (1.9a–11b). A full translation with detailed annotation is contained in Cahill 1982. For more on the history of the text, see Cahill 1986. On Du Guangting, his life and works, see Verellen 1989. On the Yellow Emperor and his battle with the Wormy Rebel, see Lewis 1990. For studies of the Queen Mother and other Chinese goddesses, see Schafer 1973, Loewe 1979, Cahill 1982, Fracasso 1988, Chan 1990. On the practice of women in Taoism, see Cahill 1990, Despeux 1990, Kirkland 1991.

---

**"The Queen Mother of the West" (Xiwang mu), from *Yongcheng jixian lu* (Record of the Assembled Immortals of the Heavenly Walled City)**

[9a] The goddess Mother of Metal is the Ninefold Numinous and Greatly Wondrous Mother of Metal of Tortoise Mountain. Some-

times she is also called the Greatly Numinous and Ninefold Radiant Mother of Metal of Tortoise Terrace. Another common name of hers is Queen Mother of the West. She is, in fact, the incarnate wondrousness of the innermost power of the west, the ultimate venerable of all-pervading yin-energy.

In old times, the energy of the Tao congealed in quietude and deepened into an organized structure. Resting in non-action, it desired to unfold and guide the mysterious accomplishments of creation, to bring forth and raise the myriad beings.

First it took the perfected true energy of the innermost power of the east and transformed it into the Lord of Wood. The Lord of Wood was born on the shore of the Bluegreen Sea, in the void of fresh-green spiritual power. [9b] Born from the energy of highest yang harmony, he rules in the east. Because of this, he is also called the Lord King of the East.

Then the Tao took the perfected wondrous energy of the innermost power of the west and transformed it into the Mother of Metal. The Mother of Metal was born on the shore of Yonder River on the Divine Continent. Jue is her surname, and Kou the clan to which she belongs. As soon as she was born, she soared up in flight. Born from the energy of highest yin spiritual power, she rules in the west. Because of this she is also called the Queen Mother of the West.

In the beginning, she derived her substance from great nonbeing. She floated along in spirit and was mysteriously hidden in the midst of the west's confused chaos of primordial energy. Then she divided the pure essential energy of the great Tao, to connect it back together again and form herself a body.

She and the Lord King of Wood and the East rule the two primal energies [yin and yang], nourish and raise heaven and earth, mold and develop the myriad beings.

The Queen Mother embodies the deepest foundation of the weak and yielding; she represents the origin of the ultimate yin. Therefore she rules over the direction of the west. She mothers and nourishes all kinds of beings, whether in heaven above or on the earth below, whether in any of the three worlds or in any of the ten directions. Especially all women who ascend to immortality and attain the Tao are her dependents.

The palaces and towers she resides in are located on Pestle Mountain in the Tortoise Mountain Range, in the splendid parks of Mount Kunlun with its hanging gardens and lofty atmosphere. [10a] Here there is a golden city a thousand levels high, with twelve-

公王東

Fig. 5. The Lord King of the East. Source: *Zengxiang liexian zhuan.*

storied jade buildings and towers of jasper essence. There are halls of radiant lucid jade, nine-storied mysterious terraces, and purple kingfisher cinnabar chambers.

On the left, the palace compound is surrounded by the Fairy Pond; on the right, it is ringed by the Kingfisher River. Beneath the mountain, the weakwater stream rushes along in nine layers, its waves and swells a hundred thousand feet high. Without a whirlwind carriage on feathered wheels, no one can ever reach here.

The jade towers rise up all the way into the heavens; the luscious terraces reach into the empyrean. The buildings' eaves are of green gems; the chambers inside of vermilion-purple stone. Joined gems make colorful curtains, while a steady bright moon irradiates them on all four sides.

The Queen Mother wears a flowered *sheng* headdress and has marvelous ornaments suspended from her belt. Her attendants on the left are immortal maidens; her attendants on the right are feathered lads. Gem-studded canopies glimmer with their mutual reflections; feathered banners shade the courtyard.

Beneath the balustrades and staircases of the palaces, the grounds are planted with white bracelet trees and a cinnabar diamond forest. There are a myriad stalks of emptiness-pure greenery, a thousand stems of turquoise-jade trees. Even when there is no wind, the divine reeds spontaneously harmonize sounds, clinking like jade belt-pendants. They naturally produce the spheric timbres of the eight harmonies.

The Divine Continent where the Queen Mother was born is southeast of Mount Kunlun. Thus the *Erya Dictionary* claims: "The land of the Queen Mother of the West is directly beneath the sun. This place and the subsolar land are the same." It also says: "The Queen Mother has disheveled hair and wears a *sheng* headdress. She has tiger's teeth and is good at whistling." [10b] Now, this describes really the Queen Mother's envoy, the white tiger spirit of the direction of metal. Such are not in fact the Queen Mother's true looks!

To ensure her power, the Heavenly King of Primordial Beginning bestowed upon her the primordial lineage record of the myriad heavens and the Tortoise Mountain registers of ninefold radiance. He empowered her to control and summon the myriad spirit forces of the universe, to assemble and gather the perfected and the sages of the world, to oversee all covenants and examine the people's quality of faith.

西王母

Fig. 6. The Queen Mother of the West. Source: *Zengxiang liexian zhuan.*

Moreover, she presides over all formal observances in the various heavens as well as at all audiences and banquets held by the celestial worthies and supreme sages. In addition, it is her duty to supervise the correcting and editing of the sacred scriptures in heaven, to reflect due divine light on the proceedings. Her responsibility covers all the treasured scriptures of Highest Clarity, the jade writs of the Three Caverns, as well as the sacred texts that are bestowed at ordination.

Formerly the Yellow Emperor [Huangdi] punished the Wormy Rebel [Chiyou] when he rose and usurped power. Before he was subdued, the Wormy Rebel brought forth many magical transformations. He raised the wind, summoned the rain, puffed forth smoke, and spat mist, so that the generals and soldiers of the Yellow Emperor's army were greatly confused. Thereupon the emperor returned home and rested in a valley of Mount Tai. Bewildered, he lay down in deep distress.

Seeing his plight, the Queen Mother sent out an envoy wearing a dark fox cloak to give him a talisman. It said:

> Great Unity just ahead!
> Heavenly Unity just behind!
> Obtain it and excel!
> Attack and overcome!

The talisman was three inches wide and one foot long. It shone like jade with a greenish lustre. Cinnabar drops like blood formed a glistening pattern on it. The Yellow Emperor hung it at his waist.

[11a] When he had done this, the Queen Mother commanded a woman with a human head and the body of a bird to go to him. She introduced herself as the Mysterious Lady of the Nine Heavens and gave the emperor the plan of cosmic yin and yang. This included information also on the five basic human intentions and the three palaces within. In addition, she bestowed upon him various arts: how to calculate the times of attack and withdrawal with the help of Great Unity and how to control all space and time through pacing the Northern Dipper in the sky. Beyond that, she taught him the way to use a number of talismans of concealment, the five divine talismans of the Numinous Treasure, and the divine writ ensuring the five kinds of victory.

Thus equipped, the Yellow Emperor easily subdued the Wormy Rebel in Middleland [Zhongji]. He then destroyed the descendents of the Divine Farmer and executed the Fiery Emperor's great-grandson at Blockspring [Banquan]. Thereafter all under heaven was greatly at peace.

The Yellow Emperor then built his capital at Dripping Deer [Zhuolu] in the Upper Valley. After he had thus been settled peacefully for a number of years, he received another envoy from the Queen Mother. This time the white tiger spirit came to him. Riding a white tiger, he descended to the emperor's courtyard. He bestowed upon him the cosmic maps of the unified empire.

Toward the end of his years, the Queen Mother moreover gave him the perfect true Tao of purity, tranquility, and non-action. Its instructions were:

> Do not stop drinking and gobbling up food—and your body
> will never be light.
> Do not stop fretting and worrying—and your spirit will
> never be pure.
> Do not stop craving for sounds and sights—and your heart
> will never be calm.

> No calm in your heart—and your spirit will never be
> numinous.
> No numen in your spirit—and the Tao cannot work its
> wonders.

> Success is not in homage to the stars or worship of the
> Dipper.
> [11b] That rather makes you suffer and exhausts your body.

> Success is in deepening the spirit powers of your heart.
> There is no effort needed—the Tao of immortality is there!

> Now you can live long!

# Chapter Three

## THE TEACHING

The teaching is another aspect of the Tao as it is active and visible in the world; in fact it is the one aspect of the Tao that is readily accessible if one only looks for it. Although beyond language, shape, or any other form of expression, the Tao as it descends into the realm of humanity takes on a whole number of different guises to save living beings.

In language, the Tao becomes manifest in the scriptures that we have on earth—translations or replicas of their original heavenly counterpart. These scriptures, revealed at different times and to members of different traditions within Taoism, are then compiled in to an organized canon. This canon also contains explanations of the scriptures, commentaries from various ages and backgrounds, encomia for the gods, descriptions of proper ritual procedures, instructions for physical and meditation practice, biographies of great masters, records of lineages, and so on. The Tao thus formulated is an encyclopedic collection of information, equally containing materials of varied levels of sacrality.

In its concrete shape, the Tao further appears as Laozi, personification of the Tao and first deity of the religion. In his various exploits around the world, called the "transformations of Laozi" because he never stays the same for long, the god establishes and reestablishes the teaching. He reveals scriptures, hands down explanations and instructions, appoints community leaders, and guides promising individuals along the path. Laozi gives shape to the Tao in several ways. He spreads the teaching in whatever form and time he may appear; he provides a concrete example for the eternal, never ending changes of the Tao itself; and he furnishes a model life for the active believer in his pursuit of the Tao. Laozi personifies the Tao; his transformations and ongoing conversions of all parts of the universe keep the teaching alive and give hope and confidence to the believers.

In other forms of expression, the Tao is accessible in the concrete physical and meditational practices of the active Taoist. This is the teaching come to life, the Tao in its most personal, most immediate form on earth. Integrating numerous different of medical and religious techniques, Taoist religious practices are a variegated mixture of activities that continue to change with the times and different schools. But in all cases a distinct path is outlined, a path that usually involves leaving ordinary society and its customs behind, at least for a time; reorganizing one's life according to yin and yang, the most pervasive rhythm of the Tao; healing the body; developing control over one's wandering mind; and joining the Tao in some form of union, ecstatic or otherwise.

While the collection of Taoist scriptural materials and the figure of the deity Laozi tend to be inclusive, if not actually universalist, the practices differ—different schools place emphasis on different techniques, and individual practitioners prefer certain methods over others. From age to age, from school to school, the canon developed and grew—is still growing in supplements today. Likewise, whenever a new religion appeared on the horizon of the Chinese empire, Laozi was made responsible for it; it was integrated under the overarching umbrella of the Tao. At the same time, practices changed and developed; some techniques were lost, others found, the composite pattern of their combination always in flux.

The selection below takes these differences into account. It begins with the *Daojiao sandong zongyuan* (The Ancestral Origin of the Three Caverns of the Taoist Teaching), which gives a summary of the organization of the Taoist canon and reports on its heavenly nature. Contained in the *Yunji qiqian*, the text dates probably to the Tang dynasty, but its description is valid for Taoist collections from their first compilations in the fifth century to today.

Second, there is the first chapter of the *Huahu jing* (Scripture on the Conversion of the Barbarians), a popular text in medieval China that was proscribed several times due to its polemical nature and has only survived in a Dunhuang manuscript. Dating from the eighth century, it shows Taoist universalism at its best, presenting the transformations and migrations of Laozi throughout history.

Two documents on the path follow. The first, the *Tianyinzi* (The Master of Heavenly Seclusion), is a summary of the path as it was undertaken in mid-Tang times. It is one of the first texts that clearly integrate the entire gamut of Taoist practices into one organized structure. It is also one of the clearest—the reason probably why it is still used among Qigong practitioners in China today.

The other contains the basic principles of the monastic school of Complete Perfection (Quanzhen) as they were set out by its founder, Wang Chongyang (1113–1170) in the twelfth century. The *Chongyang lijiao shiwu lun* (Chongyang's Fifteen Articles on Establishing the Teaching) outlines the major points aspiring Taoist practitioners must pay attention to. It integrates Buddhist monachism and places a heavy emphasis on the practice of inner alchemy. Quanzhen being one of the two major Taoist schools still active today, this text too has lost nothing of its practical relevance.

## 9. The Three Caverns

The Taoist canon that we have today was printed in 1445. While there are several supplements, one from the seventeenth, the other from the twentieth century, this canon represents the major stock of Taoist materials. It goes back to the collective activity of leading Taoists under the Ming dynasty (1368–1644) and replaces earlier versions that suffered from a persecution under the Mongol (Yuan) rulers in the 1280s.

Comprehensive canons, both Taoist and Buddhist, were first compiled upon imperial order in the late tenth century. At this time the Song dynasty had just reunified the empire and was beginning to stabilize its rule. As part of this effort, the rulers tried to salvage as much of the country's cultural heritage as was possible after two hundred years of disorder and political division. Many encyclopedias were compiled at this time. The *Yunji qiqian*, from which our text is taken, is one of them.

Before the Song, there were comprehensive collections of the teaching as well as lists of scriptures that integrated all the materials of a given tradition into an organized whole. In Taoism, the first of these is a catalogue compiled by Lu Xiujing (406–77) in the fifth century. It arranges the scriptures in the so-called Three Caverns, each representing one of the leading schools of Taoism at the time.

The Cavern of Perfection contained the scriptures of Highest Clarity (Shangqing); that of Mystery, the texts of Numinous Treasure (Lingbao); and that of Spirit, the talismans and explanations of the Three Sovereigns (Sanhuang). The first and oldest of all

Taoist schools, the Orthodox Unity (Zhengyi) or Celestial Masters (Tianshi), was relegated to the supplements. This division, patterned on the Buddhist doctrine of the Three Vehicles, has persisted to the present day.

The *Daojiao sandong zongyuan* (The Ancestral Origin of the Three Caverns of the Taoist Teaching) provides a religious and mythological backgound for the origins and organization of the canon. The text is contained in *Yunji qiqian* 3.4b-7b. It has not been translated elsewhere. Section divisions and subheadings are the translator's.

On the organization and historical development of the Taoist canon, see Liu 1973, Ofuchi 1979, Thompson 1985a, Boltz 1987.

---

*Daojiao sandong zongyuan* **(The Ancestral Origin of the Three Caverns of the Taoist Teaching)**

THE ORIGINS

[4b] In its very first origins, the Taoist school began from that which cannot be preceded. It was handed down through spontaneous impulse and response. Like the world itself, it arose from the wondrous unity of all. From wondrous unity it divided into the Three Primes. From the Three Primes it transformed and developed into the three energies—original, beginning, and mysterious. From the three energies it changed to bring forth the three forces—heaven, earth, and humanity. When the three forces were complete, the myriad beings were created.

The Three Primes are: first, the Prime of the Great Nonbeing of Coagulated Pervasion; second, the Prime of the Great Nonbeing of Red Chaos; third, the Prime of the Mysterious Pervasion of Dark Obscurity.

From the first, the Prime of the Great Non-Being of Coagulated Pervasion, developed the Lord of Heavenly Treasure. From the second, the Prime of the Great Nonbeing of Red Chaos, developed the Lord of Numinous Treasure. From the third, the Prime of the Mysterious Pervasion of Dark Obscurity, developed the Lord of Spirit Treasure. In the manifestations of the great omnipresent pervasion [of the Tao], they were transformed into separate entities. They rule the Three Clarity Heavens.

The Three Clarity Heavens are Jade Clarity, Highest Clarity, and Great Clarity. [5a] They are also known as the three heavens. As such they are also called the Heaven of Clear Subtlety, the Heaven of the Remnants of Yu, and the Heaven of Great Redness.

The Lord of Heavenly Treasure rules Jade Clarity. This is the Heaven of Clear Subtlety. Its energy is beginning and of greenish coloring.

The Lord of Numinous Treasure rules Highest Clarity. This is the Heaven of the Remnants of Yu. Its energy is primordial and of yellowish coloring.

The Lord of Spirit Treasure rules Great Clarity. This is the Heaven of Great Redness. Its energy is mysterious and of whitish coloring.

Thus the *Verses on the Vitalization of the Gods of the Nine Heavens* say: "Although these three have different names, they are ultimately one."

The Scriptures

These three lords each rule certain sections of the teaching. Venerable deities, they govern the three caverns. These Three Caverns are the Cavern of Perfection, the Cavern of Mystery, and the Cavern of Spirit.

The Lord of Heavenly Treasure revealed scriptures in twelve sections. Thereby he became the ruler of the teachings of the Perfection Cavern.

The Lord of Numinous Treasure revealed scriptures in twelve sections. Thereby he became the ruler of the teachings of the Mystery Cavern.

The Lord of Spirit Treasure revealed scriptures in twelve sections. Thereby he became the ruler of the teachings of the Spirit Cavern.

All in all there are therefore thirty-six sections of sacred scriptures in the Three Caverns.

The first, the Perfection Cavern, represents the Greater Vehicle. [5b] The second, the Mystery Cavern, represents the Middle Vehicle. The third, the Spirit Cavern, represents the Lesser Vehicle.

On the basis of the Three Caverns, altogether seven divisions of the canon developed. The Cavern of Perfection, the Cavern of Mystery, and the Cavern of Spirit are supplemented by the divisions of Great Mystery, Great Peace, and Great Clarity.

Great Mystery supplements the Perfection Cavern; Great Peace supplements the Mystery Cavern; and Great Clarity supplements the Spirit Cavern. The three supplements together also contain thirty-six sections of sacred scriptures.

The Covenant of Orthodox Unity pervades all of them. It forms the seventh division, which is also the fourth supplement. Because of this we speak of sacred scriptures contained in the Three Caverns and of mysterious teachings found in Seven Divisions. Beyond these Seven Divisions, the texts of the canon are further divided according to twelve classes:

1. Fundamental Texts
2. Divine Talismans
3. Secret Instructions
4. Numinous Charts
5. Genealogies and Registers
6. Precepts and Regulations
7. Rituals and Observances
8. Techniques and Methods
9. Various Arts
10. Records and Biographies
11. Eulogies and Encomia
12. Lists and Memoranda

Each of the Three Caverns contains these twelve sections. All in all, there are thus thirty-six sections of scriptures.

THE ENERGIES

The three energies are the beginning, primordial, and mysterious. [6a]

Beginning energy is green and resides in the Heaven of Clear Subtlety.

Primordial energy is yellow and resides in the Heaven of the Remnants of Yu.

Mysterious energy is white and resides in the Heaven of Great Redness.

Therefore we speak of the three energies—beginning, primordial, and mysterious.

From these three energies, yin and yang and their harmonious combination first developed.

From yin and yang and their harmonious combination, heaven and earth and humanity developed in their turn.

Just as the *Daode jing* says,

Tao brought forth the One.
The One brought forth the Two.
The Two brought forth the Three.
The Three brought forth the myriad beings. (ch. 42).

THE HEAVENS

Including the highest heaven with the Jade Capital of Mystery Metropolis, there are altogether thirty-six heavens. Of these, twenty-eight are within the Three Worlds, and eight are beyond them. The Three Worlds are the World of Desire, the World of Form, and the World of Formlessness.

The lowest six heavens make up the World of Desire. The following eighteen heavens are the World of Form. The four heavens above them constitute the World of Formlessness. Thus there are altogether twenty-eight heavens in the Three Worlds.

The Three Worlds are beautiful places where people can be upright and develop their strength. Once above the World of Desire, human life is extended considerably. On these higher levels, the ground is made of yellow gold; stairs are made of white jade. Pearls, jades, and valuable treasures occur naturally. [6b] Yet, although there is exceeding pleasure and happiness, people in these worlds still have not yet transcended the cycle of life and death.

This happens only above the Three Worlds. There are first four heavens called the Heavens for True Believers. These are also known as the Heavens of Sagely Disciples or the four Brahma Heavens. In these realms people have gone beyond life and death. The three calamities cannot reach them.

Above these are the three Clarity Heavens. They each house three palaces on the right, the left, and the center. These three palaces contain the heavenly hierarchy of immortal kings, dukes, ministers, earls, and officials. They are each governed by a Celestial Master, appointed by the Highest Venerable Lord.

Great Clarity contains the nine ranks of the immortals; Highest Clarity contains the nine ranks of the perfected; Jade Clarity contains the nine ranks of the sages. Altogether the heavenly hierarchy thus consists of twenty-seven ranks.

The nine ranks of immortals are:

1. Highest Immortal
2. Outstanding Immortal
3. Grand Immortal

4. Mysterious Immortal
5. Heavenly Immortal
6. Perfected Immortal
7. Spirit Immortal
8. Numinous Immortal
9. Superior Immortal

The titles in the hierarchies of the perfected and the sages follow the same pattern. Their order of rank is equally that of highest, outstanding, grand, mysterious, heavenly, perfected, spirit, numinous, and superior. [7a]

The highest heaven of all is called Grand Network. It contains the Jade Capital of Mystery Metropolis. Golden towers of purple subtlety, soaring trees of the seven treasures, cosmic unicorns and wondrous lions live in this realm. From here the heavenly venerables of the Three Worlds rule and administer the universe.

Thus altogether there are first the twenty-eight heavens of the Three Worlds followed by the four Brahma Heavens; above them there are the three Clarity Heavens, crowned in their turn by the Heaven of Grand Network. Thus there are altogether thirty-six heavens. They are governed by the three venerables.

As the *Scripture* says: "Above the Three Worlds, all is without bounds. None is higher than Grand Network. Colorful layers of clouds rise loftily above. There is only primordial beginning. People live for kalpas on end."

THE HEAVENLY VENERABLES

The Heavenly Venerables of the Three Periods are:
of the past, the Heavenly Venerable of Primordial Beginning;
of the present, the Heavenly Venerable Jade Emperor On-High;
of the future, the Heavenly Venerable Jade Constellation of the Golden Tower.

Now, the Jade Emperor On-High is the disciple of the Heavenly Venerable of Primordial Beginning. Ever since the middle of the kalpa Highest Sovereign, the Heavenly Venerable of Primordial Beginning has presided in spirit over the three periods. He has ten names:

1. Spontaneity
2. Non-Ultimate
3. Great Tao

4. Highest Perfection
5. Lord On-High
6. Lord of the Tao
7. Lofty August One
8. Heavenly Venerable
9. Jade Emperor
10. His Majesty

[Such is the ancestral origin of the Three Caverns.]

## 10. The Transformations of Laozi

The myth of Laozi's transformations was part of his deification in the Han dynasty. It is first formulated in the *Laozi bianhua jing* (Scripture on Laozi's Transformations), a text dated to the second century C.E. that has survived among the Dunhuang manuscripts.

Dunhuang is an ancient place along the silk road which was under siege in the wars at the end of the Tang. At this time, resident monks sealed a large number of manuscripts as well as invaluable artworks in its caves. The caves were discovered and opened by Western explorers in the early twentieth century and have since continued to provide a wealth of authentic information on the life and religion of medieval China.

The *Huahu jing* (Scripture on the Conversion of the Barbarians) too survived in Dunhuang. First compiled around the year 300, the text contains a polemical attack against Buddhism. It claims that when Laozi left China after transmitting the *Daode jing* he continued his wanderings throughout Central and South Asia. Everywhere he went, he converted the people to the Tao, appearing as the Buddha to them. The various religious rules of Buddhism, then, were created by him to civilize the "barbarians."

As time went on, the text was countered, proscribed, and rewritten. It continued to lay claim to all kinds of teachings, including the philosophy of Confucius and the Christianity of Mani. The text translated below consists of the first chapter of this longer scripture. It dates probably from the early eighth century, the time when Manichaeism was first acknowledged by the imperial court. It is today contained in the Buddhist canon, no. 2139 of the Taishō edition (54.1266b-67b). Its full title is *Laozi xisheng huahu jing xushuo* (Introduction to the Scripture of Laozi's Ascension to the West and Conversion of the Barbarians). Section division and subheadings are the translator's.

This text has not been translated to date. For studies of the conversion story, see Zürcher 1959, Seidel 1984, Reiter 1990, Kohn 1989d, 1991. On the deification of Laozi, see Seidel 1969.

---

**Huahu jing (On the Conversion of the Barbarians), Introduction.**

BIRTH AND VOW

[1266b] In those days, in the reign of Tangjia of Yin [King Yangjia, 1408–1401 B.C.E.] with the yearstar in *gengshen*, in the month [   ], the Highest Venerable Lord came down from the eternal realm of the Tao. He harnessed a cloud of three energies and strode on the essence of the sun. Following the rays of the nine luminaries, he entered into the mouth of the Jade Maiden of Mystery and Wonder. Taking refuge in her womb, he became a man.

In the year *gengchen*, on the fifteenth day of the second month, he was born in Bo. Nine dragons sprinkled water over him to rinse and wash his body; then they transformed into nine springs.

At that time, the Venerable Lord had white hair. He was able to walk upon birth. A lotus flower spouted under each step he took. After nine steps, he pointed to heaven with his left hand, to the earth with his right hand and announced to the people: "In heaven above, on the earth below, I alone am venerable. I shall reveal the highest law of the Tao. I shall save all things moving and growing, the entire host of living beings. I shall wander across the ten directions and reach to the dark prisons of the underworld. I shall lead all those not yet saved and all those lost in error to certain salvation."

Hidden and apparent among humanity, he served as the teacher of dynasties. Reaching in position to the Great Ultimate itself, he is highest among gods and immortals.

At the time of birth he possessed a naturally beautiful body. He was clad in heavenly garments, a divine fragrance pervaded his rooms, and brilliant sunlight radiated from him. In nine days, his body grew nine feet. Everybody, startled and amazed, recognized him for a sage.

Since he was born with the appearance of old age, he was called Laozi, "Old Child." The gods of heaven in the void, however, praise him with ten different titles. They are:

Highest Venerable Lord
Highest Venerable of Perfect Spirit and the Wisdom of Nonbeing
Teacher of Emperors and Kings

Great Officer
Great Venerable among Immortals
Father of Heavenly Beings
Highest One of Non-Action
Benevolent Master of Great Compassion
Heavenly Venerable of Primordial Beginning
Old Child

THE DECLINE OF THE ZHOU

Laozi concentrated his spirit and obscured his traces. He converted all people under heaven and explained to them the essential as well as the general methods of self-cultivation.

After more than a hundred years, the way of the king declined. He killed all those of wisdom and goodness and committed brutal atrocities without number. All the loyal ministers who tried to remonstrate were executed. Heaven sent down floods and fires [as warnings], but the king did not understand. Like this, things went on for several years. The end of the Zhou was imminent.

Thus Laozi, under the reign of King Kang [1078–1052 B.C.E.], with the yearstar in *jiazi*, joined the common officials. [1266c] To obscure his presence and hide his name, he became an archivist of the Zhou. Thus he still served the dynasty as a teacher. Then, under the reign of King Zhao [1052–1001 B.C.E.], with the yearstar in *guichou*, he decided to go west.

REVELATION

Crossing the Hangu Pass, he transmitted the *Scripture of the Tao and the Virtue* in 5,000 words, the *Wondrous True Scripture of Western Ascension*, and other sacred texts to Yin Xi [the Guardian of the Pass].

In addition, he taught him the highest methods of Great Clarity, the true writ of the Three Caverns, the talismans and charts of Numinous Treasure, the application of Great Mystery, and other secret ways. He ordered Yin Xi to teach these to people of utmost purity and humanity, so that they could undergo the transformation of wings and become spirit immortals. He commanded him to never let the transmission be interrupted.

With this he crossed over to the west. Passing through the floating sands, he reached the town of Bimo in the land of Khotan.

At that time, he raised his Tathagata staff and summoned all his followers. They appeared in an instant: There were Master

Redpine, the Elder of the Yellow Center, the Heavenly King of Primordial Beginning, the Goddess of the Great One, the Jade Maiden of the Six Heavenly Branches, the Divine Lord of the Eight Trigrams, the dragon and tiger lords, as well as large numbers of meritorious celestial officials.

Fig. 7. Laozi Meets Yin Xi, the Guardian of the Pass. Source: *Zengxiang liexian zhuan.*

In addition, there were the lads of the Golden Carriage, and those of the Benevolent Radiance, the officials of heaven and earth, as well as all the rulers of water and air, the sun and the moon, of mountains and the sea. There were the governors of yin and yang, of wood, fire, metal, and earth, as well as the gods of the five sacred mountains and the four majestic streams—and many others more.

Also present were the strongmen of the Heavenly Stems, the generals of the Floating Network, the divine kings of the Flying Heaven, as well as assorted immortals and jade maidens. All together there were more than a hundred thousand of them.

They came riding on clouds, pulled by flying dragons, or floating freely through the air. The Venerable Lord thereupon took his place behind a jade awning. There he sat on the throne of the Seven Treasures. [Attendants] burned incense of a hundred harmonies and scattered a multitude of fragrant flowers. Heavenly music was played as the wise and sagely of all the heavens came crowding around him.

THE CONVERSION OF THE BARBARIANS

Using his divine powers, he then summoned all the barbarian kings. Without question they appeared from far and near. There were numerous kings and nobles. . . . [1267a] They all came with their wives and concubines, families and other dependents. They crowded around the Venerable Lord, coming ever closer in order to hear the law.

At this time the Venerable Lord addressed the assembled barbarian kings:

"Your hearts are full of evil! You engage in killing and harm other beings! Since you feed only on blood and meat, you cut short manifold lives!

"Today I will give you the *Scripture of the Yaksa Demons*. It will prohibit meat-eating among you and leave you with a diet of wheat and gruel. This will take care of all that slaughter and killing! Those among you who cannot desist shall themselves become dead meat!

"You barbarians are greedy and cruel! You make no difference between kin and stranger. You are intent only to satisfy your greed and debauchery! Not a trace of mercy or sense of social duty within you!

"Look at you! Your hair and beards are unkempt and too long! How can you comb and wash it? Even from a distance you are full of rank smell! Bah! How awfully dirty your bodies must be!

"Now that you are made to cultivate the Tao all these things will be great annoyances to your practice. I therefore order all of you to shave off your beards and hair. According to your native customs, all your garments are made of felt and fur. By teaching you the Lesser Way, I will, by and by, lead you to more cultivated manners. In addition, I will give you a number of precepts and prohibitions, so that you gradually get to exercise mercy and compassion. Each month on the fifteenth day, you shall repent your sins."

THE ORIGINS OF BUDDHISM

Speaking thus, the Venerable Lord, by means of his divine powers, transformed himself into the form of the Buddha and came walking through the air. His body was sixteen feet tall and radiated a golden brilliance. His face, constantly turned toward the east, revealed his mindfulness of the origin.

This, as the Venerable Lord explained, is "because I came to you from the east." All those who looked at him thus were made to develop intense compassion and good-will in their hearts. "So you all, people and kings, will have an image of my face to worship every morning. Facing east, you will serve me properly."

Not long after this, he went across the Belaturgh Mountains. In the mountains there was a deep lake. Poisonous dragons were living there. They had already harmed about five hundred merchant travelers who had taken up lodgings on the lakeside. None of them survived.

I [the Venerable Lord] then sent King Koban, ruler of this land, to bring the Tao to them. Reaching the lakeside he practiced the law, and all the dragon kings were fearful and awed. Changing into human beings, they sincerely apologized for their former evils and begged the king to take them to another place to live. They did not want to harm anyone here any more. Thus, never again was anybody harmed there.

Going south, the Venerable Lord arrived in Wuchang. Perambulating the five heavens, [he recounts,] I entered the country of Magadha. My clothes were all white and I had an empty pot in my hand. Placing myself in the meditation chamber, I established the Buddhist teaching. I was called the Buddha of Purity. All the Kshatriya [warriors], Brahmins, and others worshiped me in order to attain the Tao of highest order and perfection.

之教授以浮屠

浮屠喪門

赭衣以作

髮偏袒合掌

喜心者剃髮

王率國人生

乃遣飛天神

太上說四十二章經

罪犯群胡惟喜於是

語胡王曰已告汝師赦汝

太上老君令尹喜為佛乃

第三十四化　說浮屠

Fig. 8. Laozi Has Yin Xi Appear to the Barbarian As the Buddha. Source: *Laojun bashiyi hua tushuo.*

TRAVELS EAST AND WEST

After three times eighty years, under the reign of King Mu [1001–946 B.C.E.], I returned to the Middle Kingdom of the Xia [China]. I went all the way across the land and entered the Eastern Sea. There I got as far as [the immortals' isles of] Penglai and Fangzhang and reached even to the Fusang Tree of the sun.

[1267b] For a while I stayed at the residence of the Great Emperor of Heaven. Here I organized the ranks of the immortals and established their proper hierarchy. After the reigns of another eight kings and over 240 years had passed, there came the dark age of King You. When the yearstar was in *xinyou* [780 B.C.E.], the three majestic rivers were shaken and agitated. This was a sign that soon the king's reign would perish, as the cycles were approaching the Hundred-and-Six [their end]. Nothing could be done.

Thus, I crossed over to the west again, teaching and converting all the lands. This time I went to the Western Sea, as far as the Cave, Floating and Unicorn Continents. There I summoned spirit immortals of the ten directions, including the superior among them as well as those who had only just attained the Tao. I also called the rulers of the underworld as well as those who had not yet received the teaching. There, moreover, were the floating scattered immortals as well as humans of utmost piety and perfect loyalty. I guided them all to salvation.

All these—over 80,000 people—I measured according to their merit and virtue. I weighed them in terms of their karma and retribution and accordingly awarded them their proper position in the offices of the five grades. Then I set up the twenty-seven ranks of the immortals to classify the host of celestials as either immortals, perfected, or highest sages. I furthermore placed them to reside either on sacred mountains, in rivers, or in the Three Heavens. Thus all were ranked.

THE HISTORICAL BUDDHA

Another sixty years passed. Under the reign of King Huan, with the yearstar in *jiazi* [700 B.C.E.], in the month *yiyin*, I ordered Yin Xi to stride on the essence of the moon and descend to India. There he entered the mouth of the wife of King Suddhodana. Taking refuge in her, he was born [as a human being] and named Siddharta. Rejecting his position as crown prince, he went into the mountains and cultivated the Tao. He realized the highest Tao and duly was called the Buddha.

He then set up the twelve syllabaries of the Siddha and transmitted his teaching in more than 30,000 words. Explaining the scriptures and precepts in detail, he continued to pursue the Highest Law. In addition, he destroyed the heterodox sects, all ninety-six of them. When he was over seventy, he showed his nirvana to the world.

## CONFUCIUS'S TEACHINGS

In the time of King Xiang, with the yearstar in *yiyu* [600 B.C.E.], I again returned to the Middle Kingdom. Teaching and converting the people of the world, I gave Confucius his law of rites and righteousness.

After this a king was born who, within sixty years, caused the division of the country and had to move the capital. This king was without virtue.

I therefore ascended to Mount Kunlun, and flew up to [the Heaven of] Purple Tenuity. Thus, I distributed my energy throughout the Three Worlds, nourishing them all alike.

## MANICHAEISM

Again more than 450 years passed. I strode on the radiant Tao-energy of spontaneity and descended from the world of perfection and serenity to a country called Sulin in the western jade world.

Born into a royal family, I became crown prince. But I left my family and position to enter the Tao. I was called Mani then. Turning the great wheel of the law, I proclaimed the True Law of precepts and regulations, of concentration and wisdom.

Having thus appeared three times and established two different gateways to the teaching, I finally had taught and converted all the people of the world. So I let them know the original time had come. I would ascend to the World of Light and descend into the Realm of Darkness. Wherever there was life, it would follow me and thus be saved.

## THE FUTURE

After my life as Mani, five times ninety years will pass. Then the golden energy will come to flourish, and my law will arise in its fullness. As a sagely image, arising in the west and clad in pure multicolored spontaneity, I will then once again enter the Middle Kingdom.

At this time, due to this wondrous effort, the yellow and white energies will harmonize. The three teachings will find a great reunion and be equal. All people will be joined in me, worshiping me in the chambers of concentration. Combined in root and stem, the teachings all share the same pattern. They all reveal far and wide the venerable law of the Latter-day Sage of Great Light.

The Taoists of the Middle Kingdom shall then explain cause and effect in great detail. They will provide the world with a life boat of the Vast and Encompassing Law. Through this all things moving and growing, all that contains energy, shall equally be led to salvation. This teaching will then be called the Law That Vastly Encompasses All.

## 11. The Path

Outlining the Taoist path in five distinct stages and associating each with a particular form of liberation, the *Tianyinzi* integrates the different longevity techniques and forms of meditation current in the mid-Tang period. The text is associated with Sima Chengzhen, famous patriarch of Highest Clarity and leading Taoist of his day, but its ultimate authorship remains unclear. Nobody quite knows who this elusive Master of Heavenly Seclusion was. Still, his synthesis and comprehensive discussion have continued to inspire Taoists till today.

The text is contained in DZ 1026, fasc. 672, but has been edited many times. The section headings are part of the original. For an earlier translation and study of the text, see Kohn 1987a. On Sima Chengzhen, see Section 2 ("The Tao in the World") above. On the integrated development of the immortal mind, see Kohn 1990.

---

### *Tianyinzi* (The Master of Heavenly Seclusion)

INTRODUCTION

The path of spirit immortality begins with long life. The starting point for long life is the nourishment of energy. Human beings receive energy from heaven and earth, then yin and yang harmonize it. Yin and yang spiritual and empty—this is the mind. Spirit and material souls—they govern the mind day and night, during waking and sleeping. They make sure the human body is never far from the path of immortality.

I do not know where the Master of Heavenly Seclusion came from. He wrote this treatise in eight sections to encompass the secret and the wondrous. Things found here cannot be attained through study alone.

There are the various techniques to cultivate and refine body and energy, to nourish and harmonize mind and emptiness. Its basic concept of "return to the root" goes back to Laozi; the idea of "emitting a radiance" is found with Zhuangzi. Long life and eternal vision are indeed in this text.

I have practiced the techniques of the Tao myself. Now I feel compassion for the people of the world. They often die untimely and do not live out their natural life-spans. Therefore, I decided to transmit the teaching to fellow adepts of long life. I have simplified it so that it can be practiced and referred to easily. Ever since the time of Laozi, there has only been this teaching of the Master of Heavenly Seclusion.

Sima Chengzhen

### 1. SPIRIT IMMORTALITY

All people from birth are endowed with the energy of emptiness. Originally their essence and enlightenment are of penetrating awareness, learning has no obstructions, and the "spirit" is pure. Settle this spirit within and let it shine without! You will naturally become different from ordinary people. You will be a spirit immortal! Yet even as a spirit immortal, you are still human.

To accomplish spirit immortality you must cultivate the energy of emptiness. Never let the common world defile it. Find spirit immortality in spontaneously following your nature. Never let false views obstruct your path.

Joy, anger, sadness, happiness, love, hate, and desires are the seven perversions of the emotions. Wind, damp, cold, heat, hunger, satiation, labor, and idleness are the eight perversions of energy. Rid yourself of them! Establish immortality!

### 2. SIMPLICITY

The *Book of Changes* says: "The way of heaven and earth is simple." What does this mean?

The Master of Heavenly Seclusion says: "Heaven and earth are above my head and beneath my feet. When I open my eyes I can see them. I can speak of them without complex devices. Thus I say: Consummate simplicity is the virtue of immortality."

What path should be used to seek this? He says: "Without seeking you cannot know; without a path you cannot attain the goal. All students of spirit immortality must first realize simplicity. Teachings that are marvelous, artful, and attractive only lead people astray. They do not lead to the root. They could never be my teaching."

3. Gradual Progress Toward the Gate of the Tao

In the *Book of Changes*, there is the hexagram called "Progressive Advance." Laozi speaks of the "Marvelous Gate." Human beings should cultivate inner perfection and realize their original natures. They should not expect sudden enlightenment. Rather, they progress gradually and practice the techniques in peace. The following five are the progressive gateways to the Tao.

The first is fasting and abstention.
The second is seclusion.
The third is visualization and imagination.
The fourth is sitting in oblivion.
The fifth is spirit liberation.

What does fasting and abstention mean? It means
   cleansing the body and emptying the mind.
What does seclusion mean? It means withdrawing deep
   into the meditation chamber.
What does visualization and imagination mean? It means
   taming the mind and recovering original nature.
What does sitting in oblivion mean? It means letting go of
   the personal body and completely forgetting oneself.
What does spirit liberation mean? It means spirit
   pervasion of all existence.

Practice according to these five and perfect step one, then only proceed to step two. Perfect step two, then gradually move on to step three. Perfect step three, then approach step four. Perfect step four, then finally pass on to step five. Thus you attain spirit immortality!

4. Fasting and Abstention

Fasting and abstention not only mean to live on vegetables and mushrooms. Cleansing the body is not just bathing to remove the dirt. Rather, the method is to regulate the food so that it is perfectly balanced, to massage the body so that it glows in health.

All people are endowed with the energy of the five agents. They live on things that consist of the five agents. From the time they enter the womb people breathe in and out; blood and essence circulate in their bodies. How could one stop eating and yet attain long life?

Ordinary people do not realize that to abstain from food and nourish on pure energy are only temporary measures of the Taoists. These things do not mean that we completely abstain from all grain. We speak of fasting and abstention from food, yes. But we refer to the purification of nourishment and the moderation of intake. If one is hungry one eats—but never to satiation. Thus we establish a balanced diet.

Don't eat anything not well cooked! Don't eat strongly flavored dishes! Don't eat anything rotten or conserved! These are our basic abstentions. Massage your skin with your hands so that it becomes moist and hot! This drives out the cold energy and makes the body radiate with a glow.

Refrain from long sitting, long standing, long exhaustive labor! All these are basic abstentions. They serve to balance and regulate the body. If the body is strong, energy is whole. Thus, fasting and abstention are the first gateway to the Tao.

5. SECLUSION

What is meant by seclusion? It has nothing to do with living in ornate halls, in cavernous buildings, on double matting and thick carpeting. It means sitting with one's face to the south, sleeping with one's head to the east, complying in everything with the harmonious rhythm of yin and yang.

Light and darkness should be in balance. The room should not be too high. If it is too high, yang is predominant and there will be too much light. The room should not be too low. If it is too low, yin is predominant and there will be too much darkness. The reason for this precaution is that, when there is too much light, the material souls will be harmed. When there is too much darkness, the spirit souls will suffer. People's three spirit souls are yang, their seven material souls are yin. Harm them with light and darkness, and they will get sick.

When things are arranged in the proper balanced way, we have a chamber of seclusion. Still, don't forget how various the energies of heaven and earth can be. There may be, for example, a violent yang that attacks the flesh. Or there may be a lascivious yin that overpowers the body. Be wary and guard against these!

During the progressive advance of cultivation and nourishment there is no proper seclusion unless these instructions are carried out. Thus the Master of Heavenly Seclusion says:

"The room I live in has windows on all four sides. When wind arises I close them; as soon as the wind has died down I open them again. In front of my meditation seat a curtain is suspended; behind it a screen has been placed. When it is too light I draw the curtain to adjust the brightness inside. When it gets too dark I roll the curtain up again to let light in from outside.

"On the inside I calm my mind, on the outside I calm my eyes. Mind and eyes must be both completely at peace. If either light or darkness prevails, there are too many thoughts, too many desires. How could I ever calm myself inside and out?" Thus, in studying the Tao, seclusion marks the second step.

### 6. VISUALIZATION AND IMAGINATION

Visualization is to produce a vision of one's spirit. Imagination means to create an image of one's body. How to do this? Close your eyes and you can see your own eyes. Collect the mind and you can realize your own mind. Mind and eyes should never be separate from the body; they must not harm the spirit: this is what visualization and imagination are for.

Ordinary people, to the end of their days, direct their eyes only toward others. Thus their minds wander outside. When the mind is concerned only with outer affairs, it also causes the eyes to continue looking at things outside. Brightly sparkling, their light floats around and never reflects back on themselves. How can people not become sick from this and end up dying prematurely?

Therefore, "return to the root means tranquility, and tranquility means to recover life." To recover life and perfect one's inner nature is called "the gate of all subtleties." Thus, with the step of visualization and imagination the task of learning the Tao is half completed.

### 7. SITTING IN OBLIVION

Sitting in oblivion is the perfection of visualization and imagination. It is also the utter oblivion of visualization and imagination.

To put the Tao into action but not oneself act—isn't that the meaning of sitting? To see something and not act on it—isn't that the meaning of oblivion?

Why do we speak of not acting? Because the mind remains free from agitation. Why do we speak of not seeing? Because the body is completely obliterated.

Someone asks: "If the mind is unmoving, does it have the Tao then?" The Master of Heavenly Seclusion remains silent and does not answer.

Another asks: "If the body is obliterated, does it have the Tao then?" The Master of Heavenly Seclusion closes his eyes and does not look.

Then someone awakens to the Tao and, in withdrawing, says: "The Tao is really in me. What person is this 'me'? What person actually is this Master of Heavenly Seclusion?"

Thus, self and other are both forgotten. Nothing is left to shine forth.

8. SPIRIT LIBERATION

Step one, fasting and abstention, is called liberation through faith. Without faith, the mind cannot be liberated.

Step two, seclusion, is called liberation through tranquility. Without tranquility, the mind cannot be liberated.

Step three, visualization and imagination, is called liberation through insight. Without insight, the mind cannot be liberated.

Step four, sitting in oblivion, is called liberation through absorption. Without absorption, the mind cannot be liberated.

When the four gates of faith, tranquility, insight, and absorption have been pervaded by the spirit, then we speak of spirit liberation. By "spirit" we mean that which arrives without moving and is swift without hurrying. It pervades the rhythm of yin and yang and is as old as heaven and earth.

When the three forces, heaven, earth, and humanity, are combined, changes occur. When the myriad beings are equalized, then the Tao and the Virtue are active. When the one original nature of all is realized, there is pure suchness. Enter into suchness and return to non-action.

The Master of Heavenly Seclusion says: "I am born with the changes; I will die with the changes. In accordance with the myriad beings I move; going along with the myriad beings I rest. Pervasion comes from the one original nature; perfection comes from the one original nature. Through spirit I am liberated from all: life and death, movement and rest, pervasion and perfection."

Among human beings the liberated are spirit immortals: in heaven they are heavenly immortals; on earth they are earth immortals; in water they are water immortals. Only when they pervade all are they spirit immortals.

The path to spirit immortality consists of these five progressive gateways. They all lead to one goal only.

## 12. The Way to Complete Perfection

Wang Chongyang (1113–1170), originally a military official of the Song, founded the school of Complete Perfection (Quanzhen) after he had withdrawn from service and lived in total seclusion for a decade. He was known as a rather eccentric ascetic and, once he decided to leave his meditation hut and spread the revelation he had received from Lü Dongbin, soon acquired a large following. He had seven major disciples, six men and one woman, who became the patriarchs of the sect after him.

The teaching of Complete Perfection is a mixture of Confucian formality, simple asceticism, Buddhist monachism, and Taoist inner alchemy. Due to ample imperial sponsorship, the school continued to flourish and, by the fourteenth century, had assimilated the numerous Taoist schools that had sprung up around the same time. It is the leading Taoist school in mainland China today and the only surviving form of monastic Taoism.

The *Chongyang lijiao shiwu lun* contains its basic principles in fifteen short articles. The text is contained in DZ 1233, fasc. 989. Earlier translations are found in Yao 1980: 73–85 and Reiter 1985. On the history of the school of Complete Perfection, see Yao 1980, Tsui 1991. For some of its typical features, see Hawkes 1981. On Lü Dongbin, see Section 14 ("Passing the Test") below.

---

*Chongyang lijiao shiwu lun* (Chongyang's Fifteen Articles on Establishing the Teaching)

1. CLOISTERED RESIDENCE

If you leave the family life you must first join a cloister. A cloister is a kind of residence. It provides your personal body with a foundation. When your personal body has a good foundation, your mind can gradually find peace. Then energy and spirit radiate in harmony, and you can enter the true Tao.

When movement and action become necessary, you must not overdo things and exhaust yourself, because when you overdo things and exhaust yourself, your energy will diminish. On the other hand, you can't remain entirely without movement, either, because not moving at all causes obstructions to energy and blood.

You should, therefore, find a middle way between movement and tranquility. Only then can you guard the eternal and be at peace with your lot. This is the way of residing in peace.

## 2. WANDERING LIKE THE CLOUDS

There are two different ways of wandering.

The first is to relish the spectacular scenery of mountains and rivers and enjoy the colorful bloom of flowers and trees. Someone doing so might frolic around in the variety and glitter of cities big and small or savor the towers and pavilions of temples and monasteries. He might visit friends and please himself or engage wantonly in the delights of food and fashion.

Someone who wanders like this, even if he covers a myriad miles, will exhaust his body and squander his strength. As he gazes all around at the sights of the world, his mind gets confused and his energy weakens. Such a one vainly wanders like the clouds.

The second way of wandering is to pursue inner nature and destiny and search for mystery and wonder. One who wanders like this climbs into high mountains over dangerous passes and visits enlightened teachers without tiring. He crosses distant streams with turbulent waters and inquires for the Tao without slackening.

Then, even a single saying received in the right spirit may open up complete understanding. The great realization of life and death dawns within and you become a master of Complete Perfection. As such, you truly wander like the clouds.

## 3. THE STUDY OF TEXTS

The right way to study texts is not to pursue literary quality and dazzle your eyes. Rather, extract their inner meaning in true harmony with your mind. Abandon the texts when you have extracted their meaning, their principle. And don't hesitate to abandon this in turn when you have found its deepest ground. Once this ground has been grasped, it can be consolidated in the mind.

Keep it in the mind for a very long time and its essence and inner truth will become a natural part of yourself. Mind and radiance become vast and overflowing; wisdom and spirit take off in leaps and bounds. There is nothing they do not pervade, nothing they do not understand.

Once at this level, you should further consolidate and nourish it. Yet take good care never to be hasty or nervous about the process, because there is the danger that you might lose hold over inner nature and destiny.

There are also people who do not penetrate to the deepest intention of the texts because they desire only to memorize many concepts and become widely read. Such people will chatter in front of others, bragging of their outstanding talents. With this they do nothing for their practice of cultivation, but on the contrary harm their spirit and energy. However many texts they may read, what do they truly gain in terms of the Tao?

Only by attaining the most fundamental inner meaning of the texts can you really harbor them in your depth.

### 4. The Preparation of Medicines

Herbs are the finest energy of mountains and streams, the essential florescence of grasses and trees. They may be warm, or they may be cool; one uses them to supplement or drain energy. They may be thick, or they may be thin; one uses them externally or from within.

Studying herbs in their essence allows you to support your inner nature and destiny. On the other hand, if you apply herbs blindly, you will waste your body and physical constitution.

All those who study the Tao must penetrate herbal lore. If you do not do so, you have no means to support the Tao. Yet in doing so, you must not develop attachments, for they will diminish the hidden merits of past lives. You will then hanker after material goods on the outside and waste your efforts at cultivation within.

Not only does this lead to grave transgressions and errors in this life, but it will also cause retribution in the lives to come. Oh, noble disciples of my teaching! Heed this and be very careful!

### 5. On Construction

Reed-thatched huts and grass-thatched cottages are needed to protect your body. To sleep in the open air or out in the fields is an offense to the sun and the moon.

On the other extreme, to live under carved beams and lofty eaves is what a superior disciple should not do, either. How can grand palaces and fancy halls be an appropriate way of living for a follower of the Tao? To cut down trees is to sever the precious fluid of the earth's veins, just as to beg for goods and money is to take away the life-blood of the people.

To cultivate only outside merits without pursuing inner practice is like trying to still one's hunger by drawing a cake or collecting snow for provisions. One vainly expends much effort and in the end gains nothing.

Disciples of strong determination must search for precious palaces inside their very own body. All vermilion towers outside of the body, however unceasingly one continues to erect them, one will only see them collapse and crumble. Oh, bright and perceptive worthies! Examine yourself with great care!

6. Companions in the Tao

People in the Tao join together as companions, because they can help each other in sickness and disease. "If you die, I'll bury you; if I die, you'll bury me," is their motto.

Therefore, first of all choose the right person and only then join that person as a companion. By no means join someone first and then think about him as a person.

Once you have a companion, don't develop a strong attachment to each other. Any such attachment will create a bondage to your minds.

At the same time, don't remain entirely without attachment to each other. A lack of attachment will cause a divergence in your feelings. You must find a middle way between developing personal dependence and remaining entirely unattached.

There are three kinds of people you should join and three kinds you should avoid. Go with those who have an illumined mind, deep wisdom, or strong determination. Never team up with those who do not clearly penetrate the outer projections of the mind, those who lack deep wisdom and are doltish and turbid in inner nature, or those who are deficient in determination and simply bluster about.

When you set yourself up among your fellow seekers, always act in complete accordance with your mind and will. Don't just follow your emotions, nor rely on people's outer appearance. Always only choose the lofty and illumined. This is best.

7. Sitting Straight

"Sitting straight" does not simply mean to sit with the body erect and eyes closed. That is superficial sitting. To truly sit you must maintain a mind like Mount Tai, unmovable and unshakable at all hours of the day, whether staying, walking, sitting, or lying down, in all forms of activity and repose.

Control and shut off the four gates of the senses—eyes, ears, mouth, and nose. Never let the outside world come in! If there is even a trace of a thought about activity and repose, this is no longer sitting quiet. If you can attain such a mind, although your body may remain in the world of dust, your name has already been entered in the ranks of the immortals.

Then there is no need to go far and consult others. Rather, you will be worthy and sagely within yourself. After one hundred years, with merits accomplished, you can cut off the shell and ascend to the perfected. Your pellet of cinnabar complete, the spirit wanders in the eight outer reaches.

8. CONTROLLING THE MIND

Let me explain the Tao of the mind. If the mind is always deep and tranquil, it does not move at all. It is obscure and abstruse, and never sees the myriad beings. It is dark and vague, and never knows inside or outside. There is not the slightest trace of thought or imagination. This is a concentrated mind. It needs no control.

On the other hand, if the mind actively develops in the pursuit of mental projections, it becomes all topsy-turvy, looking for the head and searching the tail. This is the confused mind. You must cut out and extirpate it thoroughly. Never let it run wild. It ruins and destroys Tao and Virtue. It harms and diminishes inner nature and destiny.

Staying, walking, sitting, and lying down—if the mind is constantly controlled, hearing and seeing, knowing and perceiving will only be its sickness and affliction.

9. REFINING ORIGINAL INNER NATURE

Ordering inner nature is like tuning the lute. If the strings are too tight they will break; if the strings are too loose they will not resonate. Find the middle way between tightness and looseness, and the lute can be tuned.

It is also like casting a sword. If there is too much steel it will snap; if there is too much tin it will bend. Find the harmonious mixture of steel and tin, and the sword can be used.

To tune and refine original inner nature embrace these two methods, and it will spontaneously be wondrous and smooth.

## 10. PAIRING THE FIVE ENERGIES

The Five Energies gather in the center; the Three Primes gather at the top.

The green dragon puffs red mist; the white tiger exhales black smoke.

The myriad spirits array themselves in rows; the [energy in the] hundred arteries flows and rushes.

The cinnabar dust radiates in brightness; the lead and mercury merge in purity.

The body is entrusted to the human world; the spirit travels in heaven.

## 11. MERGING INNER NATURE AND DESTINY

Inner nature is spirit; destiny is energy.

The relationship of inner nature to destiny is like that of wild birds to the wind. They use it to float and soar, rising lightly. Saving their strength, they accomplish their flight with ease.

Thus the *Scripture of Hidden Correspondences* says, "The way birds control their flight is through energy."

As disciples who cultivate true realization, you must rely on this concept but never allow it to get out to lesser people. Otherwise , I fear, the spirits will send down censure.

Inner nature and destiny are the roots of cultivation and practice. Refine them with caution and care!

## 12. THE TAO OF THE SAGE

To enter the Tao of the sage, first strengthen your determination for many years. Accumulate merit and unceasingly pursue the right practice. Become lofty and illumined and join the fold of the steadfast and accomplished—then you can enter the Tao of the sage.

Your body may then dwell in an ordinary house, but your inner nature will fill heaven and earth and the entire universe. The host of the sages silently protects and supports you. Immortal lords of the Great Ultimate invisibly surround you. Your name is recorded in the Purple Palace; you rank among the hierarchy of immortals.

Your physical form may still sojourn in this world of dust, but your mind already radiates widely beyond all.

### 13. GOING BEYOND THE THREE WORLDS

The Three Worlds are the World of Desire, the World of Form, and the World of Formlessness.

When the mind forgets conscious deliberation and thoughts, it goes beyond the World of Desire. When the mind forgets all the states of mental projection, it goes beyond the World of Form. When the mind does not manifest even a vision of emptiness, it goes beyond the World of Formlessness.

Leaving the Three Worlds, the pure spirit dwells in the realm of immortals and sages. Inner nature resides in the heaven of Jade Clarity.

### 14. HOW TO NOURISH THE ETERNAL BODY

The body of the law is a representation of the formless. It is neither emptiness nor existence, has neither behind nor before. It is neither low nor high, neither long nor short.

Active, there is nothing it does not pervade. Resting, it is dark and obscure without a trace. Realize this Tao and you can nourish this body. The more you nourish it, the more merits you gain. The less you nourish it, the less merits you have.

Never yearn to turn around and go back! Never hanker after the ordinary world! Then you will come and go in true spontaneity.

### 15. LEAVING THE WORLD

Leaving the world does not mean that the body departs. Rather, it refers to the mind. The body is like the lotus root; the mind is like the lotus blossom. The root is in the mud, yet the blossom is in the open air.

When you realize the Tao, your body will be in the sphere of the ordinary, but your mind will be in the realm of the sages. Nowadays, people want to avoid death forever and at the same time leave the ordinary world. They are very foolish, indeed, and have not even glimpsed the true principle of the Tao.

Now I have given you these fifteen articles in order to admonish all disciples of strong determination. Deeply take them to heart in every detail, so you know them well!

Part Two

## LONG LIFE

# Chapter Four

## DISCIPLINE

The path toward the Tao, then, consists of "long life and eternal vision," as the *Daode jing* already formulates it, and ultimately leads to immortality.

The long life part aims at the complete physical healing of the body, the harmonization and synchronization of all aspects of life with the rhythms of nature, and the recognition of the cosmic dimensions of one's own physical existence. It begins with discipline. Discipline serves to ensure the proper determination toward the Tao. It is the foundation that sets up the basic framework of mind and body in which alone the hard work of the path can be accomplished. Discipline means commitment. It means surrender to the Tao, to the scriptures, to the teaching.

Discipline appears in several concrete forms—moral uprightness, formal procedures, physical restrictions, and examinations. The key to successful discipline is the development of a strong will toward the Tao and to secure its protection. By submitting to discipline one proves one's readiness to undergo whatever is necessary to walk on the path and find one's place among the celestials.

The most fundamental form of discipline is found in the precepts and prescriptions, the basic rules that regulate the moral conscience and community behavior of Taoist practitioners. They are valid equally for lay followers and serious adepts, are in fact geared primarily toward the harmonious interaction of a large group of people, joined and living together in their will to realize the Tao.

In addition, the commitment of Taoist adepts is expressed in their undergoing of certain formal rituals. There are rites of ordination, of reporting to the gods, rites of prayer, of repentance, rites for the dead, for the living, and so on. Taoists believe that sickness and all ailments of the body are caused by the interference of malevolent demons. They can enter the body only due to the moral turpitude and sinful life of the individual in question. This being so, precepts and rituals, especially exorcisms and rites of repentence, are an essential prerequisite to the attainment of perfect health and long life.

Beyond that, individual practitioners need to have the right destiny; they have to be ready for higher attainments in terms of their cosmic standing. The concept of destiny, understood in ancient China in terms of family inheritance, was soon linked with the Buddhist notion of karma and thus became more individualized. For Taoists the necessary qualification is the possession of "immortals' bones." Only one with the right genes can ever be taught.

Even then, strong determination and a will to pursue the Tao are essential. Immortals' bones only guarantee basic good fortune, an auspicious meeting with a god or immortal, an opportunity to hear the Tao and receive the scriptures. Beyond that, the real work begins—often with a series of tests administered by the teacher to see how far the promising candidate will go. Some make it, others don't; some will be partial to higher secrets, others will have to stick to the more elementary practices.

The four selections below highlight these different aspects of discipline. There is first a list of precepts—the ten precepts, the twelve vows, and a series of 180 practical rules—from the *Chishu yujue* (Red Writings and Jade Instructions) and the *Sanyuan pin* (Precepts of the Three Primes). Both texts are from the ancient corpus of Lingbao scriptures of the late fourth and early fifth century.

Then there are the "Memorial Reading" and a set of formal "Incantations for Protection" used in the Rite of Mud and Ashes. An intense and rather ecstatic ritual of repentance, this was developed in the Lingbao school and undertaken with much splendor since the fifth century. The texts are taken from a Taoist encyclopedia of the sixth century.

Third, there are two short stories about how to be taught: the biography of the Goddess of the Great One, teacher of the Highest Venerable Lord, from a thirteenth-century collection; and the myth of the Master on the River, who reveals a commentary on the *Daode jing* to a Han emperor, from a Dunhuang manuscript. Both texts outline in exemplary clarity the conditions one must meet to be graced with immortal instruction—and the limits of this instruction.

The tests immortals-to-be have to undergo are the topic of the fourth selection. Here, too, two stories have been chosen: the biography of Fei Changfang from the *Shenxian zhuan* (Biographies of Spirit Immortals) of the fourth century; and the account of the tests of Lü Dongbin from a similar collection of the thirteenth century. In both cases, the unsuspecting possessor of the right bones meets a celestial emissary. Soon convinced that his fortune lies with the master, he follows him and is tested for his Tao-prowess. One succeeds all the way; the other fails. They both find a path just right for them and proceed to serve suffering humanity.

## 13. Precepts and Prescriptions

Taoist precepts were first adapted from Buddhism when Taoism became a country-wide communal religion in the fifth century. They always come back to the basic five: don't kill, don't steal, don't lie, don't misbehave sexually, and don't get intoxicated. Together with five other rules regarding the proper form and use of speech, they constitute the original ten precepts of the Tao.

To the precepts, a set of vows is commonly added. Patterned on the bodhisattva vows of Mahāyāna Buddhism, Taoist vows equally stress the strong determination of the practitioner to attain salvation for himself but only after all beings have been saved first. They emphasize the role of the active Taoist as a leader and savior of all suffering forms of life, as the guide and helper for all in need. They also repeat in a personalized, "I will," form of language the need to obey the teachers and honor the scriptures, to study hard and practice without laxity. Taking the precepts and vowing to pursue the path is thus the beginning of the long ascent.

Two texts are selected below, one that contains the ten precepts and twelve vows, the other a list of three sets of sixty community rules geared to the more advanced spiritual leaders (the first set actually has only forty-seven). Both documents are of Lingbao origin.

The first is the *Chishu yujue* (Red Writings and Jade Instructions), known in full as *Taishang dongxuan lingbao chishu yujue miaojing* (Highest and Wondrous Scripture of Numinous Treasure in the Mystery Cavern Containing Red Writings and Jade Instructions). It is contained in DZ 352, fasc. 178 and forms part of the original corpus of Lingbao scriptures as compiled by Ge Chaofu. The translation covers a few pages from the first scroll (1.2b–4a). The precepts have also been translated and discussed in Bokenkamp 1989.

The second gives the 180 Lingbao precepts in the *Sanyuan pin* (Precepts of the Three Primes). Here the full title is *Taishang dongxuan lingbao sanyuan pinjie gongde qingzhong jing* (Scripture on the Weight of Merit and Virtue As Based on the Precepts of the Three Primes Contained in the Mystery Cavern of Highest Numinous Treasure). The text is found in DZ 456, fasc. 202; the selection translates pages 22a–31a.

For a preliminary study of Taoist precepts, see Schmidt 1985. More detailed analyses are, so far, only available in Japanese, especially in Kusuyama 1992. On Taoist ordination ranks and procedures, see Benn 1991.

---

### *Chishu yujue* (Red Writings and Jade Instructions)

THE TEN PRECEPTS

1. [2b] Don't harbor hatred or jealousy in your heart! Don't give rise to dark thieving thoughts! Be reserved in speech and wary of transgressions! Keep your thoughts on the Divine Law!

2. Maintain a kind heart and do not kill! Have pity for and support all living beings! Be compassionate and loving! Broadly reach out to bring universal redemption to all!

3. Maintain purity and be withdrawing in your social interactions! Be neither lascivious nor thieving, but constantly harbor good thoughts! Always take from yourself to aid others!

4. Don't set your mind on sex or give rise to passions! Be not licentious in your heart but remain pure and behave prudently! Make sure your actions are without blemish or stain!

5. Don't utter bad words! Don't use flowery and ornate language! Be straightforward within and without! Don't commit excesses of speech!

6. Don't take liquor! Moderate your behavior! Regulate and harmonize your energy and inner nature! Don't let your spirit be diminished! Don't commit any of the myriad evils!

7. Don't be envious if others are better than yourself! Don't contend for achievement and fame! [3a] Be retiring and modest in all things! Put yourself behind to serve the salvation of others!

8. Don't criticize or debate the scriptures and teachings! Don't revile or slander the saintly texts! Venerate the Divine Law

with all your heart! Always act as if you were face to face with the gods!

9. Don't create disturbance through verbal argumentation! Don't criticize any believers, be they monks, nuns, male or female laity, or even heavenly beings! Remember, all censure and hate diminishes your spirit and energy!

10. Be equanimous and of whole heart in all of your actions! Make sure that all exchanges between humankind and the gods are proper and respectful!

THE TWELVE VOWS

1. [3b] I will study the perfected scriptures that set forth the Divine Law and open the liberation and salvation of all. I will bring forth a strong determination for the Tao. I vow to rise to the status of a great sage in my lives to come.

2. I will constantly practice compassion. I vow that all will learn of the Divine Law and that salvation will extend universally, without hindrance or distortion.

3. I will delight in the scriptures and teachings. I will study them widely to let my understanding deepen and to make my determination firm and enlightened. I will liberate and transform all those in ignorance and darkness.

4. I will respectfully receive the instructions of my teacher. I will spread the wonderful teachings far and wide so that all living beings might enter the gate of the Divine Law and forever depart from their paths of blindness.

5. I will cause my faith to extend to the heights of mystery and wonder. I will venerate and honor the teachings and moral injunctions. I will recite the scriptures morning and night without being lazy or remiss.

6. I will not labor for glory and fancy ornaments but break the chain of worldly causations. I will maintain a steadfast heart and resolved determination, so that all I undertake will be within the Divine Law.

7. I will diligently recite the great scriptures. I vow that all beings shall find the bridge of release and that all future life will enjoy good karma.

8. I will always maintain a mind of friendliness, free from all perverseness or falsity. I will remain without envy and ill-will, without evil and jealousy.

9. I will represent the sages in all situations where things are given life. I will pass on the teachings of the Numinous Treasure uninterrupted and without lapse.

10. [4a] I will purify my body and keep the precepts. I will observe the fasts and establish merit. Thereby I will lead the myriad beings to salvation and complete liberation.

11. I will read broadly in my studies and deeply penetrate the law contained in the scriptures. Thus I will prepare the way for heavenly beings to save all.

12. I will be with an enlightened teacher life after life. I will receive the teachings and spread them so that innumerable living beings may be saved.

---

### Sanyuan pin (Precepts of the Three Primes)

[22a] To those who pursue the highest Tao! You must not commit the following sins:

The sin to disregard the scriptures and precepts, harbor doubts or be in two minds about the teaching.

The sin to despise the sagely writings or criticize the sacred scriptures.

The sin to make light of the teachers or break the solemn oath.

The sin to slander the elders or disregard the heavenly rules.

The sin to steal the texts of the scriptures or practice without the proper teacher. [22b]

The sin to study on your own, without a teacher, or transmit the teachings without proper authorization.

The sin to illicitly collect the texts of the scriptures and pass them on to your disciples.

The sin to obtain any scriptures without the formal guidance of a teacher.

The sin to receive the scriptures without proper scriptural procedure or transmit them on other than the prescribed dates.

The sin to transmit scriptures to the wrong people.

The sin to receive instruction from a teacher of the Divine
Law without having accumulated the necessary merit.
The sin to transmit the teachings to any disciples without
having accumulated the necessary merit.
The sin to transmit the Divine Law in any way that does not
accord with the tradition of the teachers.
The sin to transmit the scriptures without properly notifying
the five divine emperors.
The sin to receive the scriptures when you don't have faith or
think lightly of the Tao. [23a]
The sin to assume merit and fame for yourself without passing
through the proper process of the sages.
The sin to neglect to honor your guides and teachers on the first
and fifteenth of each month and on the eight seasonal festivals.
The sin to neglect to observe the fasts.
The sin to neglect to purify yourself for the fasts.
The sin to take shortcuts in reciting the scriptures.
The sin to engage in disputes or fights while traveling overland.
The sin to anger or distress your teachers and elders.

To all students of the Tao and all lay followers! You must not
commit the following sins:

The sin to pick a fight with a good fellow.
The sin to speak evil or hypocrisy.
The sin to criticize your teachers, elders, or anyone else. [23b]
The sin to intoxicate yourself with wine and spirits.
The sin to kill living beings or give rise to evil thoughts.
The sin to harbor greed and passion, pride and sloth.
The sin to defile the Divine Law and the Tao.
The sin to curse demons and spirits.
The sin to kill or harm any living beings.
The sin to use fancy language or words without sincerity.
The sin to be lewd and lascivious; don't defile yourself.
The sin to steal other people's goods.
The sin to be jealous of others' wisdom or envy their abilities.
[24a]
The sin to turn your back on the love and mercy of your teacher.
The sin to cheat your teacher and turn away from the Tao.
The sin to give celestial writings to the uninitiated.
The sin to speak ill of the scriptures or the Divine Law.

The sin to turn from the commands of the scriptures.
The sin to be disobedient to your seniors.
The sin to be nasty to your juniors.
The sin to deceive your fellow students.
The sin to speak nicely while thinking something bad.
The sin to gossip about the faults of others. [24b]
The sin to make light of the three luminaries.
The sin to despise the spirits and the demons.

These sixty *[sic]* precepts are being supervised by the Twelve Officials of the Central Administrative Section of the First Office of the Department of Heaven; by the Fourteen Officials of the Central Administrative Section of the First Office of the Department of Earth; and by the Fourteen Officials of the Central Administrative Section of the First Office of the Department of Water.

To all students of the Tao and all lay followers! You must not commit the following sins:

The sin to be jealous of your fellow students.
The sin to speak flowery words or lies.
The sin to covet personal profits without ever being satisfied. [25a]
The sin to accumulate money and valuables without ever thinking of distributing them.
The sin to take pleasure in grabbing the valuables of others for yourself.
The sin to wish harm and disaster, poverty and homelessness on others.
The sin to possess knives, staffs, or any other weapons.
The sin to slaughter the six domestic animals or kill any living beings.
The sin to shoot down wild animals or birds in the sky.
The sin to burn the mountainsides in order to hunt.
The sin to set traps to catch fish.
The sin to use eating utensils made from gold or silver.
The sin to covet lucrative appointments or serve a tyrannical government. [25b]
The sin to destroy material objects for your own advancement.
The sin to throw food or drink into fresh water.
The sin to covet rich and delicious flavors, fat and meat.
The sin to covet eating foods of the five tastes.
The sin to write in a flowery style to hide your true intentions.

The sin to assemble large crowds.

The sin to harbor schemes toward another's wife or daughter.

The sin to criticize affairs of state.

The sin to harbor schemes toward another's wealth or goods.

The sin to spoil the nice things of others with coarse objects. [26a]

The sin to concern yourself with the affairs of lords and kings.

The sin to make false statements about the calendar or the movements of the stars.

The sin to burn down fields or mountain forests.

The sin to cut down trees or idly pick leaves and plants.

The sin to wander about with bad people or get too trusting with strangers.

The sin to mix with common folk or pick fights with them.

The sin to eat all by yourself when among a group, without thinking that they might be hungry too.

The sin to break up another's wedding with people of the world.

The sin to engage in entertainments of people of the world.

The sin to swear allegiance to your fellows on the outside while secretly all set to ruin these good men. [26b]

The sin to speak of your elders or superiors as faulty and bad.

The sin to expose the secrets or vulgar behavior of others.

The sin to attack good people or quarrel without end.

The sin to sneak a look at others' correspondence or pry into their secrets.

The sin to speak or walk about with a woman alone.

The sin to share mixed living quarters.

The sin to share mixed dining halls or exchange clothes with a woman.

The sin to interact with women without goodness.

The sin to think yourself great and develop pride.

The sin to take it upon yourself to revenge public injustice. [27a]

The sin to leave your family.

The sin to abort children or harm the unborn.

The sin to get too close to members of other clans.

The sin to throw poisonous drugs into fresh water and thus harm living beings.

The sin to secretly love any of your juniors.

The sin to assemble a crowd of people.

The sin to distribute writings that slander others.

The sin to presume that only you know how to properly use your inner nature.

The sin to idly set up taboos.

The sin to kill the livestock of others. [27b]
The sin to criticize the long and short of teachers and of friends.
The sin to make light of the teaching and the scriptures or any
    other words of the Law.
The sin to belittle someone else's age or sickness.
The sin to be nasty to beggars.
The sin to become high and mighty when guiding common
    people.
The sin to turn your family into a clique.
The sin to live separate from your parents and siblings.

These sixty precepts are being supervised by the Twelve Officials of the Left Administrative Section of the Left Office of the
Department of Heaven; by the Fourteen Officials of the Left Administrative Section of the Left Office of the Department of Earth;
and by the Fourteen Officials of the Left Administrative Section of
the Left Office of the Department of Water.

[28a] To all students of the Tao and all lay followers! You must
not commit the following sins:

The sin to get angry and rail at your juniors.
The sin to get angry and upbraid good people.
The sin to hinder the living to go beyond death.
The sin to forget your teacher when in wealth and honor.
The sin to neglect to recollect the Tao on the ritual days for the
    honor of the heavens.
The sin to get angry and rage at your teachers and leaders.
The sin to discuss the faults and evil of others.
The sin to ridicule the poor and humble. [28b]
The sin to encourage others to do evil.
The sin to stop others from doing good.
The sin to enhance the loss and failures of others.
The sin to approach or leave anyone impolitely, with your back
    turned toward him.
The sin to call upon the five sacred mountains and three great
    rivers without holding your ritual tablet.
The sin to defile the five sacred mountains and three great
    rivers.
The sin to take away what others value highly.
The sin to be reckless among common folk or pick fights with
    people of the world.

The sin to congratulate or condole with people of the world or seek pleasure among the common masses.

The sin to lay claim another's merit to boost your own virtue. [29a]

The sin to speak about what others eat or drink, like or dislike.

The sin to be startled and frightened when people are ailing or distressed.

The sin to be startled and frightened when wild animals are caught or shot down.

The sin to be startled and frightened with the old or very young.

The sin to take officials, chiefs, or administrators lightly.

The sin to discuss the straight or crooked ways of the people of the world.

The sin to idly discuss the rise and fall of the country.

The sin to distribute alms in a niggardly spirit.

The sin to go wandering about for pleasure and without salvational purpose.

The sin to climb up high to deceive those below. [29b]

The sin to capture and imprison wild birds or free animals.

The sin to rejoice over others' losses and mistakes.

The sin to throw thorns into people's way.

The sin to worship ghosts and spirits.

The sin to expose your naked body to the Three Luminaries.

The sin to curse the wind and the rain.

The sin to barter or borrow without returning your due.

The sin to deceive others by splendor and fancy words.

The sin to be disrespectful to the Three Treasures or irreverent toward the Heavenly Venerable.

The sin to plot against the teachers or family of others. [30a]

The sin to encourage people to be unfilial toward their parents or siblings.

The sin to proudly claim to be special or call yourself a perfected.

The sin to believe in other religions, variegated techniques, or heterodox views.

The sin to engage in studying without the proper scriptures and teacher or in any way deceive the men of spirit.

The sin to accumulate superfluous clothing instead of distributing it to the needy.

The sin to secretly copy the scriptures and precepts or idly disclose them.

The sin to adorn yourself with fancy dress or luxury objects.

The sin to ascend to the high seat without your body sparkling
clean.

The sin to be filthy or irreverent before your teacher.

The sin to neglect to offer rites and prayers when your teacher
is in mourning. [30b]

The sin to pursue worldly fame and forget all about your
teacher and family.

The sin to expect to rise to splendor when your teacher attains
noble rank.

The sin to neglect to take care of your teacher when he is sick
or in dire straights.

The sin to distance yourself from the distress of others and
rush to pursue your own pleasure.

The sin to enter or leave a chamber of the Tao without proper
formalities.

The sin to enter a chamber of the Tao to idly chat with people.

The sin to perform rites or offer prayers without transferring
merit to the Three Bureaus.

The sin to wallow in pity for the state of your own family
without considering the plight of others.

The sin to resent the Tao or blame your teacher if there is
bereavement or sickness in your home.

The sin to claim personal possession of scriptures or techniques
that you have received from your teacher.

The sin to pass on the methods of your teacher without proper
procedures and due covenant.

The sin to speak the names of the Five Emperors on the eight
days of seasonal division.

These sixty precepts are being supervised by the Twelve Officials of the Right Administrative Section of the Right Office of the
Department of Heaven; by the Fourteen Officials of the Right Administrative Section the Right Office of the Department of Earth;
and by the Fourteen Officials of the Right Administrative Section
of the Right Office of the Department of Water.

## 14. Protective Measures

Taoist ritual and talismans were used as protective measures
against the influence of demons and other evil forces from the beginnings of the religion in the second century C.E. Talismans, as the
immediate representation of celestial script, could ward off evil, un-

mask demons, convey control over forces of this world, and provide access to the realms of the otherworld. Rituals, notably purifications and invocations of the gods for protection, had the same purpose.

Purifications included not only abstentions from defiling substances and activities, but also active acts of repentance and contrition. The virtue inherent in oneself had to be brought back to its original purity, to a level close to the Tao itself. For that purpose, not only had sins and moral failures to be avoided in the future, but also those committed in the past had to be made up for.

The Rite of Mud and Ashes, described below, was such a purificatory ritual, developed in the context of the Lingbao school. It was basically an elaborate ceremonial punishment, believed to exonerate the participants from their own sins and those committed by their ancestors. This ritual would ward off calamities threatening to strike in this life and the next. It closely imitated the trials undergone by criminals condemned by the courts of the world.

The participants would appear wearing sackcloth, their faces smeared with soot. They would chant prayers of sin and repentance, then be guided by the officiant to undergo a ritual punishment. Gradually the rhythm of the chantings would increase, and the tension of the punishments would rise, until the crowd, all excited, lost control in ecstasy and began to roll wildly in the mud. The master of ceremonies then calmed them down again, to move on toward the next crescendo.

The selections below, "The Rite of Mud and Ashes: Memorial" and "Incantations to the Protective Gods [of the Five Directions]," are taken from the *Wushang biyao* (Secret Essentials of the Most High; 50.1a–2b and 6a–7b). This text is the first Taoist encyclopedia, commissioned by Emperor Wu of the Northern Zhou in 574 C.E. For a critical summary and analysis of this work, see Lagerwey 1981.

The Rite of Mud and Ashes is described in Maspero 1981: 381–86, where also a short part of the first selection is translated. On Taoist ritual in history, see Benn 1991, Schipper 1995 and 1985a. For its present form, see Saso 1972, Schipper 1975, Lagerwey 1987. The author is indebted to Lowell Skar for his critical reading of the translation.

---

### "The Rite of Mud and Ashes: Memorial," from *Wushang biyao* 50 (Secret Essentials of the Most High)

[1a] The memorial: to be read after the Nocturnal Announcement, conducted as a regular Audience Rite, and addressed to the positions and ranks as follows:

The Highest Great Tao of Non-Ultimate,
The Highest Lord of the Great Tao,
The Highest Venerable Lord,
The Highest Elder,
The Unsurpassed Venerable of Mystery,
The Heavenly Venerables of the Numinous Treasure of the Ten
  Directions,
The Host of Great Sages Who Have Realized the Tao,
The various Lords and Elders of Utmost Perfection,
The Great Ritual Masters of the Mysterious Center,
The Lords Celestial Masters,
The Highest Chancellors and High Commanders,
The Four Superintendents and Five Emperors,
The Assembled Officials of the Three Worlds,
All the Spirits and Numinous Powers,
And many others more.

I am a lowly creature, foul and filthy,
Most insignificant and most abject.

May my errors and confusion be turned into blessings!
May my life and its worth undergo a great transformation!
May the Three Caverns guide the universe's course!
May the Sacred Scriptures descend into the world!

The Three Masters have opened up salvation,
Transmitted to us all the wondrous Law,
In golden writings in jade characters,
With secret instructions of the spirit immortals.

On the day when we receive the Law,
There shall be
The end to all ignorance and blindness,
The fulfillment of all flesh and bones.

[1b] In carrying out the instructions of the scriptures,
We reverently develop kindness and compassion.
We support the masters and the elders,
Unfolding the dark so it may come to light.

We will open up salvation for all beings
And rescue them to become residents of heaven.

All our deeds will be returned in a report,
So never dare we  be lazy and remiss.

Reverently here I stand, this humble officiant _____ ,
To declare on behalf of this person _____ ,
With words sincere, since he is truly in extremes,
Genuinely pitiful and in wretched circumstances:

Reverently led forward by the hand,
We follow the instructions of the Celestial Master.
Plastered with soot, as ordered in the rules of Pardon,
We expose ourselves at the sacred altar.

Our bodies tied and roped together,
Hair dishevelled, foreheads smeared with mud,
We hang our heads, hair dangling in our mouths,
At the base of the balustrade's rail.

Performing the Pure Rite for the Great Pardon
Of Numinous Treasure's Lower Prime [festival],
We burn fragrant incense, knock our heads to the ground.
Oh please, oh please, grant mercy!

Recorded properly on this day and month, on this sacred altar
    in this institution, located in this village, this district, this
    commandery.

We, this family _____ ,
Performing the Pure Rite for the Great Pardon,
Lights lamps to display brightness,
And illuminate the heavens.

For three days and three nights,
Through all six [double-hour] periods,
We carry out repentance for our Pardon.

May our millions of forebears and ancestors,
All our fathers, mothers, uncles, brothers,
Whether dead already or to die in future,
Down to ourselves participating here,
May we all

Be free from all the evil
For kalpas still to come!

[2a] For millions of generations,
We have committed sins and accumulated burdens.
Reverently we now trust in the method of this Rite:
May our family be complete and ordered!
May we be bathed and cleansed to purity!

Thus we present this announcement for the merciful
    hearing of
The Highest Three Venerables,
The Utmost Perfected of the Ten Directions,
The Great Ritual Masters of the Mysterious Center:

Oh, extend down your spirit, shine forth your brightness
And take cognizance of these words!

We beg you, oh, issue an edict to
The Host of Officials of the Numinous Treasure,
The Powerful Divinities Attending the Scriptures,
The Assembled Officials of the Three Worlds,
And also, on this plane,
The Perfected Officers of the Earth and Land.

Order them all
To fuse together and be single-minded,
To combine their strength
And guard and protect this person and this family,
Whether big or small.

[Order them]
To come and sweep clean the sanctuary for this fast,
Our halls and residences, inside and out!
To kill off all demons and approaching robbers,
Subdue all the demons of the four directions!

To come and make
Our minds sincere, our spirit settled,
Our thoughts and ideas penetrating and aware—
As heaven is pure and the earth is vibrant.

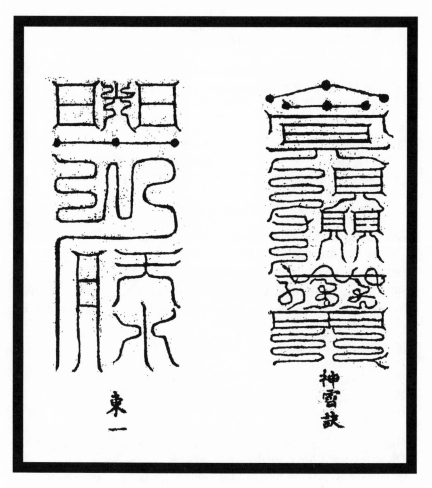

Fig. 9. Protective Talismans. Source: *Shangqing lingbao dafa*.

Thus we submit this memorial to highest hearing.

May much merit be generated by this Rite!
May there never be any hindrance or obstruction!

This person,
I have repeatedly made unworthy efforts to approach the Great
    Law,
Have worn [the talismans of] Utmost Perfection on my belt,
Still,

I am bodily bound to reside among the Five Turbidities,
In the midst of dust and filth.

My three passageways [of cosmic energy] have not been opened;
My six emotions are running wild and keep getting stronger.
Thus I have now put my trust in the precepts and prohibitions,
[2b] So I may gain more circumspection of myself.

I now rely on the Great Law of this Rite,
With its clear precepts and stern regulations,
To cause the host of officials and the lords over humanity
To all obey the order of the Law:
Illuminate my days, shine always forth for me!

As the Law wills, so I have practiced the Tao.
This I announce to merciful hearing.

---

## "Divine Incantations to the Protective Gods [of the Five Directions]," from *Wushang biyao* 50 (Secret Essentials of the Most High)

[6a] Oh, Great God of the East!
Bright Star of the Ninefold Energy of Azure Heaven!
You brilliantly illumine the Eastern Regions,
Penetratingly shine through the Nine Gates, [6b]
In your revolutions, glittering with the brightness of Pure Yang!

Oh, come and cleanse out all filth, do away with all evil vapors!
Open the light for your divine lads
To come and protect me and my house!
Restrain the demons and tie up all nasty specters!
As I rise to face the imperial lords above!

May I reverently follow the rightful Tao,
[As set forth in] the red writings and jade documents,
The talismans and instructions of the nine high heavens!

May I hitch up the dragons and get ready to rise,
Rise up to the peaceful abode of Heaven,
And soon be a flying immortal!

Oh, Fiery Star of the South!
Floating Brilliance of the Threefold Energy of Cinnabar Heaven!

In your revolutions, you shine forth and illumine all with
    Highest Yang!
Above you are, the power of Red Essence!

Oh, open the light for your divine lads,
Marshall your host of fiery soldiers,
To come and protect my three palaces within!
Behead all obnoxious powers and tie up all nasty specters,
Cut the King of Illusion into little pieces
And all that obeys the Dark Lord of the North.

May all the winds and fires in the eight directions
Blow and shine together, blending in a blaze!
How dare anyone not obey
The rightful Tao in its progression?

May I enjoy the highest merit,
Be preserved by Heaven forever and ever,
Through a million kalpas without end!

Oh, Great Whiteness of the West!
Floating Essence of the Sevenfold Energy of the Heavens!
Your radiance shines forth through the Golden Gateway,
Penetrates with brightness even the deepest dark—
The Pure Star in your midst,
Known as the Emperor of all Numen.

Oh, guard my spirits and secure my house,
Protect my body from all harm! [7a]
Oh, destroy the source of all obnoxious powers!
Let the Way of the King be upright and enlightened,
And all the halls and residences clear and dignified!

May the Three Luminaries join their radiance
And the Tao harmonize with the spontaneous flow of all!
May I fly up to the Purple Gardens
With the talismans and instructions of Numinous Treasure!

May my goodwill spread over the myriad living beings!
May my merit aid them all—
And Heaven and Earth be greatly now at peace!

護戒威神

Fig. 10. An Armed Protector God. Source: *Shangqing lingbao dafa*.

Oh, Thunderous Star of the North!
Active Power of the Fivefold Energy of Dark Heaven!
Your splendid brilliance reaches even into Great Abstrusity!
Oh, Venerable God of Black Numen!
Flying darkness in feathery garb!

Oh, come and protect all my five gateways,
Assemble the good essence and apprehend the bad!
Humbly I dare put forward this request:
Expel and scatter, destroy and behead [all evils],
As the jade talismans command!

Oh, Spiritual Perfected of Eightfold Majesty!
Seal off my gates of viciousness and all hindering obstructions,
Let me be open to the brightness of the Tao!

Shine and sparkle through my body
Like the Three Luminaries shining forth together!
May I steer the empty air and stride upon the winds,
Lift up my body into the flight of the immortals!

Oh, Protector Star of the Center!
Mysterious Perfected and Powerful Ruler
Of the Unified Energy of the Yellow Middle!
You spread brilliance and flowing brightness
Through all the Nine Heavens.

Oh, open the light for your divine lads,
Twelve in number,
For your primordial energy, clear essence of yang.
And let it float aloft in wafts of vermilion mist! [7b]

Oh, let your light pervade my residence,
Reach as far as into my very own body!
Drive out and destroy the hundred obnoxious forces,
Kill all the demons, however many millions!

May this divine incantation to the Mountain of the Center
Penetrate to Heaven and give me protection!
May the five sacred animals be securely on guard
To let me fly up and ascend to the immortals!

## 15. How to Be Taught

To be selected as one worthy to undergo the personal and individual training process of the Tao hinges on a meeting with a god or immortal. Even then, one has to prove one's worth and undergo tests. In no case must one just ask for the Tao and expect it to be given without a murmur.

The Goddess of the Great One (Taiyi yuanjun) is the teaching aspect of Laozi's mother, of the Mother of the Tao. Originally created from the primordial energies of the Tao itself, she is one with Laozi in the Tao and yet a different and independent deity. The Mother of the Tao, as described by Du Guangting of the tenth century, appears in four distinct aspects: as Jade Maiden of Mystery and Wonder she is the virginal cumulation of the Tao before she brings forth the Venerable Lord; as Mother Li she is the mother of Laozi, the Tao incarnate; as Goddess of the Great One she teaches her son the essentials of the Tao; as Great Queen of Former Heaven she resides in the higher reaches above.

Laozi, when confronted with the Goddess, is a helpless seeker for immortality, a representative of humanity in the face of the divine powers of the Tao. The same position is occupied by Emperor Wen of the Han who requests explanations of the Tao from the Master on the River (Heshang gong).

A legendary figure, whose story began to circulate around the third century, the Master on the River is associated with a commentary to the *Daode jing*. This influential document has roots as far back as the Han dynasty but in its present form goes back to an edition of the fifth century. The story how the Master transmitted his commentary is an instructive example of how the Tao can and should be taught.

The first selection on the Goddess of the Great One is taken from the *Lishi zhenxian tidao tongjian houji* (Comprehensive Mirror Through the Ages of Perfected Immortals and Those Who Embody the Tao, Supplementary Collection), found in DZ 298, fasc. 150 (1.8b–9a). This text is a huge and justly famous collection of immortals' biographies compiled by Zhao Daoyi around the year 1300. The "Supplementary Collection" contains hagiographies of goddesses and lady immortals.

The second text on the Master on the River comes from the *Laozi daode jing xujue* (Introductory Explanations to Laozi's *Daode jing*). This text, which has survived in Dunhuang, is a collection of different passages all relevant to the transmission of the *Daode jing* and dated to between the second and fifth centuries. The Heshang gong story goes back to the fourth. The Dunhuang manuscript number is S. 75 or S. 2370. For a convenient edition, see Ofuchi 1979a: 509.

On the Goddess, see Kohn 1989c. For more on the Master, see Chan 1991.

---

**"Taiyi yuanjun" (The Goddess of the Great One), from *Lishi zhenxian tidao tongjian houji* (Comprehensive Mirror Through the Ages of Perfected Immortals and Those Who Embody the Tao, Supplementary Collection)**

The Venerable Lord wandered far off to mountains and through grasslands. He searched for the true scriptures that explain how to purify the spirit [meditation] and revert the cinnabar [alchemy]. When he had almost passed Mount Lao, the Goddess of the Great One appeared to him riding a five-colored unicorn and waited upon by a host of divine attendants.

The Venerable Lord advanced to her and asked about the Tao.

The Goddess said, "The essentials of the Tao are reverted cinnabar and the golden fluid." Thereupon she imparted the secret formulas to him.

In the following year they met again on Mount Li. But at this time the Goddess of the Great One declined to reveal any further details of the divine cinnabar method.

"I am chief of all the immortals," she said, "queen of the wondrous Tao. The secret arts, mysterious and numinous, all partake in the original mystery. How could I disgrace myself by revealing them?"

"Among the people of this world," the Venerable Lord countered, "there is not a single one who really knows about death. All human beings beat their breasts and cry bloody tears. To see their misery stirs my compassion; I wish to give them divine medicine. Don't you think it should be possible that all people live long?"

"It is not possible," the Goddess replied with decision. "To live in the Tao is very difficult; one must have developed great wisdom to do so. One must become a pious, obedient, and truly sincere person. Heaven brings forth the myriad beings with good and bad traits. The good traits must be multiplied, the bad traits eradicated. It is not sufficient just to give people some medicine and make them all live long. But you already know these things; you should be careful not to give away the secrets."

The Venerable Lord thereupon practiced the Tao of spirit immortality himself. He wanted to hand down its methods to encourage future generations in their immortal pursuits. Thus he visualized the perfected, guarded the One, refined the cinnabar, and nourished his energy. Afterwards he was able to hang freely in mid-air and walk on empty space. He could easily leave being and enter nonbeing, following wherever his intention took him. Ordinary mortals can never fathom his powers.

One day he strode on a white deer, rode around the cypress in the garden, and ascended to heaven.

---

### "Heshang gong" (The Master On the River), from *Laozi daode jing xujue* (Introductory Explanations to Laozi's *Daode jing*)

Nobody knows the proper name of Heshang gong, the Master on the River. Under Emperor Wen of the Han, he set up his thatched hut near the river and spent his time reading the *Scripture of the Tao and the Virtue*.

Since Emperor Wen loved the words of Laozi, he ordered all the ministers, nobles, and vassals of his court to recite them. However, there were a few sentences he did not quite understand. No one in the empire could explain these to him.

When he therefore heard from one of his courtiers that the Master on the River also venerated the text, he sent a messenger to him with an imperial summons to come to court and explain the passage in question.

Heshang gong, however, said: "The Tao is venerable, Virtue is noble. I am afraid I cannot answer questions brought to me from afar."

The emperor therefore strode on his horse and paid him a visit.

"In all under heaven," he said, "there is no place that does not belong to me as the ruler. Among all the people living in the world, none is not my subject. There are four great halls in my palace, and I live in the greatest. You may have the Tao, but you do not have the people. You cannot make others obey your orders—why do you behave as if you could? I warn you, I can make people rich and honored or poor and despised."

All of a sudden, the Master on the River clapped his hands and stood up from his seat. Imperceptibly he rose up into the air, light as a cloud, rising from the ground more than a thousand feet. He continued to ascend to the mysterious emptiness of the sky.

After a long time, he looked down and said, "Above, I do not reach heaven, in the middle I do not belong to humanity, and below I do not live on the earth. Whatever people you may rule, Your Majesty would hardly be able to make me rich and honored or poor and despised."

Then the emperor understood. He realized that the Master was a spirit being. Sinking to the ground, he bowed deeply and expressed his apologies.

"Without virtue I am and utterly ashamed of my former conduct. My abilities amount to nothing. My grief is unbearable indeed. I may be involved in regulating the affairs of the world, yet in my heart I venerate the Tao and the Virtue. But they are described in obscure terms. There are a few places I do not understand properly. Therefore I dare to beg for your gentle kindness, oh Lord of the Tao, to explain them to me."

Upon these words, the Master on the River came down again, like the radiance of the sun penetrating the dusk, and handed the emperor a manuscript of the *Daode jing*.

"If you study this with care," he explained graciously, "all your questions will be naturally solved. Since I wrote this commentary, more than 7,000 years have passed, but I have only given it to three people so far. You are the fourth. Don't show it to anyone who isn't ready for it!"

Emperor Wen knelt humbly to receive the text. As soon as he had finished speaking, the Master vanished and was nowhere to be seen.

Note: It seems to me that Emperor Wen loved Laozi and the Great Tao very much. But none of the ordinary people around him could fully understand its meaning. Yet the emperor meditated on its far-out notions and venerated the Highest Lord. Therefore the Lord of the Tao sent down a divine messenger to teach him in particular. The messenger was to return promptly.

Then, however, he found that the emperor's mind was not yet full of pure faith. So he showed him divine transformations and made him understand the Tao properly. He intended for the emperor to perfect his Tao and find his original inner nature. People later called this messenger the Master on the River.

## 16. Passing the Test

Two classical stories, well known equally in Taoism and Chinese folklore, illustrate the need not only to profess to a sense of dedication and strong determination for the Tao but also to prove it. They each tell of a series of tests administered by immortals, apparently met accidentally, who guide potential candidates along the path. In one case, the final test is failed due to disgust, and the aspirant has to be content with the position of a demon-killer on earth. In the other, the outcome is successful and the newly developing immortal becomes a major savior of humankind.

Both figures introduced below, the Gourd Master (Hugong) and Cavernguest Lü (Lü Dongbin) are classical personages. The Gourd Master, who also inspired a key figure in van Gulik's mystery *The Emperor's Pearls*, is an immortal exiled temporarily from Heaven who makes his home inside a gourd. A microcosm, this little container sports all the luxuries and delights of a full universe, with celestial palaces and a host of divine attendants.

The Gourd Master uses his immortal powers to dispense medicine to the common people and further the attainments of more gifted ones, like Fei Changfang. When literally spiriting his disciple away, they leave a bamboo staff in his place which appears to be his corpse. This process is known as "deliverance from the corpse" and used commonly by immortals who are ready to ascend to heaven but not yet able to vanish without a trace, a much higher form of ascension. Later in the story, another bamboo staff serves as a means of transportation—another indication of the powers immortals have over the animate and inanimate universe.

Cavernguest Lü can easily be described as the most important immortal since the tenth century. To the present day, he continues to appear in planchette sessions of Complete Perfection groups in Hongkong. He is venerated wherever Chinese freely practice their religion. For centuries he has aided suffering humanity, revealing large numbers of techniques and recipes, ranging from the rules of Complete Perfection over methods of Taiji quan to new cough medicines.

Traditionally believed to have been a poet of the late Tang (ninth century) by the name of Lü Yan, the Cavernguest can be traced historically—with considerable difficulty—to stories about a wandering Taoist, happily drinking, loving, and writing poems along the waterways of central-southern China. Those waterways were the main lines of commerce in the tenth to eleventh centuries, and the stories seem to be linked with forms of advertising and a boost in business and enterprise at the time.

Later, in the thirteenth century, with the rise of popular theater, Lü Dongbin became a dramatic figure and soon developed into the central character of a group of eight. Seven men and one woman, these Eight Immortals were—with the exception of Zhongli Quan, who originally initiated Lü—all converted by him, aided in their efforts to attain the Tao. The eight, ubiquitous in all Chinese communities to the present day, stand for the happy-go-lucky vision of a life that flows effortlessly along with the course of nature. They are delightful company, drinking, singing, having fun. Their pictures are signs of good fortune and blessing, their worship—usually associated with institutions of Complete Perfection—geared toward raising the level of happiness all around.

Among the two texts selected below, the account of the Gourd Master is taken from *Shenxian zhuan* (Biographies of Spirit Immortals), chap. 5. This collection, although reedited variously later, originally goes back to Ge Hong of the early fourth century. But the Gourd Master is known not only from this. Translations of different versions of his story are contained in Giles 1948: 79–81, after the Yuan dynasty *Zengxiang liexian zhuan* (Illustrated Immortals' Biographies) as well as in Ngo 1976: 128–34 and DeWoskin 1983: 77– 81 (after the *Hou Hanshu;* Dynastic History of the Later Han Dynasty).

Lü Dongbin's meeting with the Tao and subsequent tests are told in the *Zengxiang liexian zhuan* (2.12b–13b). The translation follows Yetts 1916: 790–97. For a historical study of this Taoist immortal, see Baldrian 1986. On his role in Quanzhen Taoism today, see Tsui 1991. For material on the Eight Immortals, see Ling 1918, Yang 1958, Yetts 1916, 1922. For a discussion of "deliverance from the corpse," see Robinet 1979a. On the symbolism of the immortals, especially the microcosm of the gourd and the grotto, see Stein 1990.

---

### "Hugong" (The Gourd Master), from *Shenxian zhuan* (Biographies of Spirit Immortals)

Nobody knows the real name of the Gourd Master, but several talismans and sacred instructions prevalent today have been revealed through him. Among them are some that summon celestial armies, others that call on demons and spirits, as well as some that cure diseases. All in all, the Gourd Master delivered over twenty scrolls of texts, collectively known as the "Gourd Master Talismans."

Once there was a certain Fei Changfang, a native of Runan, who served as a guard in the marketplace. One day he saw the Gourd Master arrive from the distance, enter the market and set up a stall to sell medicine. Nobody recognized him. The drugs he sold were all equally priced, yet they cured all kinds of different diseases with the same efficacy.

As the Master instructed his customers: "Take this medicine, then each such-and-such, and within a few days you will be cured. Success is guaranteed!"

With this business, the Gourd Master made several ten thousand cash every day, of which he only kept thirty to fifty for his own use. The remainder he distributed to the poor around the marketplace, to all those starving and cold.

The Master always had a large gourd hanging in front of his medicine stall. At sunset, when the market closed, he would promptly leap into the gourd.

No one in the marketplace was able to see this, but Changfang, from his observation tower, could. Thus he knew that the Gourd Master was a very unusual person. He therefore resolved to serve him. Day in, day out, he swept the ground before the Master's stall and brought him food. The Master graciously accepted this service and did not reject it.

This went on for quite some time, but Changfang never went lax in his efforts even for a moment, nor did he dare to ask for any kind of reward. The Gourd Master knew thus that Changfang had genuine faith.

One day he told him, "Come back to me at sunset when everybody has left."

Changfang did as he was told and presented himself.

"When you see me jump into the gourd," the Master instructed him, "just follow my example and jump yourself. You will get in easily."

Changfang obeyed and indeed entered the gourd before he even noticed that anything was moving. Once inside, it was no longer a mere gourd. Everywhere he looked there were immortals' palaces, worlds upon worlds, with marvelous towers, splendid double gates, and highways between pavilions. A host of servants and attendants stood at attention.

"I am an immortal," the Gourd Master told his guest. "In the old days I used to have a position in the celestial administration. But once I failed to properly support a public affair and was punished by banishment to the world of mortals. Now, you have what it takes. Therefore you were able to see me."

Changfang knelt and knocked his head. "People of flesh and blood," he declared, "don't know how many sins they accumulate, how often they reject prosperity and happiness. Their erroneous ways should be pitied. They certainly act as if they were entering

Fig. 11. The Gourd Master and Fei Changfang. Source: *Zengxiang liexian zhuan.*

open coffins and do nothing but continually disperse their energies. They behave as if they could bring their rotten bones back to life or arise from putrefaction. They only fear the superficial stench and the corruption, never obeying the driving force at the depth. Pitiful indeed—what the world calls prosperity and happiness!"

"You are really quite outstanding," the Gourd Master agreed, "but keep quiet about your observations."

On a later occasion, the Gourd Master visited Changfang on his observation tower. "I have brought a little wine," he said, "let us drink together!"

The wine was downstairs, so Changfang sent a man down to pick it up, but he could not budge it. Changfang then sent a group of men down to hoist it up, but they could not move it either. He told the Master, who smiled and went down himself. He returned carrying the wine with a single finger. The container appeared to be slightly more than a cup, but the two men drank from it all day and could not exhaust its contents.

"I will soon be leaving," the Gourd Master announced to Changfang. "Would you like to come with me?"

"I do indeed have the strong wish to join you. There is no question about that. But I would prefer my relatives not to know that I have gone off. Is there anything we can do about this?"

"But that's easy," the Master said and handed a fresh stick of bamboo to his follower.

"Take this stick," he explained, "and go back home. Then complain of some sickness and place this stick in your bed. Come away in secret and watch what happens."

Changfang did as he was told. After he had left, his relatives believed that he had died, seeing as they did his corpse in the bed. They wailed and sobbed, and duly buried the body.

But Changfang was following the Gourd Master and soon lost all orientation of where he was.

The Master then put Changfang to the test. He left him in the midst of a pack of tigers. Curling their lips, they opened their mouths and revealed their sharp teeth, getting all ready to eat him. But Changfang showed not a trace of fear.

The next day he found himself in a stone cavern with a huge boulder, several tens of feet in size, above his head. It was suspended by nothing more than a piece of straw rope. A swarm of snakes crawled over each other for a chance to gnaw the rope in half, but Changfang did not so much as flinch.

The Gourd Master returned and patted him. "You can indeed be taught!" he said with relish.

But he tested him a third time by having him eat a pile of feces, foul with decay and full of worms several inches long. The stench and filth were awfully loathsome, and Changfang felt disgust at this.

"You will not attain the Tao of the immortals," the Master dismissed him, apologetic and with a deep sigh. "But I can grant you the powers of a demon master on earth, and you will reach a life-span of several hundred years."

He proceeded to hand him a sealed talisman in one scroll. "Carry this on your belt," he explained, "and you will be the master of all demons and spirits. Ordering them about, you can cure diseases and avert disasters."

Changfang was sad about leaving. Worse, he had no idea how to get back home. The Gourd Master thereupon gave him another bamboo staff and said, "Just stride on this and you will be back in no time."

Changfang strode on the staff and bade him farewell. In another instant, feeling as if he were awakening from a dream, he arrived back at his old home. His relatives saw him and thought he was a ghost. Only when he told his story and after they had unearthed his coffin did they believe him. Just as he had said, the coffin contained only a stick of bamboo.

The staff on which Changfang had ridden home he tossed into the Gebei Lake. He watched it hit the water and found that it was in fact a green dragon.

When he first came home, he thought he had been away only for a day or two, but according to his relatives, already a year had passed since his apparent death.

From that time on, Changfang used his talisman to control demons and cure all manner of illnesses. Often when he was sitting and chatting with a group of people, he suddenly showed signs of great rage. Asked about this, he said, "I was just reprimanding some demons."

At that time in Runan there was a malevolent demon who had been in the commandery for several years. Whenever he arrived in town, he would ride in like the grand protector, visit the district office, and pound the alarm drum. After circulating around the tribunal, inside and out, he would leave again. People felt greatly afflicted by this demon.

Once when Changfang visited the magistrate's office, the demon also arrived at the gates. The commandery forces immediately fled to safety inside the walls, so Changfang was left alone in the courtyard to face the monster. Recognizing him, the demon was so terrified that he did not dare to advance.

Raising his voice in command, Changfang called out to him: "What a handy catch! Come right here, you old demon!"

The monster stepped down from his carriage, knelt in the court-yard, and knocked his head to the ground.

"Please pardon my offense," he pleaded in a thin voice.

"You dead-beat old monster, you!" Changfang scorned him. "No sense of charity or mercy! For no good reason whatsoever you pursue your evil ways! And now you have offended our magistrate! You know very well that is punishable by death, no? Now, get back to your true shape, and be quick about it!"

The demon instantaneously turned into an old tortoise, big as a wagon wheel, with a neck stretching some ten feet. Changfang then ordered him back into human form and gave him a ritual tablet with a talisman to take to the ruler of the Gebei Lake.

The monster knocked his head and wept bitterly. Taking the tablet, he left. Changfang invited the frightened people to watch the demon's progress. They saw how he stuck the tablet into the ground on the lakeshore, wrapped his neck around it, and died.

On a later occasion, Changfang visited the coast of the Eastern Sea. There he found that the area was suffering from a three-year drought. Seeing people desperately pleading for rain, he told them, "The Dragon King of the Eastern Sea once seduced the wife of his colleague in the Gebei Lake. I punished him for it. This was three years ago and I did not think further of it. Tossing the affair aside, I forgot all about it. But this is why you've been having such a long spell of drought. I'll pardon him immediately and see that he makes rain for you without any further delay."

Before long it rained long and hard.

Changfang also possessed various supernatural powers. He could shrink the arteries of the earth up to one thousand miles and thus make distant places appear in front of one's eyes. Released from his grip, the earth would stretch back to its old shape as if nothing had happened.

---

## "Lü Dongbin" (Cavernguest Lü), from *Zengxian liexian zhuan* (Illustrated Immortals' Biographies)

[12b] Lü Yan, also known as Cavernguest Lü [Dongbin], lived under the Tang dynasty and was a native of Yongle District in Puzhou. He was later called the Master of Pure Yang [Chunyang].

When his mother gave birth to him, an unearthly perfume pervaded the house and the sounds of celestial music wafted from the sky. A white crane flew down from heaven, appeared between the curtains of her bed, and vanished again.

Even as a newly born infant, Lü's body had a golden shimmer and his flesh a radiant freshness. The crown of his head formed a high dome resembling a crane's, while his back was arched like that of a tortoise. His eyes were as brilliant as those of a phoenix, and his eyebrows extended on either side to meet the hair on the temples.

While still a child, he was very quick at learning, being able to memorize ten thousand words a day. His language was fluent and couched in classical terms. Eight feet two inches in height, he resembled the immortal Zhang Zifang. At the age of twenty, he had not yet taken a wife.

The Patriarch Ma had seen him at the beginning of his life, when he was still in swaddling clothes, and exclaimed: "This child's bones are of no ordinary mortal. Extraordinary in character, he will hold aloof from worldly affairs. Whatever hovel he happens upon he will make his home. Whenever he sees a goblet of wine he will partake of it. Mark well my words!"

Later on Dongbin wandered to Mount Lu. There he met a Taoist known as Master Firedragon [Huolong], who instructed him in acquiring supernatural invisibility by the magic sword method.

During the reign period Accomplished Prosperity [841–46], he went up twice for the imperial degree, but failed. At that time he was sixty-four years of age.

Once he wandered into a tavern in Chang'an to see a Taoist priest, dressed in a gray cap and white gown, spontaneously scribble a poem on the wall. It ran,

> Sit or lie—I always grasp a pot of wine,
> No need to tell my eyes to see the starry zone.
> Vast like heaven and like earth, I never have a name,
> Among so many mortals, I'm scattered and alone.

Impressed and attracted by the Taoist's strange appearance and unusual old age, as well as by the grace and naturalness of his verse, Dongbin bowed to him and inquired his name.

"I am Master Cloudchamber [Zhongli Quan]," he answered. "My home is the Crane Ridge in the Zhongnan Mountains. Would you like to join me in my wanderings?"

Dongbin hesitated to agree to this proposal, so Master Cloudchamber took him to an inn. While he attended to the preparation of a simple meal, Dongbin reclined on a pillow. Soon he became oblivious of his surroundings and fell asleep.

呂洞賓

Fig. 12. Lü Dongbin in His Celestial Palace. Source: *Zengxiang liexian zhuan.*

He had a dream. He dreamt that he went up to the capital as a candidate of the imperial examination and passed it at the top of the list. Starting his career as a junior secretary to one of the Boards, he rapidly rose in rank to positions at the Censorate and the Hanlin Academy. Eventually he became a Privy Councillor after he had occupied, in the course of his unbroken success, all the most sought-after and important official posts.

Twice he was married, he further dreamt, and both wives belonged to families of wealth and position. Children were born to him. His sons soon took themselves wives, and his daughters left the paternal roof for their husbands' homes. All these events happened before he even reached the age of forty.

Next he found himself Prime Minister for a period of ten years, wielding immense power. This corrupted him. Then suddenly, without warning, he was accused of a grave crime. His home and all his possessions were confiscated, his wife and children separated. He himself, a solitary outcast, was wandering toward his place of banishment beyond the mountains. He found his horse brought to a standstill in a snowstorm and was no longer able to continue the journey.

At this juncture in his dream Dongbin woke with a heavy sigh. Lo and behold! The meal was still being prepared. Laughing at his surprise, Master Cloudchamber intoned a verse.

> The yellow millet simmers yet uncooked,
> A single dream and you have reached the world beyond!

Dongbin gaped in astonishment. "Sir," he stammered, "how is it you know about my dream?"

"In the dream that just came to you," Master Cloudchamber replied matter-of-factly, "you not only scaled the dizziest heights of splendor but also plumbed the uttermost depths of misery. Fifty years were past and gone in the twinkling of an eye. What you gained was not worth rejoicing over, what you lost was not worth grieving about. Only when people have a great awakening, they know that the world is but one big dream."

Impressed by this incident, Dongbin received spiritual enlightenment. He fell to his knees before the master and entreated him for instruction in the arts of transcending the limitations of this earthly sphere.

To try his determination, Master Cloudchamber said, "Your inner stature is not yet fully developed. Before you can attain transcendence of this world, many generations shall come and pass."

[13a] Having uttered these strange words, he suddenly vanished into thin air.

After that Dongbin abandoned his semiofficial position as a literatus preparing for examination and lived in retirement.

Master Cloudchamber duly subjected him to ten tests of his immortal stamina.

The first of these occurred when Dongbin returned home after a long journey to find his entire family dead from a mortal sickness. There was no feeling of vain sorrow in his heart. Instead he manfully set about making lavish preparations for the funeral, when—lo and behold!—they all rose up alive and well.

The second time Dongbin was put on trial he had sold some copper ware to a dealer who soon wanted to return the merchandise and asked for his money back. They sought out the market inspector, and Dongbin handed over the required sum without any ado. Another day, he was negotiating the sale of some of his belongings and had come to a definite agreement about the price. This notwithstanding, the dealer wished to cancel the bargain and pay only half the stipulated sum. Dongbin acquiesced and, handing over the goods, walked away without anger or engaging in dispute.

The third ordeal took place at the time of the New Year. As Dongbin was leaving his house he was accosted by a beggar demanding alms. He handed over all he carried, cash and gifts in kind. But the beggar remained dissatisfied and threateningly demanded more, using the most abusive terms. Yet Dongbin kept a smiling face and again and again apologized to him politely.

The fourth time he was put to the test, he was looking after some sheep in the mountains. A hungry tiger came upon them, with the result that the flock scattered in all directions. Dongbin interposed his own person between the tiger and the terrified sheep. The tiger gave up the chase and crept away.

In his fifth ordeal he had retired to a simple thatched hut in the mountains to study. One day a beautiful lady came to his door, graceful and lovely and radiant with such unearthly beauty that she was positively dazzling. She explained she was a newly married bride on the way to visit her parents but had become lost. Would he allow her to rest a short while in his hut? Dongbin granted her request. She then tried in a hundred different ways to snare him from the path of virtue, but he remained steadfast and unmoved to the end.

Dongbin's character was put to a test the sixth time when, on returning home from a walk in the country, he found that during his absence thieves had carried away all his goods and chattels, leaving the house bare. Not even then was his equanimity disturbed. He just set himself to earn a livelihood by tilling the ground. One day when at work with his hoe he unearthed gold pieces to the number of several score. Yet he took not a single one, but quickly covered them all up again.

In his seventh trial he again met Master Cloudchamber who told him, "In obedience to the summons of the Celestial Emperor, I am on the way to present myself before his throne. If you behave virtuously during your abode among humankind, thus acquiring merit, you will in time reach a place similar to mine."

"My aim," Dongbin replied with another deep bow, "is not to emulate you, sir, but to bring salvation to every living creature in this world. Only when this vow of mine has been fulfilled shall I ascend on high."

The eighth ordeal occurred when he bought some potent drugs from a crazy Taoist, who used to wander about selling them in the streets. He claimed that whoever partook of his wares would instantly die, but would attain the Tao in a future existence.

As Dongbin was about to buy the drug, the Taoist warned him, "The only thing for you to do now is to make speedy preparation for your death."

Yet Dongbin swallowed the stuff without batting an eyelid, and no harm befell him.

The ninth test Dongbin had to pass came in the spring when the entire country was flooded. Together with the rest of the local population, he was seeking safety in boats. Just as they reached the middle of the waters, a violent storm burst upon them. The waves rose high, lashed into fury by the wind. All were in a panic except Dongbin, who remained erect in his seat, calm and unconcerned.

On the tenth occasion, Dongbin was sitting alone in his house, when without warning there appeared to him an innumerable host of demons in weird and terrifying shapes, all seemingly determined to beat him to death. Yet he was not in the least afraid or dismayed. Then a sharp word of command came from the sky, and the whole crowd of devils vanished.

The voice was followed by a person who, descending from above, clapped his hands and laughed with delight. It was Master Cloudchamber.

"I have subjected you to ten tests," he said, "all of which have left you utterly unmoved. There can be no doubt you will succeed in attaining the Tao. I will now disclose to you the mysteries of alchemy in order that the knowledge may enable you to save humankind. [13b] When you have continued this meritorious work for three thousand years, you will have completed your full period of probation. In addition you have to spend eight centuries in research on your own behalf. Then, and only then, will you transcend the human sphere."

"Pray, sir," Dongbin asked, "when will my transformation take place?"

"Only after three thousand years of meritorious service will you be restored to the state of your original physical purity."

"Alas!" Dongbin exclaimed, changing color with vexation. "With the prospect of having to wait three thousand years, how can I maintain my zeal for such a time?"

"Your courage," his mentor assured him with a smile, "will carry you not only over the three millennia but also over the additional eight centuries. Have no doubt!"

Thereupon he took Dongbin to the Crane Ridge and imparted to him the most profound truths and deepest mysteries of the Tao, including the secret methods of Numinous Treasure. He also presented him with a few grains of the cinnabar elixir.

While teacher and disciple were thus engaged, two immortals appeared. Each reverently held a golden tablet, the emblem of office, in their hands.

They announced to Master Cloudchamber: "The Celestial Emperor summons you to serve as the guardian of the Golden Towers in the Ninth Heaven."

Master Cloudchamber immediately climbed into the cloudy carriage provided for him, and gradually the entourage vanished into the open sky.

Dongbin in due course succeeded in mastering the Tao as taught by Master Cloudchamber. He also perfected the magic sword techniques he had received from Master Firedragon. Then he took to wandering along the banks of the Yangtse and Huai rivers.

He put the power of his magical two-edged sword to the test by ridding the country of the inundations wrought by a nasty waterdragon. He could become invisible to human eyes and transform his shape at will.

For over four hundred years he constantly journeyed around the country, visiting places as far apart as Henan and Hunan, Zhejiang and Shensi. Nobody ever recognized him. He used to call himself the Man Who Returned to the Tao [Hui Daoren].

# Chapter Five

## PHYSICAL PRACTICES

Physical exercises are the first active step taken toward the Tao. They serve to make the body healthy, to extend its lifespan, and to open it up to the free flow of the Tao.

The Tao in its tangible form on earth is cosmic energy or *qi*, a term hard to define and for which "energy" is no more than a crude approximation. *Qi* is the vital power of the Tao at work in the world—in nature, in society, in the human body. It is a continuously changing, forever flowing force, an energy that can appear and disappear, can be strong and weak, can be controlled and overwhelming. *Qi* is what moves on in the changing rhythm of the seasons; *qi* shines in the rays of the sun; *qi* is what constitutes health or sickness; *qi* is how we live, move, eat, sleep.

The goal of all physical practices is to guide and harmonize *qi*. To guide means to control, to strengthen, to increase. To harmonize is to free, to open up, to accord with nature. The first step in physical cultivation consists therefore of an effort to get on top of one's own inner energies and the patterns of one's life. Thereafter one lets go again and fully adapts to nature, begins to live spontaneously in perfect accordance with the Tao.

*Qi*, the constituting force of all-that-is, appears in the body in various forms. Its grossest and most easily accessible form is the breath. Breath is a most fundamental force of life—without breathing in air, the human organism collapses in no time. Breath is also very tangible and can be controlled without too much effort. Breath is an obvious starting point to get closer to the subtle energies of the Tao. Thus breathing exercises are commonly used as the first step, as the initial point of control and adaptation to the Tao.

Then again, *qi* occurs as the life-force that circulates throughout the body—visible first of all in the blood and tangible in the pulse. Above and beyond this, however, the Chinese traditional

133

understanding of the body includes a network of energy channels, commonly called conduits or meridians, through which pure *qi* passes independent of the blood circulation. These channels come closest to the surface of the body and become thus accessible at certain pressure points, commonly known as the points used in acupuncture.

To become aware of this flow of energy throughout the body, to learn to feel it, regulate it, and open it up to perfect smoothness is another important step in the physical practices of the aspiring Taoist. Much of this is done in meditations—the concentrated inward gaze, the increasing awareness of subtle movements within. But at the same time, the energy flow is also greatly helped by exercises—gymnastics and massages, acupuncture and moxibustion.

Yet another form in which *qi* appears in the body is the energy that arises from nourishment. To align this with the Tao, it is necessary to control what one eats: give up ordinary foods and substitute special drugs, fast for a time, adapt the diet as much as possible to the environment and seasonal changes. This again not only purifies the *qi* and increases the body's health but also helps to harmonize the person as a whole with the ongoing energy transformations of the world.

Finally, a very important form of *qi* is sexual energy, the creative force of life in its most concentrated form. Commonly called "essence" and defined as semen in men and menstrual blood in women, this too has to be brought into accordance with the Tao. While ordinary people tend to emit this energy to the outside, thus losing a valuable energy resource, Taoists train to conserve it. "Reverting the semen to nourish the brain" is the classical formula, applied to both methods of intercourse and meditational forms of sexual energy reversion.

In all these methods, the tendency is to leave the ways of the common world behind, to "revert," to reorganize, to adapt to a level subtler and more sensitive than that of ordinary existence. Higher forms of Taoist breathing are the opposite of natural breathing; gymnastics in many ways use the muscles of the body differently; Taoist diet demands the complete abstention from grains, the staple diet of the masses; and sexual practice (the way of yin and yang) calls for an inner upward movement of "essence" instead of its emission for the purpose of reproduction.

The four texts selected below introduce the major physical practices. The first, the *Yinshizi jingzuo fa* (Quiet Sitting with Master Yinshi) is a detailed description of Taoist breathing exercises by

Jiang Weiqiao of the early twentieth century. The *Daoyin jing* (Gymnastics Scripture), next, is a collection of gymnastics methods from the fourth to the sixth centuries, attributed to various famous immortals.

Third, the *Lingbao wufu xu* (Explanation of the Five Talismans of Numinous Treasure) is a fourth-century compendium of talismanic lore, myths, and longevity methods. Much of its content goes back further, to the Later Han dynasty. Its second scroll consists largely of immortality recipes.

Fourth, the *Yufang bijue* (Secret Instructions of the Jade Chamber) is a sexual manual that has survived in the tenth-century *Ishimpō* (Essential Medical Methods). The latter is a standard medical textbook compiled by the Japanese court physician Tamba no Yasuyori and dated to 984. It is a prime source for materials otherwise lost in China.

## 17. Breathing for Life

Breathing exercises go back far in Chinese history—the earliest references are found in the *Zhuangzi* and in documents excavated from tombs of the Former Han dynasty. Breathing is essential for good health and therefore for long life, and it is with breathing that the restoration of the body to its more original form begins.

The *Yinshizi jingzuo fa* (Quiet Sitting with Master Yinshi) selected below is a modern version of an ancient practice. Compiled by Jiang Weiqiao [= Master Yinshi] and first published in 1914, the text is edited in the *Daozang jinghua*, a twentieth-century supplement to the Taoist canon. It represents the personal ways of exercises and meditation developed by Jiang in an effort to heal himself.

Born in the 1870s, Jiang Weiqiao was a sickly child from the beginning. In his teenage years he became increasingly unable to lead a normal life, but neither Western nor traditional Chinese medicine could help him. His condition only improved when he found an ancient text on inner alchemy, i.e., traditional Taoist meditation and longevity techniques, and started to follow its instructions. However, as soon as he felt a little better, he stopped the exercises and soon fell back into one weakness or infection after the next.

At the age of twenty-two, he caught the tuberculosis which had killed his brother. Then he finally set out to heal himself seriously, left his wife and child to be taken care of by the family and established himself in a little meditation hut in the backyard. Within a year, a strict regimen including exercises, breathings, walks, meditations, and specific diets not only restored his health but brought him to spiritual dimensions unthought of.

This success beyond his wildest expectations led Jiang to write up and publish an account of his methods. However, he never simply copied the ancient texts and concepts but strictly reported only on his experiences, interpreting them in the scientific-technological terms current in his day. His various writings, of which the book here cited is the first, soon inspired others to follow his example. Traditional health exercises were unearthed and modified to cure everything, from the common cold to cancer. Over several decades, the movement mushroomed and grew into what is known as Qigong today. It is still flourishing.

The text is not only one of the clearest descriptions of Taoist breathing exercises in the literature. It is also an example for religion in the making, for the reinterpretation of traditional methods in the ever-changing light of the current day.

Another translation is found in Lu 1964: 171–73. This is more extensive and includes large parts of Jiang Weiqiao's autobiography as well as details on his method of meditation or "quiet sitting." On the development and practice of Qigong in contemporary China, see Miura 1989, Kohn 1993.

---

### *Yinshizi jingzuo fa* (Quiet Sitting with Master Yinshi)

Breathing is one of the most essential necessities of human life, even more so than food and drink. Ordinary people are quite familiar with the idea that food and drink are important to maintain life, that they will starve if left without it for a while. But they hardly ever turn around to think about the importance of breathing and that air is even more essential to life than anything else.

This has to do with the fact that in order to obtain food and drink people have to go to work and earn money, so they come to value these things as important commodities. Breathing, on the other hand, is done by taking in the air of the atmosphere of which there is no limit and which cannot be exhausted. There is no need to labor and pay for the air we breathe; thus people tend to overlook the importance of this function.

Yet if you stop eating and drinking, you may still survive for a couple of days, even as long as a whole week. However, if you stop up your nostrils and mouth you will be dead within minutes. This fact alone shows that breathing is far more important than food.

In discussing methods of breathing, two main types can be distinguished: natural breathing and regulated breathing.

NATURAL BREATHING

One exhalation and one inhalation are called one breath. The respiratory organs in the body are the nose on the outside and the lungs on the inside. The two wings of the lungs are positioned within the upper torso so that through the motion of the respiration the entire area expands and contracts. Such is the law of nature. However, in ordinary people, the respiration never expands or contracts the lungs to their full capacity. They only use the upper section of the lungs while their lower section hardly ever is employed at all. Because of this they cannot gain the full advantage of deep breathing, their blood and body fluids are not refreshed, and the various diseases gain easy entry. Any of this has as yet nothing to do with natural breathing.

Natural breathing is also called abdominal breathing. Every single inhalation, every single exhalation must always go deep down into the stomach area. During inhalation, when the air enters the lungs, they are filled to capacity and as a result their lower section expands. This in turn presses against the diaphragm and pushes it downward. Therefore, during inhalation, the chest area is completely relaxed while the stomach area is curved toward the outside.

Again, during exhalation the stomach area contracts, the diaphragm is pushed upward against the lungs and thereby causes the old and turbid breath to be expelled from their depth. Once it is all dispersed outside, no used air remains within. Therefore in this kind of breathing, although it makes use mostly of the lungs, it is the area of the stomach and the diaphragm which expands and contracts. This is the great method of breathing naturally by which the blood and the body fluids are kept fresh and active.

Not only during and prior to meditation should this method be employed, but always: whether walking, staying, sitting, or lying down, one can breathe deeply and naturally in any given circumstance.

*Breathing Instructions*

1. Contract the lower abdomen when breathing out. Thereby the diaphragm is pushed upward, the chest area is tensed, and all

used breath, even from the lower part of the lungs, is expelled entirely.

2. Breathe in fresh air through the nostrils. Let it fill the lungs to capacity so that the diaphragm is pushed down and the stomach area expands.

3. Gradually lengthen and deepen your inhalations and exhalations. The stomach will get stronger and more stable. Some people say that one should hold the breath for a short moment at the end of an inhalation. This is called stopping respiration. According to my own experience, this is not good for beginners.

4. As you go along, let the respiration gradually grow subtler and finer until the entering and leaving of the breath is very soft. With prolonged practice you will cease to be consciously aware of the respiration and feel as if you weren't breathing at all.

5. Once the state of non-respiration is reached, you can truly be without inhalations and exhalations. Even though you have special organs for breathing, you won't feel any longer that you are using them. At the same time the breath will by and by come to enter and leave through all the body. This is the perfection of harmonious breathing. However, as a beginner you should never try to attain this intentionally. Always obey nature and go along with what you can do.

REGULATED BREATHING

Regulated breathing is also known as "reversed breathing." It resembles natural breathing in that it is very deep and soft and should always reach as far as the stomach area. On the other hand, it reverses the movements of the stomach. The upward and downward movement of the diaphragm is accordingly different from its activity during natural breathing. It is called "reversed" precisely because it reverses the pattern proper to natural breathing.

*Practical Instructions*

1. Exhale slow and far; let the stomach area expand freely, and make sure that the stomach is strong and full.

2. Let the lower abdomen be full of breath, the chest area slack, and the diaphragm completely relaxed.

3. Inhale slowly and deeply into the diaphragm. Let the fresh air fill the lungs so that they expand naturally. At the same time contract the abdomen.

4. As the lungs are filled with breath they will press down, while the stomach, contracted, will push up. The diaphragm is therefore pressed in from above and below; its movement is thereby getting subtler and subtler.
5. When the chest area is fully expanded, the stomach region may be contracted, yet it should not be entirely empty. Independent of whether you inhale or exhale, the center of gravity must always be solidly established beneath the navel. Thus the stomach area remains strong and full.
6. All respiration should be subtle and quiet. Especially during the practice of quiet sitting it should be so fine that you don't hear the sound of your own breathing. In the old days some people claimed that inhalations should be slightly longer than exhalations. Nowadays some say that exhalations should be slightly longer than inhalations. As far as I can tell, it is best to keep their length equal.

To summarize: Independent of whether you practice natural breathing or regulated breathing, the aim is always to activate the diaphragm. In the case of regulated breathing, the diaphragm is worked by means of human power. It reverses natural breathing and thus causes the diaphragm to stretch even farther, to move even more smoothly. For this reason I never enter my meditation practice without first practicing regulated breathing for a little while.

This is also the reason why I have recommended its use in my book. Since its publication many students have begun the practice. Some found the prescribed breathing exercises useful, others didn't. For this reason, always remain aware that even though regulated breathing is controlled by the human mind, it cannot be learned by human means alone. It is not a mere distortion of natural breathing, but its development, and should be learned in accordance with nature.

BREATHING EXERCISES

Both natural and regulated breathing have the following eight instructions in common:

1. Sit cross-legged and erect; take the same posture as in quiet sitting.
2. First breathe short breaths, then gradually lengthen them.
3. All breaths should be slow and subtle, quiet and long. Gradually they enter deeper into the abdomen.

4. Always inhale through the nose. Do not inhale through the mouth. The nose is the specific organ of respiration. There are tiny hairs on the inside of the nostrils which are easily blocked and obstructed. The mouth, on the other hand, is not made primarily for respiration, and if you use it for breathing it will usurp the proper function of the nose. This in turn will lead to the gradual obstruction of the nose. More than that, by breathing through the mouth any number of bacteria and dirt particles will enter the body, and diseases are easily conceived. Therefore always keep the mouth closed, not only during breathing and meditation practice.

5. Once your breathing gets purer and warmer with prolonged practice, lengthen the individual breaths. The limit of lengthening is reached when it takes you a whole minute to breathe in and out one single breath. However, never forget that this cannot be forced.

6. The practice of slow and subtle breathing can be continued any time, any place.

7. During quiet sitting there should be no thoughts and no worries. If you have to pay constant attention to your respiration, the mind cannot be truly calm. Therefore it is best to practice breathing before and after every sitting.

8. Before and after quiet sitting, practice respiration. Pick a place that has good fresh air. Take about five to ten minutes for the exercise.

BREATHING AND THE LOWERING OF THE PIT OF THE STOMACH

In my discussion of posture above [in a separate section], I already spoke about the reason why the pit of the stomach should be lowered. Nevertheless, since this lowering is also of central importance in breathing, I come back to it now. Generally, if the pit of the stomach is not lowered, the respiration cannot be harmonized. Then the effectiveness of quiet sitting will not come to bear.

Repeating thus what I said before, students should pay attention to the following points:

1. During the breathing exercise, beginners should be aware of the pit of the stomach being firm and solid. It thus interferes with the breath, which cannot be harmonized properly. This is because the diaphragm is not yet able to move up and down freely. A beginner should overcome this difficulty with determination and not falter before it.

2. Should you become aware that your breathing is obstructed in this way, never try to force it open. Rather, let it take its natural course by gently focusing your attention on the lower abdomen.

3. Relax your chest so that the blood circulation does not press upon the heart. The pit of the stomach will then be lowered naturally.

4. Practice this over a long period. Gradually the chest and the diaphragm will feel open and relaxed. The breathing will be calm and subtle, deep and continuous. Every inhalation and exhalation will reach all the way to the center of gravity below the navel. This, then, is proof that the pit of the stomach has been effectively lowered.

## 18. Gymnastics

Chinese gymnastics are physical exercises and self-massages geared to opening up the energy channels (conduits, meridians) that crisscross the entire body. Energy, as the most accessible aspect of the Tao on earth, should pervade everything smoothly, in nature, in human society, and in the body. It should be neither overabundant nor insufficient or obstructed in any way.

By moving the limbs and torso in a particular way, combined with deep respiration, the flow of energy is regulated and pathogenic elements are expelled. Gradually the body not only becomes supple and flexible but overall health improves and longevity is attained.

Gymnastics have been popular since antiquity, as the *Daoyin tu* (Gymnastics Chart) documents. This chart, found in a Han tomb at Mawangdui (168 B.C.E.), consists of a series of illustrations of physical exercises with short captions. Even then, as still in Qigong today, the practices had colorful names: bear hangings, bird stretchings, monkey leaps, owl glares, and so on.

The *Daoyin jing* (Gymnastics Scripture) contains a collection of different methods of gymnastics popular in medieval China and each associated with a classical ancient immortal. From references to certain figures and comparisons with other texts, the methods can be dated to the fourth to sixth centuries. In its present form, however, the text has only been known since the tenth.

Its full title is *Taiqing daoyin yangsheng jing* (Great Clarity Scripture on Nourishing Life Through Gymnastics). The version used here is found in *Yunji qiqian* 34 (1a–3b and 6b–8a). Other editions of the text are contained in DZ 818, fasc. 568 and in chapter 28 of the *Daoshu* (Pivot of the Tao; DZ 1017, fasc. 641–48), a Song-dynasty compendium on Taoist health and meditation methods.

A partial translation of the *Daoyin jing* in a composite edition is found in Maspero 1981: 543–47. For a discussion of the gymnastic tradition, see Despeux 1989. The author wishes to thank Ute Engelhardt for her critical reading of the translation.

---

### *Daoyin jing* (Gymnastics Scripture)

MASTER REDPINE'S METHOD OF GYMNASTICS

[1a] Master Redpine [Chisongzi] was the Lord of Rain under the Divine Farmer [Shennong]. He could follow the wind, freely rising up and sinking down. He was active well into the time of High Toil [Gaoxin].

Today we still have his method of gymnastics, which supposedly expels the hundred diseases, extends one's years, and prolongs life. It runs as follows:

When you first rise in the morning, spread a mat and exercise facing east. Stop when your breath has reached full depth or after five respirations, if your breath is still shallow. The exercise should be undertaken regularly every day. Over a longer period, you will feel a definite improvement.

#### The Exercises

1. Stand on your mat. Interlace your fingers above your head. Stretch up, then bend to the ground. Continue for five breaths. This fills the abdomen with energy.
2. Lie down on your right side and try to touch the ground to your left with your left elbow. Then stretch the left arm as much as you can and reach beyond your head. [1b] Repeat the exercise with your right arm while lying on your left side. Continue for five breaths. This stretches the muscles and the backbone.
3. [Lie on your back.] Place both hands around your right knee and pull it up towards your waist and groin, raising your head at the same time to meet it. Repeat with the left knee. Continue for five breaths. This stretches the hips.
4. Place your right hand on your left knee, raised above your hip. Then stretch your left hand upward as far as you can. Repeat on the other side. Continue for five breaths. This expands the energy of the chest and abdomen.

子松赤

Fig. 13. Chisongzi, Master Redpine. Source: *Zengxiang liexian zhuan.*

5. Place your left hand next to your hip and pull down. At the same time, stretch your right arm upward as far as you can. Repeat on the other side. Continue for five breaths. This expands the energy in the center of the body.

6. [Sit up or kneel.] Fold your arms across your chest. Turn your head left and right. Hold your breath as long as you can. This stretches the face and ear muscles. It expels pathogenic energy and prevents it from reentering the body.
7. Link your hands behind your back and below your buttocks. Turn your torso to the right and left as far as you can. This opens the vessels of the blood-energy.
8. Interlace your fingers in front of your body. Stretch your arms forward and turn then to the right and left as far as you can. This expands the energy in the shoulders.
9. [2a] Interlace your fingers and stretch your arms above your head [with palms facing outward]. Turn left and right in an easy rhythm. This expands the energy of the lungs and the liver.
10. Fold your hands across your chest. Turn left and right as far as you can. This expels tense and restive energy from the skin.
11. Interlace your fingers and bring the hands to your shoulders, right and left. This expands the energy of the skin.
12. Stand up straight. Stretch your calves left and right [by bending over]. This expands the energy of the legs.

MASTER NING'S WAY OF NOURISHING LIFE THROUGH GYMNASTICS

Master Ning lived under the Yellow Emperor, whom he served as master of pottery. He could stack up a fire, place himself in its center, and freely move up and down with the arising smoke. At the same time, his clothes would not even be singed.

According to Master Ning, the practice of gymnastics and the guiding of energy through the body serve to expel the hundred diseases, prolong life, and prevent aging.

To practice properly, always keep your mind firmly concentrated on the One and return it to the Cinnabar Field in the abdomen. What brings people to life is the cinnabar; what affords them salvation is the act of returning.

Once the cinnabar is fully restored, you can extend your years. On the other hand, when the cinnabar is lost, the inner worms will become active and you will die early.

We practice gymnastics because they make all the pathogenic energy evaporate from our limbs, bones, and joints. [2b] Thus only good energy prevails and can become more pure and essential.

Practice the exercises diligently and with care whenever you have time between work and conversation. Either in the morning or at night is fine. Gradually your bones and joints will become firm and strong. The hundred diseases will be eliminated completely.

Whether you have caught a chill [wind-attack disorder] in your chest or are thoroughly fatigued and cannot rouse yourself;

whether you have periods of deafness when you cannot hear or find your eyes going dizzy and your mind turning mad on you;

whether you have energy moving against its proper current and rising up violently or experience severe pains in your hips—

in all cases you can actively expel the disease by practicing these exercises and guiding the energy to the place of trouble, following the proper charts and focusing it on the right spot.

By guiding the energy you will supplement the energy of your spleen and stomach systems; by practicing gymnastics you will heal your four limbs.

Thus following the Tao of natural spontaneity as diligently as you can, you will attain a state of mutual protection with heaven and earth.

*The Exercises*

1. Loosen your hair and stand facing east; make your hands into fists and hold your breath for the count of one. Then raise your arms alternately left and right and stretch them so that your hands touch your ears. [Breathe and repeat.] This will keep your hair black and prevent graying.
2. Kneel facing east and hold your breath to the count of two. Then take the middle fingers of your hands and moisten their tips with saliva. Rub them against each other for twice seven times. Then gently massage your eyes with them. [3a] This will keep your eyes bright and shining.
3. Kneel facing east and hold your breath to the count of three. Then pinch your two nostrils between your fingers. This will cure shortness of nasal breath due to too much flesh and obstructions in the nostrils.
4. Kneel facing east and hold your breath to the count of four. Clap your teeth together as often as you can. Then lean over to the front and change your legs to kneel sideways. Repeat, holding your breath to the count of six. This will take care of deafness and dizziness. Return to your original posture. Repeat, holding your breath to the count of seven. This will free you from all pain in the chest.

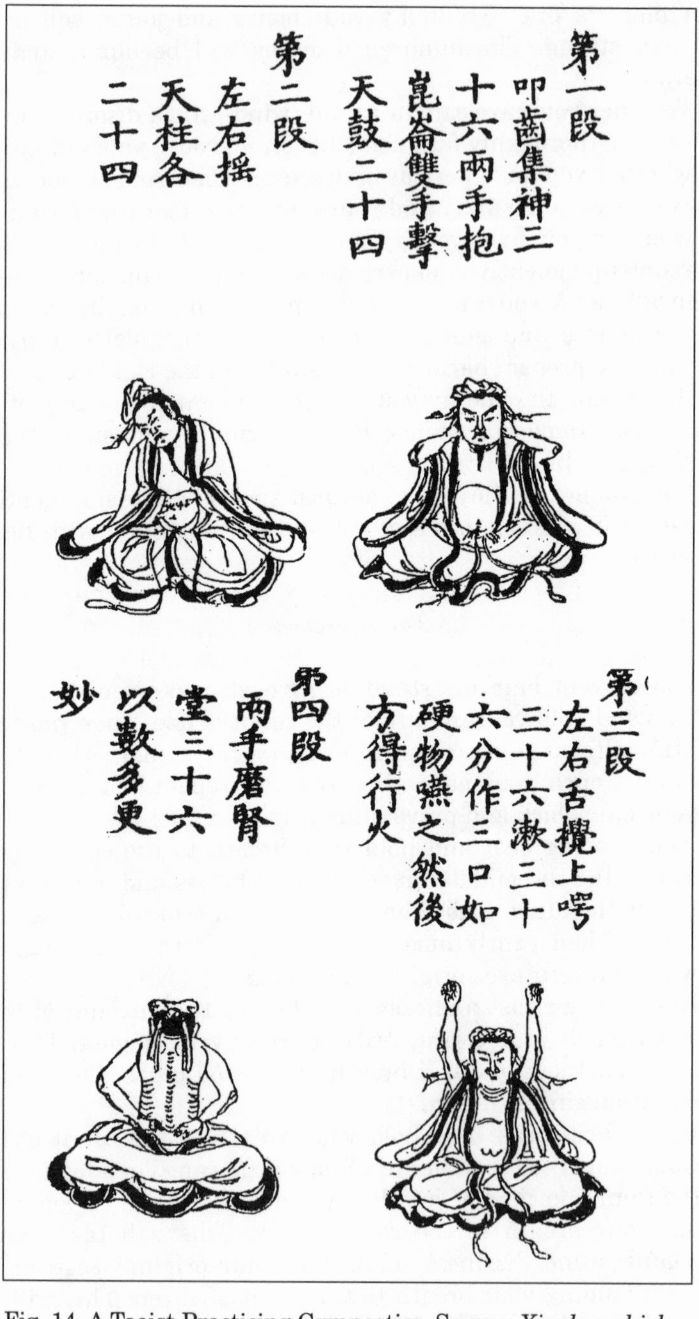

第一段
叩齒集神三
十六兩手抱
崑崙雙手擊
天鼓二十四

第二段
左右搖
天柱各
二十四

第三段
左右舌攪上齶
三十六漱三十
六分作三口如
硬物嚥之然後
方得行火

第四段
兩手磨腎
堂三十六
以數多更



Fig. 14. A Taoist Practicing Gymnastics. Source: *Xiuzhen shishu*.

5. Put both hands on your knees and stand up on tiptoe. Hold your breath to the count of eight. This will free you from all ailments above the chest, i.e., those of the head, ears, eyes, throat, and nose.

6. Make both your hands into fists and clasp them to the back of your head. Hold your breath. Rise up on your toes. Hold your breath to the count of nine. Face east. This causes energy to move up and down smoothly, opens and deepens its passage through the nostrils, and cures all emaciation and weakness.

Warning: Those who cannot follow the ways of yin and yang [3b] should not practice this.

THE WAY OF GYMNASTICS ACCORDING TO PENGZU

[6b] Pengzu was a high official under the Shang dynasty. He lived through both the Xia and Shang dynasties—altogether for over seven hundred years. He lived primarily on cinnamon and frequently practiced gymnastics. [7a] According to him, gymnastics are the best way to expel the hundred diseases, extend one's years, and increase longevity.

His method of gymnastics proceeds in ten sections of five breaths each, i.e., fifty breaths total. Repeating the exercises five times, one breathes altogether 250 times. The practice should always be undertaken between midnight and cock crow, never during the day. Also, practitioners should always eat their fill and bathe their bodies regularly.

### The Exercises

1. Loosen your clothes and lie down on your back. Stretch your hips, then close your eyes and rest for a short moment. Breathe five times. This expands the energy of the kidneys, cures diabetes, and helps the yin and yang.

2. Sit up and grab hold of your toes. Breathe five times. This expands the energy of the abdomen, cures pains and ruptures in the lower abdomen and genital area, and helps to clear the nine orifices.

3. Raise your torso and stretch your toes. Breathe five times. This expands the energy of the abdomen and the spine. It cures localized pain disorders and stiffness and makes the hearing more acute.

4. [7b] Turn your feet so the toes face each other. Breathe five times. This expands the energy of the heart and lungs. It takes care of coughs and of all ailments due to energy flowing in the reverse direction.
5. Turn your feet so the heels face each other. Breathe five times. This cleans the energies in the five network conduits. It helps the intestines and the stomach and expels all pathogenic energy.
6. Take your left shin and bend it so that it comes to rest covered by the right knee. Breathe five times. This expands the energy of the lungs. It takes care of all energy depletions caused by wind and sharpens the eyesight.
7. Stretch out both legs well down to the toes. Breathe five times. This ensures that you won't twist and cramp your muscles and tendons.
8. Lie back. Grasp both knees with your hands and pull them close to your chest. Breathe five times. This cures pain in the hips.
9. Turn both feet to the outside. Repeat ten times. This takes care of fatigue.
10. Loosen your hair and sit up facing east. Clench your hands to fists and hold your breath for a moment. Then raise both your arms above your head and alternatingly stretch them upward. Next, place your palms over your ears and, with your fingers, massage the pressure points around them. Repeat five times. This improves your eyesight, [8a] keeps your hair glossy black, and cures all ailments of the head.

### 19. Drugs and Diets

Taoist diet centers around a practice known as the "abstention from grains." Besides avoiding both meat and alcohol like their Buddhist counterparts, although for reasons of physical purification rather than moral rectitude, Taoists also avoid the staple diet of China, the grains—rice, millet, wheat, as well as beans.

The mythological reason for this abstention is the existence of three worms in the body, demonic supernatural creatures who feed on decay and are eager for the body to die altogether so they can devour it. Not only do they thus shorten the lifespan but they also delight in the decaying matter produced by the grains as they are digested in the intestines. If one is to attain long life, the three worms have to be starved, and the only way to do so is to avoid all grain.

On a more historical note, the avoidance of grain signifies the Taoist reversion and rejection of common social practices. It is a return to a time in the dawn of humanity when there were as yet no grains; it is also a return to a more primitive and simple way of eating.

Physically, abstention from grains means either nourishing on vegetables and minerals, preferably concocted into some form of drug, or living on energy. The latter is done by swallowing the saliva, another form in which the *qi* appears in the body, or by "ingesting the five sprouts," i.e., the energy of the five directions, by visualizing them congealing into pellets and entering through one's mouth into the proper part of the body.

In either case, Taoist diet has the effect of lightening the body, eliminating wastes, and stabilizing the circulation. It helps the metabolism recover its original balance and thus a more fundamental accordance with the Tao.

The selection below is taken from the *Taishang lingbao wufuxu* (Explanation of the Five Talismans of Numinous Treasure), found in DZ 388, fasc. 183 (3.21b–22a and 2.1a–3a). While the text was compiled in the fourth century, the methods are very ancient, with Lezichang, the compiler, a magico-technician and immortal of the Han dynasty. On the text and its dietetic methods, see Yamada 1989. For a general discussion of Taoist diet, see Levi 1983, Engelhardt 1987.

---

### *Taishang lingbao wufuxu* (Explanation of the Five Talismans of Numinous Treasure

[3.21b] The Third Immortal King told the Emperor:

"In the old days I followed a dietetic regimen and attained immortality. My teacher made me increase the sweet spring in my mouth and swallow it in accordance with the following incantation:

The white stones, hard and rocky, are rolling on and on.
The gushing spring, bubbling and pervasive, becomes a
    thick juice.
Drink it and attain long life—
Longevity forever longer!

"These twenty-two words—you should follow them!

"If you can actually do this and nourish on the True One without stopping, swallow from your flowery pond without interruption, then your inner energy will grow and remain strong, never to be weakened. [22a] You attain the Tao by avoiding all grains. You will never again have to follow the rhythm of the moon and plant or harvest.

"Now, the people of mysterious antiquity, they reached old age because they remained in leisure and never ate any grains.

"As the *Dayou zhang* (Verse of Great Existence) says:

> The five grains are chisels cutting life away,
> Making the five organs stink and shorten our spans.
> Once entered into our stomach,
> There's no more chance to live quite long.
> To strive for complete avoidance of all death
> Keep your intestines free of excrement!"

THE NUMINOUS TREASURE WAY OF EATING THE ESSENCE OF THE FIVE WONDERPLANTS

### Pine Resin

[2.1a] The Venerable Lord said: When a pine tree has grown for a thousand years, its resin is so concentrated that, by eating it, you can pervade all in your spirit. You can enter into the depth of the earth, hide your true identity and change your name at will.

The needles and stem of a pine tree are rather large, following the plant's roots in their shape. Its resin is also called "magnificent joy" [black amber] or again "truffle fungus."

With its help you can become immune to weapons. You can pass freely over land and through water, leave the obscure and enter the serene. You will be free from hunger and thirst and live as long as the sun and the moon.

If you can find the resin of a thousand-year-old pine, you can truly live long!

### Sesame

The Venerable Lord said: Nourish your body with this "little louse" and you will recover a healthy complexion and return to youthfulness.

Another name of this plant is "barbarian hemp." The reason for this is that it originally comes from Ferghana in the lands of the barbarians. After it had grown there wild for ten thousand years, it crossed the border and came east.

If kept deep in the earth, it is a powerful drug against all danger and fierceness. If soaked in boiled water, it can ward off wind and expel cold.

It has the most appropriate name of "giant victor." This is due to the fact that it repels all kinds of evil and demonic powers and pursues them to their end.

Take it without interruption and you will live as long as the world itself.

## Pepper

[1b] The Venerable Lord said: Pepper grows in both the regions of Shu and of Han [southwest and central China].

Since it contains the energy of great yin, it will allow you to live as long as heaven and earth, to transform and change your body at will, and to pass freely over land and through water. With pepper you can ward off dampness.

None of the many pathogenic influences will dare to come near you. As long as you eat pepper, there is not a single demon, magical evil, or poison that you cannot stop in its tracks.

If you nourish on it permanently, you can fulfill all the wishes of your heart's desire. However, you must keep the method hidden from the world, since the practice is very profound. Keep it in strict confidence and never give it away. Then you won't need a lot of gold to realize your goals.

## Ginger

The Venerable Lord said: Ginger grows in areas of strong yang, in the same regions as pepper. Both develop only in very fertile soil, preferably in remote mountain places. They grow straight up and never bow or bend, but need to be near a fresh spring of water.

Ginger contains the energy of the fiery planet [Mars] and sticks firmly to soil with its root. It turns its back toward yin and faces yang. It is as eternal as the world itself.

For these reasons it helps to ward off dampness and expels cold. It induces warmth and keeps all pathogenic influences at bay. It cuts short all illness and firmly closes the demon gateways of the body.

If you nourish on ginger all the time, you will live as long as the trigrams of Heaven and Earth themselves.

## *Calamus*

The Venerable Lord said: Calamus grows in wetlands, near deep ponds, in damp depressions, or on river banks. [2a] It may also be found on high mountains, with its roots knotted about rocks and boulders.

One inch of calamus contains nine sections or joints, which is why it is also called "numinous body." Holding on solidly to the One, it contains the myriad forms of primordial energy.

Thus calamus gives life to people, nurtures and protects essence and spirit. It drains superfluous body liquids and drives out dampness. It repels demons and dissolves all feelings of ill.

All spectres, sprites, and weird otherwordly creatures will flee from it and seek refuge in dark obscurity. Anything or anyone violent and harmful will never dare to come close.

Take it without interruption and you can live thousands and thousands of years.

## *Note*

Lezichang says: These five wonderplants can each be taken separately. They will all increase energy and secure long life. They expand one's essence and stabilize one's soul. Taking them without interruption, one can live as long as the world itself.

Thus the *Xiaojing yuanshenqi* (Guidance of Spirit According to the Classic of Filial Piety) says:

> Ginger and pepper increase energy;
> Calamus improves the hearing;
> Sesame secures long life;
> And pine resin wards off calamities.

Thus are the secret words of Confucius, the enlightened instructions of the sages.

METHODS OF THE VENERABLE LORD TO OBSERVE THE HEAVENS AND COMBINE THE FIVE WONDERPLANTS THEREBY TO RETAIN THE SPIRIT, LENGTHEN THE YEARS, TRANSCEND THE WORLD, AND LIVE FOREVER

### Recipe of the Three Heavens of Numinous Treasure
*(Compiled by Lezichang)*

[2b] Ingredients: Five parts sesame; four parts pine resin; one part pepper; three parts ginger; three parts calamus. (Best used if very fresh and full in essence.)

Have all five separately pounded by a young boy on a day ruled by the sun. Never employ any other person to do the pounding. Then, again each separately, sift them through a fine sieve. Pound again, 10,000 times.

Set in five separate vessels of red ware. Line up. Let stand overnight to collect the dew.

Next morning, at sunrise, scoop out with a sanctified dipper. Mix together, using white honey or sugar as a cohesive.

Pound again, 30,000 times, to form little pellets the size of seeds.

Next day, at sunrise, kneel facing east. Take three pellets. Pray for long life. Your prayer will be granted.

Evening, at sunset, kneel facing west. Take three pellets. Pray as before.

[Continue daily.]

During the entire process, strictly avoid all fresh fish, pork, and strong vegetables. Under no circumstances look upon dead bodies, dogs or pigs, or birthings. [3a] Be very careful!

## 20. Sexual Techniques

Taoist sexual techniques are just as ancient as the other physical practices and were also discussed in early manuscripts excavated from Han-dynasty tombs. They form an integral part of Taoist practice, both individual and communal, and especially the Celestial Masters have been frequently attacked for their allegedly orgiastic practice of "harmonizing the energies," a form of ritual intercourse.

According to the mythology, sexual techniques were first taught by a celestial lady called the Plain Maiden (Sunü) to the Yellow Emperor (Huangdi). The major sexual classic of China is accordingly called the *Sunü jing*. Many other manuals followed in its footsteps, specifiying not only various postures and methods of arousal, but also including warnings about health hazards and remedial uses of intercourse. Sexual practices have thus formed an important aspect of both the medical and religious traditions.

In Taoism, the aim of sexual techniques is to revert the "essence" to support the body instead of flowing out and being lost. Sexual arousal, and thus intercourse, in this context serves to activate the essence that lies hidden deep in the body and bring it to the surface. Only when essence is tangible can it be reverted, can—by sheer concentration and pressure applied at the right moment—the valuable substance be used to further long life.

Typically manuals are directed to the male, encouraging men to select young partners and change them frequently, making the women give up their essence but never ejaculating themselves. The interpretation of sexual vampirism has been offered for this behavior but was rejected in favor of an understanding that sees the practices as a way of creating harmony between the sexes. Some readings have even gone so far as to suggest that they pay tribute to the importance of women in Taoism.

On the other hand, ideally women can do the very same thing, using men—preferably young— to garner essence and revert it to nourish their longevity. In this case, however, Chinese folklore has created the character of the fox lady, a supernatural fairy who exploits men sexually and makes them wither away and die.

In the more meditational practices of inner alchemy, the reversal of sexual energy is undertaken in meditative fashion and without the involvement of a partner. Methods differ for men and women, but according to contemporary reports, are still undertaken successfully. Taoist nuns in particular report that, with the help of breast massages and meditational circulation of essence, they stopped menstruating and developed heightened levels of vigor and wellbeing. Needless to say that the ladies in question have by now reached venerable old age.

The text selected here is entitled "Sexual Instructions of the Master of Pure Harmony." It is from the *Yufang bijue* (Secret Instructions of the Jade Chamber), a text nowadays contained in the *Ishimpō* (Essential Medical Methods). The latter is a medical textbook by the Japanese court physician Tamba no Yasuyori and dated to the year 984. The edition used is the one published by the Renmin Weisheng Publishing Company (Beijing, 1955). Selections are from chapter 28 (pp. 635–36 and 645–46). The translation follows Wile 1992: 102–03 with minor alterations. Subheadings are the author's.

For other translations of the text, as part of a rendering of a wider selection of similar documents, see Ishihara and Levi 1970. On the *Ishimpō* and other Japanese collections on Taoist longevity techniques, see Sakade 1989. For early manuscripts on sexual techniques, see Harper 1987.

An insightful discussion of the history of sexual practices and the relations between the sexes in traditional Chinese culture is found in van Gulik 1961. Inner alchemical forms of sexual practices are discussed in Lu 1970 (for men) and Despeux 1990 (for women). For a contemporary inner-alchemical use of sexual energy to relieve stress in Western societies, see Chia 1986, 1987, 1987a. On fox ladies and the damage they may do, see Krappe 1944, Veith 1963.

---

## "Sexual Instructions of the Master of Pure Harmony", from *Yufang bijue* (Secret Instructions of the Jade Chamber)

NOURISHING THE YANG

[635] The Master of Pure Harmony [Chonghezi] says: Those who would cultivate their yang energy must not allow women to steal glimpses of this art. Not only is this of no benefit to one's yang energy, but it may even lead to injury or illness. This is what is called: "Lend a man your sword and when the time comes to roll up sleeves for a fight you cannot win."

According to Pengzu the Long-Lived, if a man wishes to derive the greatest benefit [from sexual techniques], it is best to find a woman who has no knowledge of them. He also had better choose young maidens for mounting, because then his complexion will become like a maiden's. When it comes to women, one should be vexed only by their not being young. It is best to obtain those between fourteen or fifteen and eighteen or nineteen. In any event, they should never be older than thirty. Even those under thirty are of no benefit if they have given birth. My late master handed down these methods and himself used them to live for three thousand years. If combined with drugs, they will even lead to immortality.

In practicing the union of yin and yang to increase your energy and cultivate long life, do not limit yourself to just one woman. Much better to get three, nine, or eleven: the more the better! Absorb her secreted essence by mounting the "vast spring" and reverting the essence upward. Your skin will become glossy, your body light, your eyes bright, and your energy so strong that you will be able to overcome all your enemies. Old men will feel like twenty and young men will feel their strength increased a hundredfold.

When having intercourse with women, as soon as you feel yourself aroused, change partners. By changing partners you can lengthen your life. If you return habitually to the same woman, her yin energy will become progressively weaker and this will be of little benefit to you.

The Taoist master Gray Ox [Qingniu] agrees that it is very beneficial to change female partners frequently. More than ten in one night is especially good. If one constantly has intercourse with the same woman, he insists, her yin energy will become weak. This is not only of no great benefit to the man, but will cause her to become thin and emaciated.

## NOURISHING THE YIN

[636] The Master of Pure Harmony says: It is not only that yang can be cultivated, but yin too. The Queen Mother of the West, for example, attained the Tao by cultivating her yin energy. As soon as she had intercourse with a man he would immediately take sick, while her complexion would be ever more radiant without the use of rouge or powder. She always ate curds and plucked the five-stringed lute in order to harmonize her heart and concentrate her mind. She was quite without any other desire.

The Queen Mother had no husband but was fond of intercourse with young boys. If this is not fit to be taught to the world, how is it that such an elevated personage as the Queen Mother herself practiced it?

When having intercourse with a man, first calm your heart and still your mind. If the man is not yet fully aroused, wait for his energy to arrive and slightly restrain your emotion to attune yourself to him. Do not move or become agitated, lest your yin essence become exhausted first. If this happens, you will be left in a deficient state and susceptible to cold wind illnesses.

For example, there are women who become jealous and vexed when they hear that their husbands have intercourse with another woman. Then their yin essence is aroused, they sit up indignantly, and the essential secretions come forth spontaneously. Wanness and premature aging result from this. Therefore, exercise restraint with your yin energy and be extremely careful.

If a woman knows the way of cultivating her yin and causing the two energies to unite in harmony, they can be transformed into a male child. If she does not have intercourse for the sake of offspring, she can divert the fluids to flow back into the hundred vessels [of her body]. By using yang to nourish yin, the various ailments disappear, her complexion becomes radiant and her flesh strong. Then she can enjoy long life without aging and be young forever.

If a woman is able to master this Tao and has frequent intercourse with men, she can avoid all grain for nine days without getting hungry. Even those who are sick and have sexual relations with ghosts attain this ability to fast. But they become emaciated after a while. So, how much more beneficial must it be to have intercourse with men?

[645] The Master of Pure Harmony says: If you have intercourse while indulging in emotional extremes and unbridled passion, you will suffer harm and get ill. This is obvious to those with experience in sexual relations. Because you may become ill from this, you may also be cured by it. It is quite like curing a hangover by means of more wine.

Again, if you have intercourse with your eyes open, gazing upon your partner's body, or if you light a fire so you can look at illustrated manuals, you will get dizziness in your eyes or even turn blind. To recover, have intercourse at night with your eyes closed.

If, moreover, during intercourse you place your partner upon your belly and raise your middle from below to join her, you may develop pain in the hips, tension in the lower abdomen, cramps in the feet, and strain in the back. To cure this condition, turn over so that you are on top. Then straighten your body and play at your leisure.

If you have intercourse by approaching your partner from the side and lifting her buttocks with your hands, you may get pain in the ribs. To get better, lie straight and play in a relaxed manner.

If you have intercourse with your head lowered and throat stretched out, your head will get heavy and your neck stiff. To effect a cure, place your head on your partner's forehead and not lower it.

Intercourse when overly full. If you have sex at midnight, before you have fully digested your evening meal, you may develop chest pain and fullness of energy. Indications are a pulling sensation beneath the ribs and pressure in the breast, as if it were being torn. You will lose your appetite for food and drink, feel a blocking knot beneath your heart, sometimes even vomit green and yellow bile. Your stomach will feel tense with the fullness of energy and there will be a slow and irregular pulse. Sometimes in addition there may be nosebleeds, hardness or pain beneath the ribs, and sores on the face. To heal this, have intercourse after midnight and close to the approach of dawn.

Intercourse under the influence of wine. While intoxicated, you may recklessly use force to penetrate to the extreme. This will certainly make you sick. Yellow or black jaundice and energy pains beneath the ribs are the first symptoms. If you continue like this, you will get a feeling between the thighs as if the scrotum were full of water. This extends up to the shoulders and arms. In extreme cases, there is pain in the chest and the back, coughing and spitting of blood, and rising energy. To cure this, abstain from wine and have intercourse close to the approach of dawn. Thus you can dally at leisure while relaxing the body.

Intercourse when overdue for urination. This will lead to incontinence, energy pressure in the lower abdomen, and difficulty in urinating. There is pain in the jade stalk and a frequent urge to grip it with the hand. After a moment again one feels like urinating. To get better, first urinate, then lie down and settle yourself. After a little while, have intercourse at your leisure.

Intercourse when overdue to move the bowels. This causes piles and difficulty in vacating the bowels. After some days and months there will be dripping pus and blood, and sores will appear around the anus resembling bee hives. Straining at stool, the bowels do not move in timely fashion. In this pain and bloating you find no rest even by lying down. To cure this by means of sexual techniques, rise at cockcrow and use the bathroom. Then return to your bed, settle yourself comfortably and slowly engage in playful dalliance. When your entire body is deeply relaxed, cause your partner to be slippery with secretions, then withdraw. The illness will be wonderfully cured. The same method also helps in female maladies.

Exceeding the proper measure. This results in beads of sweat the size of pearls. You will roll from side to side to let some cool air under the coverlets. When then your essence is empty and your energy exhausted, wind and harmful energies will enter the body and you will get sick. Gradually you get weaker until you are lame and cannot even raise your hand to your head. To remedy this, nourish your essence and spirit, and take regular decoctions of foxglove.

HEALING EFFORTS

The Master of Pure Harmony says: According to Wu Zidu, to improve your eyesight, wait for the impulse to ejaculate, then raise your head, hold the breath, and expel the air with a loud sound, while rolling your eyes to the left and right. Then contract your abdomen and revert the essence upward so that it enters the hundred vessels of the body.

To prevent deafness, wait for the impulse to ejaculate and then inhale deeply. Clench the teeth and hold the breath. [646] Produce a humming sound in the ears, then contract the abdomen, concentrate on your energy and circulate it mentally throughout the body until it becomes very strong. Even in old age you will never lose your hearing.

To improve the functioning of your five inner organs, to facilitate digestion and cure the hundred ills, wait for the approach of ejaculation, then expand your belly and use the mind to move the energy around the body. Next, contract your belly again so that the essence disperses and reverts to the hundred vessels. Then penetrate your partner nine times shallow and once deeply between her zither strings and grain ears. All strong and good energy will return, while all bad and ill energy will depart.

To prevent pain in the lower back, stand against a wall and stretch out the waist without letting your head incline either too far forward or too far back. Level all those places where the lower back does not make contact with the wall. During the sex act in this position you should then strive for energy circulation. In order to supplement deficiency, to nourish your body and cure diseases, you must refrain from ejaculating when the desire arises. Instead you have to recirculate your essence throughout the body. Your entire circulation will feel wonderfully warm.

# Chapter Six

## THE COSMIC BODY

Made supple, light, and healthy through the application of the various physical practices, the body becomes a more cosmic entity and is recognized as a microcosm, a universe in itself. The body, from the mere physical accumulation of different fluids, flesh, and bones, is turned gradually into a full-fledged residence of the Tao, into a cosmos within.

The advancing Taoist develops a new understanding of the body. It begins with the vision of traditional Chinese medicine of the body as a network of energy channels, pulses, moving fluids, circulation, breaths, various faculties, and inner organs. This vision centers around the so-called five orbs, five inner organs—the liver, heart, spleen, lungs, and kidneys—which are not only associated and intricately linked but structurally one with the five senses, five emotions, five forms of body tissue, five psychic centers, and so on.

The basic system that lies at the root of this vision is the cosmology of the Five Agents—wood, fire, earth, metal, and water—in conjunction with the directions, seasons, colors, tastes, grains, and many, many more. Developed first in the Han dynasty, this cosmology is fundamental to most traditional Chinese thought and has left its thorough imprint on both medical and Taoist thinking.

The five orbs in this context are the entire network associated with the five organs. Any reference made to any of them, e.g., the "liver," connotes the entire fabric of functional manifestations related to this orb. Consequently "liver" includes the working of the muscles and sinews and also corresponds to the sense of vision and the eyes, to the emotion of anger, and the seat of the spiritual soul.

More specifically, the five orbs indicate the five organs in their function as receptacles and storage spaces for the *qi*. They are furthermore associated with six intestines, i.e., gall bladder, bladder, small intestine, large intestine, stomach, and the navel or some-

161

times the triple heater. Where the orbs store, the intestines process. While the orbs are supporting and yin in quality, the intestines are productive and yang.

In Chinese medicine, health is defined as the smooth and flawless interaction of the various parts of the body, especially the network of the five orbs as it continues to interact with the seasons, the weather, the planets, society—with the entire outside world that works basically according to the same scheme of continuous alteration and change.

In Taoism, however, this is only the first step toward a more subtle and ultimately reversed union with the Tao. Where Chinese medicine is content with balancing the energy flow—reducing an overload, supplementing an insufficiency—Taoist practice moves on to develop the body back toward the level of primordial energy, to the state at the beginning of creation. The body, no longer a mere means to live harmoniously in the world, becomes a universe in itself.

The Taoist understanding of the body therefore views it as incorporating the entire cosmos. Every single part of the body corresponds to a celestial or geographical feature of the world—the body is the world. Vice versa, the world is also in the body. There are a sun and a moon, stars and planets, mountains and rivers, cities and fields, roads and passageways, palaces and towers.

And of course, there are inhabitants. The body, as much as the larger universe, is ruled and lived in by the gods—the multifaceted manifestations of spirit, the visible and accessible aspect of the Tao on earth. The body as a residence of the gods, as a network of divine halls and palaces, as a replica of the universe is the true body of the Tao, the way in which the Tao is found in everyone and everywhere.

The selections below document the varying visions of the body within Taoism. First, there is the medical system as represented in the ancient classic *Huangdi neijing suwen* (The Yellow Emperor's Classic of Internal Medicine, Simple Questions). Going back to the Han dynasty in its content, the text describes the basic workings of the orbs and their associated body functions. It is schematic but gives a clear picture of the basic idea.

Next, there is the origin myth of Pangu, whose body formed the world, as cited from the *Yunji qiqian*. This is then reversed in Taoist meditation instructions, telling the practitioner to visualize his body as the world. Two such instructions are given, one from the *Neiguan jing* (Scripture of Inner Observation) of the eighth, the other from the *Laozi daode jing xujue* (Introductory Explanations to Laozi's *Daode jing*) of the fifth century.

Third, there is an inner-alchemical journey through the land-scape within the body, describing the roads and mountains, cities and palaces. It goes back to Wang Chongyang, the founder of the school of Complete Perfection, and is contained in the *Chongyang zhenren jinguan yusuo jue* (Master Chongyang's Instructions on the Golden Gate and Jade Lock).

Fourth, then, we have the *Huangting waijing jing* (Outer Radiance Scripture of the Yellow Court), an ancient text that was most influential in Highest Clarity. It outlines the inner network of the body and defines—with commentaries at variance—the major palaces and deities therein.

## 21. The Structure of the Body

The basic Taoist understanding of the body is identical with that of traditional Chinese medicine, which in turn is based on the system of the Five Agents. They and their basic associations are as follows:

| agent | dir. | color | season | orb | emot. | sense | psych. |
|-------|------|-------|--------|-----|-------|-------|--------|
| wood | east | green | spring | liver | anger | eyes | mat. soul |
| fire | south | red | summer | heart | joy | tongue | spirit |
| earth | center | yellow | Sept. | spleen | worry | lips | will |
| metal | west | white | fall | lungs | sadness | nose | spirit soul |
| water | north | black | winter | kidneys | fear | ears | essence |

Medical thought concentrates on the fruitful or defective inter-action between these various aspects of the body and the world. It prescribes medication and exercises to balance the energy flow, but also emphasizes the correct emergence and use of the emotions and the mind.

The mind, in Chinese medical thought, is not different from the body, but flows through it as a subtler form of energy together with the energy and the blood. Emotional upheavals are therefore immediately linked with physical symptoms, either causing them or caused by them. Likewise, in Taoism the gods of the body are in no way different from the body as a material entity. However much the terminology distinguishes between spirit and matter, mind and body, there is no substantial difference nor strict delimitation be-tween the two.

The selection below describes the five orbs according to the *Huangdi neijing suwen* (The Yellow Emperor's Classic of Internal

Medicine, Simple Questions) as found in DZ 1018, fasc. 649–60. (9.13b–19a and 10.1a–7b). The text is extant today in a Tang-dynasty edition, but in content goes back as far as the Han. It is written in dialogue form, presenting the Yellow Emperor in the position of the ever-learning disciple and the ancient sage Qi Bo as the learned medical teacher.

For a complete translation of the entire text, see Veith 1972. On the history of the text, see Yamada 1979. For an introduction to the principles of Chinese medicine, see Kaptchuk 1983, Porkert 1983. For a rather difficult but substantial analysis of Chinese medical thinking, see Porkert 1974.

For histories of Chinese medical thought and practice, see Lu 1980, Unschuld 1985. On the interrelation of body and mind according to early documents, see Ishida 1989, Roth 1991.

---

**"The Five Orbs," from *Huangdi neijing suwen* (The Yellow Emperor's Classic of Internal Medicine, Simple Questions)**

9. THE SIX REGULATIONS AND THE MANIFESTATIONS OF THE ORBS

"Very good," the Yellow Emperor said. "Now, I have heard that the cosmic energies unite and take shape. Then they develop and can duly be defined in precise terms. The revolutions of heaven and earth, the transformations of yin and yang accordingly have their effect upon all living beings. Could you please explain to me the extent of this influence?"

"How brilliant a question!" Qi Bo exclaimed. "Heaven is boundless and cannot be measured; Earth is huge and without limit. Greatly pervaded by spirit and numinous power, their extent cannot be guessed!

"Grass and herbs come forth in the five colors [green, red, yellow, white, and black]; there is nothing beyond the sight of these. Grass and herbs also come forth in the five flavors [sour, bitter, sweet, pungent, and salty]; there is nothing beyond the taste of these. Within this framework, humans desire different things; they each have what they favor most.

"Heaven nourishes human beings with the five energies; Earth nourishes them with the five flavors. The five energies enter the nostrils and are stored in the orbs of the heart and the lungs. They take care that the five colors are perceived to the fullest and that the five sounds are heard properly.

"The five flavors enter the mouth and are stored in the orbs of the intestines and the stomach. As these flavors are being stored, they support the five energies. As these energies are well harmonized, they produce saliva and body fluids. As these in turn complete each other, spirit is brought forth spontaneously."

"What," the emperor then asked, "are these orbs like?"

"The orb of the heart," Qi Bo informed him, "is the root of life and all spirit transformations. Its efflorescence is visible in the complexion, while its fullness is felt in the pulse of the blood. The heart represents the greater yang within yang and corresponds to the energy of summer.

"The orb of the lungs is the root of breath and the residence of the material soul. Its efflorescence is visible in the body hair, while its fullness is felt in the skin. The lungs represent the lesser yin within yin and correspond to the energy of autumn.

"The orb of the kidneys is the root of hibernation and enclosure. Its efflorescence is visible in the hair on the head, while its fullness is felt in the bones. The kidneys represent the greater yin within yin and correspond to the energy of winter.

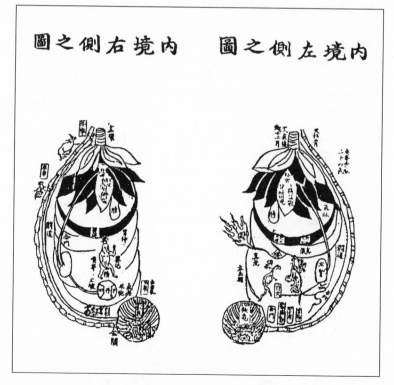

Fig. 15. The Inner Organs. Source: *Xiuzhen taiji hunyuan tu.*

"The orb of the liver is the root of all extremes and the residence of the spirit soul. Its efflorescence is visible in the nails, while its fullness is felt in the muscles. It renews the blood and the energy. The taste connected with the liver is sour, and the color associated with it is green. The liver represents the lesser yang within yang and corresponds to the energy of spring.

"The orb of the spleen and the stomach, together with those of the large intestine, small intestine, triple burner, and the bladder, is the root of all storage and the residence of the constructive energy. These orbs are called vessels. They can transform even the dregs and sediments of the food. They digest the five flavors and make them move along to their proper orb. Their efflorescence is visible in the lips and the whites of the eyes. Their fullness can be felt in the flesh. The flavor connected with them is sweet, and their color is yellow. The spleen and stomach represent the perfect yin and correspond to the energy of the earth. . . ."

## 10. THE DEVELOPMENT AND PERFECTION OF THE FIVE ORBS

The orb of the heart includes the pulse. Its splendor shows in the complexion. It rules over the kidneys.

The orb of the lungs includes the skin. Its splendor shows in the body hair. It rules over the heart.

The orb of the liver includes the muscles. Its splendor shows in the nails. It rules over the lungs.

The orb of the spleen includes the flesh. Its splendor shows in the lips. It rules over the liver.

The orb of the kidneys includes the bones. Its splendor shows in the hair on the head. It rules over the spleen.

If one eats too salty, the pulse hardens, tears appear, and the complexion changes.

If one eats too bitter, the skin withers and the body hair falls out.

If one eats too pungent, the muscles become knotty and the nails decay.

If one eats too sour, the flesh first hardens, then wrinkles and the lips become slack.

If one eats too sweet, the bones ache and the hair on the head falls out.

These are the injuries caused by the five flavors.

The heart desires bitter food.
The lungs desire pungent food.
The liver desires sour food.
The spleen desires sweet food.
The kidneys desire salty food.
These are the harmonies brought about by the five flavors.

The energies of the orbs duly appear in the complexion:
Green like grass means death.
Yellow like oranges means death.
Black like coal means death.
Red like blood means death.
White like dried bones means death.
Thus the five colors indicate death.

On the other hand,
Green like the kingfisher's wings means life.
Red like a rooster's comb means life.
Yellow like the belly of a crab means life.
White like the grease of pigs means life.
Black like the wings of a crow means life.
Thus five colors indicate life.

Life in the heart appears like a robe's vermilion lining.
Life in the lungs appears like a robe's pink lining.
Life in the liver appears like a robe's violet lining.
Life in the stomach appears like a robe's juniper berry lining.
Life in the kidneys appears like a robe's purple lining.
Thus the five orbs indicate life.

All colors and flavors belong to an orb:
White belongs to the lungs; so does the pungent flavor.
Red belongs to the heart; so does the bitter flavor.
Green belongs to the liver; so does the sour flavor.
Yellow belongs to the stomach; so does the sweet flavor.
Black belongs to the kidneys; so does the salty flavor.

Thus,
White also corresponds to the skin.
Red also corresponds to the pulse.
Green also corresponds to the muscles.
Yellow also corresponds to the flesh.
Black also corresponds to the bones.

The pulse is then connected with the eyes.
The marrow is then connected with the brain.
The muscles are then connected with the joints.
The blood is then connected with the heart.
The energy is then connected with the lungs.

The four limbs and eight joints are moving from morning to night. Only when people lie down to rest, the blood flows back to the liver.

The liver receives the blood and one can see.
The feet receive the blood and one can walk.
The palms receive the blood and one can grasp things.
The fingers receive the blood and one can lift things.

When a person is exposed to the wind, either lying down or walking about, the blood will coagulate.

When it coagulates in the skin, there is numbness.
When it coagulates in the pulse, there is obstruction.
When it coagulates in the feet, there are chills.

In all three cases, the blood enters the organs and cannot recover its proper course. Thus there are numbness and chills.

## 22. The Body as the World

Three texts document the vision of the body as the world. The first is the classical myth about Pangu, from whose body the world is first created. The story, first found in the third-century text *Sanwu liji* (Record of the Three and Five) and in the *Shuyi ji* (Tales of Marvels) of the fifth century, is here cited after its version in the *Yunji qiqian Yuanqi lun* (Discourse on Primordial Energy; 56.1b–2a). The same myth is also cited with Laozi as the creator in the *Xiaodao lun* (Laughing at the Tao), an anti-Taoist polemic of the sixth century. It documents an anthropomorphic vision of the cosmos, the close correspondence of the natural and social world to the human body.

The second selection is taken from the *Neiguan jing* (Scripture on Inner Observation), found in DZ 641, fasc. 342 (1b–3a). This Tang-dynasty set of Taoist meditation instructions documents the concrete application of the cosmic vision of the body. Placed in the mouth of the Highest Venerable Lord, it shows how every single set of universal forces enters the body and keeps it alive. The translation is taken from Kohn 1989b.

Third, there is the last section of the *Laozi daode jing xujue* (Introductory Explanations to Laozi's *Daode jing*). This is a Dunhuang manuscript listed under the numbers S. 75 and P. 2370 and conveniently edited in Ofuchi 1979: 509. The part translated here is commonly dated to the fifth century. It is an early and very clear example of how a Taoist develops his body into the cosmos in meditation. Performing purifications and assembling the protector gods around him, he places himself in the very center of all the directions, symbolized by the four sacred animals and the eight trigrams of the *Yijing*.

On Pangu and his creation, see Erkes 1942, Maspero 1981: 340. The *Neiguan jing* is translated in full and discussed in Kohn 1989b. For studies of the body in Taoism, see Schipper 1978 and 1982, Kohn 1991a.

---

### "Pangu Transforms His Body," from *Yuanqi lun*

Pangu died and transformed his body.
His breath became the wind and the clouds.
His voice became the thunder.
His left eye was the sun.
His right eye was the moon.
His four limbs changed to be the four compass points.
His five limbs became the five sacred mountains.
His blood and body fluids turned into streams and rivers.
His muscles and sinews became solid earth.
His flesh became arable land.
His hair turned into stars.
His body hair turned into grass and trees.
His teeth and bones were transformed into gold and minerals.
His marrow changed into pearls and jade.
His sweat was the rain and the moisture of the land.
The germs in his body were carried off by the wind.
They became the mass of the people.

### *Neiguan jing* (Scripture on Inner Observation)

[1b] The Venerable Lord said:
Heaven and earth mingle their essences; yin and yang engage in interchange. Thus the myriad beings come to life, each receiving

氏　古　盤

Fig. 16. Pangu, the Creator. Source: *Sancai tuhui*.

a particular life: yet all are alike in that they have a share in the life-giving Tao.

When father and mother unite in harmony, man receives life.

In the first month, essence and blood coagulate in the womb.
In the second month, the embryo begins to take shape.
In the third month, the yang spirit arouses the three spirit
    souls to come to life.
In the fourth month, the yin energy settles the seven
    material souls as guardians of the body.
In the fifth month, the five agents are distributed to the five
    orbs to keep their spirit at peace.
In the sixth month, the six pitches are set up in the six
    intestines nourishing the vital energy.
In the seventh month, the seven essential stars open the body
    orifices to let the light in.
In the eighth month, the eight luminants descend with their
    true vital energy.
In the ninth month, the various palaces and chambers are
    properly arranged to keep the essence safe.
In the tenth month, the energy is strong enough to complete
    the image.

People's feeding on primordial harmony is never interrupted. The Lord Emperor of the Great One resides in the head. He is called the Lord of the Niwan Palace. He governs the host of spirits. What makes life shine forth and lets man know of the spirits is his spirit soul.

[2a] Siming, the Ruler of Fates, resides in the heart. He regulates the prime energies of life. Wuying occupies his left, from where he regulates the three spirit souls. Baiyuan occupies the right, from where he regulates the seven material souls. Taohai resides in the navel, where he preserves the root of the essence.

What makes the various joints of the body function together are the hundred manifestations of the spirit of life. As it pervades the whole of the body, spirit is not empty. When primordial energy enters through the nose and reaches the *niwan* in the center of the head, the spirit light radiates and the body is stable and at peace. For all movement and rest, however, it fully depends on the mind. This is how life first begins.

When you now observe yourself in detail and with care, beware of the mind. As the ruler of the self it can prohibit and control everything. It is responsible for the propriety of the body spirits. The mind is the spirit. Its changes and transformations cannot be fathomed. It does not have a fixed shape.

In the five orbs, the following spirit manifestations reside:

The spirit soul in the liver;
the material soul in the lungs;
the essence in the kidneys;
the intention in the spleen;
the spirit in the heart.

Their appellations vary in accordance with their respective positions. The heart belongs to the agent fire. Fire is the essence of the south and of greater yang. Above it is governed by the planet Mars; below it corresponds to the heart. [2b] Its color is red and it consists of three valves that resemble a lotus leaf. As the light of pure spirit is rooted there, it is named accordingly.

Spirit is neither black nor white, neither red nor yellow, neither big nor small, neither short nor long, neither crooked nor straight, neither soft nor hard, neither thick nor thin, neither round nor square. It goes on changing and transforming without measure, merges with yin and yang, greatly encompasses heaven and earth, subtly enters the tiniest blade of grass.

Controlled it is straightforward; let loose it goes mad. Purity and tranquility make it live; defilements and nervousness cause it to perish. When shining it can illuminate the eight ends of the universe. When darkened it will go wrong even in one single direction. You need only keep it empty and still, then life and the Tao will spontaneously be permanent. Always preserve an attitude of non-action, and the self will prosper.

Spirit is shapeless; thus it cannot be named. All good and bad fortune, all success and failure only come from the spirit. Thus the sage will always preserve a straightforward relation to the ruler and the government, to the established rewards and punishments, and to the laws and regulations of the administration. He sets an example for others. The reason why people find it hard to submit to rules and regulations is found in their minds. When the mind is pure and calm, all the many problems of misfortune don't arise.

All ups and downs, life and death, all vicissitudes and evils arise from the mind. [3a] All foolishness and delusion, love and hate, all accepting and rejecting, coming and going, all defilements and attachments, as well as all entanglement and bondage arise gradually from becoming involved in things. Madly turning hither and thither, tied up and fettered, one is unable to get free. Thus one is bound for peril and destruction.

Oxen and horses when led properly can easily wade through the marsh. When let loose, however, they will sink in deeper and deeper and can never get out again by themselves. So they have to die. People are just like this: when first born their original spirit is pure and tranquil, profound and unadulterated. But then people gradually take in shaped objects. Those will in due course defile the six senses:

The eyes will covet color.
The ears will be obstructed by sound.
The mouth will be addicted to flavors.
The nose will always take in smells.
The mind will be intent on refusing and coveting.
The body will desire to be slimmer or fatter.

From all these ups and downs of life no one is able to wake up by himself. Thus the sages with compassionate consideration established the doctrine to teach people to reform. They made them use inner observation of the self and body in order to purify the mind.

---

### Laozi daode jing xujue (Introductory Explanations to Laozi's Daode jing)

These are the secret instructions of the Highest Lord.

First burn incense and straighten your robes, greet the ten directions with three bows each. Concentrate your mind inside and visualize Master Yin and the Master on the River, as well as Laozi, the Great Teacher of the Law.

Then open the text and recite the following in your mind:

Mysterious, again mysterious, the origin of Tao,
Above, virtue incorporates chaos and the prime.
Heaven's truth is wonderful, yet how far, alas!
Coming closer, now there is the Great Lord of Niwan.

In my room, the seven jewels come together,
Doors and windows open of themselves.
Utter in my purity, I strive for deeper truth,
Riding on bright light, I ascend the purple sky.

> Sun and moon shine to my right and left,
> I go to the immortals, find eternal life.
> All seven ancestors rise, are reborn in heaven,
> The world, how true, is the gate to virtue and to Tao.

Finish this mental recitation, then clap your teeth and swallow the saliva thirty-six times each. Visualize the green dragon to your left, the white tiger to your right, the red bird in front of you, and the dark warrior at your back.

Your feet stand between the eight trigrams; the divine turtle and the thirty-six masters bow to you. In front of you, you see the seventeen stars; your five inner orbs give forth the five energies; a network pattern streams across your body.

On three sides you are joined by an attendant, each having a retinue of a thousand carriages and ten thousand horsemen. Eight thousand jade maidens and jade lads of heaven and earth stand guard for you.

Then repeat the formula, this time aloud, and begin to recite the five thousand words of the scripture. Conclude by three times clapping your teeth and swallowing the saliva.

## 23. The World in the Body

Just as the body is the world, so also is the world in the body. Not only is there another sun and moon, are there palaces and towers, mountains and rivers, but the active practitioner can and should also wander among them, make their acquaintance, and feel at home in himself as the universe.

The *Chongyang zhenren jinguan yusuo jue* (Master Chongyang's Instructions on the Golden Gate and Jade Lock) is a text of Complete Perfection Taoism found in DZ 1156, fasc. 796. Written in a question-and-answer pattern, it consists of practical instructions Wang Chongyang, the founder of Complete Perfection in the twelfth century, gives to his disciples.

It is not a systematic or particularly well-organized text but presents a collection of methods quite parallel to each other. Some specify cures for diseases, others deal with particular situations likely to be encountered by practitioners, others again are meditation instructions, especially of inner alchemy. However, since the text seems to go back to Wang Chongyang's immediate environment, it provides a useful window to the concerns and practices of Complete Perfection Taoists. Its Buddhist influence is obvious.

The section translated below (18a–20a) describes a spiritual and mediational journey through the body. The body appears as an inner landscape, with rivers and mountains, towers and palaces, guards and gods, witches and demons. As the meditator travels along its mysterious routes, he or she is instructed to recognize the various physical features in their symbolic and spiritual dimensions.

For a discussion of the text, see Tsui 1991: 41–48 (including translations of parts other than the section chosen here). For more on the world in the body, see Rousselle 1933, Schipper 1982.

---

### *Chongyang zhenren jinguan yusuo jue* (Master Chongyang's Instructions on the Golden Gate and Jade Lock)

[18a] For those who practice this cultivation [of the Tao], there is the great road of the teaching without and the straight route within. It is just that ordinary people do not even know this is there.

As you move ahead on the inner route for three miles, you will first come to three great torrents. They are quite bottomless. How do they relate to you, past and future?

Let me explain. These three great torrents are the Three Teachings, the Three Vehicles. With their help one can be free from the Three Forms of Death, acquire the Three Treasures, and go beyond the Three Worlds.

As you then travel further, after another three miles, you will come to six deep ditches. They are so wide that you cannot proceed beyond them. What gateways do they represent?

Let me explain. These six ditches are the six bodhisattva virtues [pāramitās] with their myriad practices. They help to calm and purify the six senses, behead the six robbers [of sensual indulgence], control the six forms of sexual attraction, and establish the six stages [toward enlightenment].

Then again you move on for yet another three miles. You will see three freshly built rafts. These are the precious rafts of purity. They are near the Seven Forests, ready to transport you away from the dead.

[18b] [Traveling now by raft], another three miles further on, you will then come to a garden. This is known as the Fruitbearing Garden. It is guarded by an old man. Anyone with karma of the

past who wants to pass has first to lay it all down. You may only go on empty-handed.

Let us say you manage to move past the garden. Another three miles further on your way, you notice an enormous tree. A golden ox is tethered to it. At this point on the bank of the river, several splendid terraces appear:

Men's Yellow Gold Terrace,
Women's Phoenix Terrace,
Spirit Immortals Fishing Terrace,
Thousand-Flowers of Happiness Terrace.

Be careful and keep your eyes on them. If you don't gaze at them all the time, you will be attracted by three women near the mouth of the river. Once you move across the river mouth toward them, they will turn into evil witches. So stick to your boat and see that you get past this place as fast as possible.

Another three miles further on, there is a huge mountain. On the eastern slope of this mountain is a gray ox. This represents the energy of the Venerable Lord. On the western slope of the mountain, you can see a white ram. This is the energy of the sage Confucius. Then again, on the slope straight to the south, there is a yellow ram. This is the energy of the Golden Immortal of Great Awakening [the Buddha].

These three beasts will lead you into the mountain—the mountain is thus the assembled combination of sacred Threefold Yang. [19a] Once inside, there is a walled city called Northtown. It has four gates, each equipped with a wooden plaque with an inscription. The inscriptions read:

On the eastern gate, "Gate of Opening Radiance,"
on the western gate, "Gate of Eternal Life,"
on the southern gate, "Gate of Golden Radiance,"
on the northern gate, "Gate of the Vast Waters."
These gates are the eyes, ears, nose, and mouth.

As you enter through any of these four gates, you will see four grottoes:

The Grotto of Celestial Happiness,
the Grotto of the White Clouds,
the Grotto of Bamboo Country,
the Grotto of Eternal Life.

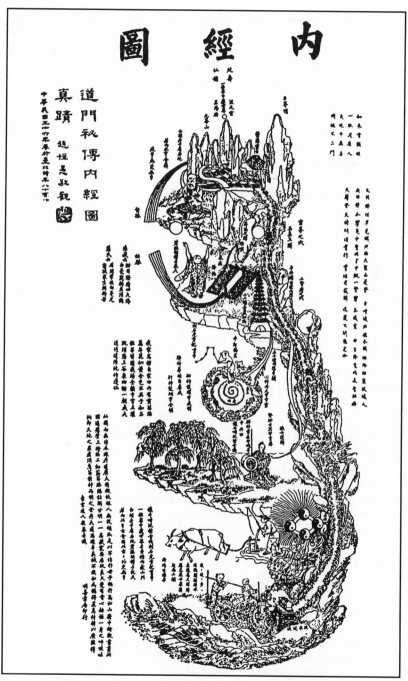

Fig. 17. The World in the Body. Source: *Neijing tu.*

As you enter further into these four grottoes, you will see four temples:

The Temple of Nonbeing and Purity,
the Temple of Mystery and Emptiness,
the Temple of the Bamboo Grotto,
the Temple of [*missing*].

These four temples represent the four karmic fruits [stages of enlightenment]:

stream-enterer,
once-returner,
non-returner,
arhat.

Such are the four temples. Resident immortals preside over them.

Move further ahead and you will notice five monasteries:

The Monastery of Fame,
the Monastery of Healing,
the Monastery of Peace,
the Monastery of Suchness,
the Monastery of Tusita Heaven.

In these five monasteries, there are five palaces:

The Twin Maiden Palace is the eyes;
the Great Dragon Palace is the mouth;
the Upper White Palace is the nose;
the Water Crystal Palace is the ears;
the Heavenly Balance Palace is the heart.

[19b] In their center is a high tower connecting the upper and the lower levels of the body through twelve stages of respiration. This tower is called the twelve-storied tower.

Each storey is also called a tower. They are:
The Tower of the Central Palace,
the Tower of the Moon Palace,
the Tower of the Heavenly Immortals,

the Tower of Collected Treasure,
the Tower of the Sagely Well,
the Tower of the Energy of the Law,
the Tower of Wondrous Sounds,
the Tower of Realizing the Tao,
the Tower of Highest Absorption,
the Tower of Luminous Yang,
the Tower of Bell and Drum,
the Tower of the Two Sages.

Each tower-level has its special time on the first day of the twelve months in every year. Thus in the human body there are towers corresponding to the twelve months. These towers are moreover related to the twelve divisions of the scriptures and the twelve earthly branches of the calendar. They divide equally among the four sides.

Also, there you can see the Nine Palaces. These represent the nine orifices of the human body. They are:

The Palace of Wind and Thunder and
the Palace of the Twin Forests in the east;
the Palace of Purple Tenuity and
the Palace of Shakyamuni in the south;
the Palace of the Holy Mother and
the Palace of the Gracious Arhat in the west;
the Palace of Brahma and
the Palace of Water Crystal in the north;
the Palace of Peace in the center.

Such are the Nine Palaces. They are arranged just as the Nine Provinces on earth.

Then again, there are smaller districts which were originally denoted as the ten continents. These are the following ten countries:

The country of Patriarch Jiao,
the country of Shakyamuni,
the country of Blossoming Flowers [20a],
the country of the Deer King,
the country of Golden Colors,
the country of Flowing Glass,
the country of Kapilavastu,

the country of Southern Depth,
the country of India,
the country of Twofold Yang.

These ten countries correspond to the ten regions on earth. In each of these regions there is one huge mountain that presides over it.

The human body truly is an amazing thing. It works hard to cure all the tough diseases which lie in wait to harm the human life.

Also, there are four large seas in the body:
The saliva is the Eastern Sea;
the blood is the Southern Sea;
the marrow is the Western Sea;
the energy is the Northern Sea.

Then again there are five great lakes:
The body at large is the Grotto Garden Lake;
the essence is the King's Lake;
the sweet saliva is the Cream Lake;
the heart is the Mysterious Lake;
the small intestine is the River Lake.

All these stand in close correspondence to the sun and the moon, the stars and the planets.

Then there are the three dissolutions. They are the weakening of the blood, energy, and essence. These three dissolutions make mountains tumble, oceans dry up, and the earth split open.

To prevent this, on the first day of each month at noontime sit and visualize the body. There is no better practice than this to gain merit.

Men thus refine their bodies and become like lads.
Women thus refine their bodies and become like girls.

As the scriptures say:

"Body and spirit are equally wondrous;
Joined in the Tao, they find their perfection."
This is just it.

## 24. The Gods Within

Another form in which the body appears is as the residence of the gods and spirits. They vitalize the human body through their presence, residing in the body as they do in the stars, in palaces and halls, towers and terraces. Rather than moving on through the inner landscape, meditation here means the focusing of attention on one or the other of these gods. The more one keeps one's concentration fixed, the less the gods will be inclined to leave. And when the gods don't leave, the body cannot die.

The text presented here, the *Huang ting waijing jing* (The Outer Radiance Scripture of the Yellow Court) is the oldest scripture in an entire group of texts called "Yellow Court Scriptures." It was compiled approximately in the third century and gives a first inkling of the powerful divine occupancy of the human body and its parallel structure to the stars.

The system becomes central in Highest Clarity Taoism. Here the most important "Yellow Court" document is the *Huang ting neijing jing* or "Inner Radiance Scripture of the Yellow Court." Longer and more elaborate, this text makes much use of the earlier, "Outer," version. It is, however, only slightly less confusing.

The text here is taken from the Song-dynasty collection *Xiuzhen shishu* (Ten Books on the Cultivation of Perfection) in DZ 263, fasc. 122–131 (58.1a–4b). The second, alternative commentary is taken from the edition in the *Yunji qiqian* (12.28b–31b). As the variations show, there is no one interpretation to the symbolic and esoteric nomenclature of bodily organs and functions.

For a convenient edition and index of both scriptures, see Schipper 1975a. A critical discussion of the texts and their relationship is contained in Robinet 1984.

On Taoist meditation after the "Yellow Court," see Robinet 1979. For a preliminary analysis of the gods and system in the "Inner Radiance Scripture," see Homann 1971.

---

### *Huang ting waijing jing* (The Outer Radiance Scripture of the Yellow Court)

Laozi, living in seclusion, composed the seven-word text.

> Laozi was born before heaven and earth; he has always been there since heaven and earth came to be. He has thirty-six titles and seventy-two names. He took refuge in the womb of Mother Li and was born after eighty-one years.

He composed the *Yellow Court Scripture* to transmit his teaching to later generations. Appearing in countless transformations, he completed his task. Always, he naturally found someone who would kneel before him to receive the instructions. If nobody had been found, Laozi would not have spoken even for ten thousand generations.

✳

Laozi is the essential soul of heaven, the lord of nature. He brought forth the divine immortals, who live on and on for ten thousand generations. He composed the seven-word text to transmit his teaching to posterity.

## Explaining clearly the human body and its relation to the gods.

Laozi rests quietly in so-being, yet at the same time floats about the eight ends of the universe. [Like the Tao] he is vague and obscure and cannot be fathomed. Continuously changing on and on, he holds the sacred talismans, controls the registers of life and death, and orders about the host of the gods.

The Tao does not have two families—to the end it always supports its servants. The Tao does not have two kin-groups— invariably it always remains with the good.

✳

The lord says that all is originally one continuous process. The whole body, from head to feet, can be brought to life. It is a single network and, as a whole, can be at peace. The Tao is not twofold. Whoever practices it is wise.

## Above there is the Yellow Court; below, the Primordial Pass.

The Yellow Court is in the head. It encompasses three palaces known as the Hall of Light, the Grotto Chamber, and the Cinnabar Field. Enter between the eyebrows toward the back of the head. After one inch, there is the Hall of Light; after two inches, there is the Grotto Chamber; after three inches, there is the Cinnabar Field. These three constitute the Upper Prime.

The Yellow Court is paired with the Grotto Chamber. Together they bring forth an infant god, who is their resident perfected. Always visualize him! Be careful not to lose the image.

The infant turns into a Perfected in the Hall of Light. Then he is called Master Cinnabar. Here, to know the perfected means to concentrate on the Hall of Light as its residence.

Practice breathing and gymnastics, close your eyes and turn your vision inward, calm your mind and concentrate your thoughts.

Merge with chaos in the limitless! Let essence revert upward and circulate in the *Niwan* [Cinnabar Field]. This will bring about the Perfected Master Cinnabar.

In the Hall of Light, the infant and the Master are like lord and minister. Further behind, in the Grotto Chamber, they are like father and mother. In the Cinnabar Field, they are like husband and wife.

According to another explanation, the Yellow Court is the spleen. It is located one inch above the Great Storehouse [stomach] in the abdomen, about three inches above the navel. The spleen is the seat of the God of the Center, the Yellow Venerable Lord. He rules from here.

The Primordial Pass is three inches below the navel. The Gate of Primordial Yang is suspended before it. When essence here is completely clear, it reflects the entire body. Never slacken in your practice of this Tao.

✳

The Yellow Court is the eyes. The father and mother of the Tao both nourish the immortal embryo. On the left, there is the Numinous Yang, also known as Splendor Brightness. On the right, there is Great Yin, also known as Mystery Radiance. All three together build the right virtue; they support each other as they develop.

Behind there are the Dark Towers; in front, the Gate of Life.

The Dark Towers are the kidneys. Like overturned cups standing on their rims, they are three inches off the navel, big on top and small below. They contain another universe, with their own sun and moon. The Gate of Life is below the navel.

✳

The Dark Towers are the kidneys. They are related to the eyes through the energy circuits. The Gate of Life is the navel. It is about three inches in size. When the sun rises and the moon sets, yin and yang are balanced. Breathe the primordial breath in and out to nourish the numinous root.

Breathe in and out and through the stove; thus energy enters the Cinnabar Field.

To breathe out means to expel the breath; to breathe in means to draw it in. The stove is the nose.

This is the essential method to expel the old and draw in the new. The vital energy then enters between the eyebrows and after three inches reaches the Cinnabar Field in the head. Thus one draws in the breath through the nose and enters it into the Cinnabar Field.

✻

Breathing out is expelling; breathing in is drawing in. Through respiration the primordial breath can enter the Cinnabar Field. The Cinnabar Field is three inches below the navel, the gate of yin and yang. This is where ordinary people produce offspring. Taoists use it to preserve their lives.

## The clear fluid in the Jade Pond waters the Numinous Root.

"Clear fluid in the Jade Pond" refers to the mouth where the saliva assembles. The Numinous Root is the tongue. One should always keep the teeth together, rinse with saliva, and accumulate it to water the tongue.

✻

The mouth is the Jade Pond, the Palace of Great Harmony. The saliva is the clear fluid, always beautiful and fresh. Saliva collected in the throat makes the sound of thunder and lightning. The tongue is the Numinous Root. Always keep it well watered.

## All can practice this, all can live long.

Practice this day morning and night without slackening. Then you can attain long life.

✻

By practicing this day and night, one will subdue the deadly forces, kill the three worms, and expel all evil demons. Body and flesh will blossom; the true energy will return. When all evils have lost their power, one will live long and radiate a brilliance.

## The gods of the Yellow Court wear red robes.

Concentrate and visualize mother and child in the spleen. See how they enter the spleen from the stomach, wearing red.

*

The tiny pupils in the eyes are a couple. The right is the king, the left is the queen. Wearing red garments, they proceed to a banquet in the palace at the rear of the Cinnabar Field. Visualize them morning and night, never relax your effort!

The Pass Gate has a strong lock; keep its doors in place.

The gate of the lower Cinnabar Field has to be locked. Don't open it wantonly.

*

Close your eyes and look inside. There is nothing that is not seen. Close your mouth and curl your tongue. This is feeding on the mother. Keep the jade flower in the throat. You will never suffer any trouble. All this is due to energy. The teeth are the doors, the tongue is the lock that keeps them in place.

The Dark Towers communicate with loftiness and eminence above.

The kidneys are located at the gate of the Dark Towers, i.e., the building of the Earth Administration. They are the storehouse of vital energy. Above they are connected with the ears. The ears are on the sides of the head, they are lofty and eminent.

*

The Tao knows of three primordial points where compassionate intention arises. The lower of these is the steadiness of the mysterious spring in the Dark Towers [testicles]. The middle one is the pair of Dark Towers of the kidneys. The upper one is the pair of Dark Towers of the ears. The latter watch over the Golden Gate and the Jade Entrance. They also communicate with heaven, in the same way as Lady Jiao plays the zither and the flute, holding and suppressing the notes *gong* and *shang*.

In the Cinnabar Field, essence and energy are subtle.

The Cinnabar Field is located three inches beneath the navel. It is about three square inches in size. Its energy is subtle and wondrous. Visualize it, and it is there; forget about it, and it is gone. It changes and disappears. Thus we say it is subtle.

✳

The Cinnabar Field is the first chamber, opposite the Hall of Light. Its essence and energy are subtle and can hardly be distinguished. Thus we say it is subtle.

## The Jade Pond with its clear fluid develops opulence.

The Jade Pond is the mouth. The clear fluid is the saliva as it accumulates there. "Develops opulence" means that saliva is collected at the root of the tongue like a pond. Thus it is opulent.

✳

In the mouth, there is saliva. It rests and moves. Only when collected on the tongue, in its white kind, is it rich and greasy like fat. Rinse with it and maintain it fresh: This is the way to long life.

## The Numinous Root is stiff and strong—grow old but never weak.

The Numinous Root is the tongue. Always keep it rolled up and the teeth strongly together. During the practice never let the tongue get tired or dry. Always visualize its god, and you will live long but never grow weak.

✳

The Numinous Root is the tongue. It governs the four directions and harmonizes the five flavors. It expels stench and invites fragrance. Bite the teeth together and preserve your energy; thus you can live by swallowing saliva.

## In the Middle Pond, a deity resides, clad in red.

Constantly visualize the infant in the heart. He is clad in red garments, finely ornamented, and resides in the middle Cinnabar Field. All exhaustion and bad fortune, all sloth and agitation, through him are made to go.

✳

Ruojing in the throat is the God of the Prime. Beneath middle harmony, the towers show the partition of the way. With his reddish glowing dress, this god becomes a friend.

Three inches below the Field is where the gods reside.

> This refers to the spleen, situated in the abdomen. Beneath the Upper Burner is the Numinous Root of the navel. This is where the gods reside.

*

> The palace of the Hall of Light is three square inches in size. The gods reside in the very center of the eye. The eyebrows are their flowery canopies; the five colors are their couches.

Inside and outside firmly kept apart—lock it twice.

> Close in essence and guard it well. Never let it leak out wantonly. To close it in properly use the Golden Tower and the Jade Lock.

*

> Energy within should go out; energy without should come in. This process takes place by way of the three passes. When both kinds of energy are kept properly separate, the Tao of heaven is in its natural order.

The interior of the Spirit Stove should be kept in order.

> The Spirit Stove is the nose. There are little hairs inside, which have to be kept in order by removing them periodically. By then breathing carefully through the nose you can expel all evil forces.

*

> This teaches to pull out the hairs in the nose. The nose guarantees the free passage of the divine Tao; thus it is a stove or residence. Practice diligently day and night; never relax your efforts!

The breath pipe suspended in the chest contains the Talisman of Essence.

> The lower part of the tongue is the Talisman of Essence. The throat is the breath pipe. Energy and essence travel up and down through it. It is also where the Upper Prime harmonizes energy to be subtle and wondrous. It is the road on which the perfected travel up and down.

*

The center of the throat is the part that rises above the chest. Primordial energy travels up and down through this area. Thus it is called the Talisman of Essence.

## Strive to steady your essence to keep naturally whole.

Close in your energy and revert your essence upward to preserve yourself intact. Never let it leak out wantonly. Revert the essence to nourish the brain—this is the Tao of no-death.

*

Keep energy together and never let it go.

## In the residence is a personage always clad in pink.

Continuously visualize the god in the heart with his pink cinnabar robe. He moves in and out. Doing this, you will be free from disaster and expel all evil.

*

The face is the inch residence, the office of the Perfected is in its center. His robes are vermilion or red; he radiates a fiery red brilliance with a pink halo.

## When you can see him, you will be sick no more.

With all your might, concentrate on the god in the heart and visualize him without interruption. When you can always see the infant within, you will be free from all sickness and disease.

*

This serves to admonish people to realize the profundity of the truth of the Tao. By merit of seeing this god, you will be free from sickness.

Part Three

ETERNAL VISION

# Chapter Seven

## THE ONE

To fully realize the cosmic qualities of one's entire self, body and mind, Taoists employ three different forms of meditation. While these three tend to go together in actual practice and always remain closely linked to both physical practices and the goal of immortality, they are well separated terminologically in the tradition itself and can also be distinguished in terms of contemporary phenomenology.

The three forms are concentrative meditation, insight meditation, and ecstatic excursions, presented below under the headings "The One," "Insight Practice," and "Ecstatic Excursions." Concentration comes first. It is a basic exercise in fixation of mind, the focusing of attention on one single spot, the cultivation of one-pointedness. The classical expression is "guarding the One." Besides simply "to concentrate," this also means to secure the presence of the gods within the body. Just as concentration in meditation practice in general is the foundation for contemplation or higher spiritual exercises, so the rooting of the gods in Taoism leads to insight and ecstatic journeys to the otherworld.

Insight is a concept borrowed from Buddhism and coupled closely with the notion of mindfulness. Here the attention is not fixed in one single spot but kept moving, either within the body or in the outside world. Practitioners notice, literally "observe," self and others and evaluate them in a particular new way, applying the worldview of the Tao to their lives and being. They gain new insights by adapting their conscious understanding of all to the point of view of the Tao.

Ecstatic excursions are travels to the realms of the otherworld that go back originally to the journeys of shamans. Leaving the physical body behind, the soul of the meditator surges up and beyond, meeting divine powers and spirits of the stars. Through

191

traversing the far reaches of the universe, by becoming lighter and softer as they adapt to celestial modes, Taoists become one with the Tao in its own plane.

Concentrative meditation, the first of the three, centers around the One. The One in Taoist cosmology signifies the state of creation, the empty circle at the beginning of all, the point of the Great Ultimate, when the Tao is no longer utterly formless and beyond and yet has not yet begun to differentiate into the creation. It is like the Tao—sometimes described as coming from it, sometimes as its origin.

This original form of oneness, of cosmic unity at the beginning of all, is known as the Great One. The Great One is a formless omnipresent principle that adepts should focus on; it is the primordial vital energy (*yuanqi*) underlying all; it is the one single element that makes beings be what they are.

While this original unity is not manifest in the body but appears as an abstraction, as a formless state of fixed unity, it becomes attainable as the Three Ones or Three-in-One. These are three original energies of the Tao, still primordial yet already leaning more toward creation and existence. They are yin and yang and the harmony between the two; they are separate and yet one, accessible in the body as distinct energies (essence, spirit, and energy), as energy centers (the Cinnabar Fields), and as gods (the Lords Three Ones), and yet still part of the original Tao.

Realizing the One therefore means recovering the original unity of the Tao, the state of creation, the pure power of life. The One appears in the body in different forms. Historically the meditation developed from visualizations of the colored energies of the five orbs, through the identification of the True One with the center of reproductive energies and original power, to the Three Ones in Highest Clarity. By the late Tang, in adaptation of Mahāyāna thinking, the One has become identified with all.

The four texts selected below represent this historical development. First, there is the *Taiping jing shengjun bizhi* (Secret Instructions of the Holy Lord on the Scripture of Great Peace), a Tang-dynasty redaction of meditation methods according to the *Taiping jing*. Since the latter was originally a Han document, the text contains descriptions of ancient methods.

Then there is the *Baopuzi* (Book of the Master Who Embraces Simplicity), a fourth-century tract on alchemical ways to immortality that also includes meditation instructions on visualizing the True One. Third, the *Jinque dijun sanyuan zhenyi jing* (Scripture of the Three Primordial Realized Ones by the Lord Goldtower) belongs to the school of Highest Clarity. It specifies ways and means to visualize and fixate the Three Ones in the body.

Finally, the *Xuanzhu xinjing zhu* (Mysterious Pearly Mirror of the Mind) of the late Tang contains two poems on the One with commentary. It gives expression to the Mahāyāna-inspired vision of the One as all.

## 25. Lights in the Body

The earliest form of Taoist meditation, as far as the texts document it, appeared in the Han dynasty and was based on the medical analysis of the body. It was the visualization of lights of different colors within different parts of the body, matching the energies of the agents with their directions and their storage place within. This practice is later known as the "ingestion of the five sprouts," in reference to the original energy of the five directions, and plays a continued part in Highest Clarity.

It is described in a rather ancient form in the first few pages (1a–3b) of the *Taiping jing shengjun bizhi* (Secret Instructions of the Holy Lord on the Scripture of Great Peace), a short collection of meditation methods of the *Taiping jing* (Scripture of Great Peace) found in DZ 1102, fasc. 755. The *Taiping jing* is the earliest revealed Taoist scripture known from the literature. A first version of the text was presented to Emperor Cheng of the Former Han in 32 B.C.E.

Revealed by a sage known as Chijingzi or Master of Red Essence, this early document was a prognostic text, revealing the impending disaster of the world and the ways in which humanity could avoid it. It appeared at a time when the Han dynasty was failing and apocryphal scriptures and prognostications of all kinds swept the country. Around the same time, the first mass religious movement is mentioned in the histories, a salvational craze centered around the Queen Mother of the West.

No organization of any historical moment evolved from it, however, until another *Taiping jing* appeared in 140 C.E. This text, a long scripture of first 50, later 170 scrolls, predicted the end of the world and beginning of a new golden age for the year 184, the next first year of the sixty-year cycle of the traditional Chinese calendar. At this time, so the prediction said, a person clad in yellow would become emperor and the realm of Great Peace, universal harmony and cosmic openness, would be inaugurated.

Inspired by this prophesy, the followers of the scripture grew into a sizable movement in the eastern province of Qi (modern Shandong). In practice and outlook they were approximately parallel to the Celestial Masters under Zhang Daoling in southwestern Shu (modern Sichuan).

Unlike the Celestial Masters, however, the Great Peace followers took the predictions to refer to them personally and, in 184, rose in rebellion. Since they wore yellow kerchiefs to fulfill the prediction, they have become known as the Yellow Turbans. Their rebellion lasted over a decade and was bloodily put down in the end. It was the beginning of the end of the Han dynasty.

The *Taiping jing*, which inspired all this bloodshed, was ruthlessly destroyed at the time and only reassembled in the sixth century from surviving fragments and the fruitful imagination of later writers. Even the version now extant is not complete. Still, what remains can, at least in certain parts, be taken as an indication of the earliest form of organized Taoism in China.

On the history and editions of the *Taiping jing*, see Kandel 1979, Mansvelt-Beck 1980, Petersen 1989, 1990. On the worldview expressed in the scripture, see Kaltenmark 1979, Hendrischke 1991, Petersen 1990a. For an account of the beliefs, practices, and rebellion of the Yellow Turbans, see Levy 1956, Michaud 1958. On the ingestion of the five sprouts, see Robinet 1979 and 1989.

---

### *Taiping jing shengjun bizhi* (Secret Instructions of the Holy Lord on the Scripture of Great Peace)

[1a] The Holy Lord said:

The three energies together are unified in the One. There is essence, there is spirit, and there is energy. These three are originally one. They are founded in heaven and earth and form the root of all human energy. Human beings receive spirit from heaven, essence from earth, and energy from the middle harmony of heaven and earth. Joined together they are the One. Thus spirit moves by riding along on energy, while essence resides in the middle between them. The three support each other and form an integrated whole.

To pursue long life you must love energy, venerate spirit, and value essence. Human beings originally come from the energy of primordial chaos. This energy brings forth essence, which in turn gives birth to spirit. Spirit brings forth light. People are also based on the energy of yin and yang. As this energy revolves it brings forth essence. Essence in turn revolves and becomes spirit. Spirit revolves and light is born.

To pursue long life you must guard energy and harmonize spirit and essence. Never let them leave your body, but continue to think of them as joined in one. [1b] With prolonged practice your perception will become finer and subtler. Quite naturally you will be able to see within your body. The physical body will become gradually lighter, the essence more brilliant, and the light more concentrated. In your mind you will feel greatly restful, delighted and full of joy. You will go along with the energy of Great Peace. By then cultivating yourself, you can turn around and go along with all without. Within there will be perfect longevity; without there will be perfect accordance with the order of the universe. Without the exertion of any muscle you naturally attain Great Peace.

To practice guarding the light of the One, when you have not yet attained concentration, just sit quietly with your eyes closed. There is no light seen in the inner eye.

Practice guarding the One like this for a long time and a brilliant light will arise. In the radiance of this light you can see all the four directions. Following it you can travel far. Using it, you can examine your person and body with penetration. The host of spirits will assemble. Thus you can transform your physical body into pure spirit.

The practice of guarding the light of the One is the root of long life. With it, you can control the myriad spirits and go beyond all through the brilliant gateway of light.

Practice guarding the One and concentrate on the light. It will first arise like fire. Be careful not to let it slip! The light will initially be red; [2a] with prolonged practice it will turn white. After another long stretch, it will be green. As you penetrate these lights, they will come nearer and nearer and eventually merge into one brilliance. Nothing is not illumined within; the hundred diseases are driven out. Guard it and never slacken! You will go beyond the world and ascend to heaven!

In guarding the light of the One, you may see a light as bright as the rising sun. This is a brilliance as strong as that of the sun at noon.

In guarding the light of the One, you may see a light entirely green. When this green is pure, it is the light of lesser yang.

In guarding the light of the One, you may see a light entirely red, just like fire. This is a sign of transcendence.

In guarding the light of the One, you may see a light entirely yellow. When this develops a greenish tinge, it is the light of central harmony. This is a potent remedy of the Tao.

In guarding the light of the One, you may see a light entirely white. When this is as clear as flowing water, it is the light of lesser yin.

In guarding the light of the One, you may see a light entirely black. When this shimmers like deep water, it is the light of greater yin. [2b]

In guarding the light of the One, you may see your own abdomen pervaded by light while the four directions are utterly in darkness. This is the light of great harmony, the Tao of great accordance.

In guarding the light of the One, you may perceive utter darkness without and total blackness within. There is nothing to hold on to, nothing to see. This is the light of human disease, disorder, and nervousness. Take medicines and drugs to remedy this, then try to see any of the seven lights described above. To do so proceed in the following way:

1. Focus on primordial energy and non-action by meditating on your body without the One. Just imagine your body as pervaded by a white light. When the flourishing energy within is quite shapeless, there is nothing that is not done, nothing that is not known.
2. Practice emptiness, nonbeing, and spontaneity by concentrating on the center of the body. There will be a white radiance both above and below, pure like jade without the smallest flaw. This is the image of primordial energy and non-action.
3. Count and measure in deep meditation all of your body, from top to toe. The distinctions between the five fingers, the exact nature of your physical body within and without—think of them as never constant. This meditation follows emptiness and nonbeing. [3a]
4. Meditate on the gods residing in the five orbs and observe how they come and go. Carefully watch their movements. If you can put their activities into words, you can predict your good and bad fortune. This practice follows counting and measuring.
5. The Great God of the Tao: Let the gods emerge from your body and mingle with the five agents and four seasons. The green, yellow, white, and black will thus equally come to be stored within. The gods emerge and enter, come and go freely as divine officials of the five agents and four seasons. Use them to subdue the hundred evil [demons].
6. The Spirits of Sensuous Attractions: Let the gods burrow deep and rout them out from the soil. The God of the Tao urges

them all toward positive efforts; still they remain half-evil.

7. The Administration of Earth: These are the deities of heaven and earth, the four seasons, soil and grain, mountains and rivers. Worship and offer sacrifices to them all. They will let you pass through all obstacles. You can traverse wherever you wish. Evil and false [demons] will be destroyed and can never resurface. [3b]

8. Foreign Gods: These are strange and alien. Their ways cannot be controlled. They make people talk foolish things. Sometimes they are similar to the perfected; sometimes they are more like evil [demons].

9. The Ancestors: They are of pure yin quality and do not belong among the perfected. They are just ordinary ghosts and spirits.

The Tao of guarding the One applied in antiquity as much as today. There have always been various kinds of people guarding the One. Those of highest wisdom guard it and go beyond the world. Those of medium wisdom guard it and become emperors and kings, faithful servants and virtuous officials. People of lesser talents practice it and are free from joy and anger. Through it, all under heaven is entirely free from bad things.

## 26. The True One

By the fourth century, the One had become a source of magical powers. The meditation had been combined with longevity practices, rituals, and alchemy. Realizing the True One, the original unity and primordial oneness of all, meant placing oneself at the center of the universe, identifying one's physical organs with constellations in the stars. The practice led to control over all the forces of nature and beyond, especially over demons and evil forces. The One as the root of all could give in a single stroke what cumbersome visualizations of protective deities and the use of magical mirrors had done before.

The section translated below is a description of the method of visualizing the True One taken from chapter 18 on "Earthly Truth" (*Dizhen*) of the *Baopuzi neipian* (Book of the Master Who Embraces Simplicity, Inner Chapters). The text is contained in DZ 1185, fasc. 868–70 (18.1a–3b).

The *Baopuzi* is the major work of Ge Hong (261–341 c.e), from whose agnomen it takes its title. The book consists of two major parts, the "Inner Chapters" and the "Outer Chapters." While the former deals specifically with methods and secret transmissions of the immortals, the latter discusses social rules, morality, and other formal aspects of the practice.

The *Baopuzi* is an important source for early Taoism, since it is rather precisely dated to about 320 C.E and can be definitely linked with the person of Ge Hong. A member of the aristocratic clans of South China who brought forth and spread the Tao of Highest Clarity, Ge Hong describes a characteristic form of southern Taoism. This, known as the Ge-family tradition, later became instrumental in the development of the Lingbao school, founded by Ge Chaofu, Ge Hong's descendent.

In preparing this rendering, I have consulted the translation of the inner chapters in Ware 1966. For an English rendering of the outer chapters and a detailed discussion of Ge Hong's life, see Sailey 1978. For an account of various ways of guarding the One, see Kohn 1989a. On the magical mirrors used to identify demons at the time, see Kaltenmark 1974, Demieville 1987.

---

### "Earthly Truth" (*Dizhen*), from *Baopuzi neipian* (Book of the Master Who Embraces Simplicity, Inner Chapters), chap. 18.

[1a] The Master Who Embraces Simplicity says: My teacher used to say,

> If you can truly know the One,
> The myriad affairs are done!

Knowing the One means that there is not a single thing that remains unknown. Not knowing the One means that there is not a single thing that can be truly known.

The Tao arises from the One; it is honored without peer. Everything resides with the One and thereby reflects heaven, earth, and humanity. Thus we speak of the Three-in-One.

Heaven obtained the One and became pure. Earth obtained the One and became restful. Human beings obtained the One and came to life. Spirit obtained the One and became numinous. Metal sinks, feathers float, mountains loom, and rivers flow—all because of the One.

Yet—we look at it and cannot see it; we listen for it and cannot hear it. Visualize it, and it is there; startle it, and it is gone. Welcome it, and there is good fortune; turn your back on it, and there is bad luck. Preserve it, and there is prosperity without end; lose it, and life declines, energy is exhausted.

As the Venerable Lord himself said:

> Obscure it is! It is vague!
> In its midst, some appearance.
> Vague it is! It is obscure!
> In its midst, some being.

[1b] This is just it. Also, the *Immortality Scripture* has,

> If you desire to extend your life,
> Guard the One and cultivate enlightenment.
> Meditate on the One!
> In extreme hunger
> The One will give you food.
> Meditate on the One!
> In extreme thirst
> The One will give you drink.

The One possesses names and distinct garments. In the male it is 0.9 inch long; in the female, 0.6. Some locate it 2.4 inches below the navel, in the lower Cinnabar Field. Some find it in the Golden Tower of the Purple Palace below the heart, in the central Cinnabar Field. Then again people place it one inch behind the space between the eyebrows, in the Hall of Light; two inches in, in the Grotto Chamber; or three inches in, in the upper Cinnabar Field.

These things are of particular concern to the Taoists, who for generations, as they continued to transmit its names, have smeared their lips with blood to seal them to secrecy.

> The One can complete yin and bring forth yang.
> The One governs heat and cold.

> Spring obtains the One and there is sprouting.
> Summer obtains the One and there is growth.
> Fall obtains the One and there is harvesting.
> Winter obtains the One and there is storing.

> The One is great beyond even the Six Harmonies.
> The One is minute beyond a hair or a sprout.

Of old, when passing Wind Mountain on the road east to the Green Mountains, [2a] the Yellow Emperor met the Master of the

Purple Chamber and received from him the *Esoteric Writings of the Three Sovereigns*. This text enabled him to summon the myriad spirits.

On his way south to the Fujian River on the slope of Round Hill, he visited the place the hundred commanders had climbed. He gathered the efflorescence of the Ruo and Qian trees and drank the waters of the Dan and Pei rivers.

In the west, he met the Master of Middleyellow and received from him the methods of ninefold augmentation. When passing through Grotto Garden, he furthermore studied with the Master of Ample Perfection and from him received various scriptures on self-perfection.

On his way north to Flood Dam, the Yellow Emperor then climbed Creeper Mountain, where he met the Lord of Greater Wei and the Lad of the Yellow Canopy. From them he received drawings of divine mushrooms. Retracing his steps back towards the royal palace, he moreover obtained the *Divine Formula of the Golden Elixir [Cinnabar]*.

Once he also reached Mount Emei. In a jade chamber there he met the Sovereign of Heavenly Truth and asked him about the Tao of the True One.

The Sovereign said:

"Already you are the ruler over the Four Seas. Now you also want to attain long life. Isn't that rather greedy?"

Their conversation cannot be described in full, so I have provided this short part only.

Now, as methods for the attainment of long life and immortality, there is only the golden cinnabar.

For the preservation of the body and the expulsion of evil, there is only the True One. For this reason, the ancients valued it in particular.

[2b] *The Immortality Scripture* says: "The *Scripture on Ninefold Reverted Cinnabar*, the *Scripture on the Golden Fluid*, and the *Formula on Guarding the One* all reside in the Five Cities on Mount Kunlun. Engraved on gold plaques, they are stored in jade boxes. These are sealed with purple mud and bear the imprint of the seal of state.

Myself, I was so fortunate as to receive this *Formula on Guarding the One* from my teacher. It goes,

Visualize the One
In the center of the North Star and deep inside yourself:

Fig. 18. Meditating under the Protection of the Dipper. Source: *Wudou tanyi tujue*.

In front—the Hall of Light [in the head];
Behind—the Crimson Palace [in the heart].
Imposing—the Flowery Canopy [the lungs];
Lofty—the Golden Pavilion [the kidneys].
Left—the *Gang* Star;
Right—the *Kui* [of the Dipper].

Rising like a wave,
Sinking like the void itself.

Use mysterious mushrooms covering the cliffs,
Vermilion herbs growing in the thickets,
Gather white jade from the mountains,
The radiance of the sun and the moon.
Pass through fire and water!
Traverse the dark and the yellow [heaven and earth]!
Enter the maze of halls and gateways,
Full of awnings in lustrous gleam!

Helped by dragon guards, tiger watchmen,
And spirit-man attendants,
Don't relax, don't give in!
Keep the One in its place!
Don't dawdle, don't rush!
Keep the One in its chamber!
Once at ease and comfortable,
The One will never leave.

Guard the One, visualize the True One!
The spirit world will be yours to peruse!
Lessen desires, restrain your appetite!
The One will remain at rest!
Like a bare blade coming toward your neck—
Realize you live through the One alone!
Knowing the One is easy—
Keeping it forever is hard! [3a]

Guard the One and never lose it!
Human limitations will not be for you!
On land, you're free from beasts,
In water from fierce dragons!
No fear of evil sprites or phantoms,
No demon will approach, nor blade attack!

This is the Great Formula of the True One.

The Master Who Embraces Simplicity says: My teacher taught
me how, with the meditations and magical practices taught in the

various scriptures on the arts of the Tao, one can dispel evils and defend oneself. Altogether there are several thousand methods:

> Cover your shadow and become invisible;
> enter a state of suspended animation.
> Bring forth things in nine mutations;
> create twelve transformations and twenty-four life-forms.
> Meditate on the gods within the body;
> look inward to make them visible.

The techniques are virtually innumerable—all of them are superbly effective and of tremendous power.

Still, sometimes the mental creation of several thousand creatures to protect oneself is a lot of trouble. It is also a great labor for the mind. Thus, to make things easy, get to know the method of guarding the One. Then you can summarily abandon all other techniques. Thus we say:

> If you can truly know the One,
> The myriad affairs are done!

There are clear instructions on how to receive the *Formula of the True One*. The lips are smeared with the blood of a white animal. [3b] One waits for a propitious day for the actual transmission. An agreement is entered into by means of white gauze and white silver. A tally of gold is notched and split. If one speaks the *Formula* lightly or transmits it without proper precaution, the gods it invokes will not respond.

> If you can guard the One, the One will also guard you. Then:
> Bare blades find no place in your body to insert their edge.
> The hundred hazards find no place to put their bad fortune.
> In defeat you can be victorious;
> In peril you can be secure.
> Whether
> in the shrine of a demon,
> in the depth of mountains and woods,
> in a place suffering from the plague,
> among tombs and graves,
> in thickets full of tigers and wolves,
> in hovels crawling with snakes and vipers—

guard the One without slackening and the multitude of evils will remain at bay.

## 27. The Three Ones

Within the Tao of Highest Clarity, the method of guarding the One was expanded to include visualizations of the Three Ones, the deities of the three primordial energies. Parallel to the essences of the Three Luminaries, i.e., the sun, the moon, and the stars, the Three Ones are guided to descend with the help of the Northern Dipper and enter the three Cinnabar Fields in the human body. With them firmly in place and their charges, the twenty-four energies of the body, in good order, life can be extended and the body developed to a cosmic stage.

The *Jinque dijun sanyuan zhenyi jing* (Scripture of the Three Primordial Realized Ones by the Lord Goldtower), is part of the Shangqing revelations. It is contained in DZ 253, fasc. 120. The same method, transmitted by the Lord Green Lad of the Eastern Sea to Master Juan, is also found in the *Suling jing* (Scripture of Immaculate Numen; DZ 1314, fasc. 1026).

For an annotated translation of the text, see Andersen 1980. For a critical discussion of the scriptures involved, the Robinet 1984. For more on the meditation, see Robinet 1979.

---

### *Jinque dijun sanyuan zhenyi jing* (Scripture of the Three Primordial Realized Ones by the Lord of the Golden Tower)

[1a] The perfected venerate the Three Ones as ultimate perfection:

> The Upper One is the Celestial Emperor;
> he resides in the body center [in the head].
> The Middle One is the Cinnabar Sovereign;
> he resides in the Crimson Palace [in the heart].
> The Lower One is the Primordial King;
> he resides in the Yellow Court [in the abdomen].

Together they supervise the twenty-four energies of the body and bring them in accord with the twenty-four deities of Great Tenuity. Through them, these energies combine in the vapor of emptiness and develop into pure spirit.

The three primordial Ones each have a thousand chariots and ten thousand horsemen; they ride in cloud chariots with feather canopies. With this entourage they frequently enter the Purple Palace and ascend to Highest Clarity. Listed in the primordial registers, their rank is that of Perfected. They fly freely through the Nine Empyreans.

Guard them firmly, and the Three Ones will become visible for you. Once visible, a thousand chariots and ten thousand horsemen will arrive [to escort you on your heavenly journey]. You can order a feather canopy and ride in a cloud chariot. You can ascend to heaven in broad daylight and rise up to Great Tenuity.

[1b] In Great Tenuity there are twenty-four energies, intermingled in chaos. Gradually they coagulate into a single energy and begin to transform. After a certain time this energy divides and floats off. Each division still contains the twenty-four perfected of Great Tenuity. Thus the Lords Three Ones are one with and yet separate from the Tao. They transform themselves independently.

Guard the Three Ones in your body and the Lords Three Ones of Great Tenuity will descend. They will appear before you and speak to you.

[Like in Great Tenuity,] in the body there are also twenty-four perfected. They are similarly created through the division and transformation of essential radiance and pure energy. Sometimes cloudy chariots come to receive these perfected and they ascend to Great Tenuity. Together with the twenty-four deities of Great Tenuity, they then celebrate a feast in Cosmic Chaos. As their joined brilliance divides and soars up, the powers within and without are joined together. They freely enter and leave Highest Clarity, leisurely stop and rest in Great Tenuity.

While guarding the Three Ones, you should also meditate on the Grotto Chamber [in the head]. [2a] In the Grotto Chamber there are the Yellow Tower, the Purple Gate, and the Chamber of the Mysterious Essence. Here the Lords Three Ones find their repose within the body.

Meditation on both [the Grotto Chamber and the Three Ones] at the same time will make the gods visible all the sooner. Practitioners of the Grotto Chamber must by all means make guarding the Three Ones the deep root of their efforts. Practitioners of the Three Ones likewise must make meditation on the Grotto Chamber the lofty ceiling of their work.

Thus the Three Ones are necessary for both, and the Grotto Chamber does service for both. Their abodes are different, yet each is equally indispensable for the attainment of the other. By realizing only one of them, however hard your efforts, you may be able to enter Great Clarity. But your rank there will be no higher than king of immortals. You will not be able to roam through Great Tenuity or float up to Highest Clarity.

Realize therefore
the Ultimate of the Upper One, emperor among the perfected;
the Perfection of the Middle One, sovereign among the
    perfected;
the wondrousness of the Lower One, king among the
    perfected.

In antiquity,
the Heavenly Sovereign attained this Ultimate and became
    the Lord of Sovereign Ultimate;
the Earthly Sovereign attained this Perfection and became
    the Lord of Utmost Unity;
the Human Sovereign attained this Wondrousness and
    became the Lord of the Manifold Wonders.

The Three Sovereigns could become one with perfection because they guarded the Three Ones. The Three Ones accordingly did not keep their shapes hidden but showed their true ultimate form to them.

[2b] The Three Ones radiate together. Only through them are people born. Therefore students of the Tao, be they the Three Sovereigns of antiquity or ordinary mortals of today, always emphasize guarding the perfected.

To guard the perfected, keep your mind simple and your spirit concentrated. Remain in deep absorption and be receptive to the mystery. The hundred thoughts must not arise; your concentrated intention should not scatter. Then, in only three months of inner vision, with focused mind and unified spirit, a divine light will appear before you, and you will first roam freely along with it. This state is reached by keeping the thoughts focused and not letting them scatter, by pulling energy together and harmonizing it. This is the perfection that comes from simplicity! It is the swiftest path to the Tao!

On the other hand, when simplicity is scattered and perfection is lost, the superficial and false begin to take over. Then a contentious mind arises and there is disorder within. In that case, the One does not appear immediately, and the gods do not respond very soon. You may not lack the desire to make them visible and come to stay, but you are not focusing hard enough and your concentration is not penetrating. Then the first flicker arises only after several years of effort.

Therefore, be conscientious! Practice fasting of the mind and keep away from the world! Concentrate your mind hard and be without conscious plans! Even then you will still have to develop sensitivity for at least three months before you can actually face the One.

The Three Primes represent the flawless perfection of the Nine Heavens, the Upright Tao of the Most High. [3a] Through them, the Great Tao of Utmost Unity brought forth the Perfected Emperor-on-High; the Mysterious Perfection of the Upright Tao gave birth to the Great Divinity Above. The Three Primes dissolved and transformed, and the One was born.

For this reason the host of the perfected return to the One. Thus the effort of attaining the mystery is fulfilled. The One is the ancestor of the Upright Tao, the original source of primordial energy.

The way of the Three Ones is to observe the Tao as it manifests in the Three Primes. To do so, first you must embrace the numinous writings and treasure the sacred scriptures:

The formula of the first One is found in the *True Scripture of Great Pervasion.*

The formula of the second One is found in the *Wondrous Scripture of Great Being.*

The formula of the third One is found in the *Highest Scripture of Immaculate Numen.*

For this reason the Upper One, the Celestial Emperor, treasures the *True Scripture of Great Pervasion.*

The Middle One, the Cinnabar Sovereign, treasures the *Wondrous Scripture of Great Being.*

The Lower One, the Primordial King, treasures the *Highest Scripture of Immaculate Numen.*

These three scriptures contain the central essence of the Tao of Perfection. They are the supreme documents of the Three Ones.

They also contain the secret formulas of Highest Clarity. Wondrous indeed! Ineffable! The Tao is not far off!

Guarding the One brings about the appearance of the Three Ones. Once you see them, you can ask for these scriptures. [3b] You are then entitled to receive the method of guarding the Three Ones. This is the first text revealed by the Lord Goldtower from the August Heaven of Highest Clarity. It contains the wondrous formulas of the host of the perfected.

> Guard the One, and it will also guard you!
> See the One, and it will also see you!
> Coming and going—think of the One!
> A thousand troubles, a myriad affairs—think of the One!
>
> Eating or drinking—think of the One!
> Happy and joyous— think of the One!
> Sad and anguished—think of the One!
> Suffering and sick—think of the One!
>
> In danger and hardship—think of the One!
> In water and fire—think of the One!
> In a carriage, on horseback—think of the One!
> In worry and agitation—think of the One!

To "think of the One" means that you keep your attention on it from beginning to end. If your thoughts tend to be still too many, then double your concentration to think of the One!

Some people suffer because their determination is not strong. They cannot maintain the concentration for long. They know all the names of the One, but cannot guard it. When they try to guard it, they cannot keep their minds on it firmly. Instead, they wallow in personal praise, forever unable to persevere in the practice. Then of course the Three Ones depart and all good, healthy energy leaves with them. Once the good energy is gone, only bad, pathogenic energy is left. When there is nothing but pathogenics in the body, why, then the day of death is close.

Some common people study the Tao, but only look for the fleeting and glamorous. They have no faith in the value of the perfected. [4a] In the beginning, they may have the will for it, but soon they deviate and end up in disgrace. This is because their determination is not firmly set. Thus pathogenic energy enters their bodies.

All rules about guarding the One warn sternly against lack of concentration. Yet even if there is concentration, there may be a lack of perseverance. And even if there is perseverance, there may be a lack of intensity. In any such case, the Three Ones will depart. Then the body will be an empty house without a master. With such a disaster, how can you last long?

Energy assembles and becomes essence. Essence is set in motion and becomes spirit. Spirit is transformed and becomes the immortal embryo. The embryo rises up and turns into a realized being. This realized being ascends and becomes an infant. He, in turn, is the perfected within.

Heaven has Three Mysteries: the sun, the moon, and the stars. They contain the Three Essentials. These help people to attain long life.

Human beings have Three Treasures: the three cinnabar fields. They contain the Three Perfected. These help people attain long life.

Thus the *Scripture of Numinous Treasure* says, "The Three Essentials in heaven, the Three Perfected on earth—these Three Treasures endure forever." This is just it.

The Upper Cinnabar Field is located between the eyebrows inside the head.

The Middle Cinnabar Field is the Crimson Palace in the heart.

The Lower Cinnabar Field is located in the adomen, three inches below the navel. Together these are the Three Cinnabar Fields.

The Upper Cinnabar Field is the residence of the Infant.

The Middle Cinnabar Field is the residence of the Perfected.

The Lower Cinnabar Field is the residence of the Immortal Embryo.

[4b] As regards the Upper Cinnabar Field, one inch between the eyebrows towards the back of head, there is the Hall of Light. One inch further inside lies the Grotto Chamber. Yet another inch reveals the Niwan Palace in the Cinnabar Field. All these are located along one line toward the back of the head. The Niwan Palace in the Cinnabar Field is perfectly square and measures one inch on each side. From here, purple energy surges up into heaven, radiating as far as ninety thousand miles.

Located in the very center of the head, the Niwan Palace is covered by the seven stars of the Northern Dipper. The Dipper's bowl is above the center, while the handle points forward and out. It changes in size and tends to blur, so always actualize it firmly in your mind.

The Infant of the Upper Prime resides right beneath the Dipper. He is also called the god of Mystery-Coagulated Heaven and known as the first among the Three Primes. He holds the position of Celestial Emperor of the Niwan Palace.

An imperial minister faces him from his right. He is the transformed spiritual essence of the teeth, tongue, and brain. He is called the god of Initial-Force Essence and known as born from harmony and mystery. He is properly invested as imperial minister.

The Celestial Emperor and his imperial minister together rule in the Niwan Palace. Both are dressed in scarlet robes, adorned with heavy embroidery. [5a] They look like newborn babies.

The Celestial Emperor holds the Highest Clarity Talisman of the Divine Tiger, while his minister has the *True Scripture of Great Pervasion* in his hand. Sitting, they either both look out or face each other.

On the inside, they watch over the Niwan Palace and guard the realms of the face, eyes, mouth, tongue, teeth, ears, nose, and hair. On the outside, they scare away the manifold demons and evil spirits of the Six Heavens. Once every five days, the three spirit souls go to pay them homage and receive instructions.

The heart is the Middle Cinnabar Field. It is called the Crimson Palace and located in the center of the heart. It is perfectly square and measures one inch on each side. From here, red vapors surge up into heaven, radiating as far as thirty thousand miles. It transforms itself and tends to blur, so always visualize it firmly in your mind.

The Perfected of the Middle Prime resides here. He is also called the god of the Spirit-Revolving Pearl and known as the master of Southern Cinnabar. He holds the position of Cinnabar Sovereign of the Crimson Palace.

An auxiliary minister stands to his right. He is the transformed spiritual essence of the four viscera. Once in the Crimson Palace, he is invested as auxiliary minister. [5b] He is called the God of Radiance Solid and known as the master of the four numinous beasts.

The Cinnabar Sovereign and his auxiliary minister together rule in the crimson palace. Both are dressed in robes of vermilion brocade. They look like newborn babies.

Fig. 19. Visualizing the Three Ones. Source: *Baosheng jing*.

The Cinnabar Sovereign holds the planet Mars in his left hand and the *Scripture of Great Protection* in his right. The auxiliary minister holds the *Wondrous Scripture of Great Being* and the eight luminaries. Sitting, they either both look out or face each other.

On the inside, they watch over the realms of the muscles, bones, five orbs, blood, and flesh. On the outside, they scare away the harmful effects of the manifold pathogenic influences.

Nurture their radiance and keep them at peace, then you may reach long life and eternal vision and fly off as an immortal into the Great Empyrean.

Once every three days the three spirit souls and seven material souls go to pay them homage and receive instructions.

Three inches below the navel is the Lower Cinnabar Field. This is the Gate of Life. The Immortal Embryo of the Lower Prime resides here. It is perfectly square and measures one inch on each side. From here, white energy surges up into heaven, radiating as far as seventy thousand miles. It changes in size and tends to blur, so always visualize it firmly in your mind.

The Lower Prime is also called the God of Beginning-Radiance Essence [6a] and known as the Glory of Primordial Yang. He holds the position of Primordial King of the Yellow Court.

A guardian minister stands to his right. He is the transformed spiritual vapor of essence and energy, saliva and body fluids. Once in the Cinnabar Field, he is invested as guardian minister. He is called the God of Light Returned-Above and also known as the mystery of valley's depth.

The Primordial King and his guardian minister together rule in the Lower Cinnabar Field. Both are dressed in robes of yellow, embroidered gauze. They look like newborn babies.

The Primordial King of the Yellow Court holds the planet Venus in his left hand and the *Scripture of the Golden Truth of the Stars Above* in his right. His minister holds the *Highest Scripture of Immaculate Numen* and the *Nine-Garden Talisman of the Light of Life*. Sitting, they either both look out or face each other.

On the inside, they watch over the realms of the four limbs, the body fluids and the blood, the intestines, stomach, and bladder. On the outside, they dispel all calamity and misfortune and get rid of the manifold evil influences. Three times a day the three spirit souls and seven material souls go to pay them homage and receive instructions.

How to Guard the Three Ones

On the day of Spring Beginning, at midnight, sit upright facing east. [6b] Exhale nine times and swallow the saliva thirty-six times.

Then visualize the seven stars of the Northern Dipper as they slowly descend toward you until they rest above you. The Dipper should sit straight above your head, with its handle pointing forward, due east. Visualize it in such a way that the stars Yin Essence and True One are just above the top of your head. The two stars Yang Brightness and Mystery Darkness should be further up. Also,

Yin Essence and Yang Brightness should be toward your back, while True One and Mystery Darkness are in front. Though the image may be blurred at first, concentrate firmly and focus it in position.

Then concentrate on the venerable Lords Three Ones. They appear suddenly in the bowl of the Dipper above your head. Before long their three ministers arrive in the same way. After a little while, observe how the six gods ascend together to Mystery Darkness, from where they move east. When they reach the Heavenly Pass, they stop.

Together they turn and face your mouth. See how the Upper Prime supports the upper minister with his hand; how the Middle Prime supports the middle minister; and how the Lower Prime supports the lower minister.

Then take a very deep breath and hold it for as long as you can. [7a] The Upper Prime and his minister follow this breath and enter your mouth. Once inside they ascend and go to the Niwan Palace in the head.

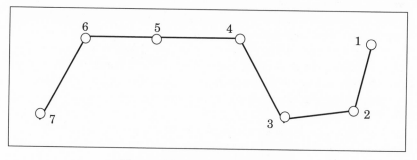

Fig. 20. The Stars of the Dipper.

1  Yang Brightness
2  Yin Essence
3  True One
4  Mystery Darkness
5  Cinnabar Prime
6  North Culmen
7  Heavenly Pass

Take another breath as deep as you can. The Middle Prime and his minister follow this breath and enter your mouth. Once inside they descend and go to the Crimson Palace in the heart.

Take yet another breath as deep as you can. The Lower Prime and his minister follow this breath and enter your mouth. Once inside they descend and go to the Lower Cinnabar Field in the abdomen.

Next, visualize the star Heavenly Pass and bring it down to about seven inches before your mouth. While this star stands guard right before the mouth, the Three Ones firmly enter into their bodily palaces.

All this complete, concentrate again on the Perfected to make sure they are all at rest in their residences. From then on, whether sitting or lying down, always keep them firmly in your mind.

At any point during the practice, if concerns and desires arise in your mind, it will push to pursue them. Then, however much the mind strains to break free, make sure to keep it firmly concentrated on the Three Ones. See that you remain at peace and in solitude! Also, if your bedroom is quiet enough, you may continue the practice well into the day.

To visualize the Three Ones on the day Summer Beginning, face south. Then proceed as outlined above.

To visualize the Three Ones on the day Fall Beginning, face west. Then proceed as outlined above.

[7b] To visualize the Three Ones on the day Winter Beginning, face north. Then proceed as outlined above.

Once you have fixated the Three Ones firmly in their residences, the practice is complete. To conclude, quietly recite the following incantation:

> All five directions the Northern Dipper rules—
> The gods arrive through the seven stars.
>
> The Three Lords come through transformation,
> Summoned by the Purple Court above.
> The Six Gods arrive in downward flight,
> To reach my Three Palaces of Cinnabar.
>
> With them I join the Emperor-on-High,
> Enter the Yellow Calm below!
> Protected by the Perfected of the heavens,
> I call the six gods of time and those of space.
>
> Immortal, may I soon float up with them,
> Ride on the vapor of the Three Clarities!
> My four limbs strong and ever more refined,
> May my five orbs forever be alive!

## 28. One in All

Under the ever-growing influence of Mahāyāna Buddhism, in Taoism too *samsāra*, the world as we know it, was identified with *nirvāna*, the realization of the Tao. Practice in this context, although still necessary, was redefined as nonpractice, noncultivation, an emergence of a reality already there rather than an active progress, a pursuit. By the late Tang dynasty, guarding the One thus was no longer a gradual process of recovery of primordiality lost, but a form of noncultivation of non-action (see Kohn 1989a).

The *Xuanzhu xinjing zhu* (Mysterious Pearly Mirror of the Mind), contained with commentary in DZ 574, fasc. 320 (and, with longer commentary, in DZ 575, fasc. 320), consists of two sets of poems revealed by Jiao Shaoxuan, the wife of a certain Lu Chui. Jiao was originally an immortal from the Heaven of Highest Clarity who came to reside in Fujian and be married to Lu. After fulfilling her earthly lifespan, she ascended back, leaving only an empty coffin behind. Her husband, finally realizing her celestial nature, begged her for instructions on the Tao. She returned once more and revealed the poems. They were published, with annotation, in 817.

---

### *Xuanzhu xinjing zhu* (Mysterious Pearly Mirror of the Mind

GUARDING THE ONE

> Attainment of the Prime of the One
> Is not a gift from Heaven.
> Realization of Great Nonbeing
> Is the state of highest immortality.
>
> Light restrained, a hidden brilliance,
> The body one with nature:
> There is true peace, won but not pursued.
> Spirit kept forever at rest.
>
> In serenity and beauty: this is perfection!
> Body and inner nature, hard and soft,
> All is but cinnabar vapor, azure barrens.
> One of the highest sages—
>
> Only after a hundred years
> The tomb is discovered empty.

## Selected Commentary

The One is without form, the beginning energy of heaven and earth, the mysterious prime of life and its transformations. As Laozi puts it, "The Tao is the prime of life."

This then is Cosmic Chaos, the initial stage before all divided, a time of obscurity and darkness without name, without appearance.

Laozi also says: "It is self-so. None knows its after; none knows its before."

Its height cannot be reached; its depth cannot be fathomed. Containing yin and emanating yang, it gives brightness to the three luminaries. So huge, it embraces heaven and earth; so minute, it fits into a blade of grass.

Whoever in the world realizes it can be said to know the Prime of the One.

To attain the Prime of the One, one must be firm even in hardship and live in solitary serenity. As one darkens the mind and refines the body, naturally spirit becomes more intense and the body more open.

Eventually bones and flesh are blended with the dark mystery; they transform to pure primordiality. Shaking off the old body like a cicada sheds its skin, you can be in several places at the same time. Leave being and enter nonbeing; sit in one moment and be standing in the next; fly all over the great void.

Once you know the One, guard it steadfastly and daily you will see the wonderful results—like an echo following a sound, like a shadow following a shape.

Once you attain the Prime of the One, embrace the Prime and guard the One; you will find your Tao complete and your spirit powerful. You can then shake off your body and ascend yonder—to Jade Clarity, to the Center of Great Mystery.

When the Tao is complete and the cosmic body attained, in your body there is no more outward force to pursue things outside; in your mind no more cunning wisdom to develop within.

All your mind is then merged with Cosmic Chaos, free from the mind of the self. All your body is then merged with Cosmic Chaos, free from the body of the self.

Just remember: as long as there is still ordinary body or mind, you cannot realize the spirit in its full power.

The fully powerful spirit and the perfected cosmic body should be deeply at rest in the womb within. The womb in men is the Ocean of Energy; in women it is the Ocean of Blood. Spirit and body should be at rest there.

As the Tao is complete, you become a perfected. You attain the cosmic body of no-body. Then the physical structure and inner nature are both hard and soft. They are soft because none in the world is softer than energy, is weaker than the Tao. They are hard because they can encompass heaven and earth and penetrate the myriad beings, even hard things such as metal and stone.

Thus you can enter the Cinnabar Vapor, the Azure Barrens, the reaches of the Three Clarities, the realm of the Jade Capital and the Golden Tower. Here the rulers and sages of Heaven have their residences—by guarding the Prime of the One you will be one of them.

"After a hundred years, the tomb is discovered empty." This is the pinnacle of the Tao, the crowning achievement of all the immortals.

Who realizes this spontaneously knows the deepest depths and farthest distances of the universe, yet would not want to display such brilliance. People of the world thus see and hear only some vague outer manifestations, some marginal ornaments that may serve as points of comparison.

Do you really think an immortal strides on a dragon, rides on the clouds, ascends to heaven in broad daylight, and that is all?

No, spirit immortals prefer to erase their traces and hide their transformations. For this reason, they leave behind some medicine or a staff in place of a corpse; they use a sword or their slippers to hide the way in which they shed their mortal skins.

By guarding the Prime of the One, this realization will soon be yours!

THE GREAT TAO OF GUARDING THE ONE

The Tao is non-action, yet does not do nothing.
Purity of mind does not come from knowledge and wisdom.
What is knowledge? What is purity?
Knowledge depends on wisdom. Purity is freedom in going
    along.
Going along, not following: this is pervasion of mind.

Pervade the One and all affairs are done!
The One is the root, affairs are its gate.
Affairs return to the One, but the One exists in
    permanence.
It exists, yet is not there—so we borrow a term and speak
    of "guard."
Just guard emptiness and nonbeing, and you will live
    forever!

### Selected Commentary

Non-action means to guard emptiness and nonbeing and the spontaneous flow of life. Be vague and obscure, pliant and vacant [like the Tao], never attached to even a single thing but totally concentrated in the mind.

The *Zhuangzi* describes this state: "Smash up your limbs and body! Drive out your perception and understanding! Cast off your physical form! Get rid of all wisdom! Thus you can join the great pervasion of all!"

In this state, within you won't know that there is this self. Without you will never be aware that there are heaven and earth. Serene and placid, you cannot hear any more sounds, cannot see any more shape. This is true non-action.

Although the Tao is in non-action, that does not mean that it does not do anything. "Do not do nothing" means that even if you guard non-action, there are still things that you will do. Also, it means that unless you actively "do" this Tao, the Tao will not be there for you. And then all the various things outside will combine to destroy your essence and spirit, ruin your inner nature and destiny.

Independent of whether you are poor and humble or rich and noble, you will not even notice how your body and spirit are pursued and plagued by outside things and affairs—until you grow weak and old and sick.

Thus the *Scripture of Western Ascension* says: "People usually consider satisfaction through sounds and sights the highest possible happiness. They do not know that satisfaction through sounds and sights is the cause of all misfortune. The sage, on the other hand, never desires anything and recovers complete freedom from desires."

It also says, "The reason why people of the world undervalue life and die early is not that heaven and earth kill them or demons and spirits do them any harm. All their misfortunes are entirely caused by themselves. They come to life, and their lives become too rich. Only those who are free of life can thus be wise to properly nourish life."

The perfect Tao is continuous spontaneous accordance. It does not come from anything or anywhere. It just is. No one knows why or how. You must merely realize non-action in the middle of plain spontaneous so-being, and spirit pervasion will be yours.

The way the Venerable Lord taught people to cultivate the Tao is the cultivation of the mind. To cultivate the mind is to cultivate the Tao. Now, the mind is the residence of spirit within the human body. When the mind remains empty and in non-action, then it will, after some time, begin to radiate with the Tao. Once there is this radiance of the Tao, the spirit will be all-pervasive [omnipresent and full of supernatural powers].

Realize this spirit pervasion and there is nothing that is not pervaded!

The Venerable Lord told Yin Xi, the Guardian of the Pass: "Just know how to guard the One, and the myriad affairs are done!"

How much more should this be the case when spirit pervades the One? By embracing the Prime and guarding the One, the self joins the shapeless and becomes one with emptiness, nonbeing, and the spontaneous flow of life. Shape without shape, it consists of nothing but the one original energy. Thus the myriad affairs are done.

Through guarding the One in all affairs, all efforts and merits return to the one original energy. Then the entire self becomes one with emptiness, nonbeing, and the spontaneous flow of life. Shapeless, this one original energy exists permanently. Yet it is not really there to be grasped. Thus we use the term "guard" to describe the practice.

Guard emptiness, nonbeing, and the spontaneous flow of life, let your body and spirit become one with the Tao, and you can live forever as an immortal.

# Chapter Eight

## INSIGHT PRACTICE

Following the successful concentration of the mind and full control over its movement, Taoists proceed to turn their focused attention on the analysis of self and world. This form of meditation, commonly described in the texts as "observation," is inspired by Buddhism and very close to its insight meditation or *vipaśyanā*. In fact, the same term is used for both in classical Chinese: *guan*, a word defined in the earliest dictionaries as "to scrutinize," "to examine carefully."

The technique involves an active, conscious introspection of one's own body and mind, reorganizing one's ideas of self to cosmic dimensions. Where a single body and mind had been struggling for control before, now the self is raised to the level of heaven and earth, raised through yang and nourished by yin, helped and guarded by the gods and spirits, patterned and working in perfect accordance with the five agents and their various correlates.

Observation, unlike concentration, can never be free from religious doctrine. Observation means to take in objects and experiences and interpret them in a new way, to gain new insights in a way that is clearly outlined by the religion.

Various levels and stages of Taoist observation can be distinguished. First practitioners are instructed to focus on the energies moving around the body and see the constantly moving nature of everything in the world. They are to realize themselves as impermanent, as part of a continuous chain of transformations of the Tao, mere particles in a huge universal rhythm of becoming and passing away, becoming and passing away.

Next, they are led to the insight that unlike over their conscious attention and concentration, they have not a trace of control over this continuously developing mass of energies. Neither their bodies nor their selves nor anything in the world is subject to their

221

say-so; nothing whatsoever can be done actively to stop or speed the unfolding of the Tao.

At the same time, however, all actions cause good or bad fortune, depending on whether or not they harmonize with the flow that nature is taking at any given point. Taoists have to learn how to maintain a high awareness of their actions together with a strong sense of detachment and equanimity. They have to be "without feelings."

Once detached from the self and the world, practitioners can start to be joyful and happy about the workings of the Tao in and around them. They gain new insights into their bodies as replicas of the universe, understand the workings of the body gods and of pure spirit as the activity of the Tao within, and find a cosmic freedom by letting themselves go with the current, with the flow.

This in turn leads to a fuller sense of oneness, of union with the Tao. Merging completely with the forces of the universe, practitioners lose themselves, forget themselves, become one with cosmic emptiness and nonbeing. The personal self and body are lost, a cosmic identity of the Tao is found and the immortal self emerges.

Observation is thus a guide to new insights into the self and the world. It is a highly complex process that is sometimes described in very abstract and sophisticated terms. It is often found as an outline of what insights adepts are supposed to gain through their training. Mostly, however, observation is described as a practical way of dealing with life and its various situations from the point of view of the Tao.

The selections below reflect these various dimensions of observation. There is first the philosophical analysis of "Two Kinds of Observation" taken from the seventh-century encyclopedia *Daojiao yishu* (The Pivotal Meaning of the Taoist Teaching). This work, strongly inspired by Buddhist Mādhyamika, distinguishes several levels and types of observation, leading practitioners from the ordinary truth of the world to the absolute truth of enlightenment.

Second, the *Jinyi huandan yinzheng tu* (Illustrated Progress to the Golden Fluid and Reverted Cinnabar), a theoretical outline of observation according to inner alchemy, is dated to the thirteenth century. Here, self and world are understood as part of several energies and forces, freely floating about and interacting with each other in complex ways.

Both the third and fourth selections describe the more concrete dimensions of the practice, answering the question what a life in the Tao would be like in its most practical terms. The section on

"True Observation" of Sima Chengzhen's *Zuowang lun* (Discourse on Sitting in Oblivion) of the eighth century describes how a Taoist of the right insight deals with sensual dependence, poverty, sickness, and death. It is written in a direct and engaging manner, full of concrete examples, not unlike the *Zhuangzi*, from which six stories are translated as a fourth selection.

## 29. Two Kinds of Observation

Under the influence of Buddhist Mādhyamika, Taoist observation reached its full philosophical height, formulated in the early Tang especially by the school of Twofold Mystery. This school of interpretation of the *Daode jing* describes the attainment of the Tao in the two stages of "mysterious and again mysterious" or "forgetting and again forgetting." In this it applies the Buddhist theory of the two truths.

The first stage leads from the wordly truth of ordinary people to the absolute truth realized by the sages, or from being to emptiness. At this stage practitioners observe that all things are ultimately empty because they do not have solidity, an intrinsic permanent nature of their own.

In the second stage both ordinary thinking and the vision of emptiness are "forgotten," i.e., understood as yet another form of comprehended, formulated, solidified truth. Absolute truth at this stage is redefined as complete nonduality: neither being nor emptiness, neither being nor nonbeing. This, however, coincides with the simultaneous existence of both: both being and nonbeing.

This system applies the "Four Propositions" of the Mādhyamika:

> affirmation of being;
> affirmation of nonbeing;
> negation of both, being and nonbeing;
> affirmation of both, being and nonbeing.

Taoists use this scheme as well as the characteristic syntax of the Mādhyamika to their own ends. It is very evident in the following description of the "Two Kinds of Observation." It is taken from the *Daojiao yishu* (The Pivotal Meaning of the Taoist Teaching), a highly Buddhist-inspired encyclopedia of the seventh century, contained (with some lacunae) in DZ 1129, fasc. 762–63. The translation covers section 17 (5.3b–6a), which seems to be incomplete.

For a discussion of observation in Taoism, see Kohn 1989b. For a summary of the worldview of the *Daojiao yishu*, see Kohn 1992: 149–54. On Twofold Mystery, see Robinet 1977, Kohn 1992. For Chinese Mādhyamika, see Robinson 1967.

---

## "Two Kinds of Observation" (*Erguan*), from *Daojiao yishu* (The Pivotal Meaning of the Taoist Teaching)

[3b] The two kinds of observation are the deep realms of concentration and insight, the mysterious gateway to emptiness and being. They are used to harmonize the mind and swiftly achieve the perfection of Twofold Mystery. Through these observations, agitation and worry will finally return to the shores of the twofold truth of the Tao. Pursuing them, one will certainly attain perfection; following them, one will certainly find liberation from all dharmas. This, then, is their perfection.

To explain: The two kinds of observation are the observation of energy and the observation of 'spirit.' The two terms 'energy' and 'spirit' refer to the inner constituents body and mind.

The body belongs to the realm of being; it is subject to the delusions of the World of Form. Thus the term 'energy' is used to refer to concentration.

The mind belongs to the realm of nonbeing; it is difficult to fathom. Thus the term 'spirit' is used to refer to the insight of emptiness.

The *Scripture of Original Time* says:

"Observation of energy and spirit means concentration and insight. 'Energy' refers to the images of energy. In observing energy, one visualizes the Three Ones. The wondrous energy and the mysterious images duly come to reside in the body.

" 'Spirit' on the other hand, refers to that which is without bent and cannot be fathomed. It appears in two different kinds of insight—that of illumination and that of emptiness. Both are impossible to think of. In a myriad ways without bent, spirit's principles are complete and unfathomable."

To summarize thus what observation means, we can say that it is to meditate and examine. In other words, one meditates and visualizes the wondrous One, on the one hand, and examines and inspects what lies beyond all phenomena, on the other.

[4a] The *Scripture on the Practice of Observation* says:

"In proper observation of all dharmas, neither attract nor reject, neither move nor rest! Enter the wondrous gateway to the One and reach the higher stages: the stage of nonbeing, the stage of no-stages, and the stage of pure virtue."

Observation of energy lies basically in properly observing the body; it consists of making it tranquil. This is concentration. The word has two meanings: first, it refers to the expedient method practiced before observation; second, it indicates the actual practice of the observation of being. All this, then, is the observation of energy.

Observation of spirit, on the other hand, is the observation of nonbeing. The *Scripture on the Practice of Observation* states it clearly:

"Observation of spirit is cultivated outside the world; observation of energy is practiced within."

To clarify the two kinds of observation of energy and spirit, one must thus distinguish between concentration and insight. This distinction, in turn, is based on the difference between body and mind and therefore refers immediately to the two realms of being and emptiness.

Observation of energy is concentration; although it pervades both emptiness and being, it is primarily concerned with the wondrous realm of being.

Observation of spirit is insight; although it pervades both being and nonbeing, it mainly deals with true emptiness.

The distinction between the two kinds of observation in terms of emptiness and being as well as the differentiation between insight and concentration are only expedient means of the masters of insight. Although it does not refer to any outer reality, it is yet of great importance in understanding observation.

In our practice, we thus first differentiate different kinds, then integrate all into the one true observation. [4b] How is this done? When all the myriad actions are equally subject to insight, then there is only the observation of emptiness. This, in turn, is the insight of true emptiness.

Realize also that in concentration and insight, one does not reach enlightenment and perfection of body and mind through the two major kinds of observation alone. Rather, there are five different sets of three levels of observation.

One such set of three is:

1. Observation of apparent existence.
2. Observation of real existence.
3. Observation of partial emptiness.

These, in fact, refer to the practitioners of the Lesser Vehicle, who are as yet unable to awaken to the full mystery. First, as long as one does not abandon all analysis and does not realize emptiness, one still accepts reality and abandons emptiness.

Then one may come to accept emptiness and abandon reality, or one may even accept emptiness and at the same time abandon it. This brings one to the two higher states and opens up the liberation through emptiness. Thus there are first these three levels.

As concerns the observation of apparent existence, 'apparent' means having a temporary appearance, whereas 'existence' refers to the embodiment of things. If you wish to gain a proper insight into observation of the host of living beings, it is very difficult to make yourself empty, but it is rather easy to make beings empty.

For example, when it comes to understanding the fact that the five aggregates [matter, sensations, perception, mental formations, and consciousness] make up oneself, how could one know which aggregate is oneself? Thus the *Zhuangzi* says: "The hundred joints, the nine orifices, the six repositories all come together and exist here. But which part should I feel closest to?"

If you don't feel very close to any one part as the one that constitutes yourself, you have begun to understand the emptiness of apparent existence. [5a] This is what we call observation of apparent existence.

Observation of real existence deals with the substance-reality of everything. Knowing already that all apparent existence is empty, you must now observe and examine the substance-reality underlying it. What actually is its substance-reality? Where does it come from? It must arise from something else. But if we assume that it arises from something else, we come to an endless chain of origination.

If we assume, on the other hand, that this chain is not endless, then substance-reality must ultimately come from emptiness. If we now assume that it arises from emptiness, we must try to grasp this emptiness. But as emptiness is nothing in itself, how can we say that it brings forth something? This way we understand that real existence cannot be accepted either. This is the observation of real existence.

Observation of partial emptiness: Here 'partial' means not yet proper, whereas 'emptiness' refers to a free and pervading way of seeing. This is practiced in order to get rid of all the numerous diseases of attachment which all beings are suffering. Thereby one gradually realizes true emptiness.

The *Scripture of Ascension to the Mystery* says:

"To renounce being, place it first above nonbeing. To embody nonbeing, emphasize the nonexistence of nonbeing."

Followers of the Lesser Vehicle merely stick to the teaching but cannot reach the remote original mind. Thus they continue to be involved with feelings and see the state of emptiness only partially. [5b] Therefore we know that the viewpoint of partial emptiness of the Lesser Vehicle is not yet proper observation.

Proper observation means to observe emptiness as emptiness and through emptiness. Only thus can one see the true emptiness of all apparent and real existence. This is why we speak of emptiness. As there is nothing beyond the apparent and real, where would emptiness come to reside? Thus we know that emptiness is empty in itself.

As the *Scripture of Original Time* says:

"True emptiness is indeed empty; empty emptiness is indeed empty."

Another set of three levels of observation consists of the following:

1. Observation of being.
2. Observation of nonbeing.
3. Observation of the Middle Way.

Observation of being refers to seeing the solidity of material existence; thus it is called observation of being. Concentrate deeply on the solidity of matter. Soon you will attain the nonbeing of all solidity. This is the same as the nonbeing of non-solidity. With no solidity at all, how can one concentrate on solidity?

Therefore the method is not to deny solidity and thus to come to non-solidity, but rather to take solidity and make it into non-solidity, to take non-solidity and make it into solidity. Doing so, you realize that what is really not solid only appears to be solid. Thus you know that what does really not exist only appears to exist.

Who practices this observation duly attains the gateway to complete observation. Then there will be no more solidity or being. This, then, is the observation of non-solidity of being. How can it not be all-pervasive?

With this you will soon see that all constructed mental states and projections of being are equally without any solidity. [6a] As you thus realize that all constructed mental projections of being are deeply unfathomable, you can truly pervade them all.

How, then, does this relate to the three levels? Embodying what is not real, there is emptiness. If it is not not apparent, then we say there is being.

If there is being, then there is both emptiness and non-emptiness. Therefore there is neither being nor emptiness. This is the level of the Middle Way.

Once constructed mental projections come to see this, your observation will follow suit. Then, while we still use language to refer to these things, we speak of observation.

Observation of nonbeing refers to seeing the non-solidity of nonbeing. This observation speaks about nonbeing being without solidity. Cutting off this linguistic help to understanding, one can never attain it. However, as long as we use this linguistic help, nonbeing remains an entity and is therefore solidity.

Pondering this, you realize that there is no way. It is neither solidity nor non-solidity, whether you take non-solidity and make it into solidity or take solidity and make it into non-solidity. Thus you know that solidity is also non-solidity, that therefore non-solidity is also nonbeing. Through this observation you can return to the gateway of completion [of the Tao].

As you observe the gateway of completion, you can realize all the three levels. How is that?

Nonbeing is also not nonbeing. On this level it is like being. Then again nonbeing is neither nonbeing nor not nonbeing. On this level it is like nonbeing. When it is like nonbeing, it is not being. When it is like being it is not like nonbeing. [6b] Both like nonbeing and not being as well as like being and not nonbeing—this is the level of the Middle Way.

Observation of the Middle Way refers to the proper embodiment of the latter. Both being and nonbeing are thus at the same time neither being nor nonbeing. This realization is the observation of the Middle Way.

Observe constructed mental projections: they are like this. Observe the physical structure of the body: it is like this. In its farthest sense, this observation looks neither at the origin of all nor at being or nonbeing in particular.

Being and nonbeing are not. Not being there, they are yet not not there. The ultimate meaning of the three levels of this observation lies just in this. Speaking about it in terms of center and sides, one could say that both being and nonbeing are the sides, while neither being nor nonbeing are the center. [This is the observation of the Middle Way.]

## 30. Energies and Elixirs

Observation according to inner alchemy sees the world less in terms of emptiness and being than through the looking-glass of energies and elixirs, metals and trigrams.

A development of the Song dynasty, inner alchemy integrates the various strands of the tradition. It makes much use of the terminology and system of the *Yijing* (Book of Changes) and applies the process of elixir concoction in operative alchemy to describe the inner spiritual development of the adepts. Its language is intentionally confusing to ensure the secrecy and integrity of the transmission.

Bound to the confidence between master and disciple, there are many different systems and styles in inner alchemy. In its most general, the process can be described as consisting of three basic stages: first, the mutation of essence to energy; second, the development from energy to spirit; and third, the merging of spirit with emptiness or the Tao.

Essence, of course is fundamentally sexual energy, located in the lower Cinnabar Field and aroused by intercourse. In inner alchemy this is reverted back to its original form, i.e., the subtler energy that flows throughout the body, by avoiding its downward movement and bringing it back upwards through massages and meditations. This leads to the development of a concentrated and purified form of essence, the pearl of immortality, the first grain of the cinnabar elixir, the first trace of the golden fluid.

In a second stage, this pearl is developed into an immortal embryo through the union of the adept's inner yin and yang forces. At this stage a set of identifications takes place:

yang = heart = fire = Li (Fire-Trigram) = pure lead;
yin = kidneys = water = Kan (Water-Trigram) = pure mercury.

In meditation as in the process of operative alchemy, these energies are revolved again and again, following an exact time schedule and being properly positioned according to the traditional stems and branches of the calendar and the compass. The cycle that is established within the body at this point includes not only the spine and breastbone, but also leads through the five orbs. It is known as the macrocosmic orbit.

At this stage the pure power of yin and yang is extracted from the various energies, and symbolized as the trigrams of Heaven and Earth (Qian and Kun). These are at the root of creation, to which the adept is gradually proceeding.

In the third and last stage, the immortal embryo, still semi-material, is transformed into the pure spirit body of the immortals, the body of pure original yang (not yang as opposed to yin), of life as such (no longer of life as opposed to death). The child is born, completed and begins an independent existence. It can ascend to the heavens and will be the form in which the practitioner survives forever.

The *Jinyi huandan yinzheng tu* (Illustrated Progress to the Golden Fluid and Reverted Cinnabar), found in DZ 151, fasc. 68, outlines this process. The text was edited by Wang Jingxuan in 1234 and has a preface by Longmeizi, dated to 1218. It belongs to the southern tradition of Song-dynasty inner alchemy in the environment of Bai Yuchan (fl. 1194–1229). Bai was born on Hainan Island, spent his youth wandering around famous mountains, and eventually settled on Mount Wuyi in Fujian. He may have been received by the emperor in  the late 1220s. Most of his writings, compiled by his students, are dated to 1212–21. The text here fits well into the known pattern of his work. It consists of twenty poems, the first seven of which are rendered below.

For a survey of inner-alchemical practices, see Needham 1983. On the philosophical understanding and theoretical system of inner alchemy, see Robinet 1989. Translations and discussions of inner-alchemical texts are found in Wilhelm 1962, Lu 1970, Baldrian-Hussein 1984, Cleary 1987, 1991, and 1992.

---

*Jinyi huandan yinzheng tu* (**Illustrated Progress to the Golden Fluid and Reverted Cinnabar**)

THE ORIGIN

Dark and obscure and without light, before even Great
    Ultimate,
The whirlwind moves with violence to bring forth true lead.
All, reaching tranquility, returns and moves again—
Thus from the limitless is born that which limits has.

The one energy emerges as the first sign from the empty;
The two forms, soon after, revolve in its firm center.
Life after life, change after change, it continues without end.
Like magic, in the cauldron there's another grotto heaven.

THE NEED TO AWAKEN

Your cast-off bones, as you look back, are piled up mountain-
    high;
The tears you shed, they now amount to the four seas'
    expanse.
The world continues to decline, running toward collapse,
The life of man, a snap it lasts, and what joy does it have?

Fig. 21. The Two Trigrams. Source: *Jinyi huandan yinzheng tu.*

Become a man, be born a woman—through a thousand
transformations.
Emerge with horns, be thickly furred—a myriad different
shapes.
Unless you do awaken to this life's truth right now,
Then, when this life is over, what will you become?

## THE TRIGRAMS OF HEAVEN AND EARTH

Chaos Primordial divided, but first was Former Heaven;
Clear and turbid then split up, and the two emblems
formed.
Earth-trigram: female; Heaven-trigram: male, each partial
energy;
Wood-dragon, metal-tiger, separate after a thousand years.

Remain alone and solitary to cultivate the Tao—
How else could you merge with soft and hard to create
mystery?
Apply yourself to unknowing, to topsy-turvy reason,
Attain this Way and a perfected you will be.

## CAULDRON AND IMPLEMENTS

To refine the cinnabar, you need cauldron and furnace.
They stand for Heaven and for Earth and must be rightly
molded.
Circumference three times five, diameter just one,
Upper rim four times eight, lower belly ample.

The cauldron's lead check carefully, its core must be right
solid,
Fiery yang will lick on it, from the base below.
No need to meet a perfected to teach you all in person,
This explains where you must settle down your center.

## LEAD AND MERCURY

Lead emerges from white metal, mercury brings forth red
sand.
Cinnabar and relatives use those to come right forward.
To transmute minerals and metals into perfection's drug,
Pick it like millet and like barley, but also check long hemp.

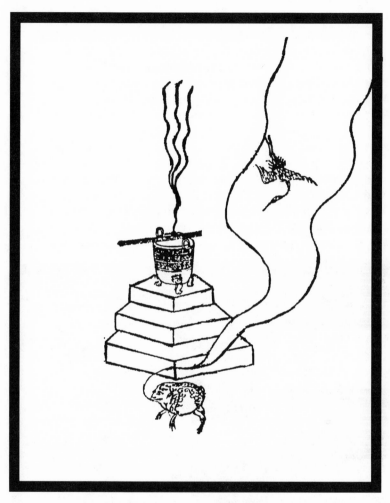

Fig. 22. The Crucible. Source: *Jinyi huandan yinzheng tu.*

The yellow male in Water-trigram is the site of mercury.
The dark maiden in the Fire-trigram is the home of lead.
Distinguish clearly who they are, what is true and false,
Then soon the true lead will sprout forth like a horse's teeth.

HARMONIZATION

Two times eight, the source is clear, the first true one
   emerges.
No more words; they come on level and are evenly balanced.

If you don't know where yin and yang find their harmony,
Then take a closer look at the positions of *zi, wu,* and *chen.*

Above *chen*, the prime's set up, making use of *si.*
Where *hai* emerges, there must also be a *yin.*
Meeting and joining equally, they establish three and five.
In harmony, there's central yellow and true perfection born.

TRUE LEAD

The one energy of Former Heaven, this is called true lead.
Never trust deluded students of a faked transmission.
A myriad transformations continue on and on, building
    karma from the start.
The single soul flies ever fast, can only trust the alms-bowl.

Fig. 23. The Dragon, the True Lead of Creation. Source: *Jinyi huandan yinzheng tu.*

Once there's a body and the solidity of life, nothing's really
   right.
Only without this life and body can there be perfection.
Hear the words of Tao tradition and learn them eagerly,
Use the true lead, but don't mistake it for ordinary stuff!


## 31. Observing Life

In another vein, observation also means to deal with the reali-
ties of life from the point of view of the Tao. How to do this is
described in some detail in the section translated below. Entitled
"True Observation" (*Zhenguan*), it forms the fifth of altogether seven
sections in the *Zuowang lun* (Discourse on Sitting in Oblivion), a
set of systematic instructions given by the Tang-patriarch Sima
Chengzhen (746–835) to his disciples.

The *Zuowang lun* outlines the ascent to the Tao in seven steps.
It begins with "Respect and Faith," emphasizing that successful
practitioners must have a firm will and strong determination to
pursue the Tao as well as full confidence in the teachers and scriptures to guide them on the way. In a second step, "Interception of
Karma," they must then leave their ordinary life behind, at least
temporarily, to stop producing any more involvement with the world
and karma for future lives.

The third step, "Taming the Mind," corresponds to the concentrative phase of Taoist meditation. Adepts are told to firmly fixate
their attention and how to deal with the various difficulties that
arise in the process. Step four, "Detachment from Affairs," sees the
first glimpses of a new vision, interpreting life and all experiences
in the light of inner nature and fate, i.e., character and karma.
Both the nature and nurture one has received in this life are seen
as the raw material the Tao has used to fashion one's self. A more
cosmic dimension of life is found.

The fifth level, "True Observation," describes the practical con-
sequences of a Tao-centered view for the dealings of one's everyday
life. In step six, "Intense Concentration," practitioners go beyond
observing self and world to attain a deeper absorption in the Tao. A
formless trance of oneness would best describe the goal at this
stage. The final step, then, is "Realizing the Tao," the attainment of
full oneness and union, the emergence of the immortal self.

The text used here is found in DZ 1036, fasc. 704 (8b–12a). A
variant version is contained in *Yunji qiqian* 94. A more original
inscription of the same title was erected in 829 before the temple

dedicated to Sima's memory on Mount Wangwu, his lifetime residence. For a full and annotated translation of the entire text as well as a discussion of its various concepts, see Kohn 1987. The rendering here is taken from the same work.

## "True Observation" (*Zhenguan*), from *Zuowang lun* (Discourse on Sitting in Oblivion)

[8b] True observation is the first mirror of the man of wisdom, the skillful examination of the able person. Probing misfortunes and blessings as they come, analyzing the good fortune and calamities of activity and rest, such a one sees ahead of life's motions and arranges things accordingly. He deeply prays and guards his concentration, serves the completeness of life. Thus he commits no action in attachment from beginning to end, nor do his principles oppose his actions. This, then, is the practice of true observation.

One bite of food or a wink of sleep can become the source of some decrease or advance; a single step or even just one word may lay the foundation for good and bad fortune. Though one might cleverly control the results, it is much better to be on one's guard against the very foundations. By observing the roots, one can know the branches.

However, one must first be free from impatient, competitive feelings. This is why we gather in the mind and detach ourselves from affairs; we let our actions decrease every day, calm the body and relax the mind. Only in such a state can one truly observe the wonders of the world. As the *Scripture of the Tao and the Virtue* has it: "Let there always be no desires so that the wonders may be observed."

Nevertheless, even a person cultivating the Tao must have clothing and food. There are affairs that cannot be given up or people one cannot leave behind. Those have to be taken care of with great humility; they should be attended to with clear vision. Don't take them as an obstruction to the Tao and let your mind develop anger and impatience. [9a] As soon as there are anger and impatience due to some affair, the mind will be sick and agitated. How, then, can it be a restful mind?

All human affairs, all clothing and food are just my boat. I want to cross an ocean, so I need a boat. After I have crossed the ocean, the reason for the boat is no longer there. But why abandon it before the trip? Clothing and food are empty illusion and certainly not sufficient provision in themselves. But in order to gain

Fig. 24. Sima Chengzhen, the author of the *Discourse on Sitting in Oblivion*. Source: *Liexian quanzhuan*.

liberation from empty illusion, one must obtain clothing and food. Although one has to look for and obtain them, one should therefore never regard them with feelings of gain or loss.

Independent of whether one has to deal with affairs or is free from them, the mind should remain constantly at rest. Join others in seeking but not in coveting; join them in achievement but not in hoarding. Without coveting you will be free from worry; without hoarding you will never experience loss. Your ways of living in the world may be like those of others, but your mind should always remain different from ordinary folk. This truly is the key to successful practice; it should be practiced seriously.

Despite a growing detachment from affairs there might still be a sickness hard to get rid of. In that case, just follow the method and observe it. There may be, for example, deep sensual attachment. That being so, observe the fact that all defilements and sensual attachments arise merely from imagination. If there is no imagination, there can never be any sensual attraction. Realize therefore that sensual imaginings are empty on the outside, [9b] while sensual feelings are foolish within. As they are nothing but foolish feelings and empty imaginings, who would be the master of sensual feelings? The *Scripture of Fixating the Will* says: "Sensuality is entirely imaginative. All imagination is ultimately empty. How can there be something like sensuality?"

Also, people should think that the attraction of a seductive woman is even more dangerous than that of a fox lady. When a fox lady seduces a man, she arouses loathing and distress. Hence men, even if they die from the contact, do not enter the evil ways. Loathing and distress keep them away from debauchery. Human beauties, however, beguile men, make them fall in love and get attached to them. They will then hanker after them with all they have. Because of their depraved thoughts, after death they fall into hell. Forever they turn away from birth in the world of human beings and from the road to happiness. As the *Scripture* says: "Why is it that people of one mind and joined as a couple in this world after death do not attain the human state together again? It is because of depraved thoughts."

Then again, why—if sensual attraction ultimately means beauty—do fish upon seeing such beauty enter deeper into the water, and birds fly off into the sky? Immortals observe sensual feelings as defilements and impurities; wise men compare them to knives and axes of punishment. In the course of your life, if you don't eat for seven days, you will die. Yet, if you remain without sensual feelings for a hundred years, you will avert the harm of an untimely departure. [10a] Realize therefore that sensual feelings are neither essential nor appropriate for body or mind. Rather, they are enemies and thieves of inner nature and destiny. Why must you be subject to affection and lust and invite disaster and destruction?

If you see another do evil and give rise to enmity and hatred in your own mind, this is just as if you were seeing someone kill himself and promptly stuck out your own neck to accept the other's blade and get killed yourself. The other person commits evil all by himself; he does not ask you to do the same. Why, then, should you reach out to take in the other's evil and make yourself sick? If you can feel enmity when you see someone do evil, then you will also react with bad feelings upon seeing someone do good. Why is that? Because in both cases your Tao is obstructed.

Now, if you suffer from poverty, observe this reality and ask yourself: "Who made me poor?" Heaven and earth are equable and regular; they protect and support all without personal aims. So if I am poor now, you should argue, it is certainly not their fault. When parents give birth to a child, they desire to see him or her in wealth and high esteem. So if I am poor now, I cannot blame it on my parents. Other people, ghosts, and spirits don't even have the time to save themselves; how then would they have the energy to make me poor?

Going back and forth, I cannot find anyone to blame for my poverty. So I know it's my own karma, my very own heaven-given destiny. I bring forth my own karma, while heaven provides me with the destiny of this life.

[10b] Karma relates to destiny like shadow and echo follow form and sound. They cannot be avoided and should not be resented. Only with wisdom can you act benevolently and realize them fully, delight in heaven and acknowledge your destiny. Then you will never lament over eventual sufferings through poverty. Therefore the *Zhuangzi* says: "Karma enters in and cannot be prevented from becoming one's own karma." Poverty and diseases come; they cannot be kept away or eliminated completely.

Thus the *Scripture* says: "Heaven and earth cannot alter their routine; yin and yang cannot revert their tasks." Looking at it from this angle, it indeed is a true destiny, not a mere mask. How could you resent it?

Your situation can be compared to the encounter of a brave knight with a band of brigands. Never feeling dread or fear, he brandishes his sword and rushes to the battle front, fighting until the robbers flee. Having thus gained merit in service, he is gloriously rewarded for the rest of his life. If now there are poverty and diseases vexing and troubling me, then these are my robbers and brigands. With an upright mind, I can be a brave knight. Examining them in wisdom and by observation, I brandish my sword. The battle is won when all vexations and forms of bondage are eliminated. To be at peace and constantly happy—this is the glorious reward.

[11a] But often, when suffering or affairs come to harass us, the mind instead of using this observation gives rise to sadness and anxiety. This, then, is like an encounter with brigands when you, rather than gaining merit in service, cast off all weapons and turn your back on the battlefield. You duly have to bear the shame of desertion and defeat. Thereby you reject happiness and invite suffering. For such foolishness, how could there be empathy?

Now, if you are suffering or have a disease, first of all observe that it originates in the body. Without a body the suffering would have no place to dwell. As the *Scripture of the Tao and the Virtue* says: "If I had no body, what suffering would I have?" Next, observe the mind. You will find that it has no true lord. Even though you search for him inside and out, you won't be able to find him anywhere.

All plans and thoughts arise only from a deluded mind. Thus when you "make your body like dried wood and your mind like dead ashes," all suffering and diseases will be eradicated. Someone who hates death, for example, should therefore think of his body as the lodge of the spirit. As the body becomes old and sick, as the power of his energy declines and gets weaker, it will just be like a house with rotting walls. Once uninhabitable, he must abandon it and look for another place to stay. The death of the body and the departure of the spirit are thus a mere change of residence.

However, when you hanker after life and loathe death, thus resisting the natural transformations, your spirit will be confused and fall into error. It will lose its proper role. [11b] Then, when you are entrusted to life again and receive the constituting energy, you will not lean to the pure and refined, but end up with turbid and disgraceful energy. Generally, all stupid and dull people, all the dumb and greedy ones, come into being like this.

Only when you do not feel exhilarated when alive or unhappy when facing death, can you fully make life and death equal. Thereby you will bring forth good karma for the future bodies to come. But by craving for a myriad different things, you will only end up with love and disease alternating. If even one limb is sick, the whole body is in discomfort and unrest. How much more so, when the mind is full of ten thousand diseases? Desiring eternal life in one body—how is it possible?

All craving and aversion arise from delusion. By accumulating delusion instead of expelling it, you obscure your vision of the Tao. Thus, relinquish all desires and abide in nonexistence! Be placid, pure, and strong—then turn to observation! Whatever you loved before will now only cause weariness and disdain.

Still, if you practice observation with a mind attached to projected reality, you will never be aware of bad feelings in yourself. Only when your mind is utterly detached from projected reality can you observe the phenomenal world and truly understand right and wrong. In fact, you are just like a sobered man. Freshly awakened, he can now see the evil he did while he was drunk, deeds of which he was completely unconscious before.

Thus the *Scripture of Ascension to the Mystery* says: "I uproot and cast off worldly life and give up the world completely." [12a] And the *Scripture of Western Ascension* has: "Sight and hearing of eyes and ears keep you always in a state of tension. The joys of nose and mouth and all the other senses must be given up." Even the Venerable Lord himself gave up the world and cast aside all ordinary life.

Realize, then, that smell and taste have to be given up! They are nothing but a steady flow of craving and desires! How, thus liberated, could you ever think of the fishmonger's shop as stinking?

## 32. Glimpses of the New Mind

The everyday activities of the newly emerging Taoist mind are already described, in a more humorous and literary form, in the ancient philosophers. Especially the *Zhuangzi* has quite a collection of stories, rightfully famous, that describe the workings and intricacies of thinking with the Tao.

In the six stories selected below from a variety of chapters, the boundaries of the ordinary mind are transcended. Whether one is human or an animal, whether one is dreaming or awake, whether one has feelings or remains unattached to all, whether one is better off alive or dead—all the various habitual patterns of reaction and classification of the common human mind are not only questioned but actively discarded and replaced with something else.

Taoist practitioners learn to understand their place in the world as part of the fate they brought with them, but they also realize that the common ways of dealing with the self and the world lead to mechanical solutions and thus to a mechanical understanding that destroys the naturalness of life. Refusing the ways of the world, yet accepting her or his own being in it, the successful Taoist can remain untouched by the vicissitudes of life, can forget the world and go wandering off, free and easy, in the reaches of the Tao, in the origins and beginning of all.

The rendering relies on Watson 1968. For more on the *Zhuangzi*, see Section 4 above ("Ineffable Knowledge").

---

*Zhuangzi.* **Six stories from chapters 2, 5, 6, 12, 18, 21.**

ONE

Once in the past, Zhuang Zhou dreamt that he was a butterfly, flitting and flying around, content with himself and doing what he liked. He didn't know he was Zhuang Zhou. Suddenly he woke up. There he was, firm and clearly Zhuang Zhou. But he did not know whether, in fact, he was Zhuang Zhou who had dreamt he was a butterfly, or a butterfly now dreaming he was Zhuang Zhou. Between Zhuang Zhou and a butterfly there must be some difference! These are the different transformations of beings. (chap. 2)

TWO

"Can a human being truly be without feelings?" Huizi once asked Zhuangzi.

"Indeed."

"But a person who is without feelings—how can you say he is a human being?"

"The Tao gave him a human face; heaven gave him a human body," Zhuangzi said. "Why not call him human?"

"But once you have called him human, how can he be without feelings?"

"That's not what I mean by feelings. When I talk about having no feelings, what I say is that a person does not allow preferences and aversions to enter and do harm. Instead, he always follows the natural course of things and does not push life along."

"But—" Huizi hesitated. "If he never pushes life along, how does he keep himself alive?"

"The Tao gave him a human face; heaven gave him a human body. He doesn't let likes and dislikes enter and harm himself. You, now—you place your spirit on the outside. You exhaust your essence, leaning on a tree and moaning, slumping at your desk and drifting off. Heaven picked out a human body for you, and you use it to gibber about sophistries!" (chap. 5).

THREE

Master Chariot and Master Mulberry were friends. Once it rained for ten days without interruption. Master Chariot said to himself, "Master Mulberry will be feeling ill in this weather!" So he took some food to his friend to eat.

When he got to Master Mulberry's door, he heard a sound, either singing or crying, while someone was plucking the zither:

> Father?
> Mother?
> Heaven?
> People?

It was as though the voice would break any moment and the singer were rushing to finish the lines.

Intrigued, Master Chariot entered. "What do you mean—singing like that?"

"I was thinking," Master Mulberry answered. "What was it that brought me to this terrible poverty? Really, I couldn't come up with an answer! For instance, my own father and mother—how could they wish me to be poor? Or heaven and earth—they cover and support all equally well. How could they be so partial toward me and make me poor? So I've been searching and searching to understand how this has come to pass, but I can't find any answer. Still, I somehow got here, to this terrible state. It must be fate." (chap. 6)

FOUR

Zigong had been traveling in Chu in the south. On his way back he passed through the state of Jin. Walking by the south bank of the Han River, he saw an old man about to prepare his vegetable plot for planting.

The man had hollowed out a hole to enter the well. From there he came out, carrying a heavy pitcher full of water, which he then poured over his plot. Moaning and catching his breath, he exerted much strength with only very little to show as a result.

"There is a machine for this, "Zigong said to him. "In one day it waters a hundred such plots. It needs very little strength and yet has great results. Don't you want one?"

The gardener looked up and faced Zigong squarely. "How does it work?"

"It's a device made by chiseling a piece of wood. The back end is heavy, while its front is light. It heaves the water as though pouring it out, so fast that it seems to be boiling over! It is called a well sweep."

The gardener flushed with anger, then laughed derisively. "I have heard my teacher say," he said with decision, "where there are machines, there inevitably are machine affairs; where there are machine affairs, there inevitably are machine minds. With a machine mind in your breast, the pure and simple in your nature cannot develop. And when the pure and simple cannot develop, you won't have any peace, in spirit or in life. Without peace in spirit and in life, the Tao will no longer support you. It's not that I don't know about your machine—I would be ashamed to use it!"

Zigong blushed with chagrin, bent his head, and did not answer. After a while, the old gardener said, "Who are you, anyway?"

"I am a disciple of Confucius."

"Oh! That means you are one of those who try to extend their learning in order to imitate the sages of old—always heaping nonsense on the common people, plucking the zither's strings and wailing sad songs, hoping to sell your name to the world!

"Really! You'd do better to forget your spirit and energy, drop off your body and bones! Then you might get along a bit! As it is, you can't even control your own self—how can you presume to order the world! Be off with you, now! Don't meddle with my business!" (chap. 12)

FIVE

Zhuangzi once went to Chu. On the way he saw a hollow old skull that looked all dried out and withered. Poking it with his horse whip, he talked to it.

"Oh, well now, were you greedy in life and lost all reasonable measure, and thus ended here? Were you involved in the destruction of your state or beheaded by an ax, and thus ended here? Did you behave unlawfully and were ashamed to cause your parents and family disgrace, and thus ended here? Did you suffer extreme cold and hunger, and thus ended here? Or did your springs and autumns just number so many that you ended here?"

When he had finished speaking, Zhuangzi pulled the skull to the side of the road. Using it for a pillow, he lay down and went to sleep.

In the middle of the night, the skull appeared to him in a dream.

"Your chatter is like that of a rhetorician," it said to Zhuangzi. "When I look at what you say, it is just full of entanglements with the world of the living. In death, there are none of these! Would you like to hear about the dead?"

"I'd be delighted," Zhuangzi responded with enthusiasm.

"Well," the skull began, "among the dead, there is no ruler above and no minister below. Nor are there the labors of the four seasons. Free and easy, we take heaven and earth as our springs and autumns. You might even be a king facing south on his throne, yet you could not surpass this!"

Zhuangzi did not believe a word. "Now wait," he said. "Let's say, I got the Department of Destiny to restore your body to you, to make you some bones and flesh, to return you to your parents and family, to give you back your old home and friends—wouldn't you want that?"

The skull frowned deeply and wrinkled its brow. "Why in all the heavens would I want to throw away the happiness of a king and go back to the toils of being human?" (chap. 18)

Six

Confucius called on Laozi. Laozi had just taken a bath and was sitting with his long white hair spread over his shoulders to dry. Utterly unmoving, he looked like a statue. Confucius, unseen, stood waiting. After a little while, he made himself known.

"Dear me!" he exclaimed. "Did I see right? Was that really true? A moment ago your body and bones seemed rigid like a withered tree. You seemed to have forgotten the world, left humanity entirely, and were standing in absolute aloneness!"

"Oh, yes, indeed," Laozi agreed. "My mind was wandering in the beginning of all things."

"What do you mean?"

"The mind may struggle for it, yet can never understand it. The mouth may twist itself for it, yet can never describe it. Still, this once, I will try to give you a general idea.

"Perfect yin," Laozi continued, "is stern and frigid. Perfect yang is bright and glittering. The stern and frigid comes from heaven. The bright and glittering develops from earth. As the two forces mix and join in harmony, living beings are born.

"Perhaps there is something or someone who pulls the strings that hold it all together, but, if so, none has ever seen its form.

Things dissolve and develop, grow full and get empty, are dark one moment, bright the next; the sun rises and sets, the moon changes according to its phases—every day things proceed along their way, yet no one has ever seen the effort that underlies their movements.

"Life arises from somewhere. Death returns someplace. Ending and beginning follow one another without interruption—yet no one knows their ultimate limits. If not like this—who would be the ancestor of it all?"

"Hmm," Confucius said thoughtfully. "I wonder, though, what it is like to wander around in this way?"

"It means," Laozi replied, "to attain perfect beauty and perfect happiness. Attain perfect beauty and wander around in perfect happiness, and you may be called a perfect one."

"How, pray, could I go about this?"

"Well, beasts that feed on grass do not suffer from a change of pasture. Creatures that live in water do not suffer from a change of stream. They accept lesser changes without losing their overall constancy. Like that, don't let joy and anger, grief and happiness enter your breast!

"Now, all the myriad beings under heaven have an underlying oneness. Attain this One and become one with it! Then your four limbs and hundred bones will just be so much dust and sweepings. Life and death, beginning and end will be a mere day and night to you. Nothing whatsoever can confound you—how much less the trifles of gain or loss, good or bad fortune!

"Someone may discard his servants as if they were so much earth or mud, for he knows himself worthier than the servants. Worth lies within yourself and should not be lost due to external changes. Therefore, observe that the myriad transformations of the world continue to change without even the trace of a limit! How could they ever distress your mind?

"As one who practices the Tao you will certainly understand all this!"

"Your virtue, sir," Confucius said, deeply impressed, "is a true match to heaven and earth. Yet even you learn from perfect words and cultivate your mind. Who, then, even among the lords of old, could ever have been truly free?"

"No, indeed!" Laozi exclaimed. "The murmuring of the flowing water is its natural talent, something it does in non-action. One who is similar has a relation to virtue that does not need cultivation. It is so strong that beings cannot separate him from it. It is as natural to him as heaven is naturally high, as earth is naturally low, as the sun and the moon are naturally bright. What is there to be cultivated?" (chap. 21)

# Chapter Nine

## ECSTATIC EXCURSIONS

Ecstatic excursions are spirit trips into the otherworld. Adepts prepare themselves with purifications and ritual measures, chant specific incantations and visualize the perfected. Then they haul their souls out of their body and ecstatically ascend into the higher reaches of the universe.

Taoist ecstatic excursions are a formalized development of the spirit travel of the shamans of old. Shamans are people who can easily traverse the gap between the worlds of the seen and the unseen, the human and the divine. They undergo specific initiatory rites and receive detailed instructions on the structure and organization of the otherworld. Then they open themselves to the spirits—and either the gods come to them, in forms of possession, or they go out to the gods, in a spirit journey.

Shamanistic practices are documented in one form or another in all parts of the world. Although the classical case, Central Asia as described by Mircea Eliade, has not been known before the nineteenth century, the techniques and cosmologies associated with shamanism are thought to be very old. In ancient China, the phenomenon is clearly present in the Warring States and Han periods. Opinions about its importance in Chinese neolithic and bronze-age cultures (Xia and Shang dynasties) differ.

In Taoism, the shamanistic practice of spirit journeys to the otherworld is linked with the concrete journeys emperors of old made through their realm. By imperial circuit to all parts of the world, the rulers established their power. They made their presence felt and at the same time acquainted themselves with the far reaches of the world, collected marvels and received tributes.

The circuit, whether through earth or through heaven, is thus a way of knowing and possessing all-there-is. It is a method of reaching out to the more wondrous parts of the world, of going beyond the known and reaching into the unknown, of leaving the common world behind and attaining the position of the Tao.

The Tao in this context is localized. It is a place beyond all known regions, a place that is both deepest darkness, usually associated with the north, and highest light, the power of the south. Yet however much the Tao is found in these locations, it is more. It is the ultimate center of all, everywhere and nowhere at the same time, the perfect nothingness and emptiness beyond, and yet deeply within all being.

To attain the Tao through ecstatic excursions, the soul and spirit of the Taoist must be freed completely from the concerns of this world. Concentrating the mind and visualizing the gods, adepts make first acquaintance with the Tao in its statuary, imaginable state. Observing reality and going along with the moving energies of the world, they then adapt themselves to the eternally transforming, forever changing nature of the Tao. This is a more subtle level, a deeper closeness to the Tao. By rising up completely beyond the world and ecstatically traversing the earth, the stars, and the heavens, adepts finally reach the center of the Tao, arrive on its homeground, find it in its most essential form.

Journeys through the heavens are described either in poetry or in meditation instructions. They reach from the pre-Han into the modern period, never tiring to praise the mystery and delight of the worlds beyond.

The selections below give a representative sample. There is first the most classical of all ecstatic journeys in Chinese religion and literature, the "Far-off Journey" (*Yuanyou*) of the *Chuci* (The Songs of Chu). A collection of semi-ritual songs, this work is among the foremost documents of shamanism in pre-Han China. Compiled by Qu Yuan, a poet from the south, the poems are roughly dated to the third century B.C.E. They are standard pieces of Chinese literature and have strongly influenced poetry and song.

Next, there is the *Tianguan santu* (Three Ways to Go Beyond the Heavenly Pass), a set of meditation instructions from the school of Highest Clarity dating from the fifth century. Here adepts are given detailed visualization patterns and incantations, with which they can induce the deities of the Dipper, the astral constellation that represents the center and therefore the Tao in the sky, to let them pass up and beyond the world. The key to the excursions here is the transfer of the adepts' names from the registers of death into those of eternal life.

Third, there is another set of Shangqing meditation instructions, this time for the visualization of a jade maiden who will deliver divine essences mouth to mouth and even descend to join the adept in intimate embrace. The text, the *Xuanzhen jing jue* (Scripture of the Mysterious Perfected) dates from the Tang dynasty and was revealed by the Queen Mother of the West.

Fourth, then, there is an inner-alchemical vision of the ecstatic excursion. The immortal sleep exercises of the Taoist master Chen Tuan of the tenth century are famous for their length and power. They are outlined in his Taoist biography, written around the year 1300. The Tao here is found in sleep, the sleep of the perfected, which is a form of frolicking about with the immortals.

## 33. The Far-off Journey

The *"Yuanyou"* (The Far-off Journey), from *Chuci* (The Songs of Chu), can be dated to the third century B.C.E.. It is ascribed to Qu Yuan, poet and official of South China, who drowned himself in sorrow when he was rejected by his overlord. His death is associated with the Dragon Boat festival and thus with the midsummer time, the "double five" (fifth day of the fifth month) of the Chinese calendar.

In this poem, the poet describes a visionary journey that takes him from the sorrows and afflictions of his unhappy life on earth through various physical practices and concentration efforts into the realm of the gods and immortals. Not only one among them but a guest beyond the clouds, he soon turns into an emperor himself, commanding thousands of chariots and giving orders to the Rain God, Lord Wind and other celestials of high standing. Traversing the world in all the cardinal directions, he reaches the far ends and goes beyond, to finally find Clarity and the Great Beginning.

For an annotated translation of the text, contained in a rendering of the entire collection, see Hawkes 1959. For shamanism in the *Chuci*, see Waley 1955. On Qu Yuan and the traditions associated with him, see Schneider 1980.

---

## "The Far-off Journey" (*Yuanyou*), from *Chuci* (The Songs of Chu)

Saddened by the hardships of the common world,
How I wish to rise up and travel ways far-off!
My own strength is feeble; there is no support—
What could I stride on to float up and away?

Encountering nothing but foulness and defilement,
I am alone and miserable—who could I talk to?

At night I lie restless, never sleeping,
My soul roving about till the approach of dawn.

Thinking of the infinity of heaven and of earth,
I cry with the eternal toil of human life.
People of the past I cannot reach;
People of the future I will never know.

Pacing with restlessness, I yearn to get away,
Confused and close to madness, I long for the eternal.
My mind goes wild, strays off without control;
My heart melancholy, I am ever sadder.

Then suddenly my spirit, off, never to come back,
My body, like a withered tree, left behind alone.

I look within, try to get back my grip,
To find the place where life's energy arises:
All vastly empty and tranquil, there is serenity.
Quietly in non-action, spontaneous truth is found.

I hear how Master Redpine cleansed the world's defilements
And wish to follow the model he has left.

Honoring the blessed virtue of the perfected,
I admire all who in the past have become immortal.
Taking off in a transformation, they were never seen,
While still their name and nature continue on and on.

Oh, how Fu Yue went to live among the stars!
How Han Zhong succeeded to realize the One!
Oh, for the body to slowly fade off in the distance—
To leave the human crowd behind, to vanish so completely!

Oh, to follow the flow of energy, rising ever upward—
Swift as the spirit, wondrous as a ghost!
To see the world get hazy, look back from far-off—
All dazzling essence, flashing back and forth!

Oh, to go away from all the dust to greater purity—
Never to turn back to the old home!
To escape all the afflictions and never fear again—
None in the world knows how this truly is!

And here I am, afraid of the passing of the seasons,
With every rising of the sun on its westward move.
A subtle frost descends, sinking ever downward,
I fear my fragrant freshness will fade all too soon.

Oh, to leave it all for free and easy journey
Through years eternal that will never end!
Here, who would enjoy with me my remaining fragrance,
Walk through the country air and share my depth with me?

Gaoyang, my hero, is removed ever farther,
Where will this life, so lonely, lead me to?

Then again, as spring and autumn hurry,
How can I always stay in my old home?
The Yellow Emperor cannot become my model,
But I can follow Jumping Wang to please myself.

So I eat the six energies and drink the nightly dew,
Rinse my mouth with yang itself and swallow morning light.
Guarding the purity of the spirit light within,
I absorb essence and energy, drive out all that's coarse.

Wandering in the wake of the gentle wind,
I reach the Southern Nest without a single stop.
I meet with Master Wang and pause to speak to him,
Inquire about the harmony and virtue of the One.

"The Tao can only be received," he says,
"It never can be given.
"So small that it has no within,
"So big it has no bounds.

"No twists at all inside your soul,
"And it will come spontaneously.
"Focus on energy and open up to spirit—
"Let them grow in you at the midnight hour.

"Wait for the Tao in emptiness,
"Clear even of non-action.
"All living species rise from this,
"It is the Gate of Virtue."

Having heard this precious teaching, I move on,
Swiftly getting to wherever I am going.
I meet the winged ones on Cinnabar Hill,
Tarry in the old land of No-Death.

In the morning I wash my hair in the Sun's Own Valley;
At night I rest at the Ninefold Yang.
I sip the subtle fluid of the Flying Spring
And hold the shining brightness of the Glittering Gem.

My face, like jade, is flushed with radiant color;
My pure essence is starting to grow strong.
My solid body dissolving into softness,
My spirit's ever subtler and more unrestrained.

How fine the fiery virtue of the Southern Land!
How lovely the winter blooming of the Cassia Tree!
How desolate the mountains with no beasts upon them!
How solitary the wilderness with not a single man!

Holding to my sparkling soul, I climb to the empyrean;
Clinging to the floating clouds, I ride up further high.

I order heaven's gate-keeper to open up the locks;
Pushing the sacred portals wide, he lets me look ahead.
I call upon the Rain God then to lead the onward way,
Ask him to guide me to Great Tenuity.

I reach the walls of Twofold Yang and the Imperial Palace,
Meet the Week Star and inspect the Clear Metropolis.
In the morning I set off from the Court of Heaven,
Arrive at night already at the Subtle Village.

Marshalling a whole ten thousand chariots,
I rise with them in slow and grand procession.
Harnessing eight dragons, coiling and in twists,
I bear a cloudy banner flapping in the wind.

I set up a bright standard, rainbow-made,
Five colors dazzling, so variegated.
The yoke-horses bow and toss their heads in splendor;
The trace-horses arch and curve with pride.

Confusion reigns and mixed disorder,
As the colorful and overflowing train sets out.

I hold my reins, adjust my whip,
Decide to go visit Goumang of the East.
Crossing the Great Brightness, I wheel over to the right,
Send Flying Wind to announce him our coming.

Yang in its first gentle flashes, not quite bright,
We ford the waters of the Pool of Heaven.
The Lord Wind drives ahead of us,
To blow the dust away, make all clear and cool.

Phoenixes wing along, bearing up my pennant,
As we pass Rushou, the Western Sovereign.
I seize the Broom Star for a banner,
And lift the Dipper's Handle as my baton.

Plunging and soaring, we go up and down,
Wandering on the floating waves of unsteady mist.

As the daylight fades into gathering darkness,
I summon the Dark Warrior to join as our leader.
The God of Literary Glory follows, marshalling the progress,
Selecting all the gods for their different places.

Far-off the road stretches, on and on,
Carefully, stopping in places, we ascend to lofty heights.
On my left the Rain God guides us on the way;
On my right the Thunder God serves as bodyguard.

Thus I go beyond the world, forget all about returning:
My mind all unrestrained pushes up and away.
Deep within so full of joy and spontaneous delight,
Oh, how merry I am now, so perfectly happy!

Traversing fresh blue clouds, I am floating freely,
Yet suddenly I glimpse the old village down below.
My groom homesick, my own heart full of sadness,
Even the trace-horses look back—none would go any further.

Thinking of my dear old friends in my imagination,
I heave a heavy sigh and brush the tears away.
Slowly again I float, rising ever farther:
Suppressing now my will, keeping myself controlled.

I point to the God of Fire and gallop straight to him,
Wishing to journey to the world's southern end.
I gaze on wilderness beyond all known directions,
Float on and on over watery expanse.

The Blessed Melter of the South stops me on the way,
So I go back by phoenix and visit the River Consorts.
They play the "Pool of Heaven" and sing me "To the Clouds";
Both ladies then perform the Nine Songs of Shao.

Asking the Xiang goddesses to play their zithers for me,
I bid the Sea God dance with the River God.
They pull up water monsters to step forward with them,
Their bodies coiling and writhing in ever swaying motion!

Gracefully the Lady Rainbow circles all around them;
The phoenixes soar up, stay hovering above—
The music swells ever higher, into infinity.

At this point I leave to wander yet again;
With my entourage, I gallop far away.

At the world's far end at the Gate of Coldness,
I race the rushing wind to Clarity Springs.
I follow Zhuanxu of the North over piled-up ice,
Turn from my path to pass through Mystery Darkness.

Striding on cosmic mainstays, I look back behind me,
Summon Qian Lei the Creator to appear,
To go in front of me on the level way.

Thus I tour all four outlands,
Traverse all the six regions,
Up to the Cracks of Heaven,
Down to the Great Abyss.

Below just lofty openness, there is no more earth;
Above just empty vastness, there is no more heaven.

I look but my vision blurs, nothing to be seen;
I listen but my ears are numb, nothing to be heard.

Going beyond non-action, I reach the Clarity,
Become a neighbor of the Great Beginning.

## 34. Trips through the Stars

In Highest Clarity Taoism, the ecstatic journey serves to newly integrate self and Tao, body and cosmos on a higher level. From an ordinary human, with the travel to the otherworld, a fully cosmicized being emerges. Practitioners increasingly make the heavens their true home, wander freely through the far ends of the universe, and gain control not only over their own life and death but over the transformations of the cosmos at large.

The practice is highly formalized and begins with purifications and prayers. It includes incantations to the various gods, mostly those of the Dipper, the ruling constellation of the center, asking them to convey the adept to the heavenly regions, delete his name from the registers of death and make him a full resident among the celestials.

The text translated here, *Tianguan santu* (Three Ways to Go Beyond the Heavenly Pass), is found in DZ 1366, fasc. 1040. The first twelve pages are rendered, short in text due to the numerous illustrations.

For more on ecstatic excursions in Highest Clarity Taoism, see Robinet 1979, 1989. On the stars and their role, see Schafer 1977. For a more general discussion of ecstatic practice and shamanism in Taoist mysticism, see Kohn 1992.

---

### *Tianguan santu* (Three Ways to Go Beyond the Heavenly Pass)

[1a] To practice the Tao of excursions to the seven stars [of the Dipper], first summon the Jade Emperor and his nine lords and let their mysterious essence radiate within your body. Block off the root of death, calm your mind, and darken the room. Let neither wind nor dust disturb you, but in solitude face the other realm.

Watch carefully for the first glimmer of sunrise, then burn incense on your right and left sides, scatter the smoke and let it form a cloud in the courtyard. Concentrate your mind and make a strong effort to control your thoughts. Visualize the gods in creative imagination, but do not fall asleep.

Fig. 25. Invoking the Celestials. Source: *Tianguan santu.*

Practice this for seven years; then a jasper carriage with a flying canopy and cinnabar shafts will come to receive you and take you to ascend through the Heavenly Pass.

The route of blocking death is to the northeast; the route of entering the registers of life is to the south. Immortals call them the way of hard attainment and the truth of easy descent. Once you have a golden tablet and jade name for yourself, you will attain the full power of this Tao.

Practice in particular on the days *renyin, bingyin, jiazi, jiawu, xinwei,* and *xinchou* [i.e., days 1, 3, 8, 31, 38, and 39 of the 60-day cycle], since these are the times of highest harmony. [1b] The Jade Emperor always gives orders to his immortals-in-attendance and to the jade lads on these days. Also, at those times, he examines and decides on the golden tablets, jade names, and registers of all students of immortality, which are kept in the Eastern Palace of Green Florescence. Therefore, practice with a determined will on these days in particular, applying yourself with utmost penetration and strong impulse.

The Jade Emperor is the overlord of the Northern Emperor who resides in the Six Palaces [of the dead] at Fengdu. He is the chief authority that can eliminate your name from the registers of death.

You can have your name recorded in the registers of life at the Gate of Humanity. You can traverse the seven stars after passing through the Gate of Demons. And you can go beyond the mysterious pivot of the universe by opening the Heavenly Pass.

In all cases, first undertake purifications and fasts, make an effort to control your thoughts, and focus your mind firmly on the mystery. Close your eyes and visualize the gods within. Clap your teeth thirty-six times.

First, meditate on the Great Star. This is Yang Brightness of Mystery Pivot, the spirit soul and spirit of the Heavenly Pivot. Here the Nine Lords of Highest Mystery reside.

They wear robes of flying-cloud brocade; on their heads they have the caps of mysterious morning light. They descend from the center of the Dipper and enter your body.

Now recite:

Oh, Yang Brightness of Mystery Pivot!
Spirit Soul and Spirit of the Heavenly Pivot!
Oh, Nine Lords of Highest Mystery!
Merge and transform into one single spirit! [2a]

Cut off my route to death at the Gate of Demons!
Open my registers of life in the Southern Office!
Let my seven souls be free from the three bad rebirths!
Let me come to life again as an immortal!
Let me traverse the sevenfold essence to reach mysterious
    darkness!
Let me bodily go beyond all through the Heavenly Pass!

Exhale deeply twenty-seven times.

Continue this practice without slackening; then you will be invited up to heaven as a guest of the Jade Emperor, or the celestials themselves will come down to you on a cloud of purple haze. You will be guarded by jade maidens of gleaming efflorescence and by jadelads of radiant sunlight. Twelve maidens and lads will be your attendants.

[2b] Next, meditate on the second star, the Prime Star. This is Yin Essence of Northern Womb, the spirit soul and spirit of the Celestial Jade. Here the Nine Lords of Highest Jade reside.

They wear flying skirts of yellow brocade; on their heads they have caps of mysterious morning light. They descend from the center of the Dipper and enter your body.

Exhale and recite:

Oh, Yin Essence of Northern Womb!
Spirit Soul and Spirit of the Celestial Jade!
Oh, Nine Lords of Highest Jade!
Merge and transform ten thousand times into one single
    spirit!

Delete all my yang sins from the registers of Great Yin!
Transfer all my yin energy into the Realm of Great Yang! [3a]
Let me traverse the seven stars to cut off death!
Let me open up the six harmonies at the Heavenly Pass!

Let me free my ancestors for seven generations from the
    three bad rebirths!
Let us all come back to life in the Southern Palace!

Exhale deeply twenty-seven times.

[3b] Third, meditate on the True Star. This is the Highest True One of Ninefold Ultimate, the Lady of the Upper Prime. It is the material soul and essence of the Heavenly Pearl. Here the Nine Lords of Highest Simplicity reside.

They wear flying robes of green brocade; on their heads they have caps of mysterious morning light. They descend from the center of the Dipper and enter your body.

Exhale and recite:

Oh, Highest True One of Ninefold Ultimate!
Lady of the Upper Prime!
Material Soul and Essence
Of Heavenly Pearl and Celestial Jade!
Oh, Nine Lords of Highest Simplicity!

Fig. 26. Reaching Out to the Deities of the Dipper. Source: *Tianguan santu.*

Merge and transform ten thousand times into one single
　spirit!

Eradicate all roots of my old karma!
Cut off the source of the death for me! [4a]

Let my eyes be bright and of penetrating vision!
Let them mirror everything without end!
Let me communicate with the truth of the mystery!
Let its essence flow into my body!

Let me reach out to the august Dipper's handle!
Let me fly all the way across its seven stars!
Let me stride on light and ride on air!
Let me end only in time with heaven itself!

Exhale deeply twenty-seven times.

[4b] Fourth, meditate on the Pivotal Star. This is Mystery Darkness of Jade Pearl, the spirit soul and essence of the Heavenly Pillar. Here the Nine Lords of Highest Emptiness reside.

They wear flying robes of purple brocade; on their heads they have caps of mysterious morning light. They descend from the center of the Dipper and enter your body.

Exhale and recite:

Oh, Mystery Darkness of Jade Pearl!
Spirit Soul and Essence of the Heavenly Pillar!
Oh, Nine Lords of Highest Emptiness!
Merge and transform ten thousand times into one single
    spirit!

Let me safely go beyond the seven stars!
Block of the Gate of Demons!
Cut out all my energy of death!
Open wide the Heavenly Pass for me! [5a]

Let me traverse the Northern Dipper from the Mysterious
    Pivot!
Let me pass beyond life's energy to the west-power of the
    Earth!
Let me leave the Northern Emperor behind on Mount
    Fengdu!
Let me register my name forever in the Southern Office!

Exhale deeply twenty-seven times.

[5b] Fifth, meditate on the Net Star. This is Cinnabar Prime of Heavenly Peace, the spirit soul and numinous power of the Jade Beam. Here the Nine August Lords of Highest Mystery reside.

They wear flying robes of cinnabar brocade; on their heads they have caps of mysterious morning light. They descend from the center of the Dipper and enter your body.

Exhale and recite:

Oh, Cinnabar Prime of Heavenly Peace!
Spirit Soul and Numinous Power of the Jade Beam!
Oh, Nine August Lords of Highest Mystery!
Merge and transform ten thousand times into one single
    spirit!

Bring the essence of the seven stars,
So it freely descends into my body! [6a]
Let it revolve three and four times,
So the Seven Primes be opened!

Let me seal off the gate of death in the northeast!
Let me receive the hall of life in ninefold mystery!
Let me register my name forever in the Eastern Flower
    Palace!
Let me become an attendant on the Jade Lord of Morning
    Light!

Exhale deeply twenty-seven times.

[6b] Sixth, meditate on the Mainstay Star. This is North Culmen
of Destiny Pivot, the spirit soul and numinous power of Open Yang.
Here the Nine Lords of Highest Cinnabar and August Emptiness
reside.

They wear flying robes of vermilion brocade; on their heads
they have caps of mysterious morning light. They descend from the
center of the Dipper and enter your body.

Exhale and recite:

Oh, North Culmen of Destiny Pivot!
Spirit Soul and Numinous Power of Open Yang!
Oh, Nine Lords of Highest Cinnabar and August Emptiness!
Merge and transform ten thousand times into one single
    spirit!

Open the Mysterious Gate of Heavenly Unity
Above at Triple Charter! [7a]
Transfer me past the Six Palaces of the Northern Emperor
Below at Mount Fengdu!

Let me govern and control all the officials of Darkness!
Let me exterminate the roots of all nine kinds of death!

Let me revolve the three stars and return to the four!
Let me transfer my name to the seven primes!
Let me forever preserve myself without end!
Let me be as old as the Dipper is itself!

Exhale deeply twenty-seven times.

[7b] Last, meditate on the Passgate Star. This is the Heavenly Pass of Mysterious Yang, the great brightness of Vacillating Radiance. Here the Tao Lords of the Highest Jade Emperor reside.

They wear flying gauze robes of cinnabar brocade; on their heads they have caps of mysterious morning light. They descend from the center of the Dipper and enter your body.

Exhale and recite:

Oh, Heavenly Pass of Mysterious Yang!
Great Brightness of Vacillating Radiance!
Oh, Tao Lords of the Highest Jade Emperor!
Merge and transform ten thousand times into one single
   spirit!

Summon the Morning Emperor above,
The Ninefold Perfect Lord!
Let me leave the Ninefold Darkness and Deep Chaos
Through the Heavenly Pass! [8a]

Let me liberate my ancestors for seven generations!
Let me float freely through the clouds of mystery!
Let me dissolve all roots of death in the Dark North!
Let me register my name in the jade records of the Eastern
   Flower Palace!

Exhale deeply twenty-seven times.

[10b] Note: In the illustrations found in this volume, unless specifically mentioned otherwise, all perfected personages should be imagined wearing blue caps, red capes, pink robes, and dark red shoes. They all stand on five-colored clouds. For purposes of visualization, think of the perfected as wearing blue caps, yellow robes, green capes, and having a fresh youthlike countenance. In addition, the interior of halls and palaces should be imagined as golden in color and furnished with suitable decorations and ornamentations.

THE METHOD OF GOING BEYOND DEATH THROUGH THE NORTHERN
EMPEROR OF THE SIX PALACES ON MOUNT FENGDU

Mount Fengdu is located in the North, in the position of the celestial stem *gui*. Therefore the Northeast is known as the Gate of Demons [*gui*], the root of the energy of death. The mountain is 2,600 miles high and 30,000 miles in circumference. [11a] Its grotto heaven begins right beneath the mountain; it measures 15,000 miles in circumference.

Above and below, there are palaces and residences of demons and spirits. On top of the mountain are the Six Palaces, with another set of them deep inside the grotto. Each palace is about 1,000 miles in size. They are the palaces of the demons and spirits of the Six Heavens.

First, there is the Dark Heavenly Palace of Infamy and
   Death;
Next, there is the Ancestral Heavenly Palace Where All
   Faithfulness is Killed;
Third, there is the Military Heavenly Palace Where Even the
   Morning Light Has to Endure Offenses;
Fourth, there is the Heavenly Palace of Thoroughly Shining
   Energy of Guilt;
Fifth, there is the Heavenly Palace of the Seven Misdeeds of
   the Ancestors' Souls;
Last, there is the Heavenly Palace of Frequently Repeated
   Presumptions of Office.

The Six Palaces are governed by the Northern Emperor. They are the Six Heavens of the demons and the ghosts of the dead. Here the institution that governs people's death is located. [11b] In all cases, a death summons is issued at these Six Palaces on Mount Fengdu.

For this reason, the Emperor of Heaven often delivers all those who pursue life and practice excursions to the seven stars to the realm beyond the Heavenly Pass. For them, he opens the Palace of Life at the South Culmen and seals off the Gate of Death in the Northeast.

After you have completed the visionary excursion [to the Six Palaces], clap your left teeth nine times and call out the names of the Six Palaces. Then recite the following incantation:

Fig. 27. The Six Palaces of the Dead. Source: *Tianguan santu.*

I am a minister of the Lord Emperor of Heaven.
My name is registered in Jade Clarity.
From there on down to the Six Heavens,
To all the demon palaces of the Northern Emperor,
All realms are under my control.
They are all part of my jurisdiction—
How would any demon dare to go on living there?

Watch out!
On the right of my belt, I carry the talisman Easy Fall!
On the left, I have the talisman Fire Bell!
I can throw fire as far as ten thousand miles!
I can awe and control as many as ten thousand souls!

Any criminal will at once be executed!
Any offender will at once be punished!
Whenever the Lord Emperor has an order,
I will immediately hasten to carry it out!

This concludes the exercise.

If you recite this incantation only once, the radiance of heaven will be startled into action and the myriad evil specters will be captivated and bound. If you recite it three times, all demons and calamitous forces will be destroyed and the names of the dead will be taken from the registers of the Six Heavens. Then the Heavenly Pass will open, and people will come back to life in the palace of the South Culmen.

[12a] You can study the Tao without learning the names of the palaces on Mount Fengdu where the demons and spirits of the dead reside. However, in that case you will not properly seal off the root of death. Even if you continue to practice for ten thousand years, you will not succeed in becoming immortal. Only with this can the excursion to the seven stars be concluded properly!

## 35. Divine Loves

The complementary form to ecstatic excursions into the heavens and palaces of the otherworld is the ecstatic, frequently sexual, encounter with gods descending to this level of existence.

Going back far in Chinese history, intimate meetings with gods and goddesses were sought after fervently by the shamans of old, as several songs in the *Chuci* (Songs of Chu) document. Here as in Taoism later, the practitioner purifies himself or herself, sets up a proper sacred space, adorns his or her body, and entices the deity to descend with melodious incantations and seductive dances. The lover comes, the union is attained, but after a sojourn forever too short the deity returns to the heavenly abodes. The human lover left behind is full of sadness and longing, praying for another chance at such a divine encounter.

In Highest Clarity, the ancient shamanistic practice is turned into a formal meditation procedure. Adepts visualize the pure energy of the sun or the moon, then imagine a goddess in its midst. The goddess grows stronger and more vivid with prolonged practice until she is felt present in the flesh. Pressing her mouth to his, she dispenses celestial vapors to increase the adept's vitality. After a long courtship and regularly repeated visualizations, she will even lie with him.

The technical meditation instructions combined with the songs of the shamans of old were continued in Tang poetry. Here Taoist priestesses express their desire for an ecstatic meeting with a divine lover; seekers of the Tao spend their nights in temples willing a divine maiden to join them on their mat; poets sing of the union's delight and sorrow at the parting.

The text translated here, the *Shangqing mingtang xuanzhen jing jue* (Scripture of the Mysterious Perfected from the Hall of Light of Highest Clarity, with Practical Instructions) is among the technical manuals of Highest Clarity, dating probably from the Tang dynasty. It is found in DZ 424, fasc. 194 and contains a variety of different methods for the ingestion of celestial energies. The love encounter is described in the beginning (1a–4b).

A translation of the technical instructions with ample annotation is found in Schafer 1978. For sexual encounters of shamans and goddesses in ancient China, see Hawkes 1974. Translations of Tang poetry on the same topic are found in Cahill 1985, Schafer 1978a. For more ecstatic poetry of the same period, see Schafer 1981 and 1985.

---

## *Shangqing mingtang xuanzhen jing jue* (Scripture of the Mysterious Perfected from the Hall of Light of Highest Clarity, with Practical Instructions)

[1a] The Greatly Perfected Goddess of the Nine Numina of the White-Jade Tortoise Terrace, the Queen Mother of the West, gave us the *Scripture of the Mysterious Perfected from the Hall of Light.* It runs:

> All Highest, Full of Mystery,
> Where the two energies pervade their brilliance—
> The Mysterious Perfected radiates within.
> The Hall of Light spreads clarity without.
>
> Swallow the essence of the two luminants,
> So spirit and essence live forever.
> Rise up to aid the Ruler of Fates;
> Inspect and control the myriad numina on earth.
>
> Your six fluorescences full to overflowing,
> You penetrate to see the yellow repose of all.

These forty characters were carved by the Highest Lord on the southern railing of Phoenix Terrace. Only disciples of the assembled perfected can ever receive them in teaching; only those listed with the Ruler of Fates can ever receive them in transmission.

THE PRACTICE OF THE MYSTERIOUS PERFECTED

> Visualize the sun or the moon in your mouth. [1b]
> During bright daylight, visualize the sun.
> In the depth of night, visualize the moon.
> When it is neither day nor night, visualize either,
> But make a clear distinction between them.
> The color of the sun is red.
> The color of the moon is yellow.
> The sun has nine rays of purple light.
> The moon has ten rays of white light.

[2a] Make the sun or the moon stand right in front of your mouth, about nine feet away. The rays of their light should be directed straight toward your mouth so they can easily enter.

Now visualize a young lady in the sun or the moon. On her head she is wearing a purple cap; her cloak and skirt are of vermilion brocade. She calls herself Jade Maiden of Cinnabar Morning Light of Greatest and Highest Mystery. Her taboo name is Binding Coil, and she is also known as the Secret Perfected.

From her mouth she now emits a red energy, which fills the space between the light rays of the sun or the moon. See how the light rays merge and combine with the morning light of the Jade Maiden. When they have amalgamated completely, let them enter your mouth.

[2b] Hold on to the light and swallow it; then visualize the Jade Maiden emit another stream of light. Practice this nine times ten, then stop.

Now visualize the Jade Maiden and order the luminants of either the sun or the moon to press intimately on your face. Make the Jade Maiden press her mouth tightly upon your own, and allow her energy fluids to enter deeply into you.

Softly utter the following incantation: [3a]

> Oh, Purple Perfected of Great Empyrean,
> Hidden Goddess of the Hall of Light!
> Oh, Living Essence of the Sun and the Moon,
> Binding Coil, Jade Maiden!
> Oh, goddess born prior even to emptiness,
> Known as the Secret Perfected!

Your head is crowned by purple radiance,
A numinous cap of lotus leaves.
Your body is wrapped in a brocade cloak,
A flying skirt of vermilion cinnabar.

Oh, come out of the sun and enter the moon,
You celestial light of enchanting fragrance!
May your mouth emit red energy—
Oh, let it drip into my Three Primes!

May my face gaze upon the Well of Heaven,
Softer become my spirit soul, strong my material parts.
May the mysterious fluid come floating to me
And the embryo essence within grow to completion!

May my five orbs within develop florescence!
May my pupils be open to look back inside!
May I inspect and control the myriad spirits!
May I be a flying immortal near the Ruler of Fates!

Following this incantation, visualize the mouth of the Jade
Maiden spouting forth salival fluid. Let it flow into your own mouth.
Then rinse with this fluid and swallow it. Perform this ninety times,
then stop.

Once this is accomplished, just calm your mind and open your
thoughts. At this point you can perform the practice frequently, no
longer subject to various limitations.

[3b] However, make sure that as long as you visualize the
moon, you do not work on the sun, and vice versa. At the same
time, see that you visualize them both in equal measure and at
their proper times.

If you do not meet the proper time for ingestion [of the celestial
energy], then visualize the two luminants take up residence in
your Hall of Light. The sun on the left, the moon on the right, let
their radiance and brilliance merge to radiate out of the pupils of
your eyes. Let their two energies shine forth into the four directions and penetrate your entire being in free flow.

Then again, you can also visualize the sun and the moon in
your Hall of Light on a regular basis and without waiting to ingest
the energy of either. Doing so, you can make use of their combined
power.

[4a] Practice this for five years, and the Jade Maiden of Greatest Mystery will descend to you and lie down to share your mat. The Jade Maiden might even divide her shape for you into a host of like jade maidens who will serve your every whim.

This is due to the proper accordance of impulses, to the right combination of essences. It is the pure transformation of life, the essential vision of the true inner forms of all.

With this you have reached the perfect state of superior essence, the wondrous response to the divine impulse.

The perfected officers on high have developed this method of the sun's morning light and the practice involving the two luminants in order to allow human beings to pervade the universal numen and reach utter perfection. People with this practice can embody pure life and develop a jade-like glow.

[4b] With this you can command the myriad spirits and ascend to the halls of the emperor-on-high.

## 36. Ecstatic Sleep

"Sleep" exercises are a meditation that is practiced lying down. Popular since the Song, it is specifically used to circulate and revert energy according to the rules of inner alchemy.

Practitioners should first sit cross-legged and clap their teeth, then summon the gods in the body. Once concentration is thus established, they lie down on their side, either right or left, with their hands forming particular positions (mudras) of protection and with one leg bent slightly under the other. Further instructions include to close the mouth, lower the eyelids, and press the tip of the tongue against the upper palate.

Once in the right position, the various gateways of energy within the body are opened while those to the outside are firmly closed. Then the energies of the fire and water trigrams, the dragon and tiger, lead and mercury are circulated, leading eventually to the creation of an immortal embryo who in turn can ascend to the heavens. While the young one frolics about, the body of the practitioner lies in suspended animation.

Chen Tuan (died 989) was a Taoist master of the Five Dynasties and early Song who resided for most of his life on Huashan, the western sacred mountain. He is well known for his prognosticatory skills, his *Yijing* exegesis, and his months-long sleep practice. Inspiring many schools and traditions, he was later linked not only with various forms of inner alchemy and Qigong practice, but also with the development of Neo-Confucianism, in particular with Zhou Dunyi's "Diagram of the Great Ultimate."

The text below describes his sleep experiences according to the biography contained in the *Lishi zhenxian tidao tongjian* (Comprehensive Mirror Through the Ages of Perfected Immortals and Those Who Embody the Tao). This work, found in DZ 296, fasc. 139–48 (47.9a–11a) is among the most extensive works on the lives of the immortals. It was compiled by Zhao Daoyi (fl. 1294–1307) around the year 1300.

For a discussion of Chen Tuan, his life and legend, see Knaul 1981, Kohn 1990a. On Chen Tuan's role in the development of Neo-Confucianism, see Li 1990. For his later legends, including a transfer to Japan and involvement with the Huangbo (Obaku) school of Zen, see Russell 1990, 1990a. For more on sleep exercises, see their discussion in the Ming-dynasty manual *Chifeng sui* (The Marrow of the Red Phoenix), translated in Takehiro 1990 and Despeux 1988.

---

**"The Sleep of the Perfected," from the Biography of Chen Tuan, *Lishi zhenxian tidao tongjian* (Comprehensive Mirror Through the Ages of Perfected Immortals and Those Who Embody the Tao)**

[9a] From time to time, Master Chen walked around the mountain and down into the villages. To this day, there are people who have met him. Also there still are the monastery and residence of the Master in the western part of the Huashan range.

In the old days, the Master used to hike around much with a villager by the name of Cui Gu. Once a young monk by the name of Jin Li, who also spent his time hiking around sacred mountains, came to see Cui Gu.

"I would like to come along when you go to see Master Xiyi one of these days."

"Please be patient for a little while," Gu answered. "The Master is currently deep in sleep. You can meet him as soon as he comes out of it."

"When will this be?"

"There is no way of telling, maybe in half a year, maybe in three or four months. The Master hasn't even rested for a single month yet. So, if you have anything else to do in the meanwhile or any other places to visit, please do so and come back here later."

Thereupon Li left and only returned to Mount Hua after more than a year. He went to see Gu and was admitted to join him in a visit of the Master. Entering together, they bowed deeply. Li greeted the Master with utmost reverence.

He then addressed him: "I have ventured before to come to Mount Hua. My heart ached to meet you. But at that time you were deep in sleep and had not yet woken up. May I ask: Does the sleep also have Tao? [9b] If you would please be so kind as to instruct me in this matter and illuminate me in things unfathomable to my poor brain!"

The Master made a noise that sounded like laughter, squared his shoulders, pulled up his legs into a cross-legged posture, and let his dignified countenance relax.

"There is no need for you to be anxious or worried. It is like this. In the rhythm of activity and rest that governs our everyday life one cannot but know desires. It is very difficult to be liberated from life and death, to step outside of the wheel of rebirth.

"An ordinary person eats to satiation and then takes plenty of rest. He or she is mainly worried that the food should not be too rich, eating when he feels hungry and sleeping when he feels tired. His snore is audible all over the place. Yet, then, at night, when he should be sound asleep, he wakes up unaccountably. This is because fame and gain, sounds and sights agitate his spirit and consciousness; sweet wine and fried mutton muddle his mind and will. This is the sleep of ordinary folk.

But I practice the sleep of the perfected,
Store up the breath of gold and drink the juice of jade.
I lock the golden gate within, so it cannot be opened;
I close the door of earth inside, so it can not be broken.

The green dragon guards the Eastern Palace;
The white tiger stands before the Western Hall.
Perfected energy circulates in my Pond of Cinnabar,
And spirit water revolves around my five inner orbs.

I call the gods of *jia* and *ding* to adjust the time;
I summon all the hundred spirits to guard the inner chamber.
[10a]

Then my spirit
Leaves to ascend to the Nine Palaces above,
Frolics in the sky's azureness;

With it, I step on emptiness as if on solid ground,
Rise up as easy as if falling down.

Imperceptibly, I float around with the gentle winds;
Whirling, I appear with the easy-going clouds.
Sitting quiet, I reach the purple realm of Mount Kunlun;
With ease I pass through lucky places and the grotto
     heavens.

I inhale the flowery essence of the sun and moon;
I sport in the wondrous landscape of vapors and of haze.
I visit the perfected and discuss the principles beyond;
I join immortals and we go off to visit far strange lands.

As I see the green sea turning into soil,
I point at yin and yang and yell with exultation.

Delighted, I wish to return:
My feet step on clear wind,
My body floats on rays of light—
This is perfected sleep!

"Not knowing the movements of the year-star and the moon, how can one be saddened by the changes and alterations of the affairs of this world? Since you so politely asked me, I will summarize the gist of perfected sleep in a poem:

> In eternal sleep
> The world is energy.
> The soul all gone,
> No movement in the body.
>
> Coming back to consciousness — where is there a self?
> I wish my mind to wander once again
> And laugh about the grimy world of dust.
> How can I ever know that I am really there?

"Another good way of putting it is as follows [10b]:

> Superior beings do not dream;
> they sport with the immortals.
> The perfected never sleep;
> they float up with the clouds.

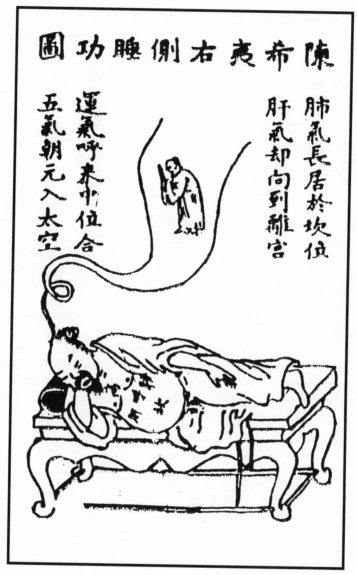

Fig. 28. Master Chen Practices Ecstatic Sleep. Source: *Chifeng sui.*

A cauldron full of drugs brings eternal life;
A hollow gourd contains a whole new world.
You want to know what is in sleep and dream?
It's well the highest mystery among men!

Thus, great dreams have great awakening;
Small dreams have only small.
Sleep the sleep of all that is perfection;
Dream the dreams of wide eternity—
None are there at all that would be of this world!"

This concluded his instructions. "I will sleep again shortly," the Master said. "If you do not have any other plans, please do not hesitate to come again in a few days and I will show you a practical example."

With this the Master left.

Li was dumbfounded like a block of wood. He felt as if he was waking from a state of deep intoxication. He had no idea how he managed to finally stumble out of the door.

Ultimately he returned to his lodgings and in due course came back to see the Master again. This time the Master discussed the secret ways of nourishing life with him and expounded the concepts of perfect wonder. He thereby clarified the profound principles of Great Mystery.

He ended by saying: "On that and that day, I will sleep again. Please come to see me then."

Li came on the appointed day. When he arrived he found the Master already asleep. He noticed that he slept while lying flat on his back, no inhalation or exhalation of breath was perceptible, and yet his face showed a rosy and radiantly healthy complexion. [11a] Li paid respects before the bed and went on his way.

Part Four

IMMORTALITY

# Chapter Ten

## IMMORTAL PERSONALITY

The fully accomplished immortal, easy traveler to the stars and companion of the perfected in the realm of the Tao, is still human. For the time being he or she has still to come back to the world of humanity, has to live among ordinary people, to deal with life in its various forms. Only after the lifespan decreed at this time has ended or when a summons to celestial office arrives, do immortals finally leave this world and ascend off and away for good. They then become one of the heavenly host, are given a rank in the hierarchy above, and serve in the celestial administration of this and the other world.

As long as they are still with ordinary mortals, however much their heads and minds and feelings might rest above the clouds, immortals are human beings with particular characteristics; they are people with the mind of immortals, with powers and behavior patterns unlike the ordinary.

Definitions and descriptions of this immortal personality differ. Most commonly, living immortals are described as perfected. They are realized ones in that they have fulfilled their full potential, true persons in that they have become truly human. Such people are qualified by their unshakable equanimity in all situations. The perfected among us do not hasten after gain, do not take pride in their achievements, do not worry about their ventures, and do not despair in failure.

They are calm and uninvolved, yet take action in just the way that is best for any given situation. With their hands on the pulse of nature, they are compassionate and understanding, compliant and gentle, helpful and upright. They seem to do the most outstanding feats with ease and no particular effort, fully in control of themselves, yet charming in their compliance with others.

Their personalities are completely unified. Forgetful of themselves, they have no trace of ego, of selfish interests left in them. Their minds at-one with the Tao, living immortals are in tune with nature and true companions of the world.

If one or the other of these wonder people takes up an active social role, he or she will become a center of society, a sage. Ideally the ruler or at least a close adviser to the ruler, such a sage does not need to do much actively to make the world a better place. In fact, the more he remains in non-action, the more the Tao that is concentrated in him can freely radiate and thereby create harmony and openness for all.

Without any effort, sages become models and foundations of the world as we know it. At one with the natural radiance of heaven, they spread sweetness and light wherever they go. Despite their elevated social position, they continue to behave with humility and in a withdrawing manner. Sages are whole persons whose government is beneficial to all. Their personality is one of complete openness, a free passageway for the cosmic energy of the Tao to flow from the root of creation to the benefit of all.

One with the Tao, living immortals also have various supernatural powers. The Tao itself is beyond life and death, time and space, light and darkness, and so are its perfected.

Many of their powers are similar to the abilities of shamans. Taoist immortals heal the sick, exorcise demons or beasts, make rain or stop it, foretell the future, prevent disasters, call upon wild animals as helpers, and remain unharmed by water and fire, heat and cold. Control over the body, a subtle harmony with the forces of nature, as well as an easy relationship with gods and spirits, ghosts and demons are equally characteristic of successful shamans as of the immortals of the Tao.

In addition, however, living immortals may also engage in more magical activities, feats that characterize them as wizards. They are shape-changers who can appear in any form they please. They can multiply themselves into many different people and be present in more than one place at the same time. They can become visible and invisible at will and travel thousands of miles in an instant. Controlling not only themselves, they also have power over nature. They can make rivers flow backward and mountains tumble. Plants, animals, and people die at their command and come back to life if they tell them to. They transport buildings to far-off places, open up mountains and reveal grottoes. In all these arts, immortals use their powers less for the benefit of humankind than for their own pleasure, as a demonstration of their might.

Sometimes they also use these powers to make fun of people or to extricate themselves from a difficult situation. In that case, the living immortal comes close to the figure of the trickster, someone who does not take life and death quite seriously and plays around with the world as he pleases.

Linked to this feature of the immortal personality is the type of the happy-go-lucky fellow who hangs out drinking and playing games, chess for a preference, writes silly verses on the walls of taverns, and shocks contemporary citizens with his unconventional behavior. So far beyond that they seem completely out of their normal minds, such immortals appear as weirdos and eccentrics. They sing at funerals, pinch wine and meat from the gods at sacrifices, drink and make merry whenever they get the chance, and laugh at anything and everything.

Accepting life and death as a single flow, they take neither seriously and make the best of all they meet. Their happy attitude, their playful way of being is characteristic of the popular image of the immortal today. It is frequently expressed in pictures of the Eight Immortals, shown playing and drinking together in merry company, that are often found on good-luck cards and in restaurants. Immortals that appear in modern films also tend to be of this type.

The selections below illustrate these character traits of the immortals. There is first the description of the perfected of old from the *Zhuangzi*, followed by sections on the sage from the *Daode jing*. Third, their magical powers are presented in several immortals' biographies from the fourth-century *Shenxian zhuan* (Biographies of Spirit Immortals) and *Soushen ji* (Record of Spirit Inquiries). Fourth, finally, some anecdotes about and a poem by Liu Ling, eccentric drinker of the third century, reveal the behavior of uninhibited personalities and society's reaction to it.

## 37. The Perfected

The *Zhuangzi* gives a convincing psychological description of the workings of the immortal mind. The perfected or realized one, free from worries and the ordinary emotions of life, in this understanding is not unlike the mystic described in the various religious traditions of the world.

Mystics all over are said to place their faith in something higher than themselves, to go along with life and never be afraid of death. Utterly equanimous in all situations, they have freedom and peace within, trust in the deity and compassion for all creatures without. Their state of mind can in fact be described in the terms of contemporary psychology as a state of complete being, of wholeness rather than deficiency.

Never striving for anything, never regretting anything, the mystic encompasses a personality fully human, fully at-one. Larger than life, he is yet the complete realization of life; one with the deity, with the Tao, he is yet more human than before.

The mystical ideal of the *Zhuangzi* provides a standard for the aims of the religious Taoist. The oneness of mind and Tao, the peace and serenity of the Tao within are forever a shining goal along the path, a sign of realization and immortality—at least in the spirit.

The translation relies on Watson 1968. For more on the *Zhuangzi*, see Section 4 above ("Ineffable Knowledge").

---

## "The Perfected of Old" and "The Great Man," from *Zhuangzi*, chaps. 6, 11, 24.

What, then, is a perfected?

The perfected of old did not fight it if he had little, did not grow proud if he had much. He never planned his affairs. Someone like this would make a mistake and not feel bad about it; he would attain success and not claim credit for it. Someone like this would climb into high places and not get nervous. He would enter water and not get wet; he would enter fire and not get burned. All this is because his knowledge could reach to the Tao itself.

The perfected of old slept without dreaming and woke without worrying. He ate without delighting in the taste and breathed very deep. In fact, a perfected breathes all the way to his heels, while ordinary people breathe only as far as their throats. Bent and burdened, they gasp out words as if they were retching. Involved deeply with passions and desires, their connection with heaven is shallow indeed.

The perfected of old did not know how to delight in life, nor did he know how to loathe death. He came to be without pleasure and went back to nonbeing without refusal. He came in an instant, he went in an instant, and that was all. He never forgot where he began; he never pursued where he would end. He received life and enjoyed it. But then he forgot about it and returned it when the time came. This is what we mean by not using the mind to repel the Tao, nor using humanity to assist heaven. Such indeed is the perfected.

In someone like this, the mind is concentrated, the expression serene, the forehead broad. His coolness is like autumn, his warmth like spring; thus his joy and anger go along perfectly with the four seasons. He perfectly matches the needs of all living beings—no one knows his limits. Therefore, when a true sage engages in warfare, he may destroy a country, but he will not lose the hearts of the people. His advance benefits ten thousand generations, but he has no egoistic love for any particular person. . . .

The perfected of old bore himself with dignity and did not budge. He appeared to lack, yet he would receive nothing. He was upright in his correctness but never insistent. He was strong in his position yet never showed off.

> Mild and cheerful—he seemed joyous.
> Reluctant—he would not help himself.
> Annoyed—he let it show in his face.
> Giving—he found rest in his virtue.
> Tolerant—he seemed like the common world.
> Imposing—he would never be controlled.
> Withdrawn—he seemed to prefer his solitude.
> Bemused—he forgot what he was going to say.

For him penalties were the body of life, rites its outer wings; for him wisdom was to be in accordance with the times, and virtue to follow the natural course.

Because for him penalties were the body of life, he was compassionate in killing. Because for him rites were the outer wings of life, he always went along with the world. Because for him wisdom was to be in accordance with the times, there were things he would not help himself but do. Because for him virtue was to follow the natural course, his words had head and tail and always made their point.

And yet—people truly thought that he made strong efforts to be like this!

Therefore, in the perfected of old, all liking was unified into one and all disliking was unified into one. His being at-one was unified and his not being at-one was unified. When he was at-one, he acted as the companion of heaven. When he was not at-one, he acted as the companion of humanity. Heaven and humanity not fighting each other within—this is the perfected!

Life and death are fate—regular as the succession of night and day. They are a matter of heaven! Nothing that human beings could do anything about. A matter of beings' inner nature!

Someone may take heaven as his father and love it with all his being—how much more should he do for the highest of all? Someone may take the ruler as his superior and be ready to die for him with all his being—how much more should he do for the truth of all?

When a spring dries up, the fish lie together on the ground. They spray each other with moisture and wet each other with spittle. Still, how much better were it if they could forget each other in the rivers and lakes! In the same way, people praise the benevolent ruler Yao and condemn the tyrant Jie. But how much better were it if they could forget either and transform themselves naturally with the Tao! (chap. 6)

Now, he who has the earth possesses a great being indeed. As he possesses a great being, he cannot be considered a mere being himself. He is a living being, yet he is not a mere being. Thus he can treat beings truly as beings in their own right. It is clear indeed! One who treats beings truly as beings in their own right is not a mere being himself! How could he merely rule the hundred clans in all under heaven and nothing else?

Rather, he freely leaves and enters the Six Harmonies of the universe and wanders through the Nine Continents at his leisure. He goes alone and comes alone—he can be called a lone possessor. One who possesses alone—he has reached perfect eminence.

The teaching of the great man is like a shadow following a shape, an echo following a sound. When questioned he answers, and exhausting all he has, he truly becomes the companion of the world.

Yet at the same time he dwells in the echoless and moves in the shapeless. Throwing off the rush and bustle of the world, he floats around the beginningless, passes in and out of the boundless. Like the sun, he has no beginning nor end. His face and body are joined with Great Unity. In face, he is Great Unity!

Such a one has no self. Selfless, how could he regard having something as possession? No, it was the gentleman of antiquity who had his eyes on possession. One who has his eyes on nonbeing—he is the true friend of heaven and earth. (chap. 11)

The sage embraces heaven and earth. His benefit reaches to all under heaven. Yet no one knows who he is or what family he belongs to. For this reason, in life he holds no rank, in death he has no posthumous titles. Events do not assemble around him, names do not get attached to him—such is the great man. . . .

He who understands this greatness does not seek, does not lose, does not reject, does not change himself for the sake of beings. He returns to himself and is never exhausted; he follows the ways of old and never perishes. Such is the sincerity of the great man! (chap. 24)

## 38. To Be a Sage

The ideal human being in the *Daode jing* is understood more politically. The sage here is not only socially responsible but a key figure to the integrated functioning and wholeness of government and society. It is through him that the Tao can spread throughout the world, that the spontaneous flow of natural goodness can work for the benefit of all.

In the *Zhuangzi*, there is a distinction between the sage (*shengren*) and the lord (*junzi*), the former being unobtrusive and withdrawing, a little bird which no one notices and who works his good in solitude. The latter, on the other hand, is a proud man, politically ambitious, rich and noble, full of troubles and the worries of the world.

The *Daode jing* has the two coincide in its vision of the sage, a vision which becomes dominant in the later tradition. The ideal Taoist ruler is a sage-lord who will bring integrity to his subjects, harmony to their families, prosperity to their land, and Great Peace to all under heaven. Utterly open to the flow of the Tao, this ruler spreads its power for the sake of all.

For more on the *Daode jing*, see Section 1 above ("The Tao That Can't Be Told").

---

### *Daode jing* (Scripture of the Tao and the Virtue)

The sage rests in affairs in non-action,
And practices the teaching of no words.
The myriad beings are active through him—
He does not turn away from them.
They live through him—
He does not take possession of them.

The sage acts in the world,
But does not depend on it;
His task accomplished,

He does not stay with it.
And because he does not stay,
It remains. (chap. 2)

Do not exalt the worthy!
And the people will not compete.
Do not value rare goods!
And the people will not steal.
Do not display desirable things!
And the people's hearts will remain at peace.

Such is the government of the sage:
He frees their hearts
And fills their stomachs.
He weakens their ambitions
And strengthens their marrow.

He always causes the people to be unknowing,
Free from desires,
So that the smart ones will not dare to impose.

He acts in non-action,
And there is nothing that is not well done! (chap. 3)

Leave off learning! Be without worry!
Leave off sageliness! Get rid of wisdom!
The people will benefit a hundredfold.
Leave off benevolence! Get rid of righteousness!
The people will recover true obedience and caring love.
Leave off skill! Get rid of profit!
There will be no more thieves and robbers.

Still, these are outer attitudes and not yet sufficient.
Therefore, let the people always follow these rules:

Manifest plainness!
Embrace simplicity!
Reduce selfishness!
Have few desires! (chap. 19)

Yield and you will be whole!
Bend and you will be straight!

Let go and you will be rich!
Grow old and you will be new!
Have little and you will be gaining!
Have plenty and you will be confused!

Therefore the sage embraces the One
And becomes the model for all under heaven.

Not presenting himself, he is radiant.
Not thinking himself right, he is famous.
Not pushing himself forward, he is meritorious.
Not pitying himself, he is eminent.

He never competes—
None under heaven can compete with him!

The ancients said:
"Yield and you will be whole!"
Are these mere empty words?
They are not!
The sage is whole. He follows this. (chap. 22)

Good traveling leaves not track nor trace.
Good speaking has not flaw nor bent.
Good reckoning uses not counters nor devices.

A door well shut needs no bolts, and yet cannot be opened.
A knot well tied needs no extra rope, yet cannot be undone.

Therefore the sage
Is always there to help the people—
He rejects no person.
Is always there to help all beings—
He rejects no creature.

Thus it is said:
He is at-one with universal light.

For him, good people are the teachers of the bad;
The bad their work material.
He neither values the teachers
Nor passionately loves the material.

Knowing that, however wise, a person may be greatly
   deluded.
Such is his essential mystery. (chap. 27)

Know the male and keep to the female;
Be the depth of the world.
As the depth of the world,
Universal virtue will never leave,
And you return to be a small child!

Know the bright and keep to the dark;
Be the model for the world.
As the model for the world,
Universal virtue will never err,
And you return to be without limit!

Know glory and keep to humility.
Be the ground of the world.
As the ground of the world,
Universal virtue will suffuse you
And you return to be perfectly simple!

In most people,
Simplicity is lost and things take over.
But when the sage uses it,
He becomes a leader among officials.
Therefore his rule is great—
It never cuts the network of the world. (chap. 28)

The sage has no ordinary mind;
He makes the people's mind his own.

The good, I treat with goodness;
The bad, I treat with equal goodness.
Thus my virtue is full of goodness.

The honest, I treat with honesty;
The dishonest, I treat with equal honesty.
Thus my virtue is full of honesty.

The sage in the world
Unites with the entire world

And makes it his mind,
Joins the hundred clans
And makes them his eyes and ears.
They are all his children. (chap. 49)

The still is easy to grasp.
The open is easy to plan.
The brittle is easy to crack.
The tiny is easy to lose.

Act before there's need!
Order before there's chaos!

A huge thick tree grows from a tiny shoot.
A nine-storied tower rises from a heap of earth.
A thousand-mile journey starts with the first step.

Act with intention and you will fail!
Grasp hold firmly and you will lose!

Therefore
The sage rests in non-action and never fails,
Is without grasping and never loses.
People handle affairs and fail close to success.
Take care of the end as much as of the beginning!
There will be no failure!

Therefore
The sage wishes to be free from desires
And does not value rare goods.
He learns to be free from learning
And recovers what the multitude has passed.

He aids the spontaneous development of the myriad
     beings—
Never dares to act. (chap. 64)

True words are not beautiful;
Beautiful words are not true.
A good man does not argue;
Who argues is not a good man.
A wise man has no knowledge;
Who knows is not a wise man.

The sage does not accumulate:
The more he does for others,
The more he gains himself.
The more he gives to others,
The more he has himself.

The way of heaven:
Always benefit, never harm!
The way of the sage:
Always work, never compete! (chap. 81)

### 39. Magical Powers

Magical supernatural powers, be they of shamans or of wizards, appear most clearly in the biographies of the immortals. There are many such collections in Chinese literature, stereotyped rather early and repetitive in their standard patterns.

The *Shenxian zhuan* (Biographies of Spirit Immortals) is the second early collection of such biographies after the Han-dynasty *Liexian zhuan*. Originally written by Ge Hong (263–343) in the fourth century, it was lost later and reassembled in the sixth century. Today it is edited in the *Daozang jinghua* (5.11).

The *Soushen ji* (In Search of the Supernatural) is a collection of tales of the marvelous from approximately the same time. It was put together by Gan Bao (ca. 320 C.E.) and is today available in an edition from Shijie shuju (Taipei, 1970). The story is taken from the first chapter.

I have consulted the *Shenxian zhuan* translation in Güntsch 1988. Liu An's and Zuo Ci's biographies partly follow Giles 1948. For studies of the *Soushen ji*, see Bodde 1942, DeWoskin 1977.

More details on the arts and powers of the immortals are found in Robinet 1979a and 1986, DeWoskin 1990. For a discussion of the symbolism of the microcosm, the habitat, and attributes of the immortals, see Stein 1990.

---

### *Shenxian zhuan* (Biographies of Spirit Immortals)

THE MASTER WITH THE YELLOW PUPILS

The Master with the Yellow Pupils had the family name Ge and the personal name Yue. He was good at curing and healing. Even at a distance of one thousand miles, if he only knew the name of the sick person, he could cure him. All would get well, even if he never saw the patient's body.

He was also very good at exorcising with the help of cosmic energy. He would get rid of tigers, wolves, and all kinds of nasty insects. None of them would dare move when he was around, nor would birds dare to fly off.

He could make the river flow backwards as far as one mile. He easily reached the age of 280 years, at which he was still able to lift a ton without any trouble.

He walked as fast as other people rode on horseback. Around his head there frequently was a five-colored halo, which made him look about ten feet tall.

At times of drought he could enter deep into the springs and summon forth dragons. Controlling them, he ordered them to ascend to the sky and produce rain. Numerous times he worked miracles like that.

One day he said farewell to his family and friends, strode on a dragon, and left. He never came back. (10.40b)

The Lady of Great Mystery

The Lady of Great Mystery had the family name Zhuan and was personally called He. When she was a little girl she lost first her father and after a little while also her mother.

Understanding that living beings often did not fulfill their destined lifespans, she felt sympathy and sadness. She used to say: "Once people have lost their existence in this world, they cannot recover it. Whatever has died cannot come back to life. Life is so limited! It is over so fast! Without cultivating the Tao, how can one extend one's life?"

She duly left to find enlightened teachers, wishing to purify her mind and pursue the Tao. She obtained the arts of the Jade Master and practiced them diligently for several years.

As a result she was able to enter the water and not get wet. Even in the severest cold of winter she would walk over frozen rivers wearing only a single garment. All the time her expression would not change, and her body would remain comfortably warm for a succession of days.

The Lady of Great Mystery could also move government offices, temples, cities, and lodges. They would appear in other places quite without moving from their original location. Whatever she pointed at would vanish into thin air. Doors, windows, boxes, or caskets that were securely locked needed only a short flexing of her finger to break wide open. Mountains would tumble, trees would fall at the pointing of her hand. Another short gesture would resurrect them to their former state.

One day she went into the mountains with her disciples. At sunset she took a staff and struck a stone. The stone at once opened wide, leading into a grotto-world fully equipped with beds and benches, screens and curtains. It also had a kitchen and larder, full with wine and food. All was just like it would be in the world of everyday life.

The Lady of Great Mystery could travel ten thousand miles, yet at the same time continue to stay nearby. She could transform small things to be suddenly big, and big things to be small. She could spit fire so big it would rise up wildly into heaven, and yet in one breath she could extinguish it again.

She was also able to sit in the middle of a blazing fire, while her clothes would never be even touched by the flames. She could change her appearance at will: one moment she was an old man, the next a small child. She could also conjure up a cart and horse to ride back and forth in if she did not want to walk.

The Lady of Great Mystery perfectly mastered all thirty-six arts of the immortals. She could resurrect the dead and bring them back to life. She saved innumerable people, but nobody knew what she used for her dresses or her food, nor did anybody ever learn her arts from her. Her complexion was always that of a young girl; her hair stayed always black as a raven. Later she ascended into heaven in broad daylight. She was never seen again. (7.27a)

LIU AN AND THE EIGHT WORTHIES

Liu An, the Prince of Huainan, used humble words and high rewards to invite many guests to his house. He was especially fond of scholars of the Tao and masters of magic, and he got them to come, be they even a thousand miles away.

One day, eight old men with white beards and eyebrows appeared at his gate. When the gatekeeper saw them, he immediately stole away to inform the prince, who ordered him, as if on his own initiative, to put some difficult questions to the newcomers.

"Uppermost in my lord's mind," he said accordingly, "is the wish to pursue the Tao of extending one's years, living a long life, and never growing old. Next, he wishes to find great scholars who understand things broadly, analyze their deep meaning, and delve

Fig. 29. Liu An Ascends to Heaven with His Dog and Rooster. Source: *Zengxiang liexian zhuan*.

into the wonders of the world. Third, he wishes to attract strong men full of courage, who can lift heavy tripods and wrestle tigers with bare arms.

"Now you, sirs, are already advanced in years. It looks as though you do not have the magic means of warding off decay. Nor do you seem to have any extraordinary courage. How, therefore, could you penetrate the mysteries of the Three Sovereigns and Five Emperors of antiquity, understand the Eight Simplicities of the Trigrams and the Nine Continents of the World? How would you be able to investigate profundities, exercise control over things at a distance, thoroughly assimilate universal principles, and perfect your inner nature? As you are wanting in those requirements, I dare not announce you to my lord."

The Eight Worthies smiled. "We have heard," one of them said in response, "that the prince greatly venerates wise men and never tires to leave his meals and jump out of his bath to rush to their service. Even to those of small skill he is kind and allows everyone to come to his house.

"In antiquity, people valued the study of the nine times nine and cultivated such arts as the imitation of birds' cries and dogs' barks. When they bought a horse on the market, they seriously hoped to purchase a magic steed like the racer of King Mu. When they served in office, they were honestly concerned to live up to Master Guo in caring for the welfare of their state.

"Now, we are old and common, and do not have the qualities the prince is looking for. We just came here from afar because we would like to meet His Highness. It may not be much use, but then—it may not do any harm, either. Why, then, should you bar these old men from access to your lord?

"Of course," he added with a shrug, "if the prince saw that we were young, he would assume that we possessed the Tao. Since we have white hair, he automatically takes us for foolish old men! I'm afraid he is rather shortsighted: neither drills into stone in order to find jade nor dives into depths in order to find pearls.

"So, then, if he dislikes us old—well, then we shall become young!"

Scarcely had he spoken these words, when all eight of them turned into youths of fourteen or fifteen. Their coils of hair became black and silky; their complexions looked rosy like peach blossoms.

The gatekeeper, much amazed, went and told the Prince. Hearing the news, he never even put on his shoes but rushed out to welcome them. He conducted them up to the Terrace of Contemplating Immortality, where he drew brocade hangings and arranged ivory benches. He lit the incense of a hundred harmonies and placed before them tables of gold and jade.

The Prince paid them deference as if he were their disciple. Facing north, he knocked his head and said: "I am a man of mediocre ability. Ever since I was a child I have loved the Tao and its virtue. Fettered by the duties of the world and drowning in mundane affairs, I cannot escape from my worries and go off, shouldering my satchel, to live in the mountains and forests.

"Yet," he went on with a sigh, "morning and evening I hunger and thirst, yearning deeply for the radiance of the spirit. I long to wash away the dirt and mud of this world. Alas, that the sincerity within myself is so shallow! That the determination in my bosom is not stronger! But the arts of the Tao have been so far beyond me as if they were the Milky Way itself!

"Now, however, I have come into unexpected good fortune: You, my Lords of the Tao, have condescended to grace my abode with your presence! Oh, that it should be my fate to be elevated like this! I am happy yet anxious, excited yet nervous about what I should do.

"Therefore, with all my heart, I beg you, Lords of the Tao, to have pity and instruct me. Then, though now merely a crawling insect, I shall borrow the wings of a heron and soar up into the sky."

The eight youths promptly turned into old men again. They told the Prince: "Our knowledge is insignificant. We have only borrowed the learning of our elders. Still, we have come to join you after we heard that you are fond of scholars. Now, we still have to find out what it is you want to learn.

"One of us, for example, is able to call up wind and rain without effort, to raise clouds and mists in an instant. He can trace lines across the lands and they become rivers, scoop up soil and make mountains.

"Another of us can cause tall mountains to collapse, the sources of deep springs to run dry. He can tame tigers and panthers, summon scaly monsters and dragons to appear, and press demons and spirits into his service.

"The third among us can divide his body and transform his appearance, become visible or invisible at will. He can hide away whole armies, and turn midday into night.

"Another of us can ride the clouds and tread on empty air, cross the sea and walk on flowing waves. He can go in and out of the spaceless and travel a thousand miles in one breath.

"The fifth among us can enter flames unscathed and plunge into water without getting wet. He is invulnerable to swords or arrows. He feels no cold in winter frosts, nor sweat in the heat of summer.

"Yet another of us can perform a myriad transformations. Bird, beast, grass, tree—as the fancy takes him, he can become each and any of the myriad beings. He can move mountains and bring rivers to a halt. He can transport palaces and move houses around as he pleases.

"The seventh among us can prevent disasters and save others from danger. He can protect people from all thinkable harm. He also knows how to extend the years and increase longevity, to live a long life and attain eternal vision.

"The last of us, finally, can boil mud into gold and congeal lead into silver. He can fuse the eight minerals into a liquid from which pearls fly aloft like steam. He can ride in a cloud chariot drawn by a team of dragons and thus float even above the Heaven of Great Clarity.

"Now, you Prince, must decide which of these powers you will want to acquire."

Liu An reverently served the Eight Worthies from morning to night. He had them well provided with meat and wine, and carefully examined each of their claims. A thousand changes, ten thousand transformations, all sorts of strange arts—there was none that they did not master to perfection!

Later they bestowed upon him the *Cinnabar Scripture* in thirty-six scrolls, so that he could prepare the elixir of immortality. . . .

People living at the time report that, when Liu An and the Eight Worthies at last took their departure from this earth, the vessel containing the dregs of the elixir was left behind in the courtyard. The contents were duly finished by the dogs and poultry of the establishment, with the result that they too sailed up to heaven. Thus roosters were heard crowing in the sky, and the barking of dogs resounded among the clouds. (4.14a–15a)

---

## *Soushen ji* (In Search of the Supernatural)

ZUO CI AND THE GENERAL

Zuo Ci, also known as Yuanfang, was from Lujiang in Anhui. From an early age, he possessed a high insight into the workings and marvels of the spirit.

Once the general Cao Cao invited him to a banquet. Looking round his guests with a smile, Cao said: "I am embarrassed of the poor provision made for this high company today. What we lack are some perch from the Wusong River."

"That's easy," Zuo said and called for a bronze bowl filled with water. Once he had the bowl, he started to fish in it with a bamboo rod. After a little while he had caught a perch. Cao Cao clapped his hands vigorously, and everyone was greatly astonished.

"One fish," Cao then said, "won't go around. It would be good to have two."

So Zuo cast his line again and soon caught another fish. Both were over three feet long and tasted deliciously fresh.

Cao Cao had them cut up before his eyes, then had the dish handed to all the guests at his table.

"Now that we have got our perch," he said thoughtfully, "it is a shame we have no fresh ginger from Sichuan with it."

"That too can be obtained," Zuo assured him.

Suspicious lest he should buy some nearby, Cao Cao added a demand. "Some time ago," he said, "I sent a man to Sichuan to buy brocade for me. Please instruct your messenger to tell my agent to buy two more bolts."

Zuo's messenger departed and, in a moment, was back again with the fresh ginger. "I saw the general's agent," he reported. "I met him in a brocade shop and gave him the order."

More than a year later, Cao's agent came back. Sure enough, he had bought two more bolts. On being questioned, he said: "About a year ago, on such and such a day, I met this man in a brocade shop. He informed me of your new order."

On a later occasion, Cao Cao, together with a group of over a hundred scholars, went on an excursion outside the city. Zuo provided a single jar of wine and a single piece of dried meat. Pouring from the jar with his own hands, he poured out wine for all the guests. There was not one of them who did not drink and eat to repletion.

Cao Cao thought this very strange and had the matter investigated. He sent round to inspect the wine shops and found that the day before they had all been cleared of their stocks of wine and meat. This angered him and he secretly determined to put Zuo to death.

The latter was in the general's palace. But when they came to arrest him, he just walked straight into a wall and vanished without a trace. Then Cao hired a number of men to capture him. One

Fig. 30. Zuo Ci Greets the Immortals' Crane. Source: *Zengxiang liexian zhuan.*

of these saw him in the marketplace. On the point of seizing him, suddenly all the people there were transformed into Zuo's exact likeness. No one could tell which one was he.

Later on, some of the hired men found Zuo on the slope of Southtown Hill. Again they pursued him, and he fled among a flock of sheep, turning into an animal himself.

The general realized that Zuo would not be caught this way. So he told his men to go among the sheep and make the following announcement: "Lord Cao will not put you to death. He only wanted to try the power of your magic. Now that you have passed the test, please come and talk to us!"

Suddenly one old ram bent its forelegs, stood upright like a human being, and said in a human voice: "What a fluster you are in!"

"There!" Cao's men cried excitedly. "That ram is the one we want!"

But as they made a dash for him, the entire flock of several hundred turned into rams. They all bent their forelegs, stood upright like humans, and cried: "What a fluster you are in!"

Nobody knew which one to capture.

## 40. The Virtue of Wine

A classical example of the carefree drinker and eccentric nobleman is found in Liu Ling of the third century (–265). One among a group of like-minded men, the so-called Seven Sages of the Bamboo Grove, he spent his life in leisure, drinking, singing, making poetry with his friends, and forgetting about the politically troubled times he lived in.

To a certain extent, he and his friends were helped in this effort by a drug called Cold-Food-Powder. Taken in small amounts with wine, it would lift up the senses into ecstasy but make the body feel extremely hot, so that takers would feel compelled to take off all their clothes and immerse themselves in cold water.

While not himself counted among the immortals, Liu Ling is recognized as an example for the happy and carefree behavior of people who have gone beyond. Like many in his group, he dreamt of an existence as a full perfected, wishing to be like the great man who could leave it all behind for the pleasures of heavenly rambling.

The poem that extols the virtues of the great man and his wine is taken from *Wenxuan* (Literary Selections), chapter 47. The two biographical incidents are mentioned in the *Shishuo xinyu* (A New Account of Tales of the World).

The rendition is reprinted from Mather 1976. On the Seven Sages, see Holzman 1956, 1978. For more on drugs in medieval Chinese society, see Wagner 1973. The translation of the poem is taken from Kohn 1992.

*Jiude song* (In Praise of the Virtue of Wine)

> There is Master Great Man—
> For him heaven and earth are a single morning,
> A thousand years just a short moment.
> The sun and the moon are mere windows for him,
> The Eight Wilds are his pleasure garden.
>
> He travels without wheels or tracks,
> Sojourns without house or hearth.
> Heaven is his curtain and earth his seat;
> He indulges in what he pleases.
>
> Stopping, he grasps his wine-cup,
> Holds fast to his goblet;
> Moving, he carries a casket,
> Holds a jar in his hand.
> His only obligation is toward wine,
> But of that he knows plenty.
>
> Some noble princely courtier
> And an official in seclusion
> Come to hear my song,
> To deliberate its worth.
>
> Flapping wildly their sleeves,
> Pulling up their robes,
> Anger in their eyes,
> They loudly gnash their teeth.
>
> They explain to me
> The rules of ritual and order,
> Raise for me their lances
> To show what's right and wrong.

The Master, however, only
Holds up his jar
And goes on with his wine,
Cherishing his cup
To the last lees.

With ruffled whiskers he sits,
Legs spread indecently apart;
The yeast becomes his pillow,
The sediments his mat.

Utterly free from yearnings and from worries,
Always happy and full in his contentment—
Without ever moving he gets drunk,
Then, with a start he sobers up.

Listens quietly,
But does not hear the boom of rolling thunder;
Watches intently,
But does not see towering Mount Tai.

Unaware of the cold biting his flesh,
Unmoved by the afflictions of common greed.

Looking down he watches:
The myriad beings bustle there about
Like tiny pieces of duckweed
Floating on the Han and Jiang.

The two courtiers stand as servants at his sides,
Like caterpillars near a sphinx.

---

## "On Liu Ling," from *Shishuo xinyu* (A New Account of Tales of the World)

On many occasions Liu Ling, under the influence of wine, would be completely free and uninhibited. Sometimes he would take off his clothes and sit naked in his room.

Once some people came to see him and chided him for this behavior. Liu Ling retorted, "I take heaven and earth for my pillars and roof, and the rooms of my house for my pants and coat. And now, what are you gentlemen doing in my pants?" (23.6)

Liu Ling was once suffering from a hangover and was extremely thirsty. He asked his wife for some wine.

However, she had poured all the wine away and smashed all the vessels. "You are drinking far too much!" she pleaded, tears in her eyes. "This is no way to preserve your life! Oh, if you would only stop!"

"A very good idea," Liu Ling agreed. "But I am unable to stop all by myself. It can only be done if I pray to the ghosts and spirits and take an oath to stop drinking from now on. So, please get ready the wine and meat for the necessary sacrifice."

"As you wish," his wife said. She duly set out wine and meat before the spirits and requested Liu Ling to kneel down and take his oath.

Ling duly knelt and prayed:

> "Heaven brought forth Liu Ling
> And took "wine" for his name.
> At one gulp he downs a gallon—
> Five dipperfuls to ease the hangover.
> As for his wife's complaint,
> Be careful not to listen!"

Thereupon he drained the spirits' wine and ate all the meat. Before he knew it, he was drunk again. (23.3)

# Chapter Eleven

## ASCENSION

The transition from a realized life on earth to an eternal existence in the glory and delight of the heavens is the process of ascension. Ascension is the key phase that separates immortals as realized human beings from immortals as members of the administration of heaven and attendants on the higher deities of the Tao.

Ascension is moreover a strong symbol of the going-beyond of all individuality and social integration of the world. Whether a given immortal observes his or her own funeral, whether a high Taoist master formally prepares and exhibits his or her "transformation," or whether the person just vanishes to the great consternation of all around—in all cases ascension signifies the ultimate break with the world of humanity, the transcendence of all that's ordinary, common, normal, in body as well as in mind.

Ascension comes in different forms. The highest way to ascend is by celestial chariot. Receiving a summons to office among the heavenly bureaucrats, the immortal readies himself or herself and, on the day appointed, is formally met by a dragon-drawn cloudy chariot and escorted up to heaven by a large entourage of celestial guards, supernatural horsemen, and divine lads. The most famous ascension of this kind is that of the Yellow Emperor, who mounted on a huge celestial dragon together with seventy of his followers, some people trying to cling to the dragon's beard and claws in a desperate effort at eternal life.

The second most powerful way of ascension is by just vanishing completely. Again, a divine invitation is received, but rather than in a formal reception, the immortal ascends upward on his own, using clouds and streams of air to support himself. Here, too, the celestial-to-be announces his or her supernatural state and gets ready for departure, but the entire setting is decidedly less formal. This form of ascension, not as celebrated and rather less well prepared, often leaves friends and family in a state of confusion. How can one be sure there wasn't foul play by some nasty demon?

A third way of ascension is by "deliverance from the corpse." This is a rather crude way to leave, since it requires that the immortal leave some physical token of his or her worldly presence behind. This shows that he or she is quite able to dissolve completely into the heavenly spheres. Typically, in such cases there is a corpse—unless substituted by a bamboo staff or sword—but unlike that of an ordinary dead person, this body does not decay. Far from smelling offensive in any way, the corpse is fragrant; pink clouds come to hover around it, and strands of celestial music are heard. Most classically, this is the way Taoist masters go, announcing their "transformation" and leaving the world sitting erect in deep meditation.

In terms of methods, there are several ways to undertake an ascension. The most effective and immediate is by swallowing a cinnabar elixir, a concoction of various metals and minerals, but ultimately identifiable as a mercury compound. The stronger the elixir, the more instantaneous is the transformation. Operative alchemy in traditional China is not only a formalized and ritualized process of replicating the creation of the universe and an attempt to find the philosophers' stone, but the safest way to be ready for the celestial summons at the moment it comes. Elixirs are highly poisonous, but ascending immortals knew where they were going.

Another way is to produce an inner elixir by way of internal alchemy. Here an immortal embryo is created, an agent that combines all the celestial elements of the practitioner and that will travel freely through the otherworldly realms. When the summons comes or the natural lifespan of this body ends, the embryo ascends once more, this time for good.

Then again, there is the way of dissolution, a more meditative method in which the adept transforms his or her self and body to ever subtler energies and eventually loses self completely in the overall stream of the Tao. Rather a gradual process, ascension here is the opening of the earth-bound body and mind to a more subtle being, the gradual floating away of the self and merging into the nothingness of the Tao.

The selections below show these various types and ways of ascension. There is first the description of the nine elixirs from the fourth-century *Baopuzi* (Book of the Master Who Embraces Simplicity), a highly technical exposition of the methods and aims of operative alchemy.

Next, there is Zhang Boduan's *Wuzhen pian* (Awakening to Perfection), one of the classics of inner alchemy, dated to the eleventh century. Third, Sun Simiao's *Cunshen lianqi ming* (Visualization of Spirit and Refinement of Energy) is a short but clear description of the immortal process of self-transformation and the gradual stages of dissolution into the Tao. It is dated to the seventh century.

Fourth, there are three reports on actual ascensions. One, from the *Shenxian zhuan* (Biographies of Spirit Immortals) of the fourth century, records the adventures of one who ascended in a cloudy chariot and come back to tell about it. The second, the *Huang xianshi Qutong ji* (Record of Immortal Master Huang and Lad Qu), is a late Tang record on the strange events surrounding the sudden disappearance of Lad Qu, a young Taoist adept. The third is a short description of the typical transformation of a Taoist master (in this case a mistress), an excerpt from the tenth-century biography of the Flower Maiden from Du Guangting's *Yongcheng jixian lu* (Record of the Assembled Immortals of the Heavenly Walled City).

## 41. Alchemical Transformation

Alchemy, the concoction of a cinnabar or elixir, is the prime method to prepare for ascension. Cinnabar, a reddish mineral dust found along riverbanks, transmutes into mercury when heated. If combined with silver, it turns into a highly poisonous mixture that will deliver anyone instantaneously into the otherworld.

The taking of such an elixir, upon receiving the celestial summons, is in fact a form of ritual suicide. However strong the belief in a continued existence in the upper reaches of the universe, however desirable the transformation, there is no belying the physical death that Taoists have to undergo at the time of ascension. Only, of course, death at this point is no longer death, suicide no longer suicide. The physical transformation is a form of liberation and the ultimate fulfillment of a longstanding effort.

There is a logic behind mercury poisoning and the replenishing of the body with metals and minerals. Since these substances are themselves non-decaying, they are believed to prevent from decay whatever they come in contact with, more so when actually ingested. There is no doubt that Taoists with their diet of grain-avoidance had to rely a great deal on vegetal and mineral substances to maintain health and strength. Nor is it questionable that, taken in small amounts, the various substances they used are quite helpful and form an important part of medicine in China and elsewhere.

The compound drugs produced on the basis of cinnabar are thus a direct continuation of the crude and more innocuous drugs used for medical purposes and in supplementing Taoist diet. Alchemy, in its pharmacological dimension, is thus linked immediately to Chinese medicine and traditional dietetics. At the same time, alchemy is a highly ritualized undertaking that has a primarily religious goal. The concoction of cinnabar elixirs thus integrates the various strands of the Taoist tradition as much as it is a pinnacle of the Taoist career.

The description of the various recipes below is taken from the chapter "Gold and Cinnabar" (*Jindan*) of the *Baopuzi neipian* (Book of the Master Who Embraces Simplicity, Inner Chapters: 4.2a–11b). This text, compiled by Ge Hong (263–343) in the early fourth century, is contained in DZ 1185, fasc. 868–70.

The translation of its more technical sections relies closely on Ware 1966. The outer chapters are rendered in Sailey 1978. For a study of the *Scripture of the Nine Tripods' Cinnabar* and other early texts, see Pregadio 1991.

For a short survey of the development of Chinese alchemy, see Akahori 1989. A detailed historical survey is found in Needham et al. 1976. For more on alchemical methods, apparatus, and theoretical system, see Needham et al. 1980. A translation and analysis of a Tang-dynasty alchemical tract is found in Sivin 1968. For a study of alchemy in Highest Clarity Taoism, see Strickmann 1979.

---

## "Gold and Cinnabar" (*Jindan*), from *Baopuzi neipian* (Book of the Master Who Embraces Simplicity, Inner Chapters)

[2a] Once in the past, Zuo Ci was meditating in the Heavenly Pillar Mountains, when a spirit being revealed several immortal scriptures on gold and cinnabar to him. At the time, however, the political chaos at the end of the Han dynasty prevented him from concocting the elixir. Instead he fled his mountain retreat, crossed the Yangtse and went east with the intention to select a famous mountain and cultivate the Tao he had received.

At this place my father's cousin, Ge Xuan, now known as an immortal himself, received the texts from Zuo Ci. In all, he received the *Scripture of the Great Clarity Cinnabar* in three scrolls, the *Scripture of the Nine Tripods' Cinnabar* in one scroll, and the *Scripture of the Golden Fluid Cinnabar*, also in one scroll.

In the following my teacher, Zheng Yin, was my uncle's disciple. He received these texts from my uncle, but since he was from a poor family, he lacked the means to purchase the ingredients. I in turn was his pupil, sprinkling and sweeping his courtyard for a long time. [2b] Eventually, on Mount Horsetrack [Maji], we set up a sacred area and swore to a covenant. Thus I received the scrolls from him together with secret oral instructions, which may never be written down.

Previously these writings had not existed in this area. They all came from Zuo Ci, who transmitted them to my uncle. He in turn passed them on to Zheng Yin, from whom I received them. Therefore other followers of the Tao know nothing about them, while I have had them for over twenty years. However, my resources have not been sufficient to enable me to follow their instructions. For this I can feel only deep regret.

On the other hand, those who have accumulated gold in their coffers and gathered mountains of cash do not know that these methods for attaining immortality exist. Even if they heard about them, not one in ten thousand would believe them. . . .

[3a] Gold and cinnabar preparations are such that the longer they are heated, the more wondrous are their transformations. Even after a hundred firings, gold does not melt away, nor does it decay, no matter how long it is buried. By taking these two substances we refine our bodies so that we neither grow old nor die. Actually, this seeking of external substances to make ourselves more solid is much like a fire that does not die as long as the fuel maintains it. It is like feet smeared with verdigris that will not decay in water because the strength of the copper serves to protect the flesh. On entering the body, however, gold and cinnabar permeate the blood and energy systems. They do not merely provide an external help. . . . [3b]

Say, you only know some idle chatter about wondrous drugs but have not been accepted by a teacher and yet you desire to ascend to heaven by using some cheap medicine. Would this not be the same as spurring a lame donkey in pursuit of a strong wind? Like crossing a huge river by poling a reed boat? [4a] There are many lesser recipes for edible cinnabar, which vary greatly in effect due to the different quality of their preparation. Although there are good and bad ones among them, in all cases the number of cyclical transformations is insufficient. They are like wine that has been fermented once: it can in no way compare to the pure clear wine that has been fermented nine times.

It is a fact, however, that the least of the minor cinnabars is far superior to even the best of herbal and plant medicines. When roasted, all herbs turn to ashes, but cinnabar, when heated, produces mercury, which after a number of successive transformations reverts to cinnabar. It is thus far better than herbal and plant medicines. This is why cinnabar can produce longevity in people. The spirit immortals have long perceived this principle. How infinitely different are they from ordinary men! . . .

[6a] The *Scripture of the Yellow Emperor's Divine Cinnabar of the Nine Tripods* says: "The Yellow Emperor took this elixir and ascended to the immortals."

It also states: "Through breathing exercises and gymnastics, by taking herbs and plant medicines, you may extend your years, but you will not avoid death in the end. [6b] Only taking the divine elixir will give you long life without end and allow you to live as long as heaven and earth themselves. You will be able to rise on clouds and drive dragon chariots, to freely travel up and down and reach the heaven of Great Clarity!"

The Yellow Emperor transmitted this divine process to the Master of Mystery [Xuanzi] and warned him: "This is a highly powerful Tao! It must be transmitted only to wise people. If a person lacks the necessary qualities, even if he offers you jade piled as high as a mountain, never divulge it!"

On the other hand, if you actually receive it, you must first throw a golden human statuette and a golden fish into an eastward-flowing stream as a pledge. At the same time, you must close a formal covenant with your teacher by smearing your lips with blood. Make sure that nobody who lacks immortal's bones even observes the process!

To prepare the cinnabar itself, first find an uninhabited place on a sacred mountain! Under no circumstances, take more than three companions!

Then begin by purifying yourself for one hundred days. Wash your body and hair in water enriched with the five fragrances and make yourself utterly clean! Never approach any defiling or dirty object or let ordinary people come anywhere near you! Let no disbelievers know of your plans! If they denounce the divine medicine, successful preparation will be impossible. Yet, once it has been successfully prepared, you can raise your entire family to become immortal, not just your own self!

[7a] Worldly folk do not prepare divine elixirs but have great faith in herbal medicines—although they decay when buried, get

mushy when cooked, and burn when roasted. Since these substances cannot even keep themselves alive, how could they ever give life to human beings?

There are nine cinnabar elixirs essential for the attainment of long life. But they are not something that anyone can or should observe or hear about. The masses, in their frantic creeping about, know only how to hanker after honors and riches. How, really, would they be different from walking corpses?

Throughout the preparation of the elixir you must continue to perform offerings and make sacrifices to the gods and spirits. For more details, see the separate chapter below, complete with illustrations and instructions.

The first elixir is known as Cinnabar Florescence. It starts with the preparation of tin oxide. From several dozen pounds each of realgar solution, kalinite solution, Turkestan salt, lake salt, arsenolite, oyster shells, red bole, soapstone, and white lead, prepare Six-One Lute. Then fire the elixir for thirty-six days. Take it for seven days and you will be an immortal.

Also, you can make a pill of this elixir by mixing it with some glue. Then place it in a raging fire, and it will soon turn into gold. You can also produce gold by mixing 240 half-ounces of the elixir with 100 pounds of mercury and firing it. If the gold forms, you know the true medicine is done. [7b] If it does not form, reseal the medicine and fire it again for another thirty-six days. This never fails.

The second elixir is called Divine Cinnabar or Divine Talisman. Take it for one hundred days and you will be an immortal. To cross streams or pass through fire, smear the soles of your feet with it and you will be able to walk over water. After taking only three spoonfuls of it, the three deathbringers and nine worms in your body will disappear. All your illnesses will be cured.

The third elixir is called Divine Cinnabar. Take a spoonful for one hundred days and you will be an immortal. It will also confer deathlessness if given to livestock. More than that, it also wards off all weapons. Take it for one hundred days, and immortals and jade maidens as well as the demons and spirits of streams and mountains will come to serve you.

The fourth elixir is called Reverted Cinnabar. Take a spoonful of it for one hundred days and you will be an immortal. Vermilion birds and celestial phoenixes will soar and hover above you; jade maidens will come to your side. Take one spoonful of this and mix it with one pound of mercury. Heat it and it will immediately turn into gold. Smear coins and goods with it, and they will return to you the very same day they are traded. [8a] Use it to draw a character above anyone's eyes, and the hundred demons will flee in terror.

The fifth elixir is called Dietetic Cinnabar. Take it for thirty days and you will be an immortal. Demons and spirits will come to serve you; jade maidens will make their appearance.

The sixth elixir is called Refined Cinnabar. Take it for ten days and you will be an immortal. When mixed and fired with mercury, it too turns into gold.

The seventh elixir is called Tender Cinnabar. Take one spoonful for one hundred days and you will be an immortal. If taken mixed with raspberry juice, it is a strong aphrodisiac that will cause even men of ninety to beget children. Mixed with lead and fired, it turns into gold.

The eighth elixir is called Fixed Cinnabar. Take it and you will immediately be an immortal. Hold a piece about the size of a jujube seed in your hand, and the hundred demons will flee in terror. Use it to draw a character over a doorway, and no evil powers will dare approach it. Thieves and bandits, tigers and wolves will all be put to flight.

The ninth elixir is called Cold Elixir. Take one spoonful for one hundred days and you will be an immortal. [8b] Immortal lads and maidens will come to serve you. You will be able to fly without feathers or wings.

Acquire any one of these nine elixirs and you will be an immortal! There is no need to prepare all nine. Which one you prepare depends entirely on your preference. After taking any one of them, if you wish to ascend to heaven in broad daylight, you can do so. If you wish to remain on this earth for some time, you can come and go freely wherever you wish, no matter what the barriers. Nothing and nobody will harm you.

There is also the *Scripture of the Divine Cinnabar of Great Clarity*. This method comes from the Primordial Lord. The Primordial Lord was the teacher of Laozi, while the text was part of the *Great Clarity Scripture of Observing the Heavens*. This consisted originally of nine scrolls. But the first three of these were never transmitted or taught. The second set of three was permanently submerged beneath the three springs of heaven, since nobody in the world was found worthy to receive them in transmission. The last set of three, finally, constitute the *Scripture of the Divine Cinnabar*. It consists of the top, middle, and bottom scrolls.

The Primal Lord is the chief of the gods and immortals. He harmonizes yin and yang, gives orders to demons and spirits, wind and rain. He drives a chariot with nine dragons and twelve white tigers. [9a] All the immortals of the world are his subordinates; yet he claims to have achieved his rank through studying the Tao and taking a cinnabar elixir. If even to him it did not come naturally, how much more effort must it take for ordinary mortals!

The *Scripture* says: "When a superior person attains this Tao, he or she becomes an official in heaven. When a medium person attains this Tao, he or she will join the immortals on Mount Kunlun. When an inferior person attains this Tao, he or she will live a very long life on earth."

Indeed, common folk are ignorant and have no faith; they say this is all empty talk and, from morning to night, engage solely in occupations that will inevitably lead to their death. They do not even attempt to pursue long life! How then can even heaven itself force such people to live?

The only things ordinary mortals know are fine food, nice clothes, sensual pleasures, riches and honors. Take care not to speak of the divine elixir in front of those who give free reign to passion and lust and are therefore bound to die in a short while. It will make them mock the process of the Tao and ridicule perfection. If you transmit the *Cinnabar Scripture* to an undeserving person, you will suffer bad luck yourself. If, however, you find a true believer, you may share the finished medicine. Beware! Don't pass the recipe to anybody without due consideration!

What use does a person of the Tao have for lords and kings? As soon as the elixir is done, not only do you have a very long life, but you can even make your own gold. [9b] However, when you have achieved this, you must expend one hundred pounds of the gold on a great sacrifice to the gods. For specific instructions regarding this ceremony, see the particular scroll. The rules here are different from those used in the nine tripod elixirs mentioned above.

Allocate the following sums to the deities listed below:

| | |
|---|---|
| to Heaven | 20 pounds |
| to the Sun and the Moon | 5 pounds |
| to the Great Dipper | 8 pounds |
| to the God of the Great One | 8 pounds |
| to the God of the Well | 5 pounds |
| to the God of the Stove | 5 pounds |
| to the Lord of the River | 12 pounds |
| to Earth | 5 pounds |
| to various ghosts and spirits | 20 pounds |

Then place the remaining twelve pounds in a sound leather pouch and, on a propitious day at the peak hour of the market in the city, drop it silently among the crowd. Leave the place without a single glance backward. Any gold you make over and above the hundred pounds, use as you please. But if you don't use the first portion of the gold to serve the gods, you will surely incur disaster.

[10a] The *Scripture* also says:

> The Tao of long life and immortality
> Does not depend on offerings
> Or service to the spirits;
> Nor does it lie with gymnastics,
> Various bendings and stretchings.
>
> The essence of ascension to immortality
> Is the divine cinnabar alone!
> Knowing it is not easy!
> Doing it is truly hard!
> Produce it and you can live forever!

Recently, at the end of the Han dynasty, Master Yin the Longlived [Yin Changsheng] concocted the elixir of Great Clarity and attained immortality. He began as a student of the Confucian classics and was very gifted by nature. He composed poetry and also a eulogy and introduction for the *Scripture of the Divine Cinnabar*. In the latter, he gives a clear account of his early studies of the Tao under a teacher. He also lists forty-odd acquaintances of his who became immortals as well.

The making of the elixir of Great Clarity is somewhat more difficult than that of the Nine Tripod Elixirs described above. However, it represents a superior method for ascending to heaven in broad daylight. Here you may light the fire only after preparing fortified vinegar, red crystal salt, calomel, a mixture of lead, gold, and mercury, as well as special talismans, and the Three-Five divine solution.

This elixir, once cycled, brings immortality in three years.
This elixir, twice cycled, brings immortality in two years. [10b]
This elixir, thrice cycled, brings immortality in one year.
This elixir, four times cycled, brings immortality in half a year.
This elixir, five times cycled, brings immortality in 100 days.

This elixir, six times cycled, brings immortality in forty days.
This elixir, seven times cycled, brings immortality in thirty
days.
This elixir, eight times cycled, brings immortality in ten days.
This elixir, nine times cycled, brings immortality in three
days.

Place the elixir, which has been cycled nine times, in a reaction
vessel and expose it to the sun after the summer solstice. When the
container becomes hot, introduce a pound of cinnabar beneath the
lid. Even while you are watching, with the full power of the sun
shining upon it, the whole content will suddenly glow and sparkle
with all the colors of spirit radiance. It will immediately turn into
reverted elixir. If you take even a single spoonful, you will straight-
away rise to heaven in broad daylight. But make sure that you seal
this nine-cycle elixir in an earthenware crucible and heat it by a
chaff fire, at first gently, then with more intensity.

The nine cyclical mutations are different according to the varying speed of their effectiveness. [11a] The fewer transformations
the elixir has undergone, the weaker the medicine will be. In that
case you will have to take it for a longer period and immortality
will come more slowly. The more cycles it undergoes, on the other
hand, the stronger the medicine will become. Even if you take it
only for a few days, you will become an immortal instantaneously.

## 42. The Inner Elixir

The *Wuzhen pian* (Awakening to Perfection) is one of the most
important Taoist texts since the Song and a fundamental manual
of inner alchemy. It combines the three teachings of Taoism, Buddhism, and Confucianism, emphasizing the double cultivation of
both inner nature and fate, of inner spirituality and physical longevity, without foregoing the moral teachings of Confucius. In this
sense, the text places its ideas above and beyond those of each of
the three teachings taken individually.

The *Wuzhen pian* was originally written by Zhang Boduan (ca.
983–1082), a military adviser to a high official of the Song. Its
preface is dated to 1075, its postface to 1078. In style not unlike
the *Cantong qi* (Triple Unity), an alchemical classic based on *Yijing*
exegesis and full of hexagram symbolism, the text is rather cryptic
and difficult to understand.

The multiplicity of layers and meaning have led to manifold interpretations and commentaries ever since the text became popular in the mid-twelfth century. It is extant in numerous editions within and without the Taoist canon. The version used here is found in *Xiuzhen shishu* (Ten Books on the Cultivation of Perfection) in DZ 263, fasc. 122–31 (27.1a–14b).

For an early translation of the text, see Davis and Chao 1939. A recent English version of the text, including the commentary by Liu Yiming of the Qing dynasty, is found in Cleary 1987. An extended review of this is found in Baldrian-Hussein 1990.

---

## *Wuzhen pian* (Awakening to Perfection)

### 1

First take the power of heaven and earth and make them
    into your crucible;
Then isolate the essences of the sun [raven] and the moon
    [rabbit].
Urge the two things to return to the Tao of the center
    [yellow];
Then work hard to attain the golden elixir—how would it
    not come forth?

### 2

Secure your furnace, set up your crucible; always follow the
    power of heaven and earth.
Forge their essence and refine their innermost power,
    always keeping well in control of your yin and yang souls.
Congealing and dissolving, the incubating temperature
    produces transmutation.
Never discuss its mystery and wonder in idle conversation!

### 3

Don't waste your effort in building an oven of muddy
    cinnabar!
To refine the medicine, just look for the crescent-moon
    furnace within.
Spontaneously and of itself it has heaven's way of true
    firing;
There is no need for purple coal or blowing bellows.

### 4

In the crescent-moon furnace, jade blossoms grow;
In the vermilion crucible, mercury flows evenly along.

Only after harmonizing them with great firing power
Can you plant the central [yellow] sprout to gradually ripen.


### 5

Swallowing saliva and breathing exercises are what many
    people do,
Yet only with the method of this medicine can you truly
    transform life.
If there is no true seed in the crucible,
It is like taking water and fire and boiling an empty pot.


### 6

Harmonize your inner lead and mercury to produce the
    elixir;
Whether big or small, there is no harm; both areas are quite
    safe.
If you wonder what the true lead may be—
It is moonlight shining every day on the western river.


### 7

Before you have refined the reverted elixir, do not enter the
    mountains,
Since on the mountains, in and out, there is no lead for you.
Rather, the supreme treasure is in everybody's home;
It's just that folk are ignorant and never recognize it.


### 8

When bamboo breaks, use bamboo to repair it!
To hatch a chicken, use an egg!
To match up different species is a waste of effort;
Much better, add to your spiritual potential with true lead.


### 9

To use lead thus, don't use ordinary lead;
Use true perfected lead alone, and throw it out when used.
This is the deep secret of using lead.
Use it and then don't use it—these are veritable words.


### 10

"Empty the mind and fill the belly"—such profundity of
    meaning!
Just, to empty your mind, you must know it first.

Fig. 31. Dragon and Tiger Join the Practitioner. Source: *Jinyi huandan yinzheng tu.*

Similarly, to refine your lead, you must first fill the belly:
Understand this to protect the mass of gold that fills your
    halls within.

11

In a vision, I visited the innermost power of the west and
    ascended to the ninth heaven;
A perfected gave me a scripture about the origin of things.
The text was simple and easy, not too many words;
Just teaching how to refine true mercury and lead.

12

[It said that] the Tao, from emptiness and nonbeing,
    brought forth the energy of the One;

Then, from the energy of the One, it gave birth to yin and
    yang.
Yin and yang then combined to form the three;
The three in turn multiplied and produced the myriad
    beings in their prosperity.

### 13

The lightning of true water boils and thunders in the realm
    of metal and of water;
True fire arises from Mount Kunlun—these are our yin and
    yang.
The two restored and harmonized in proper ways
Make the elixir grow naturally, pervade the body with its
    fragrance.

### 14

True fire and water, if returned without the proper timing,
May contain the four cosmic emblems, yet there will be no
    elixir.
It is only when these two embrace the true earth and center
That the elixir can be reverted properly.

### 15

Next, the sun, in the position of true fire, turns into a
    female.
Water, in the palace of the moon, then becomes a male.
If you do not know the meaning of inversion here,
Stop engaging in lofty discussion with your restricted views.

### 16

Take the central solid core in the position of true water,
Let it drip into the palace of true fire, have it change the yin
    in your abdomen.
From this transformation develop your own inner power of
    heaven!
Then you may be hidden in obscurity or fly through the
    cosmos—all as you desire!

### 17

True thunder, dragon and mercury, comes from the realm of
    fire;
True lake, tiger and lead, is born in the realm of water.

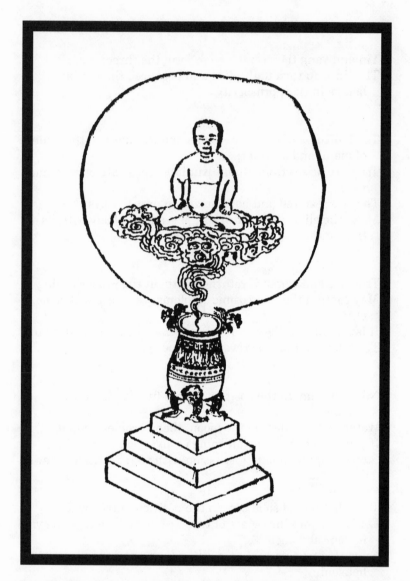

Fig. 32. The Immortal Embryo Emerges. Source: *Jinyi huandan yinzheng tu.*

Both processes follow the principle of "the child giving birth
    to the mother";
With them, the complete essences of all the five agents are
    joined in the center.

18

The red dragon and black tiger take up their positions in the
  west and east;
The four cosmic emblems join together in the position of the
  center.
The processes of "return" and "approach" can now be
  started;
Who says the golden elixir will not be soon achieved?

19

The white tiger in the western mountains begins to go wild;
The green dragon in the eastern sea is no match for him.
Both beasts interlock and fight hard to the death.
They turn into a mass of purple golden frost.

20

On the peak of Sacred-Flower Mountain, the male tiger
  roars;
At the bottom of Sun-Mulberry Ocean, the female dragon
  howls.
The matchmaker of the center spontaneously knows how to
  join them together;
They become husband and wife, sharing the same core.

21

When the half-moon rises bright over the horizon
And you can hear the dragon howl, the tiger roar,
Immediately apply your mind well to cultivate the two for
  eight more cycles.
Within an hour, you can see the elixir take shape inside.

## 43. Gradual Dissolution

Sun Simiao (ca. 581–682) was an alchemist, Taoist, and physician of the seventh century. Born near the capital Chang'an, he
was a sickly child and due to this developed a strong interest in
healing, diets, alchemical procedures, and Taoist practices. Training under various masters, he eventually settled on Mount Taibo,
not far from his original home.

Received by various emperors, Sun Simiao became well known
and, after his transformation in 682, was venerated as the divine

King of Medicines, a hagiography still active today. He is the author of various famous medical books, notably the *Qianjin fang*
(Prescriptions Worth a Thousand Ounces of Gold).

His *Cunshen lianqi ming* (Visualization of Spirit and Refinement of Energy) is translated here after the version in *Yunji qiqian*
33.12a–14b. Another complete version of the text is contained in
DZ 834, fasc. 571.

The main body of the work consists of a description of the five
phases of the mind and the seven stages of the body. This also
forms an important section of the *Dingguan jing* (Scripture on
Concentration and Observation), found in DZ 400, fasc. 189, in
*Yunji qiqian* 17.6 b–13a, as well as in the appendix to the *Zuowang
lun* (Discourse on Sitting in Oblivion; 15b–18a).

For an annotated translation of these various texts, see Kohn
1987. For more on Sun Simiao, see Sivin 1968, Engelhardt 1989. A
translation of the *Qianjin fang* is contained in Despeux 1987. The
translation here is taken from Kohn 1987. Section headings are the
translator's.

---

## *Cunshen lianqi ming* (Visualization of Spirit and Refinement of Energy)

OUTLINE

[12a] The body is the habitation of spirit and energy. As long as
spirit and energy are there, the body is healthy and strong. As soon
as spirit and energy scatter, the body dies. Therefore, if you wish to
preserve yourself whole, first calm spirit and energy.

Understand: energy is the mother of spirit; spirit is the son of
energy. Only when energy and spirit are together can you live long
and not die.

If you, therefore, wish to calm the spirit, first refine primordial
energy. When this energy resides in the body, spirit is calm and
energy is like an ocean. With the ocean of energy full to overflowing, the mind is calm and the spirit stable. When this stability is
not scattered, body and mind are gathered in tranquility. Tranquility then attains to concentration, and the body continues to exist
for years eternal.

Just stay all the time with the deep source of the Tao, and you
will naturally become a sage. Then energy pervades spirit and all
mental projections; [12b] spirit pervades all insight and destiny.
With destiny established and the body preserved, you can unite

both with your true inner nature. Then you will reach an age as old as the sun and the moon! Your Tao is perfected!

PREPARATION

You wish now to learn the technique of refining your energy as described. For this, first abstain from eating all grains! Then focus your mind calmly on the ocean of energy, visualize the spirit in the Cinnabar Field, gather in your mind, and make your thoughts tranquil. When the ocean of energy is full, you will always feel naturally satiated.

Thus you cultivate mental one-pointedness. One hundred days mean a minor achievement; three hundred days bring you to a major level. Only after this can you enter the five phases of the mind, and only after these are completed can you undergo the seven stages of the body.

Then you will be nothing but pure spirit and numinous power, changing ever and ever and naturally existing throughout all the world's coming and going. Whether confronting a steep cliff or a thousand miles' distance, you can go or stay without obstruction.

As long as energy does not scatter, your ocean of energy will always be full, your spirit will be at peace in the Cinnabar Field, and your body and mind will continually be stable. Naturally you will develop a youthful complexion, which will remain despite whatever changes may occur in the bodily structure. Thus you become an immortal! Then you can appear and disappear from the ordinary world at will, freely pass through the all-pervading numinous power. You will be called "one gone beyond the world," or a "realized one." Equal in years to heaven and earth, you will be as old as the sun and the moon.

This method does not require that you nourish on energy, swallow saliva, or undergo any particular hardships. When you must eat, you eat; when you need rest, you rest. Thereby you live forever in freedom and without obstruction.

Through the five phases of the mind and the seven stages of the body you duly enter the core of the Tao, using deeper concentration and observation. [13a]

THE FIVE PHASES OF THE MIND

1. The mind is very agitated and only rarely tranquil. With your thinking conditioned by a myriad different projections, you

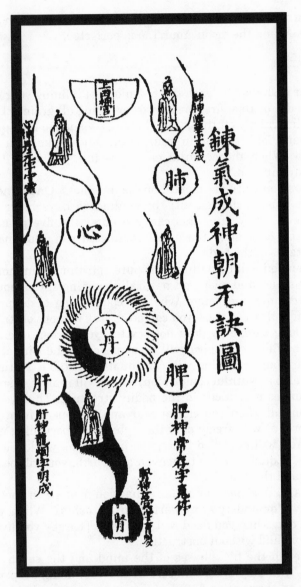

Fig. 33. Refinement of Energy and Perfection of
Spirit. Source: *Xiuzhen taiji hunyuan tu.*

accept this and reject that without any constancy. Dreads and
worries, plans and calculations keep racing on inside your mind
like mad horses. This is the ordinary mind.

2. The mind is somewhat tranquil and still much agitated. If, for once, you curb agitation and find tranquility for a moment, the mind scatters again immediately. You find it very hard to control and subdue the mind, to curb its agitation and entanglement. Still, this is the first small progress toward the Tao.

3. The mind is half agitated and half tranquil. The tranquil mind already resembles the unified mind, but this tranquility continues to scatter. Tranquility and diffusion are about equal, but you have begun to pay attention to the mind's agitation and entanglement. Gradually you see it getting calmer and more harmonious.

4. The mind is rather tranquil and only occasionally agitated. You gradually succeed in gathering it in, and whenever it gets agitated, you check it at once. The mind becomes fully one-pointed, and as soon as one-pointedness is lost, you recover it immediately. [13b]

5. The mind is entirely oriented toward the pure and tranquil. Whether involved in affairs or free from them, there is no agitation either way. With a powerfully controlled mind, you put a stop to all scattering and enter deep concentration.

Only after you are firmly established on phase five, can you enter the seven stages. Just leave all to the natural process and let it realize itself spontaneously. There is nothing to be actively done.

THE SEVEN STAGES OF THE BODY

1. All diseases you inherited from former lives gradually vanish; your body grows light, your mind radiant! The mind is now completely at peace within, the spirit is tranquil, and the energy at peace. The four elements are joined in great harmony; the six emotions are deeply serene.

   With the mind resting peacefully in the mysterious realm, continue to practice one-pointedness and inner concentration. Then joy and exultation are daily new—this is called "realizing the Tao."

2. Now you leave the limits of ordinary life and recover a youthful appearance! Your body in a state of joy, your mind constantly at peace, you numinously attain a vision of the deep and mysterious. At this stage, better move to another part of the country, choose a spot and settle down. It is better not to be a too old acquaintance with the local folk. [14a]

3.  Extend your years to a thousand: you become an immortal! As you travel extensively to all the famous mountains, flying or walking in spontaneity, azure lads are your guards and jade maidens your pleasure. As you step high on mist and haze, colored clouds support your tread.
4.  Refine your physical form to pure energy, so that it may radiate throughout the body. You are now a realized one! You appear and disappear in the common world in accordance with spontaneous change. Your glittering clarity radiates of itself, night and day in equal brightness. With immortals in attendance, you traverse through grottos and palaces.
5.  Refine the energy to pure spirit and become a spirit being! Changing and passing on spontaneously, you are utterly boundless, with a power that can move heaven and earth, remove mountains, and drain the sea.
6.  Refine the spirit to unify with the world of form and become a perfect one. As you numinously pervade all existence, your appearance and shape are no longer definite. [14b] You change according to occasion, appear in different forms, and go along with all-that-is.
7.  Finally you go beyond all beings in the body, whirl out of all relations! Now you can reside next to the Jade Emperor of the Great Tao in the numinous realm! Here the wise and sagely gather, at the farthest shore, in perfect truth. In creative change, in numinous pervasion, you reach all beings. Only with this level have you truly reached the source of the Tao! Here all the myriad paths come to an end! This is called the final ultimate!

WARNING

People nowadays study the Tao less and less every day. They do not even achieve the first stage, so how would they ever realize the numinous pervasion of all?

Instead, they continue to wallow in ignorance and passion, hold on to their defilements and personal dispositions with fierce determination. As the four seasons move along in their course, their bodies and appearances continue to decay until they collapse and return to nothing. To call this "realizing the Tao"—what hypocrisy!

On the other hand, embryo respiration together with inner observation allows one to preserve spirit and retain the body. These methods, while transmitted through lines of patriarchs, in their beginning were conceived and revealed by truly realized ones.

The methods were then preserved orally only and never put down in writing. If you, as a virtuous person of perfection, learn of them by chance, by all means be very diligent and take great care to preserve them! Without doubt, let only the wise and worthy encounter their sagely wisdom!

## 44. Eyewitness Accounts

The actual events during and surrounding an ascension into heaven are documented in various eyewitness accounts. Ascension, one finds, can be quite sudden and unexpected, a great shock to family and friends, and even the Taoist master might be flabbergasted. Then again, it may be well planned and publicly announced, a serious, stately transformation.

The first case described below is that of an ordinary citizen who, by virtue of his solicitude and healing efforts, is granted an audience at the courts above. He is received together with his wife in a cloudy chariot, meets the immortals, and only visits the earth again after four hundred years. At this time he gives a first-hand account of his adventures.

"The Life of Shen Xi" is taken from Ge Hong's *Shenxian zhuan* (Biographies of Spirit Immortals) of the fourth century. The text is found in *Daozang jinghua* 5.11 (8.33ab) as well as in *Yunji qiqian* 109.6b–8a.

Then there is the case of a young and inexperienced, if very diligent and eager, Taoist apprentice who vanishes without a trace right under the noses of his astonished fellow seekers. Only his own words and a number of strange supernatural occurrences at the time indicate that he has in fact ascended and not been abducted by some evil force.

The story is contained in the *Huang xianshi Qutong ji* (Record of Immortal Master Huang and Lad Qu), which in turn is found in chapter 689 of the *Quan Tangwen* (Complete Tang Literature) (9a–11b). For a study, see Sunayama 1987.

Third, we have the report of a Taoist priestess transforming herself right before her disciples. Her behavior is typical of that of Taoist masters in general. In addition to the common pattern, however, her corpse is liberated too and ascends to heaven right through the ceiling.

The account of "The Flower Maiden" comes from Du Guangting's *Yongcheng jixian lu* (Record of the Assembled Immortals of the

Walled City) of the tenth century. The text appears in *Yunji qiqian* 115.9b–12a.

Shen Xi's story follows Giles 1948. See also Güntsch 1988. The Flower Maiden's transformation is adapted from Cahill 1990, consulting also Kirkland 1991.

---

### "The Life of Shen Xi," from *Shenxian zhuan* (Biographies of Spirit Immortals)

Shen Xi was a native of Wu district in Jiangsu. He studied the Tao in Sichuan, attaining the magical powers of dissolving calamity, healing disease, and bringing relief to the people. However, he knew nothing of the drugs of immortality. Still, his merit and virtue found favor in the sight of heaven and the gods of heaven knew him well.

On one occasion, Xi and his wife, Lady Jia, were returning from a visit to the family of their daughter-in-law when they encountered three chariots. One was drawn by a white deer, another by a green dragon, and the third by a white tiger. There was a throng of horsemen in dark red uniforms, armed with lances and swords. They crowded the narrow road, filling it with light and glitter.

Their leader addressed Xi: "Are you Shen Xi?" Xi was dumbfounded and did not know what to make of this. "Yes," he replied. "But why do you ask?"

"Mr. Shen, sir," one of them explained, "you have meritoriously served the people. The Tao is forever present in your heart, and from your earliest childhood, your behavior has been free from blame. However, your allotted lifespan is short and will soon be exhausted. So the Yellow Venerable Lord has sent down three immortal officials with their chariots to escort you to heaven.

"The gentleman in the chariot with the white deer is Bo Yanzhi, a palace official.

"The gentleman in the chariot with the green dragon is Sima Sheng, a lord of transcendence.

"The gentleman in the chariot with the white tiger is Xu Fu, a master of ceremony."

Presently the three immortals came forward in their feathery robes. They held their official tablets in their hands and bestowed on Shen a tablet of white jade, a green jade scepter, and a set of red jade characters, which he could not read. After this formal ceremony, they took him to heaven.

His ascension was witnessed by a number of field laborers in the vicinity. They did not know what to make of it. After a little while there came a thick mist, and when it cleared away, the whole company had disappeared. All that remained were the oxen which had drawn Shen's carriage. They were peacefully grazing in the fields.

Someone recognized the animals as belonging to the Shen household and informed his family that he and his wife had vanished. Fearing that they had been carried off to the deep mountains by evil spirits, family and servants searched in every direction for a hundred miles around. But they did not find them.

Over four hundred years later, Shen Xi unexpectedly revisited his native village. He sought out one of his descendents, a man called Shen Huaixi, who explained that he had heard his elders speak of a certain ancestor who had become immortal. But, he said, this ancestor had never come back.

Shen stayed with his descendant for about a month. During that time, he recounted his first experience of ascension.

"Although I was not brought before the Emperor of Heaven himself," he said, "I did get to meet the Venerable Lord, who is his right-hand man. The attendants instructed me not to make any formal acknowledgments, but simply to take my seat in silence.

"The celestial palace seemed composed of an insubstantial, luminous haze, shot through with an enormous variety of colors too fantastic to describe. There were hundreds of attendants, mostly female. In the gardens grew trees bearing pearls and jade; all sorts of immortality herbs and magic mushrooms sprouted in great profusion.

"Dragons and tigers," he continued, "assembled in groups and frolicked in their midst. I could hear a tinkling sound, like that of copper and iron ornaments, but I've never discovered where it came from. The walls on all sides shone with a bright glow; they were covered with talismanic inscriptions.

"The Venerable Lord himself was about ten feet in height. His hair hung loose, and he wore an embroidered robe. His entire person radiated light. After a while, several jade maidens brought in a golden table with jade goblets and set it before me. They told me that this was the divine cinnabar elixir. Whoever drinks it is exempt from death. Both my wife and I were given a cup and promised a long life of ten thousand years.

"Next we were told to make a formal obeisance to the Venerable Lord but offer no thanks. When we had finished the divine medicine, they brought us two dates as large as hens' eggs, and several five-inch slices of something that looked like dried meat. 'Return to the world of mortals for a time,' they told us, 'and there cure the manifold diseases of humanity. Whenever you wish to ascend again, just write out this talisman and hang it on the end of a pole. Then someone will come and get you.'

"So they said, and handed me the talisman and an immortal recipe. Soon afterward I fell into a drowse. Suddenly I seemed to wake as if from a long sleep and found that I was back on earth. Many times I have tried it on sick people. The recipe really works!"

---

### *Huang xianshi Qutong ji* (Record of Immortal Master Huang and Lad Qu)

[9a] In Peach Spring [Taoyuan] district of Langzhou Prefecture, there was the Peach Blossom Monastery [Taohua guan]. Immortal Master Huang Dongyuan [Grotto Source, the fifteenth patriarch of Highest Clarity] from the Southern Peak lived there. He had a disciple named Qu Baiting [Cypress Garden].

At the early age of fourteen he had experienced great harmony. Although not quite rid of all craving and desires, he was in no way arrogant and harbored a serious determination to leave the world.

[9b] In the fourth year of Great Succession, a year of the dog [770], he came from his home in Thunder Creek [Chenqi] and knocked his head to the ground beneath the Master's canopy. He said he wished to withdraw to this sacred place of the Tao and was ready to do the most menial labor of slaves.

The Immortal Master felt a deep sense of compassion and regarded him with kindness. He took him on.

Lad Qu had to live among the apprentice boys and children, yet he was extremely diligent in his service. He was rather uncomely and not handsome at all, but his character was unusually reverent and solemn.

Every day, morning and evening, when the Immortal Master performed the devotions for the Tao, Lad Qu would attend to the rites with a grave face, burn incense, beat the musical stones, knock his head to the ground, and kneel immovable for extended periods—all as if he were approaching his father or his lord. Like this he went on for several years and never slackened in his efforts.

Occasionally Lad Qu would also go off wandering by himself. He would enter grottos along the valleys and explore deep hidden places. Often he would stay out for several nights in a row before he returned, but the Immortal Master allowed him his freedom.

Once Lad Qu returned and said: "I have stumbled upon a most fascinating place. I have seen gods and sages. I have looked upon cloudy vapors forming fancy plants, wondrous buildings, strange food. All this makes me feel weak and pliant; I feel unlike myself somehow and not happy. Oh, Master, would you please come with me so we can look upon this place together?"

"Ah, well," the Immortal Master replied, "I'm sure the realm of the numinous immortals is somewhere close by. But you are still so young! Really, the place you have described, it can't be all like this."

Some time later Lad Qu was among a group of disciples who went to the market in High Hill [Xiangyang] to purchase the ingredients necessary for the concoction of the elixir. Right inside the market gate, he was suddenly overcome by the bustle and noise of the trading crowd and collapsed. All went dark to his eyes so he couldn't see; his spirit and energy were sluggish and as if dead drunk. Only after the first night of the trip home did he come around again.

[10a] Asked what had happened, he raised both hands in supplication and said, "It has by now been a long time that people have lost the great simplicity of old. Common folk today wear round caps and square shoes. They best each other only in cheating and artifice; they trade with each other only for their personal profit. I just could not bear it."

The Immortal Master heard of these words and was very astonished. He did not, after that, dare to employ Lad Qu as a common servant, but would politely ask him for his service. The Immortal Master even intended to go with the Lad to that immortals' grotto, but due to rain and muddy paths they never made it in the end.

In the summer of the eighth year [of Great Succession], a year of the ox [773], in the evening of a dragon day in the fifth month [27th], Lad Qu put on formal dress, paid reverence to the gods and stepped outside into the courtyard. He said that a numinous appointment was waiting for him and that he could not linger much longer. Only when, some time in the future, the sun and the moon would appear together in the constellation Quail's Head, would he again come back to this place.

The Immortal Master indulged him with even more kindness, since he had never heard such a thing before. In his dormitory, however, there was a young fellow student of his, the Taoist Zhu Lingbian [Numinous Deliberation]. He was greatly afraid that the Lad's spirit had been captured and was now under attack by an evil sprite. He wished to write out a talisman in cinnabar ink to exorcise the demon.

Lad Qu, however, was not pleased at this. Drawing himself up proudly, he proclaimed:

> The various planets of time come to meet me—
> Even the yearstar is descending now!

On the side of the courtyard, there was a huge chestnut tree, not more than a couple of yards from where everybody was standing. Lad Qu now turned his back to the crowd and very slowly walked over to stand beside the tree. From there he gradually dissolved and vanished into thin air. [10b] When this happened, there was a tremendous sound, like the howling of a tornado or the deep rumbling of thunder.

The Taoists were amazed and startled. Words failed them to describe the events. They had no idea what was happening to them. When they gathered themselves together again, they rushed off to tell the folks in the next village. All together they formed a tight circle and started to search for the Lad everywhere. Over a thousand cliffs and into deep gullies they went. But all they met was deadly quiet; there was not a single sound.

Then, when they had gone west for a mile or two, they came across a huge snake. Majestic it was and fierce and very imposing. Lying right across the path with its fat belly, it was blocking their way. Nobody dared to go near it.

Then again, they went to search the eastern part of the area. Here they found the trace of the right foot of some extraordinary beast with eight claws. They broke off eight poles of new bamboo and planted it criss-cross next to the strange footprint.

Like this, there were a number of wondrous signs, but of Lad Qu not a single trace remained.

---

## "The Flower Maiden," from *Yongcheng jixian lu* (Record of the Assembled Immortals of the Heavenly Walled City)

In the ninth year of Kaiyuan [721], Huang Lingwei, known as the Flower Maiden, wished to ascend through transformation. So she said to her disciples: "My journey to immortality is coming

Fig. 34. On the Way to the Immortals. Source: *Neijing yushu.*

close. I cannot stay here much longer. After my body has been transformed, do not nail my coffin shut, but just cover it with crimson netted gauze."

The next day she came to an end without even being sick. Her flesh and muscles were fragrant and clear; her body and energy were still warm and genial. A strange fragrance filled the court-yard and halls.

Her disciples followed her orders and did not nail the coffin shut. Instead, they simply covered it with crimson netted gauze.

Suddenly they all heard a massive clap of thunder. When they looked at the coffin, there was a hole about as big as a hen's egg in the gauze, and in the coffin itself only her shroud and some slips of wood were left. In the ceiling of the room, there was a hole big enough for a person to pass through.

They duly presented an offering of a gourd at the place of her ascension. After several days it sprouted creepers and grew two fruits that looked like peaches.

Each time the anniversary of her death came around, wind and clouds swelled up and suddenly entered the room.

# Chapter Twelve

## IMMORTAL LIFE

Once the immortal has ascended, he or she takes up a proper position within the celestial hierarchy above. Ranked in nine levels, in close imitation of the imperial bureaucracy on earth, celestials are Tao-kings of various levels, rulers of the Brahma-Heavens, the realms for true believers, governors of the Three Worlds—of Formlessness, of Form, and of Desire. They occupy the positions of kings, dukes, and ministers, and are classified according to sages, perfected, and immortals.

Each rank within this hierarchy has to conform to a particular style of dressing, using only specific colors, fabrics, and materials, and is obliged to appear with certain typical objects and specific insignia of rank and office. All this is just like the imperial bureaucracy on earth, where every single detail of a person's life was determined exactly in accordance with his rank and standing. Among the celestials, of course, the fabrics are much finer than their earthly counterparts, the utensils made from divine materials, the garb consisting of cloud-stuff, mists, and rays of morning light.

Garbed and ranked properly, the immortal then has to get to work. There is for them no such thing as pure leisure, although those of higher rank enjoy that, too. As a beginner in the celestial spheres, the immortal will be positioned in a specific department of the heavenly administration, seeing to the proper organization and recording of events in heaven and earth.

There is, very important, the Department of Destiny, which administers the lifespans and fates of human and other beings. There is the Department of Pestilence, which takes care of the proper distribution of plagues and illnesses among the living, punishing the sinful and relieving the good. There is the Department of Rain and Wind, largely in the hands (or better, claws) of dragons, which is responsible for the timely appearance of the natural forces that make the crops grow and give the soil its rest.

Then there is the Department of the Earth Prisons, also known as hells. This consists of ten judicial courts and affiliated prisons, which judge and punish the dead for their misdeeds during life. The last section of this Department is the Court of Rebirth, where people are equipped with a body for their next life, all in close cooperation with the Department of Destiny. Then there is the Celestial Treasury, where people are given the loan of life and where their repayments or further debts are closely monitored. And many others more.

Immortals serve in these departments in various bureaucratic functions, gradually attaining higher rank and developing in status. The main difference from the officials in the world is that immortals hold more power and have more ease, that they are unburdened by the sorrows of physical existence, and that they need not to worry about the well-being of either family or ancestors. Other than that, the rules are the same. Exemplary performance in office is lauded and rewarded with promotion, and mistakes are punished; serious errors may lead to banishment among mortals—as was the case with the Gourd Master described in Section 16 above.

Then again immortals, once they have served with merit in various offices, may take some time of leave. They may whirl around the heavens in free enjoyment of movement and the journey; they may also, for the pure fun of it, go back to the world of mortals, be born as emperors and kings, as court ladies or as wandering mendicants. Already immortal to begin with, they are strange figures among mortals and can fly off again any time. Immortals returning to the world are just as before they left it, but with a celestial certainty behind them that makes ascension less urgent. Given the toil they face in the administration above, it is small wonder that some, like Master Whitestone, decide to prolong their stay on mortal shores.

However, even those eccentrics among immortals have the guarantee of eternal life and the knowledge of the ultimate joy of immortality. They know they need only to ascend to be full members of the parties, banquets, and audiences among the heavenly host. With dragons and phoenixes dancing and singing, with the celestial halls decked out in miraculous splendor, with the peaches of immortality in full ripeness and the elixir pure ambrosia, with delightful jade maidens and celestial lads hovering to serve one's every whim—the paradisiacal joys of the immortal life eventually entice even the most earth-bound back to the heavens. The administration once forgotten, celestials dress up in their fancy garb and dance and sing to their heart's delight. This, then, is the ultimate reward of the seeker's quest, the end of the Taoist journey, the paradise won and never to be lost.

The four texts below give a glimpse of these various aspects of immortal life. First, the *Fafu kejie wen* (Rules and Precepts Regarding Ritual Garb) is an eighth-century description of the ranks, robes, and regalia of the heavenly host, as revealed by the Highest Lord to the Celestial Master.

Second, the *Lingbao tianzun shuo luku shousheng jing* (Scripture on the Loan for Life from the Celestial Treasury Following the Words of The Heavenly Venerable of Numinous Treasure) of the twelfth century outlines the workings and organization of the Celestial Treasury. It specifies the sums received at birth, the amounts necessary for future human rebirth, and gives the names of the officers in charge of each transaction. It describes the workday routine of the lower level of immortal administration.

Third, there are eight short biographies of immortals on earth, six taken from the oldest collection of immortals' lives, the *Liexian zhuan* (Immortals' Biographies) of the second century C.E., two more from the *Zengxiang liexian zhuan* (Illustrated Immortals' Biographies) of the thirteenth century.

Fourth, a celestial audience, banquet, and general entertainment is described in the words of the *Santian zhengfa jing* (Scripture on the Proper Law of the Three Heavens), a scripture of the Celestial Masters, dated to the fifth century, which is largely based on the worldview of Highest Clarity.

## 45. Celestial Garb

A detailed account of the proper garb and adornment of the celestials and their earthly Taoist counterparts is contained in the *Fafu kejie wen* (Rules and Precepts Regarding Ritual Garb). Consisting of the dialogue between the Celestial Master and the Highest Lord, the text claims revealed status and is set in a formal audience of the human master with the divine ruler.

The *Fafu wen* is dated to 712. It was edited and recorded by the ritual master Zhang Wanfu, an important officer of Highest Clarity Taoism under the Tang emperor Xuanzong. The text is found in DZ 788, fasc. 563.

On Zhang Wanfu and his ritual involvement with the Tang court, see Benn 1991. For more on the garb of the immortals, see

Schafer 1978a. On celestial fashions and their changes between the Han and Six Dynasties periods, see Spiro 1990.

---

## *Fafu kejie wen* (Rules and Precepts Regarding Ritual Garb)

THE CELESTIAL MASTER'S QUESTIONS REGARDING RITUAL GARB

[1a] The Highest Lord gave the Tao to Zhang Daoling, the Law Master of the Three Heavens and Perfected of Orthodox Unity. Thereafter he ordered the jade maidens of his cloudy palace to emerge. They wore

> Lotus caps of ninefold radiance with precious gleam,
> Brocade robes of five colors, interwoven with cinnabar,
> Immortals' gowns of cloudy brocade, patterned in red,
> Feathered skirts of flying brocade, light like soaring
>     phoenixes,
> Brocade skirts of seven colors, made from precious cloudy
>     matter,
> Embroidered slippers of green florescence, studded with
>     pearls.

They also had

> Ritual tablets of azure jasper,
> Wrappers containing the seven treasures,
> Ornate belt hangings of flowing essence,
> Ear pendants of bright carnelian,
> Sitting cushions with embroidered dragons,
> Incense burners with jasper phoenixes,
> Jade benches with intertwining dragons,
> Kingfisher whisks with variegated unicorns,
> All-wish scepters with brilliant radiance,
> Fifteen different kinds in all.

They presented these things to the Celestial Master.

The Celestial Master put on his formal ritual gown, cap, and belt. With all five limbs touching to the ground, he paid obeisance to the Highest Lord and asked:
[1b] "I have not yet gotten to know the superior realm of the Three Clarities and all the various worlds. As for the sages, per-

fected, and immortals, what differences are there in their garb? What ranks are there in their descent? Ignorant I am and do not yet understand these matters. Yet I dearly wish to know the distinctions. Pray, would you give me an explanation?"

The Highest Lord replied:
Clothes are the outer display of the person. In accordance with each individual's endowments, status and rank they differ. Each one has his proper observances and rites.

Basically there are nine ranks. I'll explain them to you. Listen very carefully.

First, the Tao-King of Grand Network, the Heavenly Venerable of Primordial Beginning, wears

A precious cap of ten thousand transformations and nine colors,
A spontaneous-cloud robe of a thousand kinds of meeting and separating,
A flowery skirt of green brocade, ten revolutions and nine transformations,
A precious cape of variegated colors, sevenfold light and fourfold radiance,
Pearly slippers with the ten jewels and transformations of the five species.

The perfected attending him to the right and left are all attired in the same fashion.

Second, the Tao-King of Jade Clarity, the Heavenly Venerable of No-Shape, wears

A precious cap of one thousand transformations and seven colors,
A flying-cloud robe of a hundred kinds of meeting and separating,
A floating skirt of azure brocade, nine revolutions and seven transformations, [2a]
A brocade cape of flowing mist, sevenfold light and fourfold radiance,
Embroidered slippers with cinnabar cloud and transformations of the seven treasures.

The perfected attending him to the right and left are all attired in the same fashion.

Third, the Tao-King of Highest Clarity, the Heavenly Venerable of No-Name, wears

> A precious cap of one hundred transformations and five
> colors,
> A flowing-empyrean robe of ten kinds of meeting and
> separating,
> A misty skirt of yellow brocade, eight revolutions and five
> transformations,
> A brocade cape of flying brilliance, sevenfold light and
> fourfold radiance,
> Jasper slippers of spontaneity and transformations of the
> five colors.

The perfected attending him to the right and left are all attired in the same fashion.

Fourth, the Tao-King of Great Clarity, the Heavenly Venerable of Great Unity, wears

> A precious cap of ten transformations and lotus essence,
> A florescent five-cloud robe of nine kinds of meeting and
> separating,
> A feathery skirt of purple brocade, seven revolutions and
> four transformations,
> A cinnabar cape of mysterious brilliance, sevenfold light and
> fourfold radiance,
> Patterned slippers of master and disciple and transforma-
> tions of spontaneity.

The perfected attending him to the right and left are all attired in the same fashion.

Fifth, the Elevated Rulers of the Four Brahma-Heavens, the Heavenly Venerables of Non-Appearance, wear

> Flowery caps of flowing essence and radiant sunlight,
> Bejeweled robes with dark phoenix patterns,
> Flying skirts of bluegreen brocade with cinnabar feathers,

Fig. 35. A Taoist God in Full Regalia. Source:
*Neijing yushu.*

[2a] Precious capes of planetary clouds and fivefold light,
Slippers of flying dragons transformations.

The perfected attending them to the right and left are all attired in the same fashion. They may also be attired in

> Purple robes with green skirts,
> Azure robes with cinnabar skirts,
> Green robes with light red skirts,
> Cinnabar robes with yellow skirts,
> Yellow robes with plain skirts,
> And skirts of deep red brocade with dragon patterns.

All these are the outfits worn by the perfected in attendance.

Above the four Brahma-Heavens, all garments are made from
flying clouds and floating mists, pure spontaneity and wondrous
energy. They are brought forth from the precious radiance of the
nine colors. There are a myriad varieties, long and short, big and
small. All are coordinated with their specific position in due accordance with their rank.

Some are so bright that they radiate in the eight directions,
filling all with their pervading brilliance. Their celestial luminosity
reaches far and near; pure transformations they are of spontaneity.
Others again are made form the nine radiances and their brilliance, splintered into ten thousand facets.

Then again there are some thickly embroidered with dragons
and phoenixes, with the flowing shapes of mountains and rivers.
Changing a thousand times and transforming ten thousand times,
they cannot be described.

> Now, as for the
> cities and townships,
> palaces and halls,
> towns and terraces,
> plants and animals,
> carriages and utensils,
> pennants and awnings,
> and all kinds of ritual implements—

They are all made from pure spontaneity and appear in accordance with prevailing causes. None of them have any material
solidity whatsoever. They appear and disappear without constancy.
[3a]

Sixth, the immortals, perfected, and sages of the Heavens of Formlessness and their heavenly emperors wear

> Precious caps of flying clouds,
> Unsewed robes of the nine colors,
> Flowery skirts with bluegreen dragon patterns,
> Brocade capes of the five colors,
> Jasper slippers with auspicious phoenixes.

These are all brought forth by spontaneity itself. As you try to think of them, they disappear.

> As regards their
> palaces and halls,
> terraces and towers,
> carriages and utensils,
> toys and ornaments,
> gardens and flowers,
> musical instruments and other ritual implements—

You should know that they are all just like this.

Seventh, the various immortals, perfected, and sages of the Heavens of Form and their heavenly emperors wear

> Morning-light caps of lotus flowers,
> Brocade robes of flying clouds,
> Flying skirts of dark red mist,
> Brocade capes of flowing planet light,
> Patterned slippers with jasper phoenixes.

Even though things here have form and a certain solidity, still they are in nothing like those produced on earth. They are rather like those made from pure spontaneity.

As regards their residences, carriages, and other implements, imagine them just as you like. They will come to life in your meditation. However, they do keep changing of their own accord and do not compare to anything permanent.

Eighth, the various immortals, perfected, and sages of the World of Desire wear

> Caps of pearls and jade, [3b]
> Robes of the five clouds,
> Azure skirts of flying florescence,
> Feathery capes of flowing light,
> Patterned slippers with the nine radiances.

All that arises in this world is either taken directly from the various heavens or received from the spirit immortals. Thus their products are not the same. In this lower world, there is labor and toil.

As regards their residences and halls, carriages and other implements, they are also like this.

Ninth, all the spirit immortals, divine representatives, and perfected officials as well as the guardians of the earth and other celestial administrators residing in the numinous places on the mountains as well as within the grotto heavens of the five and others sacred peaks wear

> Caps studded with the seven treasures,
> Misty robes of the nine radiances,
> Flowery skirts of flying green color,
> Embroidered capes of cloudy brocade,
> Patterned slippers with phoenixes on them.

These garments are all made from fine silks and brocades, which are brought forth in the various heavens and ornamented with the precious objects of the lower regions. Often they are produced by transformational refinement, in no way like anything made in the human world.

The divine personages themselves stride on phoenixes and cranes, put dragons to the reins and tigers, white deer and wondrous lions, an entire host of numinous beasts and divine birds. They ride in chariots of floating clouds and with jasper wheels; they hold up streamers and display their staffs, grasp talismans and present their registers. [4a] Thus they arrive anywhere on impulse—rising up as perfected and immortals, or descending to teach and to transform [the world]. In all cases, they are garbed according to occasion, just as is the custom among humanity.

Then again they may descend as perfected and immortals or rise up to pay court to the rulers of the heavens. Whatever they wear and ride is part of the higher realms and changes with true spontaneity. Indeed, you will find your senses reel; it is too immeasurable.

## 46. The Administration of Heaven

Immortals serve in the celestial administration of heaven and earth, beginning as low-level clerks and serving their way up, just as in the bureaucracies of this world. The lowest administrative level is that of hell, where the souls of sinners are prepared for rebirth.

Hell in Chinese religion is a concept integrated from Buddhism. According to ancient Chinese beliefs, the souls of the dead assembled in an underworld country, known as the Yellow Springs. During the Han dynasty, with the establishment of an all-encompassing imperial administration, the abode of the dead was associated with merit and demerit. It was then located to Mount Taishan in Shandong and linked with the north, the realm of pure yin.

Only with the spread of Buddhism did ideas of organized hells and punishments develop in China. In Highest Clarity, for the first time there are the six palaces of the dead in Fengdu, where sinners are judged and can expiate their evil deeds. Later, ten integrated courts of hell developed as well as a detailed bureaucratic system linking the fate of the individual with his or her constellation of birth.

The *Lingbao tianzun shuo luku shousheng jing* (Scripture on the Loan for Life from the Celestial Treasury Following the Words of the Heavenly Venerable of Numinous Treasure) is a popular document of the Southern Song (twelfth century), which describes the fate of the individual in monetary terms. Everyone receives a loan from the Celestial Treasury in order to come to life. This loan has to be repaid by good deeds and in spirit money; otherwise, one will fall ever deeper into debt and thus unhappiness and hell.

The text is contained in DZ 333, fasc. 167. It is set in the context of a celestial audience that the Heavenly Venerable of Numinous Treasure gives to his ample court. Written in a flowery dialogue style, it is patterned on Mahāyāna Buddhist sutras. Its ideas can be related to the emergence of a full-fledged monetary economy in the twelfth century, but are still popular today.

For a French translation and detailed analysis of the celestial treasury, see Hou 1976. For an English summary and review, see Seidel 1978. On the celestial administration in ancient China, see

Levi 1989. For more on Chinese hells, see Eberhard 1967, Goodrich 1981, Thompson 1989.

---

## *Lingbao tianzun shuo luku shousheng jing* (Scripture on the Loan for Life from the Celestial Treasury Following the Words of the Heavenly Venerable of Numinous Treasure)

[1a] At that time the Heavenly Venerable of Numinous Treasure was in the World of Floating Network, in the Land of Pure Brightness. He was sitting under the Tree of the Seven Treasures on the Mountain of Good Accumulated. With him were innumerable followers: flying celestials and divine kings, countless immortals and the host of the sages. Thus he proceeded to preach the wondrous Law.

The Venerable emitted a brilliant radiance of the nine colors. It illuminated all the ten directions. Living beings everywhere were receiving good and bad retribution for their deeds, whether noble or humble, rich or poor.

The great host were astonished that all living beings would equally receive such karmic retribution, but they did not dare to ask about it.

At that time there was a perfected called Radiant Wondersound. Rising from his seat, he straightened his cap and gown, knocked his head on the ground, and prostrated himself before the Presence.

"My lord," he addressed the Heavenly Venerable, "we have just been so fortunate as to witness how Your majestic radiance illuminates all the ten directions. Whether man or woman, whether rich or poor, whether noble or humble—all receive suffering and happiness in different measure. Why is it that all living beings are subject to such variety in karmic retribution?

"Bowing down low, I pray to Your sagely grace. Oh, have compassion for our need and bestow upon us Your valuable instruction!"

[1b] The Heavenly Venerable said:

"Very good! Very good indeed! Sit back down, please. Then compose yourself, calm your spirit, concentrate your mind, and listen carefully!"

The Heavenly Venerable said:

"All living beings of the ten directions in their fate depend on the officials of heaven; in their bodies they are subject to the administration of earth. The day anyone receives a human body, he or she is registered with the administration of earth.

"The underworld officials at this time lend him or her a sum for receiving life, a loan from the Celestial Treasury. The more people save on their account in the underworld, the richer and nobler they will be on earth.

"Those who are poor and humble are debtors who never repay. They get in worse from kalpa to kalpa, since the underworld officials have to borrow on the account [every time they are reborn]. In the case of those who are impoverished in the world of humanity, the underworld officials have already used up all the yang credit and are now supplying the account with yin.

"Thus it is that in the world there are differences in retribution between noble and humble, rich and poor, happy and miserable. Consider it well!"

The Heavenly Venerable said:

"Once in the past I presented a Treasure Tree to High Highness, the Northern Emperor in Fengdu. He planted it in his Dark Capital to help him judge more clearly the good and bad retribution coming to all living beings. [2a]

"Whenever someone is about ready to be reborn with a human body, he takes three sagely arrows and three divine bows and hands them to the man or woman in question. He then lets them shoot at the Treasure Tree.

"If they hit the eastern branch of the tree, they will be reborn in a long-lived body and with high position and income.

"If they hit the southern branch of the tree, they will be reborn in a very healthy body and with exceptional longevity.

"If they hit the western branch of the tree, they will be reborn in a beautiful body and with riches and honors.

"If they hit the northern branch of the tree, they will be reborn in a miserable body and with humility and poverty.

"Thus this Treasure Tree as We just described is a very useful mirror to judge people's karmic standing and necessary retribution.

"Those who, in this life, properly venerate the Three Treasures, give ample donations, organize rituals, chant the scriptures, and perform all manner of good deeds—those, in other words, who follow Our teaching and conscientiously recite this scripture and burn spirit money to repay their celestial loan for life—they will all be born in male bodies for three lives to come.

"Also, when they die again, they will not fall into the earthly prisons [hell]. And, when they are ready to be fitted with their next body in Fengdu and get to shoot at the Treasure Tree, We will personally use Our divine powers to prevent them from hitting the northern branch. This way they will definitely be born again in a strong body and with noble rank.

"Those, on the other hand, who in this life are avaricious and greedy, foolhardy and obstinate, do not believe in the scriptures and the Law, [2b] never make any payments on their debt, are jealous and envious of others, fail to remember doing good and only perform evil deeds, will be listed among the registers of sinners. The officials of Heaven will subtract from their account and their debt will mount.

"The fact is, those who do not repay the loan they received for their life from the underworld officials and cheat other people into the bargain upon death will fall into the earthly prisons. Only after ten thousand kalpas [of punishment] will they be reborn, and then only as wild beasts or domestic animals. Only over many life cycles will their karma improve again.

"When such people then arrive in Fengdu and are ready to shoot their arrow at the Treasure Tree, they will naturally hit the northern branch. They have at this point reached the human stage, but they are still impoverished and humble. Such is the retribution for those who do not believe in the karma of good deeds."

The perfected again addressed the Heavenly Venerable: "It is not quite clear to me yet which department each human being in his or her life is subject to. Which division of the Celestial Treasury gives out his or her loan for life? And to which division of the Treasury should he or she repay it?

"Your venerable explanation was superbly enlightening. However, in my ignorance I have not perfectly understood this point. May I count myself so fortunate as to receive in Your gracious answer a clear distinction between the different cases?"

The Heavenly Venerable said:

"The life of humanity is administered by officials. They are arranged in divisions according to a twelve-year roster. [3a] In each of the divisions, there is one senior administrator particularly responsible for the Treasury.

"I shall now give you the divisions, the names of the officials, and the sums paid out in each case.

"People born in the year of the rat owe 13,000 strings of cash to the first division of the Treasury. The official in charge is named Li [Plum].

"People born in the year of the ox owe 20,000 strings of cash to the second division of the Treasury. The official in charge is named Tian [Field].

Fig. 36. A Celestial Official. Source: *Shangqing lingbao dafa*.

"People born in the year of the tiger owe 80,000 strings of cash to the third division of the Treasury. The official in charge is named Lei [Thunder].

"People born in the year of the hare owe 80,000 strings of cash to the fourth division of the Treasury. The official in charge is named Li [Willow].

"People born in the year of the dragon owe 50,000 strings of cash to the fifth division of the Treasury. The official in charge is named Yuan [Robe].

"People born in the year of the snake owe 70,000 strings of cash to the sixth division of the Treasury. The official in charge is named Ji [Record].

"People born in the year of the horse owe 260,000 strings of cash to the seventh division of the Treasury. The official in charge is named Xu [Permit].

"People born in the year of the sheep owe 100,000 strings of cash to the eighth division of the Treasury. The official in charge is named Zhu [Red]. [3b]

"People born in the year of the monkey owe 40,000 strings of cash to the ninth division of the Treasury. The official in charge is named Che [Cart].

"People born in the year of the rooster owe 50,000 strings of cash to the tenth division of the Treasury. The official in charge is named Zheng.

"People born in the year of the dog owe 25,000 strings of cash to the eleventh division of the Treasury. The official in charge is named Cheng [Perfect].

"People born in the year of the boar owe 9,000 strings of cash to the twelfth division of the Treasury. The official in charge is named Gang [Neck]."

The Heavenly Venerable said:

"These twelve officials of the Treasury supervise the registers of the celestial loan for people's current life. In addition, anyone who has obtained a human body should pledge a certain sum [to be used at rebirth] to the original constellation under which he or she has been born. This, too, should be entered in the account registers of their celestial loan as well as in the records of the underworld officials."

The perfected rose again and asked another question. "I am," he said, "as yet unaware of the names, position, and sums involved in the pledges to the original constellations. May I again presume upon Your grace to grant me an explanation?"

The Heavenly Venerable smiled fondly and said:

"Excellent! You do indeed exhaust your strength for the benefit of all that lives.

"I will gladly explain to you the adminstration of the twelve original constellations, the sums involved in the pledge, and the names of the officers in charge. [4a]

"People born in the year of the rat have Liu Wenzhen as constellation officer. They need to pledge 7,000 strings of cash toward renewed human rebirth.

"People born in the year of the ox have Meng Hou as constellation officer. They need to pledge 9,000 strings of cash toward renewed human rebirth.

"People born in the year of the tiger have Zhong Yuan as constellation officer. They need to pledge 6,000 strings of cash toward renewed human rebirth.

"People born in the year of the hare have He Yuan as constellation officer. They need to pledge 10,000 strings of cash toward renewed human rebirth.

"People born in the year of the dragon have Li Wenliang as constellation officer. They need to pledge 6,400 strings of cash toward renewed human rebirth.

"People born in the year of the snake have Cao Jiao as constellation officer. They need to pledge 1,000 strings of cash toward renewed human rebirth.

"People born in the year of the horse have Zhang Si as constellation officer. They need to pledge 9,000 strings of cash toward renewed human rebirth.

"People born in the year of the sheep have Sun Gong as constellation officer. They need to pledge 4,000 strings of cash toward renewed human rebirth. [4b]

"People born in the year of the monkey have Du Zhun as constellation officer. They need to pledge 8,000 strings of cash toward renewed human rebirth.

"People born in the year of the rooster have Tian Jiaoyou as constellation officer. They need to pledge 5,000 strings of cash toward renewed human rebirth.

"People born in the year of the dog have Cui Jianjin as constellation officer. They need to pledge 5,000 strings of cash toward renewed human rebirth.

"People born in the year of the boar have Wang Zhuang as constellation officer. They need to pledge 6,000 strings of cash toward renewed human rebirth."

The Heavenly Venerable announced to the host of the four classes:

"Good people of the world, be they men or women, should take joy in the scriptures and the Law, give ample donations and provide money for the needy. They should rely on this scripture and set up religious ceremonies, performing proper worship by burning incense, scattering flowers, lighting lamps and burning candles.

"With serious reverence they should pay obeisance to the Three Treasures and the Great Tao, venerate the countless immortals and the host of the sages. In all the six periods they should practice the rites of the Tao, turn and chant the scriptures, observe the fasts and make the proper sacrifices. They should furthermore prepare a sum of money to repay the celestial loan for their present life and set aside a sum to be pledged to their original constellation for human rebirth.

"To this end they should take the matching tablets for both sums and burn them to transfer the sums to the appropriate division of the Treasury. [5a] If they do all this, they will in retribution receive great good fortune, glory, and honor in this life. Even in the lives to come they will never suffer hardships or be bent by trouble.

"Those among living beings, however, who do not believe in predetermination through karmic causes but, on the contrary, produce nothing but bad karma, will fall into the depth of the Nine Springs [hell]. There they will suffer terribly.

"Such is the retribution of happiness and misery in life and death. Consider it well!"

At that time, the perfected Radiant Wondersound together with the countless immortals and the host of the sages, including also Yama, the Northern Emperor of Fengdu, the underworld officials and administrators of the Celestial Treasury, the officers of the original constellations—everyone in the huge assembly—knelt to knock their heads on the ground, then raised their eyes to the Venerable Countenance. Then they withdrew with proper ceremony.

Thereafter the perfected Radiant Wondersound transmitted the teaching to the world of humanity. With it he is saving both the living and the dead.

*Praise and spread the wonderful teaching!*
*Believe and practice!*

## 47. Sojourn Among Mortals

The way immortals behave in the world after they have already ascended is documented in a variety of collections on their lives. Usually coming down for a short visit, they put affairs to right and help out mortals in unexpected ways. Eccentric and otherwordly in every way, their lives yet remain linked, at least at times, with the events and affairs of this world.

The *Liexian zhuan* (Immortals' Biographies) is the oldest collection of such immortals' adventures that has come down to us. Originally written by the Han-dynasty official Liu Xiang (77–76 B.C.E.), the text was lost and later reassembled. The edition extant today can be dated to the second century C.E. The text consists of eighty short sketches of immortals' lives. It is contained in DZ 294, fasc. 138.

The *Zengxiang liexian zhuan* (Illustrated Immortals' Biographies) is a Yuan-dynasty collection, extant in a Qing edition. It contains fifty-five biographies of immortals with a characteristic picture for each. In addition the text has a chapter with selections from various Taoist scriptures, illuminating the Taoist path and worldview of the immortals.

I have consulted the complete translation of the *Liexian zhuan* in Kaltenmark 1953 and relied on Giles 1948 in the biographies of the Horsemaster, Master Anqi, the Hairy Lady, Dongfang Shuo, and Master Whitestone. For the problems of human historians with immortals returning, see DeWoskin 1990. For some examples of the appearance and behavior of immortals in more recent years, see Blofeld 1973.

---

## *Liexian zhuan* (Immortals' Biographies)

### THE YELLOW EMPEROR

The Yellow Emperor [Huangdi] was personally called Xianyuan. He ruled the hundred gods, who would all pay homage to him and serve his every whim.

Even when only a small child, he was already able to speak. Later he developed sageliness and could foretell the future. He would understand the deep inherent structure of all things.

He was also the Master of Clouds, and as such had the body of a dragon.

Choosing for himself the day of his disappearance from the world, he said farewell to his courtiers and his people. After his death, he was buried on Bridge Mountain.

Later, there was a landslide on the mountain and his tomb split open. However, there was no corpse in the coffin. Only his sword and slippers remained.

The *Immortal Scripture* says:

The Yellow Emperor mined copper on Head Mountain and melted it into tripods at the foot of Mount Thorn. When the tripods were finished, a dragon, with whiskers streaming, descended to receive him into heaven.

The emperor duly strode on the dragon's back and up they went.

His numerous courtiers and ministers, who were standing by, immediately grabbed hold of the dragon's whiskers so they would be borne up, too. Some even got hold of the emperor's bow. However, after some time, the dragon's whiskers came loose and the emperor's bow dropped to the ground.

In the end, the courtiers and ministers thus did not manage to follow him into heaven. Watching their sovereign rise up higher and higher, they broke into loud cries of lamentation.

For this reason, later generations called the place of the emperor's ascension the "Tripod Lake" and named his bow the "Cry of Lament."

## LORD HORSEMASTER

Lord Horsemaster [Mashi Huang] was a horse doctor under the Yellow Emperor. He knew the vital symptoms in a horse's body, and on receiving his diagnosis the animal would immediately get well.

Once a dragon flew down before him with drooping ears and open mouth. Horsemaster said to himself, "This dragon is ill and knows that I can cure him."

Thereupon he inserted an acupuncture needle in its gums just below the upper lip and gave it a decoction of licorice to swallow. The dragon promptly recovered.

Afterwards, whenever the dragon felt unwell, it issued from its watery abode and presented itself for treatment. One morning the dragon came, took Huang on its back and bore him away.

## THE FLUTEPLAYER

The Fluteplayer [Xiao Shi] lived under the reign of Lord Mu of Qin. He was so good at playing the flute that he could attract peacocks and white cranes to the palace gardens.

Lord Mu had a daughter by the name of Playful Jade. Playful Jade loved the Fluteplayer, and Lord Mu duly consented to their marriage.

Every day the Fluteplayer would teach his wife how to imitate the cry of the phoenix. After several years, she could indeed make a sound very much like that of the phoenix.

At that time, two of the sacred birds, a male and a female, alighted on one of the palace buildings. Lord Mu appropriately changed its name to "Phoenix Terrace."

The young couple went to live there and did not leave it for several years. One day, they both followed the phoenix pair and flew off.

Later the people of Qin established a shrine to the "Phoenix Lady" in their capital. Still today, from time to time, one can hear the Fluteplayer's song!

MASTER ANQI

Master Anqi came from Fu village in Langya district of the Shandong peninsula. He used to sell herbs on the shore of the Eastern Sea. People at the time called him Old Father Thousand Years.

When the First Emperor of the Qin dynasty made a journey to the East, he asked to see Anqi and talked with him for three days and three nights. The emperor then bestowed on him over 100,000 pieces of gold and precious jewels.

On his departure, however, Anqi left the gifts in the village office together with a note to the emperor. Here he said that he was sufficiently rewarded with a pair of red jade slippers. He then added: "In a few years, come to look for me on the paradise island of Penglai!"

The First Emperor immediately sent out to sea an expedition numbering several hundred people, led by Xu Shi and Lu Sheng. However, before they reached Penglai they encountered violent storms and had to turn back.

Shrines in honor of Master Anqi have been erected since in a dozen places along the coast near Fu village.

THE HAIRY LADY

The Hairy Lady [Maonü], also known as Jade Mistress, has been seen by hunters on Mount Hua for several generations. Her body is covered with hair.

安期生

Fig. 37. Master Anqi on His Way to Sell Medicines. Source: *Zengxiang liexian zhuan*.

She claims that she was among the palace ladies of the First Emperor and first fled to the mountain when the Qin dynasty collapsed.

There she met the Taoist Spring Valley [Gu Chun], who taught her how to live on pine needles. As a result of this diet, she was free from cold and hunger, and her body became so light that it seemed to fly.

For over 170 years the mountain cliff where she makes her home was filled with the sound of her zither.

DONGFANG SHUO

Dongfang Shuo came from Yanci village in Pingyuan district of the Shandong peninsula. For a long time he lived south of the Yangzi as a scribe. After several decades, under the reign of Emperor Wu of the Former Han dynasty, he sent in a memorial on the needs of the state and was given a court appointment.

By the time of Emperor Zhao, some people thought he was a sage; others found him ordinary. His behavior varied between depth and shallowness, brazenness and withdrawal. At times his words were full of loyalty, then again he made jokes. Nobody could figure him out.

At the beginning of the reign of Emperor Xuan, Dongfang Shuo left his post to avoid the disorders of the time. He put down his official cap and quit his stately residence, drifting off to wherever chance might take him. Later he was seen in Guiji, selling herbs in the region of the five lakes.

Among wise men some suspected that he was really an incarnation of the essence of the planet Jupiter.

---

## *Zengxiang liexian zhuan* (Illustrated Immortals' Biographies)

THE HEMP LADY

The Hemp Lady [Magu] was the younger sister of the immortal Wang Fangping. Under Emperor Huan of the Han dynasty, Wang descended from heaven to visit the family of Cai Jing.

He told him: "You have the ability to go beyond the world. This is why I have come today to teach you. However, your energy is low and your flesh is strong. Therefore you cannot ascend bodily into heaven, but rather have to prepare yourself for deliverance from the corpse."

麻姑

Fig. 38. The Hemp Lady and Her Deer. Source: *Zengxiang liexian zhuan.*

Wang duly gave him essential instructions and left again.

Later Jing developed a fever that seemed to burn his entire body. After three days his flesh began to dissolve so that his bones were sticking out. Lying down in his bedroom, he covered himself with a blanket, when he vanished all of a sudden. His relatives looked in and found only a shell under the blanket, somewhat like the skin of a cicada.

Over ten years later he unexpectedly returned to his family. He told them: "On the seventh day of the seventh month, Lord Wang will grace our house with his presence. We should prepare several hundred pitchers of wine to feast him."

On the appointed day Wang indeed arrived, floating down from heaven. He was sitting in a carriage drawn by five dragons. Preceding and following him were attendants carrying banners and flags, as if he was a five-star general. As soon as he had landed, the entourage vanished.

Jing and his family duly paid their formal respects to the visitor. After that, Wang sent off someone to invite his sister, the Hemp Lady. When she arrived, all found her a young girl of about eighteen years. She wore her hair tied into a topknot on the top of her head, but some stands were left untied and flowed down well to her waist. She wore a robe of brocade and a wide embroidered skirt, with colors so bright and radiant they dazzled the eye.

When everybody had taken their seats, a fantastic banquet on dishes of gold and jade was served, including such delicacies as unicorn meat.

At the time Jing's wife had just given birth. When the Hemp Lady saw her, she immediately said: "Ah! Please stop and don't come near me!" Then she asked for a bit of rice, which she spread all over the floor. As soon as it hit the ground, every grain turned into cinnabar.

Wang laughed when he saw this. "Oh, my dear sister," he said, "you still play the games of a child!"

"Well, after all," the Hemp Lady responded, "since we've last seen each other the Eastern Sea has only changed three times into mulberry fields. And now the waters around Penglai are already growing shallow again!"

"Indeed," Wang agreed. "All the sages are saying that the sea is turning to dust again soon!"

The Hemp Lady had hands that looked like the claws of a bird. Seeing them, Cai thought to himself, "If one had an itch on the back, wouldn't it be nice to be scratched by these claws!"

Wang immediately read his thoughts and was furious. He turned to whip his host, scolding him: "The Hemp Lady is a divine personage! How could you even think of her claws scratching your back?"

Soon after, Wang left and the Hemp Lady too took her leave. (2.11b)

MASTER WHITESTONE

Master Whitestone [Baishi sheng] was a disciple of the venerable Master Middleyellow [Zhong Huang]. In the days of the long-lived Pengzu, he was already more than two thousand years old. However, he had no longing to ascend to heaven; instead he aspired only to a long life on earth.

Among drugs he preferred liquid gold, but his family was poor and he could not obtain it. So he raised pigs and herded sheep, and after about ten years had amassed a fortune of ten thousand pieces of gold. This enabled him to buy the drug and take it.

Later it was his habit to boil white stones and use them for food. This led him to make his home on Whitestone Mountain. Thus he was called Master Whitestone. Sometimes he would also eat dried meat; then again he would abstain from all grains.

He was able to walk as far as three or four hundred miles in one day. Though hundreds of years old, he still looked like he was about thirty. When someone asked him why he did not wish to ascend to heaven, he replied: "I'm not at all sure I should enjoy myself as much in heaven as I do in this world right here!" (1.17b)

## 48. Feasting in Paradise

The ultimate joy of the immortal life is the easy, leisurely feasting among the crowd of the celestials. Imperial lords invite to fancy banquets, dragons and phoenixes sing and dance, jade maidens and celestial lads serve divine snacks—a life of delight and beauty, of song and pure joy.

The *Santian zhengfa jing* (Scripture on the Proper Law or the Three Heavens) as we have it today, contained in DZ 1203, fasc. 876, is a text of the Celestial Masters of the fifth century. Its original version was part of the revelations of Highest Clarity and contained the eschatology of this school.

Today the text begins with a description of the origins of the nine heavens, the creation of the world and of humanity, and the

生石白

Fig. 39. Master Whitestone on His Mountain. Source: *Zengxiang liexian zhuan.*

proper establishment of the gods. It continues with an audience given by the Highest Lord to his two favorite advisers, Lord Goldtower and the Green Lad, both important deities of Highest Clarity. The audience takes the form of a celestial banquet, during which the three lords engage in joyful song.

On the text, see Robinet 1984. For more on the delights of the heavenly halls, see Kroll 1985.

---

### *Santian zhengfa jing* (Scripture on the Proper Law or the Three Heavens)

[3b] The Imperial Lord Goldtower, the Latter-Day Sage, and the Lord Green Lad, the First Minister, three times in every month, at the time of the pure fasts, climb into a cloudy chariot. It is made from blue and rosy tinged clouds mixed with the flowing light of the nine numina. It is covered with a canopy of green feathers. Following the thousand perfected of Mulberry Forest, they ascend to the palace of the highest numinous capital. There they pay homage to the Perfected Father and attend various feasts in the gardens of jade.

The Highest Lord of the Great Tao at one such time was with the Sagely Lord of Ninefold Mystery [Goldtower] and with the Lord Green Lad, the First Minister. Together they climbed up the Jade Hall in the Jasper Palace. Serving maids waited upon them—they numbered several billion. Flying dragons and poisonous beasts stood guard at the numinous portals. Huge scaly dragons, thousands of feet long, spread their claws as wide as the entire garden. Flowing radiance shone brightly in the eight directions, brilliantly illuminating the entire Heaven of Jade Clarity. Banners and canopies were hanging from the walls; flags were flowing as incense wafted throughout.

Soon jade pipes began to sing in the vast emptiness. The dense crowd of divine beings raised [their voices] in sound. Ten thousand echoes swelled the music so it pervaded and delighted even the Nine Primes. While the host of immortals yodeled away their cloudy songs, unicorns danced and phoenixes cooed. A magnificent concert rose, an offering to the kings in emptiness. Its jasper quality moved all and everything throughout the Three Clarities.

The company was served with sweet wine from flowing rosy clouds and with fruits shining like metal and diamonds. Variously they listened to the ongoing flow of the variegated streams and looked out even beyond the end of the great dark sea.

[4a] Then the Highest Lord pulled over a zither stringed with cloud and jade. He strung it and began to play. The emerging jade sound was so splendid in its full radiant beauty that it pervaded the great empyrean. Then he sang a verse on the divine phoenix, a poem on the nine numina. The song went:

Subtler than the energy of ninefold mystery,
They pervade the depth of the Three Clarities.
All wondrous transformations go with life's eternal cycle,
As the sounds of the abyss penetrate on-high.

Sixfold awareness begins with the mysterious pass;
Not yet clear, it is just beginning.
Leading gradually up to the Jade Emperor's garden,
It opens up the principles of Great Emptiness.

The purple light irradiates the Terrace of Mystery,
A flowing brightness, infinite and without end.
Even a great kalpa has its end well numbered:
Hundred-and-Six—it turns over and begins anew.

The pleasure of the gods is not limited in years,
We cherish and we grieve—for our late-born children.

With this, the song of the Highest Lord ended. The Imperial Lord of Ninefold Mystery took up the theme. He sang,

I take my whip and grasp the reins of the nine dragons,
Ride up to visit the Jade Emperor's gardens.
Great Emptiness and its energy of ninefold mystery
Transform as patterned through all three numina.

Above I join the tower of mysterious morning light
Where all bodies and lives receive their first prime essence.
[4b] Then I move on to the Hall of Great Cloud's Glow,
Let my glance flow on to years infinite.

Divine light penetrates even the passes of deep darkness,
Purifies the womb, restores the body's strength.
We cherish and we grieve for the five sons of the turbid
And let our lives flow along with the morning's newly born.

With this, the song of the Sagely Lord of Ninefold Mystery ended. The Lord Green Lad, the First Minister, in turn took it up and sang:

The Nine Heavens pervade the fibers of the Primes;
Transforming, they produce energy without bounds.
The three numina purify the dark and then shine forth,
The six essences follow in their cycles, then they cease to be.

Cinnabar empyrean vanishes in empty pervasion;
The three perfected go beyond even where's no time.
Look down, look up—the Great Imperial Halls
Realize the true way of the Three Heavens now!

Massively they wash away the bad luck of all Six Heavens.
Properly they set up then a life without defilement.
Reaching up all the way to the great perfected,
They save the world completely, under the rule of Yao.

Just about to awaken, there are the end-born children,
Aware now that they kept a tryst with darkness.
They eradicate the sufferings of the three bad rebirths;
Soaring up, they take hold of the dragons' reins.

Like bubbling foam, they reach to Highest Clarity.
How could there ever be obstacles to their way?

[5a] With this the song ended. Thereupon the Highest Lord proceeded to discuss the True Law of the Three Heavens with his companions, the Sagely Lord of Ninefold Mystery, the Latter-Day Sage, and the Lord Green Lad, the First Minister, telling them how to abolish the rule of the Six Heavens forever with the use of precious formulas and the proper spells. For the two lords he clarified and explained all the celestial rules and regulations and ordered them to go and instruct the masses of later [human] learners and help them to attain the state of the perfected.

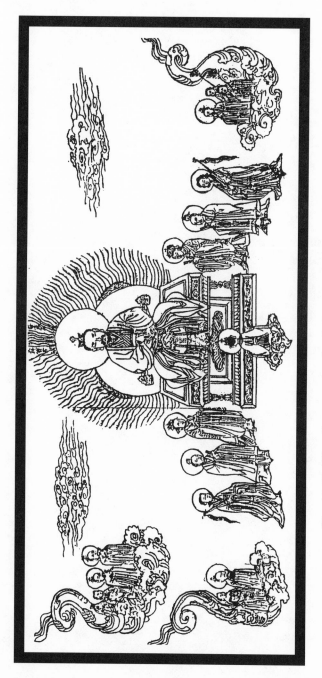

Fig. 40. Holding Court among the Gods. Source: *Sancai dingwei tu.*

# LIST OF CHINESE TEXTS TRANSLATED

# BIBLIOGRAPHY

Akahori Akira. 1989. "Drug Taking and Immortality." In *Taoist Meditation and Longevity Techniques*, ed. Livia Kohn, 71–96. Ann Arbor: University of Michigan, Center for Chinese Studies Publications, 61.

Allan, Sarah. 1991. *The Shape of the Turtle: Myth, Art and Cosmos in Early China*. Albany: State University of New York Press.

Allinson, Robert E. 1990. *Chuang-Tzu for Spiritual Transformation*. Albany: State University of New York Press.

Andersen, Poul. 1980. *The Method of Holding the Three Ones*. London and Malmø: Curzon Press.

Baldrian-Hussein, Farzeen. 1984. *Procédés secrets du joyau magique*. Paris: Les Deux Océans.

Baldrian-Hussein, Farzeen. 1986. "Lü Tung-pin in Northern Sung Literature." *Cahiers d'Extrême-Asie* 2:133–70.

———. 1986a. "Review of *Understanding Reality* by Thomas Cleary." *Harvard Journal of Asiatic Studies* 50:335–41.

Benn, Charles D. 1991. *The Cavern Mystery Transmission: A Taoist Ordination Rite of A.D. 711*. Honolulu: University of Hawaii Press.

Bergéron, Marie-Ina. 1986. *Wang Pi: Philosophie du non-avoir*. Taipei, Paris, Hong Kong: Institut Ricci.

Blofeld, John. 1973. *The Secret and the Sublime: Taoist Mysteries and Magic*. New York: Dutton.

Bodde, Derk. 1942. "Some Chinese Tales of the Supernatural." *Harvard Journal of Asiatic Studies* 6:338–57.

Bokenkamp, Stephen. 1983. "Sources of the Ling-pao Scriptures." In *Tantric and Taoist Studies,* ed. Michel Strickmann, 2:434–86. Brussels: Institut Belge des Hautes Etudes Chinoises.

———. 1986. "The Peach Flower Font and the Grotto Passage." *Journal of the American Oriental Society* 106:65–79.

———. 1989. "Death and Ascent in Ling-pao Taoism." *Taoist Resources* 1.2:1–20.

———. 1990. "Stages of Transcendence: The *Bhumi* Concept in Taoist Scripture." In *Chinese Buddhist Apocrypha*, ed. Robert E. Buswell, 119–46. Honolulu: University of Hawaii Press.

Boltz, Judith M. 1987. *A Survey of Taoist Literature: Tenth to Seventeenth Centuries*. Berkeley: University of California, China Research Monograph 32.

Bynner, Witter. 1944. *The Way of Life According to Lao tsu*. New York: Perigree.

Cahill, Suzanne. 1982. "The Image of the Goddess: Hsi Wang Mu in Medieval Chinese Literature." Ph.D. diss., University of California, Berkeley.

———. 1985. "Sex and the Supernatural in Medieval China: Cantos on the Transcendent Who Presides Over the River." *Journal of the American Oriental Society* 105:197–220.

———. 1986. "Reflections on a Metal Mother: Tu Kuang-t'ing's Biography of Hsi-wang-mu." *Journal of Chinese Religions* 13/14 :127–42.

———. 1990. "Practice Makes Perfect: Paths to Transcendence for Women in Medieval China." *Taoist Resources* 2.2:23–42.

Chan, Alan. 1990. "Goddesses in Chinese Religion." In *Goddesses in Religions and Modern Debate*, ed. Larry W. Hurtado, 9–81. Atlanta: Scholars Press.

———. 1991. *Two Visions of the Way: A Study of the Wang Pi and the Ho-shang-kung Commentaries on the Laozi*. Albany: State University of New York Press.

Chan Wing-tsit. 1964. *A Source Book in Chinese Philosophy*. Princeton: Princeton University Press.

Ch'en Ku-ying. 1981. *Lao-tzu: Text, Notes, and Comments*. San Francisco: Chinese Materials Center.

Chia, Mantak. 1986. *Chi Self Massage: The Taoist Way of Rejuvenation*. Huntington, NY: Healing Tao Books.

———. 1987. *Awaken Healing Energy through the Tao*. Huntington, NY: Healing Tao Books.

———. 1987a. *Taoist Ways to Transform Stress into Vitality*. Huntington, NY: Healing Tao Books.

Cleary, Thomas. 1987. *Understanding Reality: A Taoist Alchemical Classic by Chang Po-tuan*. Honolulu: University of Hawaii Press.

Cleary, Thomas. 1991. *Vitality, Energy, Spirit. A Taoist Sourcebook*. Boston: Shambhala.

———. 1992. *The Secret of the Golden Flower: The Classic Chinese Book of Life*. San Francisco: HarperCollins.

Davis, Tenney L., and Chao Yün-ts'ung. 1939. "Chang Po-Tuan of T'ien-t'ai, His Wu Chen P'ien, Essays on Understanding of the Truth." *Proceedings of the American Academy of Arts and Sciences* 73:97–117.

Demiéville, Paul. 1987. "The Mirror of the Mind." In *Sudden and Gradual: Approaches to Enlightenment in Chinese Thought*, ed. Peter N. Gregory, 13–40. Honolulu: University of Hawaii Press, Kuroda Institute Studies in East Asian Buddhism, 5.

Despeux, Catherine. 1987. *Prescriptions d'acuponcture valant mille onces d'or*. Paris: Guy Trédaniel.

———. 1988. *La moélle du phenix rouge. Santé et longue vie dans la Chine du seizième siècle*. Paris: Editions Tredaniel.

———. 1989. "Gymnastics: The Ancient Tradition." In *Taoist Meditation and Longevity Techniques*, ed. Livia Kohn, 223–61. Ann Arbor: University of Michigan, Center for Chinese Studies Publications, 61.

———. 1990. *Immortelles de la Chine anciénne. Taoisme et alchimie feminine*. Paris: Pardes.

DeWoskin, Kenneth. 1977. *Six Dynasties Chih-kuai and the Birth of Fiction*. Princeton: Princeton University Press.

———. 1983. *Doctors, Diviners, and Magicians of Ancient China*. New York: Columbia University Press.

———. 1990. "Xian Descended: Narrating Xian among Mortals." *Taoist Resources* 2.2:70–86.

Dragan, Raymond. 1989. "Ways to the Way: A Review of Bibliographies on Taoism." *Taoist Resources* 1.2:21–27.

Eberhard, Wolfram. 1967. *Guilt and Sin in Traditional China*. Berkeley and Los Angeles: University of California Press.

Engelhardt, Ute. 1987. *Die klassische Tradition der Qi-Übungen. Eine Darstellung anhand des Tang-zeitlichen Textes Fuqi jingyi lun von Sima Chengzhen*. Wiesbaden: Franz Steiner.

———. 1989. "Qi For Life: Longevity in the Tang." In *Taoist Meditation and Longevity Techniques*, ed. Livia Kohn, 263–94. Ann Arbor: University of Michigan, Center for Chinese Studies Publications, 61.

Erkes, Eduard. 1942. "Eine P'an-ku Mythe der Hsia-Zeit." *T'oung-pao* 36:159–74.

Fracasso, Ricardo. 1988. "Holy Mothers of Ancient China." *T'oung-pao* 74:1–46.

Fung Yu-lan, and Derk Bodde. 1952. *A History of Chinese Philosophy.* 2 vols. Princeton, Princeton University Press.

Giles, Lionel. 1948. *A Gallery of Chinese Immortals.* London: John Murray.

Girardot, Norman. 1983. *Myth and Meaning in Early Taoism.* Berkeley: University of California Press.

Goodrich, Anne S. 1981. *Chinese Hells.* St. Augustin: Monumenta Serica Monograph.

Goullart, Peter. 1961. *The Monastery of Jade Mountain.* London: John Murray.

Graham, A. C. 1960. *The Book of Lieh-tzu.* London: A. Murray.

———. 1980. "How Much of *Chuang-tzu* Did Chuang-tzu Write?" In *Studies in Classical Chinese Thought. Journal of the American Academy of Religion,* Supplement 35:459–501.

———. 1981. *Chuang-tzu: The Seven Inner Chapters, and Other Writings from the Book of Chuang-tzu.* London: Allan and Unwin.

———. 1982. *Chuang-tzu: Textual Notes to a Partial Translation.* London: University of London.

———. 1990. "The Origins of the Legend of Lao Tan." In *Studies in Chinese Philosophy and Philosophical Literature,* 111–24. Albany: State University of New York Press. Originally published 1981.

Gulik, Robert van. 1963. *Sexual Life in Ancient China.* Leiden: E. Brill.

Güntsch, Gertrud. 1988. *Das Shen-hsien-chuan und das Erscheinungsbild eines Hsien.* Frankfurt: Peter Lang.

Harper, Donald. 1987. "The Sexual Arts of Ancient China As Described in a Manuscript of the Second Century B.C." *Harvard Journal of Asiatic Studies* 47:459–98.

Hawkes, David. 1959. *Ch'u Tz'u: The Songs of the South.* New York and Oxford: Oxford University Press.

———. 1974. "The Quest of the Goddess." In *Studies in Chinese Literary Genres,* ed. Cyril Birch, 42–68. New York: Columbia University Press.

———. 1981. "Quanzhen Plays and Quanzhen Masters." *Bulletin d'Ecole Francaise d'Extrême-Orient* 69:153–70.

Hendrischke, Barbara. 1991. "The Concept of Inherited Evil in the *Taiping jing.*" *East Asian History* 2:1–30.

Henricks, Robert. 1989. *Lao-Tzu: Te-Tao ching.* New York: Ballantine.

Holzman, Donald. 1956. "Les sept sages de la foret des bambus et la société de leur temps." *T'oung-pao* 44:317–46.

————. 1976. *Poetry and Politics: The Life and Works of Juan Chi (210–263).* Cambridge: Cambridge University Press.

Homann, Rolf. 1971. *Die wichtigsten Körpergottheiten im Huang-t'ing-ching.* Göppingen: Alfred Kümmerle.

Hou Ching-lang. 1975. *Monnaies d'offrande et la notion de trésorerie dans la réligion chinoise.* Paris: Memoires de l'Institut des Hautes Etudes Chinoises, 1.

Ishida, Hidemi. 1989. "Body and Mind: The Chinese Perspective." In *Taoist Meditation and Longevity Techniques,* ed. Livia Kohn, 41–70. Ann Arbor: University of Michigan, Center for Chinese Studies Publications, 61.

Ishihara, Akira, and Howard S. Levy. 1970. *The Tao of Sex.* New York: Harper & Row.

Kaltenmark, Maxime. 1953. *Le Lie-sien tchouan.* Peking: Université de Paris Publications. Reprinted 1988.

————. 1960. "Ling-pao: Note sur un terme du Taoïsme réligieux." *Mélanges publieux par l'Institut des Hautes Etudes* 2:559–88.

————. 1969. *Lao-tzu and Taoism.* Stanford: Stanford University Press.

————. 1974. "Miroirs magiques." In *Mélanges de Sinologie offers a M. P. Demiéville,* 2:91–98. Brussels: Institut Belge des Hautes Etudes Chinoises.

————. 1979. "The Ideology of the *T'ai-p'ing-ching.*" In *Facets of Taoism,* ed. Holmes Welch and Anna Seidel, 19–52. New Haven: Yale University Press.

————. 1981. "Quelques remarques sur le 'T'ai-shang Ling-pao wou-fou siu'." *Zimbun* 18:1–10.

Kandel, Barbara. 1979. *Taiping jing: The Origin and Transmission of the 'Scripture of General Welfare'—The History of an Unofficial Text.* Hamburg: Gesellschaft für Natur- und Völkerkunde Ostasiens.

Kaptchuk, Ted J. 1983. *The Net that Has No Weaver: Understanding Chinese Medicine.* New York: Congdon & Weed.

Kirkland, Russell. 1991. "Huang Ling-Wei: A Taoist Priestess in T'ang China." *Journal of Chinese Religions* 19:47–73.

Knaul, Livia. 1981. *Leben und Legende des Ch'en T'uan.* Frankfurt: Peter Lang.

Kobayashi, Masayoshi. 1992. "The Celestial Masters under the Eastern Jin and Liu-Song Dynasties." *Taoist Resources* 3.1:17–46.

Kohn, Livia. 1987. *Seven Steps to the Tao: Sima Chengzhen's Zuowanglun.* St.Augustin/Nettetal: Monumenta Serica Monograph 20.

———. 1987a. "The Teaching of T'ien-yin-tzu." *Journal of Chinese Religions* 15:1–28.

———, ed. 1989. *Taoist Meditation and Longevity Techniques.* Ann Arbor: University of Michigan, Center for Chinese Studies Publications, 61.

———. 1989a. "Guarding the One: Concentrative Meditation in Taoism." In *Taoist Meditation and Longevity Techniques*, ed. Livia Kohn, 123–56. Ann Arbor: University of Michigan, Center for Chinese Studies Publications, 61.

———. 1989b. "Taoist Insight Meditation: The Tang Practice of *Neiguan*." In *Taoist Meditation and Longevity Techniques*, ed. Livia Kohn, 191–222. Ann Arbor: University of Michigan, Center for Chinese Studies Publications, 61.

———. 1989c. "The Mother of the Tao." *Taoist Resources* 1.2:37–113.

———. 1989d. "Die Emigration des Laozi. Mythologische Entwicklungen vom 2. bis 6. Jahrhundert." *Monumenta Serica* 38:49–68.

———. 1990. "Transcending Personality: From Ordinary to Immortal Life." *Taoist Resources* 2.2:1–22.

———. 1990a. "Chen Tuan in History and Legend." *Taoist Resources* 2.1:8–31.

———. 1991. *Taoist Mystical Philosophy: The Scripture of Western Ascension.* Albany: State University of New York Press.

———. 1991a. "Taoist Visions of the Body." *Journal of Chinese Philosophy* 18:227–52.

———. 1992. *Early Chinese Mysticism: Philosophy and Soteriology in the Taoist Tradition.* Princeton: Princeton University Press.

———. 1993. "Quiet Sitting With Master Yinshi: Religion and Medicine in China Today." *Zen Buddhism Today* 10.

Krappe, Alexander. 1944. "Far Eastern Foxlore." *California Folklore Quarterly* 3:124–47.

Kroll, Paul W. 1985. "In the Halls of the Azure Lad." *Journal of the American Oriental Society* 105:75–94.

Kusuyama Haruki. 1992. *Dōka shisō to dōkyō*. Tokyo: Hirakawa.

LaFargue, Michael. 1992. *The Tao of the Tao-te ching*. Albany: State University of New York Press.

Lagerwey, John. 1981. *Wu-shang pi-yao: Somme taoïste du VIe siècle*. Paris: Publications de l'Ecole Française d'Extrême-Orient.

———. 1987. *Taoist Ritual in Chinese Society and History*. New York: Macmillan.

Lau, D. C. 1982. *Chinese Classics: Tao Te Ching*. Hong Kong: Hong Kong University Press.

LeBlanc, Charles. 1978. *Chapter Six of the Huai-nan-tzu*. Hong Kong: Hong Kong University Press.

———. 1985. *Huai-nan-tzu: Philosophical Synthesis in Early Han Thought*. Hong Kong: Hong Kong University Press.

Legge, James. 1962. *The Sacred Books of China: The Texts of Taoism*. New York: Dover.

Levi, Jean. 1983. "L'abstinence des céréals chez les taoïstes." *Etudes Chinoises* 1:3–47.

———. 1989. *Les fonctionnaires divins*. Paris: Seuil.

Levy, Howard S. 1956. "Yellow Turban Rebellion at the End of the Han." *Journal of the American Oriental Society* 76:214–27.

Lewis, Mark E. 1990. *Sanctioned Violence in Early China*. Albany: State University of New York Press.

Li Yuanguo. 1990. "Chen Tuan's Concepts of the Great Ultimate." *Taoist Resources* 2.1:32–53.

Lin Yutang. 1948. *The Wisdom of Laotse*. New York: Random House.

Ling, Peter. 1918. "The Eight Immortals of the Taoist Religion." *Journal of the Royal Asiatic Society, North China Branch* 49:53–75.

Liu Ts'un-yan. 1973. "The Compilation and Historical Value of the *Tao-tsang*." In *Essays on the Sources of Chinese History*, ed. D. Leslie, 104–20. Canberra: Australian National University Press.

Loewe, Michael. 1979. *Ways to Paradise: the Chinese Quest for Immortality*. London: Allan and Unwin.

Loon, Piet van der. 1984. *Taoist Books in the Libraries of the Sung Period*. London: Oxford Oriental Institute.

Lu Gwei-djen. 1980. *Celestial Lancets: A History and Rationale of Acupuncture and Moxa*. Cambridge: Cambridge University Press.

Lu Kuan-yu. 1964. *The Secrets of Chinese Meditation*. London: Rider.

———. 1970. *Taoist Yoga — Alchemy and Immortality*. London: Rider.

Mair, Victor H. 1983. *Experimental Essays on Chuang-tzu*. Honolulu: University of Hawaii Press.

Major, John S. 1984. "The Five Phases, Magic Squares, and Schematic Cosmography." In *Explorations in Early Chinese Cosmology*, ed. Henry Rosemont, 133–66. Chico, CA: Scholars Press, American Academy of Religion.

Mansvelt-Beck, B. J. 1980. "The Date of the *Taiping jing*." *T'oung-pao* 66: 149–82.

Maspero, Henri. 1924. "Légendes mythologiques dans le *Chou King*." *Journal Asiatique* 20:1–101.

———. 1981. *Taoism and Chinese Religion*. Trans. by Frank Kierman. Amherst: University of Massachusetts Press.

Mather, Richard B. 1976. *A New Account of Tales of the World: The Shih-shuo hsin-yü*. Minneapolis: University of Minnesota Press.

Michaud, Paul. 1958. "The Yellow Turbans." *Monumenta Serica* 17:47–127.

Miura Kunio. 1989. "The Revival of Qi: Qigong in Contemporary China." In *Taoist Meditation and Longevity Techniques*, ed. Livia Kohn, 329–58. Ann Arbor: University of Michigan, Center for Chinese Studies Publications, 61.

Needham, Joseph, et al. 1976. *Science and Civilisation in China*, vol. 5, no. 3. Spagyrical Discovery and Invention: Historical Survey, from Cinnabar Elixir to Synthetic Insulin. Cambridge: Cambridge University Press.

———. 1980. *Science and Civilisation in China*, vol. 5, no. 4. Spagyrical Discovery and Invention: Apparatus, Theories and Gifts. Cambridge: Cambridge University Press.

———. 1983. *Science and Civilisation in China*, vol. 5, no. 5. Spagyrical Discovery and Invention: Physiological Alchemy. Cambridge: Cambridge University Press.

Ngo Van Xuyet. 1976. *Divination, Magie et Politique dans la Chine anciénne*. Paris: Presses Universitaires de France.

Ofuchi Ninji. 1974. "On *Ku Ling-pao ching*." *Acta Asiatica* 27:33–56.

———. 1979. "The Formation of the Taoist Canon." In *Facets of Taoism*, ed. Holmes Welch and Anna Seidel, 253–68. New Haven: Yale University Press.

———. 1979a. *Tonkō dōkei. Zuroku hen* (Taoist Scriptures from Dunhuang). Tokyo: Kokubu shoten.

Pas, Julian F. 1988. *A Select Bibliography on Taoism.* Stony Brook, NY: Institute for the Advanced Study of World Religions.

Petersen, Jens O. 1989. "The Early Traditions Relating to the Han-dynasty Transmission of the *Taiping jing.*" Part 1. *Acta Orientalia* 50:133–71.

———. 1990. "The Early Traditions Relating to the Han-dynasty Transmission of the *Taiping jing.*" Part 2. *Acta Orientalia* 51:163–216.

———. 1990a. "The Anti-Messianism of the *Taiping jing.*" *Journal of the Seminar for Buddhist Studies* 3:1–36.

Porkert, Manfred. 1974. *The Theoretical Foundations of Chinese Medicine.* Cambridge: MIT Press.

———. 1983. *The Essentials of Chinese Diagnosis.* Zürich: Acta Medicinae Sinensis.

Pregadio, Fabrizio. 1991. "The *Book of the Nine Elixirs* and Its Tradition." In *Chūgoku kodai kagakushi ron*, ed. Yamada Keiji, 539–636. Kyoto: Jimbun kagaku kenkyujo.

Reiter, Florian C. 1985. "Ch'ung-yang Sets Forth His Teachings in Fifteen Discourses." *Monumenta Serica* 36:33–54.

———., ed. 1990. *Leben und Wirken Lao-Tzu's in Schrift und Bild. Lao-chün pa-shih-i-hua t'u-shuo.* Würzburg: Königshausen & Neumann.

Robinet, Isabelle. 1977. *Les commentaires du Tao to king jusqu'au VIIe siècle.* Paris: Mémoirs de l'Institut des Hautes Etudes Chinoises, 5.

———. 1979. *Méditation taoïste.* Paris: Dervy Livres.

———. 1979a. "Metamorphosis and Deliverance of the Corpse in Taoism." *History of Religions* 19:37–70.

———. 1984. *La révélation du Shangqing dans l'histoire du Taoïsme.* 2 Vols. Paris: Publications de l'Ecole Française d'Extrême-Orient.

———. 1986. "The Taoist Immortal: Jester of Light and Shadow, Heaven and Earth." *Journal of Chinese Religions* 13/14: 87–106.

———. 1989. "Original Contributions of *Neidan* to Taoism and Chinese Thought." In *Taoist Meditation and Longevity Techniques*, ed. Livia Kohn, 295–328. Ann Arbor: University of Michigan, Center for Chinese Studies Publications, 61.

——. 1989a. "Visualization and Ecstatic Flight in Shangqing Taoism." In *Taoist Meditation and Longevity Techniques*, ed. Livia Kohn, 157–90. Ann Arbor: University of Michigan, Center for Chinese Studies Publications, 61.

——. 1991. *Histoire du Taoïsme: des origins au XIVe siècle*. Paris: Editions Cerf.

Robinson, Richard. 1967. *Early Mādhyamika in India and China*. Madison: University of Wisconsin Press.

Roth, Harold D. 1991. "Psychology and Self-Cultivation in Early Taoistic Thought." *Harvard Journal of Asiatic Studies* 51:599–650.

——. 1991a. "Who Compiled the *Chuang-tzu?*" In *Chinese Texts and Philosophical Contexts*, ed. Henry Rosemont, Jr. 79–128. La Salle, IL: Open Court Press.

——. 1992. *The Textual History of the Huai-nan Tzu*. Ann Arbor: Association for Asian Studies Monographs.

Rousselle, Erwin. 1933. "Zum *Nei-ching-t'u*." *Sinica* 8:207–16.

Russell, Terence. 1990. "Chen Tuan at Mount Huangbo." *Asiatische Studien / Etudes Asiatiques* 44:107–40.

——. 1990a. "Chen Tuan's Veneration of the Dharma: A Study in Hagiographic Modification." *Taoist Resources* 2.1:54–72.

Sailey, Jay. 1978. *The Master Who Embraces Simplicity: A Study of the Philosophy of Ko Hung (A.D. 283–343)*. San Francisco: Chinese Materials Center.

Sakade Yoshinobu. 1989. "Longevity Techniques in Japan: Ancient Sources and Contemporary Studies." In *Taoist Meditation and Longevity Techniques*, ed. Livia Kohn, 1–40. Ann Arbor: University of Michigan, Center for Chinese Studies Publications, 61.

Saso, Michael. 1972. *Taoism and the Rite of Cosmic Renewal*. Seattle: Washington University Press.

Schafer, Edward H. 1973. *The Divine Woman*. Berkeley and Los Angeles: University of California Press.

——. 1977. *Pacing the Void*. Berkeley and Los Angeles: University of California Press.

——. 1978. "The Jade Woman of Greatest Mystery." *History of Religions* 17:387–98.

——. 1978a. "The Capeline Cantos: Verses on the Divine Loves of Taoist Priestesses." *Asiatische Studien / Etudes Asiatiques* 32:5–65.

———. 1981. "Wu Yün's 'Cantos on Pacing the Void'." *Harvard Journal of Asiatic Studies* 41:377–415.

———. 1985. *Mirages on the Sea of Time. The Taoist Poetry of Ts'ao T'ang.* Berkeley: University of California Press.

Schipper, Kristofer. 1965. *L'Empereur Wou des Han dans la legende taoïste.* Paris: Publications de l'Ecole Française d'Extrême-Orient, 58.

———. 1975. *Le Fen-teng: Rituél taoïste.* Paris: Publications de l'Ecole Française d'Extrême-Orient.

———. 1975a. *Concordance du Houang-t'ing king.* Paris: Publications de l'Ecole Française d'Extrême-Orient.

———. 1978. "The Taoist Body." *History of Religions* 17:355–87.

———. 1982. *Le corps taoïste: Corps physique—corps social.* Paris: Fayard.

———. 1985. "Vernacular and Classical Ritual in Taoism." *Journal of Asian Studies* 65:21–51.

———. 1985a. "Taoist Ritual and Local Cults of the T'ang Dynasty." In *Tantric and Taoist Studies,* ed. Michel Strickmann, 3:812–34. Brussels: Institut Belge des Hautes Etudes Chinoises.

Schmidt, H. H. 1985. "Die hundertachtzig Vorschriften von Lao-chün." In *Religion und Philosophie in Ostasien. Festschrift für Hans Steininger,* ed. G. Naundorf, K. H. Pohl, H. H. Schmidt, 149–59. Würzburg: Königshausen und Neumann.

Schneider, Laurence. 1980. *A Madman of Ch'u: The Chinese Myth of Loyalty and Dissent.* Berkeley and Los Angeles: University of California Press.

Seidel, Anna. 1969. *La divinisation de Lao tseu dans le Taoïsme des Han.* Paris: Ecole Française d'Extrême Orient.

———. 1969a. "The Image of the Perfect Ruler in Early Taoist Messianism." *History of Religions* 9:216–47.

———. 1978. "Buying One's Way to Heaven: The Celestial Treasury in Chinese Religions." *History of Religions* 17:419–32.

———. 1983. "Imperial Treasures and Taoist Sacraments: Taoist Roots in the Apocrypha." In *Tantric and Taoist Studies,* ed. Michel Strickmann, 2:291–371. Brussels: Institut Belge des Hautes Etudes Chinoises.

———. 1984. "Le sutra merveilleux du Ling-pao suprême, traitant de Lao tseu qui convertit les barbares." In *Contributions aux études du Touen-houang,* ed. Michel Soymié 1984:305–52. Geneva: Ecole Française d'Extrême-Orient.

———. 1990. *Taoismus: Die inoffizielle Hochreligion Chinas*. Tokyo: Deutsche Gesellschaft für Natur- und Völkerkunde Ostasiens.

Sivin, Nathan. 1968. *Chinese Alchemy: Preliminary Studies*. Cambridge: Harvard University Press.

Smith, Thomas E. 1990. "The Record of the Ten Continents." *Taoist Resources* 2.2:87–119.

———. 1992. "Ritual and the Shaping of Narrative: The Legend of the Han Emperor Wu." Ph.D. diss., University of Michigan, Ann Arbor.

Soymié, Michel. 1968. "Bibliographie du Taoïsme: études dans les langues occidentales." *Dōkyō kenkyū* 3:246–317.

———. 1969. "Bibliographie du Taoïsme: études dans les langues orientales." *Dōkyō kenkyū* 4:225–87.

Spiro, Audrey. 1990. "How Light And Airy: Upward Mobility in the Realm of Immortals." *Taoist Resources* 2.2:43–69.

Stein, Rolf A. 1990. *The World in Miniature: Container Gardens and Dwellings in Far Eastern Religious Thought*. Trans. by Phyllis Brooks. Stanford: Stanford University Press.

Strickmann, Michel. 1978. "The Mao-shan Revelations: Taoism and the Aristocracy." *T'oung-pao* 63:1–63.

———. 1979. "On the Alchemy of T'ao Hung-ching." In *Facets of Taoism*, ed. Holmes Welch and Anna Seidel, 123–92. New Haven: Yale University Press.

———. 1981. *Le Taoïsme du Mao chan: chronique d'une révélation*. Paris: Collège du France, Institut des Hautes Etudes Chinoises.

Sunayama Minoru. 1987. "Ku Dōtosenkō: Chūban Tō no shidaifu to Mōzanha dōkyō." *Tōhōshūkyō* 69: 1–23.

Takehiro, Teri. 1990. "The Twelve Sleep Exercises of Mount Hua." *Taoist Resources* 2.1:73–94.

Thompson, Laurence. 1985. *Chinese Religion in Western Languages: A Comprehensive and Classified Bibliography . . . through 1980*. Phoenix: University of Arizona Press.

———. 1985a. "Taoism: Classic and Canon." In *The Holy Book in Comparative Perspective*, ed. Frederick M. Denny and Rodney F. Taylor, 204–23. Columbia: University of South Carolina Press.

———. 1989. "On the Prehistory of Hell in China." *Journal of Chinese Religions* 17:27–41.

Tsui, Bartholomew P. M. 1991. *Taoist Tradition and Change: The Story of the Complete Perfection Sect in Hong Kong*. Hong Kong: Christian Study Centre on Chinese Religion and Culture.

Unschuld, Paul. 1985. *Medicine in China: A History of Ideas*. Berkeley and Los Angeles: University of California Press.

Veith, Ilza. 1963. "The Supernatural in the Far Eastern Concepts of Mental Diseases." *Bulletin of the History of Medicine* 37:145.

——. 1972. *The Yellow Emperor's Classic of Internal Medicine*. Berkeley and Los Angeles: University of California Press. Originally published 1949.

Verellen, Franciscus. 1989. *Du Guangting (850–933)—taoïste de cour a la fin de la Chine mediévale*. Paris: Collège du France, Memoires de L'Institut des Hautes Etudes Chinoises, 30.

Wagner, Rudolf. 1973. "Lebensstil und Drogen im chinesischen Mittelalter." *T'oung-pao* 59:79–178.

——. 1980. "Interlocking Parallel Style: Laozi and Wang Bi." *Asiatische Studien / Etudes Asiatiques* 34:18–53.

——. 1986. "Wang Bi: 'The Structure of the Laozi's Pointers'." *T'oung-pao* 72:92–129.

——. 1989. "The Wang Bi Recension of the *Laozi*." *Early China* 14:27–54.

Waley, Arthur. 1934. *The Way and Its Power*. London: Allen and Unwin.

——. 1955. *The Nine Songs: A Study of Shamanism in Ancient China*. London: Allen and Unwin.

Ware, James R. 1966. *Alchemy, Medicine and Religion in the China of* A.D. *320: The Nei P'ien of Ko Hung*. Cambridge: MIT Press.

Watson, Burton. 1968. *The Complete Works of Chuang-tzu*. New York: Columbia University Press.

Welch, Holmes, and Anna Seidel, eds. 1979. *Facets of Taoism*. New Haven: Yale University Press.

Wile, Douglas. 1992. *Art of the Bedchamber: The Chinese Sexual Yoga Classics Including Women's Solo Meditation Texts*. Albany: State University of New York Press.

Wilhelm, Richard. 1962. *The Secret of the Golden Flower*. New York: Harcourt, Brace and World. Originally published Zurich, 1929 .

Wong, Eva. 1992. *Cultivating Stillness: A Taoist Manual for Transforming Body and Mind.* Boston: Shambhala.

Yamada Keiji. 1979. "The Formation of the *Huang-ti nei-ching.*" *Acta Asiatica* 36:67–89.

Yamada, Toshiaki. 1989. "Longevity Techniques and the Compilation of the *Lingbao wufuxu.*" In *Taoist Meditation and Longevity Techniques,* ed. Livia Kohn, 91–122. Ann Arbor: University of Michigan, Center for Chinese Studies Publications, 61.

Yang, F. S. 1958. "A Study of the Origin of the Legend of the Eight Immortals." *Oriens Extremus* 5:1–20.

Yao Tao-chung. 1980. "Ch'üan-chen: A New Taoist Sect in North China During the Twelfth and Thirteenth Centuries." Ph.D. Diss., University of Arizona, Phoenix.

Yetts, Percifal. 1916. "The Eight Immortals." *Journal of the Royal Asiatic Society* 1916:773–807.

———. 1922. "More Notes on the Eight Immortals." *Journal of the Royal Asiatic Society* 1922:397–426.

Yoshioka Yoshitoyo. 1979. "Taoist Monastic Life." In *Facets of Taoism,* ed. Holmes Welch and Anna Seidel, 220–52. New Haven: Yale University Press.

Yü Ying-shih. 1964. "Life and Immortality in the Mind of Han-China." *Harvard Journal of Asiatic Studies* 25:80–122.

Zürcher, Erik. 1959. *The Buddhist Conquest of China.* 2 Vols. Leiden: E. Brill.

———. 1980. "Buddhist Influence on Early Taoism." *T'oung-pao* 66:84–147.

# INDEX